"I WANT EVERYONE IN THE WORLD TO KNOW THAT I AM THE BEST FIGHTER IN THE WORLD." —Mike Tyson

Today everyone does know that Mike Tyson is the best fighter in the world. And though much of his controversial private life has become public, there is still a shroud of mystery surrounding him. Who is Mike Tyson and what makes him tick? Is this awesome destroyer in the ring an inarticulate innocent or a predator with a con man's tongue? Did he leave the mean streets of Brooklyn behind, or does he still live by the law of the jungle? Is he victim or victimizer?

This hard-hitting book gets to the bottom of the boy-man who fought his way to the top. It reveals a past shadowed by crime. It details endless managerial battles. It exposes a marriage rocked by more destructive fighting than any he's seen in the ring. And it tells perhaps the most remarkable story in the annals of boxing—of a youth who at the age of thirteen was ripped from his roots and shaped by a master to be one thing and one thing only . . . the heavyweight champion of the world.

BAD INTENTIONS
THE MIKE TYSON STORY

by
Peter Heller

A SIGNET BOOK

NEW AMERICAN LIBRARY

A DIVISION OF PENGUIN BOOKS USA INC.

Copyright © 1989 by Peter Heller

Bad Intentions previously appeared in an NAL Books edition published
by New American Library and simultaneously in Canada by
Penguin Books Canada Limited.

Published by arrangement with Robson Books Limited,
Bolsover House, 5-6 Clipstone Street, London W1P 7EB, England.

SIGNET TRADEMARK REG. U.S. PAT. OFF. AND FOREIGN COUNTRIES
REGISTERED TRADEMARK—MARCA REGISTRADA
HECHO EN DRESDEN, TN, U.S.A.

SIGNET, SIGNET CLASSIC, MENTOR, ONYX, PLUME,
MERIDIAN and NAL BOOKS are published by
New American Library, a division of Penguin Books USA Inc.,
1633 Broadway, New York, New York 10019

First Signet Printing, March, 1990

1 2 3 4 5 6 7 8 9

PRINTED IN THE UNITED STATES OF AMERICA

For Michelle and Lindsey
Who make it all worthwhile

Contents

ACKNOWLEDGMENTS

No work of contemporary nonfiction can be properly completed without the insights, help and cooperation of many people with particular pieces of knowledge or information they are willing to share. Because many insiders have shared such knowledge with me but prefer to remain anonymous, I will respect their wishes. I offer posthumous thanks to my dear friend of twenty years, Jim Jacobs, who shared much of his knowledge of boxing with me, as well as many behind-the-scenes insights into the management of fighters in general, and Mike Tyson in particular. I also thank the late Cus D'Amato for the time he gave me during the final dozen years of his life.

Others who shared their knowledge and information with me include Camille Ewald; Jay Bright, Kevin Rooney; Jeff Levine; Michael Marton; John Halpin; Harry Markson; Mickey Duff; Bill Cayton; Steve Lott; Ted Atlas; Bob Stewart; Reuben Givens; Loraine Miller; Butch Lewis; Richard Stickles; Joe Bruno; Nat Loubet; Teddy Brenner; Steve Dunleavy; Holly Robinson; Tony D'Amato; Fred Chetti; Lee Bordick; Wallace Matthews; Tim Layden; Ernie Butler; Joe Mahoney; Paul Grondahl; Phil Paul, and Lee Pollock. In addition, I would like to thank Mike Tyson for the time he periodically allowed me to spend with him in Catskill from 1986 to 1988.

Thanks are also due to my editor in Great Britain, Liz Rose, who did a wonderful job under extreme deadline pressure; to my friend and partner, Judd Maze, for allowing me to use him as a sounding board during the completion of this manuscript in 1988 and 1989, and who often kept me on the right track; to my colleagues at ABC News, Pat Roddy and John Snyder, who tolerated me during the writing of this book, and to my friend of more than twenty years, Edgar Rodriguez, who facilitated the transporting of manuscript material between New York and London. In addition, my appreciation goes to the Turnberry Isle Yacht and Country Club in North Miami, Florida, which provided wonderful ambiance during the preparation of a portion of this manuscript.

Although much of what is contained in this book was derived from first-hand interviews and research, the following sources were of great help in filling the gaps, and use of them as research sources is hereby acknowledged: for information on Don King: Thomas Hauser's book, *The Black Lights* (1986, McGraw-Hill); "Don King's Boxing Monopoly" by Jack Newfield (*Village Voice*, September 13, 1983); Ed Schuyler's Don King profile for the Associated Press on February 17, 1989; Bill Brubaker's "The Fight Came" (Part 2) *Washington Post*, February 20, 1989; "Don King's Tight Grip on Boxing" by Glen Macnow, (*Philadelphia Inquirer*, June 26, 1988); *Mean Business* by Stephen Brunt (1987, Viking-Penguin Canada, Ltd.). For information on Bill Cayton: the Gannett-Westchester Newspapers profile on Bill Varner on May 10, 1988. For information on Cus D'Amato: *Victory Over Myself* by Floyd Patterson and Milton Gross (published 1962 by Bernard Geis Associates); "Fury, Fear, Philosophy" by Norman Mailer, in the September 1988, issue of *Spin* magazine; "Hail, Hail, The Gang's All Here" by Robert Boyle, (published in *Sports Illustrated* magazine, February 20, 1961); *Floyd Patterson, Heavyweight King* by Jack Newcombe, (published 1961, by Bartholomew House). For information on Ruth Roper and Robin Givens: *Jet* magazine for June 22, 1988, and January 4, 1988; "Robin and Marryin'," in the August 8, 1988, issue of *US* magazine; "Tyson Turmoil" in the November, 1988, issue of *Vanity Fair* magazine; "The Lady And The Champ" in the July, 1988, issue of *Life* magazine, and "The Woman And Tyson" by Mitch Gelman and Jonathan Mandell, in the October 5, 1988, edition of *Newsday*. For information on Jim Jacobs, the June, 1988, issue of *Handball* magazine; "Really The Greatest" by Robert Boyle, in the March 7, 1966, issue of *Sports Illustrated* magazine; "The Ring Leader" by Joshua Hammer, in the April, 1986, issue of *Manhattan, Inc.* magazine. For information on the IBC, *Jim Norris And The Decline of Boxing*, by Barney Nagler, (published 1964 by Bobbs-Merrill). For information on the WBA, WBC, and

IBF, "Time To Clean Up Boxing Again," and "Fighting the Rulers of the WBA" by Pat Putnam, published in 1981 in *Sports Illustrated*; "The Alphabet War," in the December 1988, issue of *Ring* magazine; "The Fight Game" (Part 1) by Bill Brubaker, in the February 19, 1989 issue of the *Washington Post*, as well as Tom Hauser's *The Black Lights*. For information on Donald Trump, "Flashy Symbol of An Acquisitive Age," by Otto Friedrich and Jeane McDowell in the January 16, 1989, issue of *Time* magazine; "The People's Billionaire" by Glenn Plaskin in the February 26, 1989, issue of the *New York Daily News;* "The Billionaires" in the September 12, 1988, issue of *Forbes* magazine; and "The Art of the Steal" by Rick Hornung, in the August 9, 1988, issue of *The Village Voice*. In addition, the *New York Daily News,* including stories by Mike Katz and Bill Gallo; *The New York Times,* including stories by Phil Berger and Dave Anderson; *New York Newsday,* including stories by Wallace Matthews; the *New York Post,* including stories by Mark Dionno and Michael Marley, were used as sources of corroboration from 1985 to 1989, as well as the magazines *Sports Illustrated, People,* and *Time* during that same period.

—Peter Heller
New York City
May 3, 1989

PROFESSIONAL RING RECORD

Michael Gerard Tyson
"Iron Mike" "Catskill Thunder"
Born June 30, 1966, Brooklyn, NY

1985

March 6	Hector Mercedes, Albany, NY	KO-1
April 10	Trent Singleton, Albany, NY	KO-1
May 23	Don Halpin, Albany, NY	KO-4
June 20	Rick Spain, Atlantic City, NJ	KO-1
July 11	John Alderson, Atlantic City, NJ	KO-3
July 19	Larry Sims, Poughkeepsie, NY	KO-3
Aug. 15	Lorenzo Canady, Atlantic City, NJ	KO-1
Sept. 5	Michael Jack Johnson, Atlantic City, NJ	KO-1
Oct. 9	Donnie Long, Atlantic City, NJ	KO-1
Oct. 25	Robert Colay, Atlantic City, NJ	KO-1
Nov. 1	Sterling Benjamin, Latham, NY	KO-1
Nov. 13	Eddie Richardson, Houston, Texas	KO-1
Nov. 22	Conroy Nelson, Latham, NY	KO-2
Dec. 6	Sammy Scaff, Madison Square Garden, NY	KO-1
Dec. 27	Mark Young, Latham, NY	KO-1

1986

Jan. 11	David Jaco, Albany, NY	KO-1
Jan. 24	Mike Jameson, Atlantic City, NJ	KO-5
Feb. 16	Jesse Ferguson, Troy, NY	KO-6
Mar. 10	Steve Zouski, Uniondale, NY	KO-3
May 3	James "Quick" Tillis, Glen Falls, NY	W-10
May 20	Mitch "Blood" Green, Madison Square Garden, NY	W-10
June 13	Reggie Gross, Madison Square Garden, NY	KO-1
June 28	William Hosea, Troy, NY	KO-1

July 11	Lorenzo Boyd, Swan Lake, NY	KO-2
July 26	Marvis Frazer, Troy, NY	KO-1
Aug. 17	Jose Ribalta, Atlantic City, NJ	KO-10
Sept. 6	Alfonzo Ratliff, Las Vegas, Nevada	KO-2
Nov. 22	Trevor Berbick, Las Vegas, Nevada	KO-2
	(Won WBC World Heavyweight Championship)	

1987

Mar. 7	James "Bonecrusher" Smith, Las Vegas, Nevada	W-12
	(Won WBA World Heavyweight Championship)	
May 30	Pinklon Thomas, Las Vegas, Nevada,	KO-6
	(Retained WBC/WBA Heavyweight Championship)	
Aug. 1	Tony Tucker, Las Vegas, Nevada	W-12
	(Won IBF World Heavyweight Championship)	
Oct. 16	Tyrell Biggs, Atlantic City, NJ	KO-7
	(Retained undisputed World Heavyweight Championship)	

1988

Jan. 22	Larry Holmes, Atlantic City, NJ	KO-4
	(Retained undisputed World Heavyweight Championship)	
Mar. 21	Tony Tubbs, Tokyo, Japan	KO-2
	(Retained undisputed World Heavyweight Championship)	
June 27	Michael Spinks, Atlantic City, NJ	KO-1
	(Retained undisputed World Heavyweight Championship)	

1989

| Feb. 25 | Frank Bruno, Las Vegas, Nevada | KO-5 |
| | (Retained undisputed World Heavyweight Championship) | |

TOTAL BOUTS	WON	LOST	KO's
36	36	0	32

Boxing is entertainment, so to be successful a fighter must not only win but he must win in an exciting manner. He must throw punches with bad intentions.
                        —Cus D'Amato
                            teacher/mentor of Mike Tyson

No matter what anyone says, no matter the excuse or explanation, whatever a person does in the end is what he intended to do all along.
                        —Cus D'Amato

BAD INTENTIONS
THE MIKE TYSON
— STORY —

Chapter 1

Preliminaries

Monday, June 27, 1988. Convention Hall. Atlantic City, New Jersey. The job of a good boxing manager is to serve his fighter to the best of his ability; to gain every physical, psychological and financial edge he possibly can for his warrior. For twelve years, Butch Lewis had done all this for Michael Spinks. But shortly before 11:00 P.M., just minutes before Spinks was to enter the ring for the most climactic fight of his career, Butch Lewis did his fighter no service at all. While in the dressing room of Spinks's opponent, Mike Tyson, an aide to Lewis noticed a small lump under the surgical tape around the wrist portion of Tyson's left glove. It is customary for boxers to have a representative in the locker room of the opponent to observe the ritual of hand-wrapping and gloving-up, even though impartial officials are assigned to observe that all is done within the rules. Lewis's aide summoned the flamboyant promoter.

Lewis was in his customary fight-night attire: a white, double-breasted jacket, white collar and matching bow tie—but no shirt. Bare-chested under his jacket, the only thing that Lewis sported between his white bow tie and his waist was a thick gold chain with a diamond charm hanging from it. With an eye to publicity, the camera-conscious Lewis had hit upon the affectation of going shirtless several years earlier. Curiously, whereas the manager reveled in media attention, his fighter, a man who had won an Olympic gold medal, the undisputed Light-Heavyweight Championship of the World, and then made history by becoming the only light-heavyweight champion to win the Heavyweight Championship, shied away from publicity and crowds.

When Lewis attempted to enter Tyson's room to see the lump for himself, Tyson's people and an inspector for the New Jersey Boxing Commission refused him entry. Larry

Hazzard, chairman of the Jersey commission, was summoned from ringside to deal with the impasse. Inside the dressing room, it was determined there was indeed a lump, either by design or by accident, under the tape on Tyson's glove. Lewis was concerned that the lump, caused by the knotting of the laces under the tape, might—again, by design or by accident—result in a cut or laceration to his fighter's face. And, as he was later to admit, once the situation had arisen, he also saw an opportunity to "try to pull a little psych" on Tyson. Tempers flared while outside the world was waiting to see a fight, but Lewis was adamant. "It ain't gonna be a fight if we don't do somethin' about this knot," he told Tyson's trainer. Hazzard agreed there was an abnormality under the tape and ordered the taping to be redone and the lump smoothed out. If part of Lewis's motive was to psych Tyson out, however, he achieved exactly the opposite result. Tyson's people saw a rage build in their fighter.

Outside in the main hall, unaware of the reason for the delay, 21,735 spectators plus several hundred writers, reporters and officials of the New Jersey Boxing Commission and the WBA, WBC, and IBF—boxing's three sanctioning organizations—waited, growing restless. For the preceding hour, they had been lulled into indifference by a fight between the top two contenders in the heavyweight division, Carl "The Truth" Williams and Trevor Berbick, the Jamaican fighter Tyson had defeated a year and a half earlier to win the WBC portion of the title. The crowd hardly cared when Williams was announced the winner after a dull, plodding contest.

That match over, they had sat through the endless introductions of celebrities and fringe celebrities. Sean Penn . . . Madonna . . . Natalie Cole . . . Jack Nicholson . . . the "Rocky" threesome of Carl Weathers, Burt Young and Dolph Lundgren . . . Chuck Norris . . . Don Johnson . . . Marvin Hagler . . . Billy Crystal . . . Matthew Broderick . . . Judd Nelson . . . Sugar Ray Leonard . . . and on and on. This fight was real estate mogul Donald Trump's show. He had paid for it—$11 million—and had flown in his celebrities from the East River heliport on Manhattan's East Side, some 130 miles to the north. He had treated them to a private prefight party at his hotel adjoining the Convention Hall that spared them the necessity of watching three hours of preliminary bouts. As fight time drew near, Trump's guests were ushered to their seats in the fenced-in ringside area known as the "celebrity corral." Everyone who meant something to Trump had to be introduced, from financier Carl Ichan to New York Yankees owner George Steinbrenner—which brought a crescendo of booing and catcalls for perhaps the most unpopular owner of any major sports franchise in history—to Jesse Jackson, then a candidate for the Democratic presidential nomination. When Tyson's wife, actress Robin Givens, was introduced, a torrent of loud booing reverberated through the enormous arena, the public letting her know as she sat there at ringside with her mother and Donald Trump and all the beautiful people just what they thought of her. Maybe you've been successful pulling the wool over Tyson's eyes, they were saying, but you haven't fooled us.

Meanwhile, back in the dressing room, the impasse was being resolved, as the crowd began to wonder what was causing the delay. Tyson shadow-boxed to stay loose, listened to blaring rap music on a tape player and seethed inside. Larry Hazzard said he could find nothing wrong with the glove. Lewis was insistent, until Spinks's trainer, the aging master and universally respected Eddie Futch, also told him there was nothing wrong with it. Lewis finally relented, but as he left the room, Tyson turned to his trainer Kevin Rooney and, channeling his fury from Lewis to the man he could shortly vent it on, said of Spinks, "You know, I'm gonna hurt this guy," and then slammed a rapid one-two combination of punches against the dressing room wall for emphasis.

At 11:20 P.M., the challenger, Michael Spinks, made his way to the ring. As the lights dimmed and the crowd anticipated the entrance of the fighters, the unmistakable electricity that always builds in an arena before this moment began to be palpable. The theme from *Rocky*—used how many times by how many fighters?—heralded the entrance of both men. Spinks climbed through the ropes first, robed, wearing white trunks and white shoes, both knees taped with Ace bandages. As the underdog, he had strong sentimental support from the crowd. Next, with his trainer Kevin Rooney leading in the long walk down the aisle, came the champion. Rooney's arms were raised high over his head. Tyson, by contrast, was impassive, seemingly oblivious to the spectators surging into the aisle around him, seeking to glimpse, to touch, the champion before The Big Fight. As usual, he wore no robe, or socks, only his customary black satin trunks and black leather shoes, his red leather gloves with white surgical tape around the wrists identical to those of Spinks. He climbed into the ring between the ropes, bouncing, flexing and loosening up, getting the feel of the ring under his feet.

Across the ring, Spinks was calm, quiet, perhaps too quiet. He had never had any qualms about openly admitting the fear that all fighters feel, whether or not they acknowledge it. He was still wearing his robe, standing in his corner, not loosening up—perhaps a strategic mistake—as Tyson flicked jabs into the air while the prefight announcements continued.

Standing in the ring was Muhammad Ali, flanked by Donald Trump and the unmistakable figure of the flamboyant and controversial promoter Don King. In a time now past, King had made millions for Ali—and millions for himself along the way—and now he paid the faded legend $10,000 to put in an appearance every time Tyson fought. Tonight, Ali was wearing a conservative suit and tie, spectacles, and a blank expression. His affliction with Parkinson's disease has been widely known for several years. Tonight, who knew what thoughts raced through his mind, what memories of past glories in rings throughout the world when he was at the center of attention? One thing was certain: The engaging Ali smile and the twinkle in his eyes were also just memories. He was introduced to the most thunderous ovation of the night, but he could only feebly acknowledge the cheers with a half-hearted lifting of his arm and then walk unsteadily from corner to corner, offering a perfunctory word of encouragement to each fighter.

Spinks's robe was now off as he was being introduced: "212¼ pounds . . . 31 and 0 . . . 21 by knockout . . ." At thirty-one years of age, he was nine years older than Tyson, who paced back and forth, his mouthpiece already in place, anxious to get on with the event ahead. Then Tyson was introduced: 218¼ pounds . . . 34 and 0 . . ."—Tyson continued to pace—". . . the undefeated, undisputed heavyweight champion of the world, 'Iron' Mike Tyson."

At last, the preliminaries were done with. Veteran referee Frank Cappuccino signaled both men to the center of the ring. Futch accompanied Spinks; Rooney went with Tyson. Both fighters avoided the stare-down, that traditional show of false bravado between fighters. They did not make eye contact. Cappuccino's instructions were brief: "You both were given your instructions in the dressing room. Any questions? Touch gloves. Good luck to both of you." Both men returned to their corners. At last the final high moment of drama had arrived, the time when the adrenalin pumps not only for the fighters, but for the crowd as well. The cornermen cleared out of the ring, and a swell of sound began to rise from the crowd. Spinks dropped to one knee in his corner for a final moment of prayer, while across the ring, Rooney hugged Tyson and whispered a few last words of strategy and encouragement. Butch Lewis shouted the same at his man, Spinks. Already nearly half an hour behind schedule, Cappuccino impatiently hurried everyone along, yelling "Let's go, let's go, let's go." The bell rang, and the fight which many thought would never happen, the fight that everyone knew must happen, had begun.

Chapter 2

Little Fairy Boy

People who are born round don't die square.
—Cus D'Amato

Living on the edge, running the streets. That was what the young boy loved best. Even now, years later as a man, it's where he loves to return, where he feels free, where the sense of danger is a natural high, yet where he feels safe because he knows the streets are his turf. He is a product of the streets, a creature of the streets—not the tree-lined suburban streets of lawns and private homes, not the neatly paved streets of terraced houses and apartment buildings of the middle class, but the mean streets, the city streets of Brooklyn.

Mike Tyson was born to these streets. They were what he knew from the day he drew his first breath of life, June 30, 1966. It is always hotter on the city streets than in the country, and it always seems to be hotter in the ghetto streets than elsewhere in the city. It was already hot, July hot, when Lorna Tyson brought home Michael, her second son, to their tenement apartment in Bedford-Stuyvesant. In the streets, children ran free, ran wild, in and out of the water gushing all day from the fire hydrants, the only way to stay cool where there were no swimming pools and no air conditioners to cool tenement apartments. His father, Jimmy Kirkpatrick, was a strapping black man forty-two years of age, over 200 pounds, a construction worker. Jimmy, too, was wild, liked to run free. He never got around to marrying Lorna, so Lorna's maiden name, Tyson, was the one entered on Michael's birth certificate. There were two other children, Rodney, five years older than Mike, and, in between the two boys, sister Denise.

When Mike was just two years old, the family fell apart. Jimmy developed a heart condition and was hospitalized; when he came out he could no longer work. Unable to support his family, he felt strangled, smothered, boxed in.

He needed to be free, and so he left. The streets of Bedford-Stuyvesant are not a good place, especially for a family floundering without its breadwinner, its man, its father. For Lorna, with three children and no means of support, there was only one answer. Welfare. Public Assistance. That is how the Tysons survived. It was a comedown, for Lorna Tyson had education, but the burden of seeing to it that she and her children survived was a full-time job where they lived, so she couldn't work.

Things got worse, and as Mike was nearing his tenth birthday, Lorna was forced to move her brood further into the depths, to the section of Brooklyn known as Brownsville. Watts . . . Chicago's South Side . . . Houston's Fifth Ward . . . Fort Apache, The Bronx—some of America's most notorious addresses, and Brownsville ranked right up there with the worst of them. In any jungle the strong prey on the weak. Mike Tyson was one of the weak ones. Small for his age then, he was an easy victim for the predators of this urban jungle. He spoke softly, with a lisp, so they called him "fairy boy." He was there to be beaten up. Even the girls beat him. If he had some money, they took it from him. If he was wearing a jacket someone wanted, it was gone in a flash and all he could do was to run home and cry. Lorna cared about Mike, and she hurt for him. It tore her up inside when he came home in tears, but there was nothing she could do out on the streets of Brownsville to shelter him from the hurt, the humiliation, the taunting: "Fairy boy, gimme that dollar. . . . Fairy boy, run home and cry to yo' momma befo' I kick yo' ass." But even at home he found no refuge. When Lorna was not there, Rodney took his turn beating up his baby brother.

In the winter, they slept with their clothes on. There was no heat and no hot water. And sleep was uneasy, because they had to be always on the alert for smoke. Maybe someone would start a fire in another apartment to try to keep warm. Or maybe someone would set the building on fire on purpose. After all, if you got burned out, then the city had to take care of you, send you and your family somewhere to sleep that was warm, give you food, maybe find you a better place to live.

The family moved from Herzl Street to Amboy Street,

and Brownsville continued to nurture Mike Tyson. His playground was the inside of abandoned tenements or the empty lots strewn with rubble, broken bottles, discarded refrigerators, rusting, burned-out car hulks, bricks from the apartment buildings that had once stood on those lots. He saw things that no ten-year-old should see. Junkies dead from overdosing. People beaten with baseball bats or shot with guns. Yet, shielded by his mother as best she could, his sister his primary playmate, he remained gentle, and therefore a victim, in the midst of all this violence, violence that his mother abhorred, that she hoped against hope she could keep him from succumbing to. What are the odds that a young boy could rise from a cesspool like this to become the richest, the strongest, the most exalted athlete in the world? 100,000 to 1? 500,000 to 1? a million to one?

Friendless, he turned to animals and began to keep a pigeon coop. When his pigeons flew, the young boy watched them in the sky, marveling at their freedom, their ability to soar above the filth and danger and rubble. He loved those birds more than anything: (Indeed, he would continue to raise and fly pigeons even when he became heavyweight champion of the world. He kept his makeshift coop on the roof of an abandoned building. Accustomed to staying out all night, sleeping sometimes in deserted tenements, now he sometimes stayed with his birds. These were his babies, just as he was Lorna's, and he loved them the same way. He stroked them, cared for them when they were sick.

Then, one day it happened: the turning point. Would Mike Tyson have gone on to become heavyweight champion of the world ten years later had it not occurred? Who knows. There have been several turning points in his life, without which, by his own admission, he would probably have ended up in jail instead of winning the most coveted individual title in sport. For young Mike Tyson, the little "fairy boy" of Brownsville, this was certainly the first of those decisive moments. A teenage bully, the kind of anonymous punk that the neighborhood breeds so well, approached him at his pigeon coop. He didn't want the birds, had no interest in them. He was just out for some fun at the expense of someone weaker, smaller and helpless. He grabbed one of the pigeons. Mike pleaded with him to give it back, to let it go, but the older boy just laughed and taunted him with the bird. Then, suddenly, the older boy took the pigeon's head and twisted it around until its neck snapped and the head was torn off. He tossed the lifeless body at Mike's feet and watched as its legs and wings twitched, even with its head gone. In an instant, without thinking, just reacting, Mike pounced on the bigger boy. For the first time in his life, he fought back. Someone had unknowingly crossed over the line, and from that moment on there would never be any return for Mike Tyson to the meek little kid he had been. Fighting was new to him. He didn't know what to do, but his instincts, his blind rage, the surge of revulsion at what this bully had done, his fear, his pent-up emotions, all spilled over, and he attacked like a cornered animal, gouging, pulling, kicking, punching. He would admit, many years later, that he loved the feeling, that he still relished the memory of it. It was the first time he emerged triumphant by using his fists.

As Mike's reputation in the streets spread, he was no longer regarded as the lisping, effeminate little "fairy boy." He gained a new respect; he could sense it, and it gave him a feeling of acceptance, of self-worth as judged by the law of the streets. Suddenly, as he began to run with a gang called the Jolly Stompers, the streets were his turf. Bristol Park . . . Pitkin Avenue . . . Rockaway Avenue . . . Herzl Street . . . Lincoln Terrace Park . . . all of it, all of Brownsville, was now his territory. He was a gladiator, a warrior. The prey had now become the predator, getting his thrills from making others his victims. He got a natural high, taking from others. He was at this point eleven years old and rapidly becoming a cunning street criminal. His sister recalls that he became one of the best pickpockets in Brooklyn, able to remove a wallet or a wristwatch so deftly as to go completely undetected. Sometimes it was a less sophisticated theft—just snatching a necklace or a gold chain from someone's neck and running.

In Public School 396, he had been so poor that the teachers sometimes gave him shoes, and when these wore out he had to put cardboard inside them to cover the holes. However, with the money from his crimes, he could now buy his own shoes and have cash in his pocket besides. Never mind that he caused his mother grief and anguish over whether he would kill someone—or wind up dead in the gutter himself. Inevitably, Mike and his gang soon graduated to holding up stores. There were small neighborhood markets and the storefront check-cashing service where they could lay in wait for those newly flush with cash. Mike was still only eleven, too small to handle a gun, so he was the bagman, loading up the gang's spoils and then running. Sometimes the police would come and the gang would scatter, Mike running, his heart pumping with fear and exhilaration as the adrenalin raced through his veins, using his turf, his streets, as a familiar sanctuary, ducking into the burned-out shell of a windowless, deserted building, darting up the stairs into an abandoned apartment, scattering the rats and vermin as he hid, safe from the police, who prudently refrained from risking their lives in vacant tenements at twilight. He would sit quietly and wait, feeling his heart pounding inside his chest, enjoying the almost sexual charge of doing wrong, of being chased, and of escaping. Later in life, he would tell interviewers that though he did bad things, in his heart he was good, implying, somehow, through some convoluted reasoning, that his behavior should be excused, because "inside" he was pure. But neighbors remember him as "a bad-ass kid." When he wasn't with his gang, he'd commit his crimes solo. In the opinion of one young woman who grew up with him in Brooklyn, "That boy is a devil. You can see the devil in his eyes. He always was bad. I don't care how much money he makes, he'll always be a devil, he'll always be evil."

Escape from the police was not possible every time, and Mike began to get caught. However, there are more street criminals, more youthful offenders and juvenile delinquents than there are places to house them, and the system is too overloaded to deal effectively with all the underage recidivists who plague the sidewalks. When Mike was caught, he would be sent to various juvenile detention centers in Brooklyn, only to escape or be released and sent home to his mother who asked him, "Why? *Why*?" And then, to return to his now familiar way of life, a life he had learned to love. He knew he would be caught again, knew that if he lived long enough it was only a matter of time before he ended up in a prison cell, but he liked what he was doing too much to stop.

He would wait by bus stops, and as the buses began to pull away from the curb, he would reach in through the open windows and pull chains off women's throats. He would offer to help women loaded down with groceries to carry their bags, then hand them back and grab their purses. He and his gang of Jolly Stompers would roll drunks at night, take their money and pull the rings from their fingers and the watches from their wrists. Tyson blames no one else for his behavior. "I wasn't sucked in by anyone else. I wanted to be sucked in," he has said.

Now he was nearly twelve years old, getting bigger, and now he could handle a gun. A pistol replaced his fists. A pistol was much more of a status symbol in Brownsville, and putting a pistol in a shopkeeper's face was even more of a kick. Now he was playing for higher stakes. But higher stakes carry higher risks, and the next time he was caught, he finished up in the Spofford Detention Center in the Bronx, and escape from Spofford was tougher than Mike anticipated, so there he stayed.

Muhammad Ali was then the heavyweight champion of the world, and one day he came to visit the kids in Spofford. Mike Tyson saw Ali in the flesh that day for the first time. Like everyone else, he knew the legend from television, the magazines, but here he was, larger than life, close enough for Mike to reach out and touch, being mobbed by the screaming kids, giving out autographs, talking to them about being good, doing right, leading good lives when they left there. Mike saw the way people responded to him, looked up to him, listened to him. He saw the smiling faces of the guards, the counselors as they looked at Ali, and he said to himself, "That's what I want to be, I want to be champ of the world some day." And then, Ali was gone, and Mike returned to reality.

By now, his past had caught up with him. Barely twelve years old, he already had a rap sheet that could have belonged to a much older offender. Lorna could not handle him, hard as she tried, and he was becoming increasingly dangerous. It was decided that it would be best for all concerned if Mike was removed from the streets of Brownsville. He was sentenced to be incarcerated at the Tryon School for Boys in the mountains of upstate Johnstown, New York, nearly 200 miles from the hollow tenement skeletons and cracked pavements of his beloved Brooklyn streets.

Chapter 3

The Discoverer

*There are very few new things in this world, very few.
That's why people that are young, if they're smart, try to
profit from the experience of an older guy so they won't
have to go through all the pain and suffering. But a certain
amount of pain and suffering is good, because it makes
a person think they've learned.*

—Cus D'Amato

The formal structure at Tryon was a new experience for
Mike and one he didn't take to very well. For all intents and
purposes Tryon was a prison, although it was not called so
because those sent there were not adults in the eyes of the
law. There were three so-called "open" cottages, where the
boys had privileges and discipline was relatively relaxed.
Then there was Elmwood, the confined cottage, where the
kids who made trouble, the kids who needed a tight rein,
were sent. Before long, Mike Tyson would be headed for
Elmwood.

During his first weeks at Tryon, he began to lash out. He
had little confidence in himself, and he was on new, unfamiliar ground, where instinct told him he had to establish
himself. As the counselors put it, Mike began "acting out."
At first it was fights with the other boys, then it escalated to
threatening a teacher—anything to make himself look good
in the eyes of his peers.

One theory is that kids who act out like this are asking to
be disciplined, asking for some order to be imposed on their
lives and on their inner turmoil. Perhaps this is what Mike
Tyson was crying out for. But there may have been another
reason why he wanted to be sent to the disciplinary cottage.
He had heard that one of the head counselors at Elmwood
had been a fighter, and a pretty good one at that. His name
was Bobby Stewart. Five years earlier, in 1974, Stewart had
won the U.S. National Golden Gloves Light-Heavyweight
Championship by defeating Michael Dokes. (Dokes would
later go on to win the WBA Heavyweight Championship of

the World.) Bobby Stewart turned pro, had a modest career of a dozen fights or so, most of them in small towns like Latham, New York, and then quit and went to work for the Tryon School, not far from his home in upstate New York. Mike Tyson remembered that day Muhammad Ali came to Spofford in the Bronx, remembered how he'd thought how great it would be if he could be a champion some day, too. Maybe a guy like Bobby Stewart held the key, could show him, teach him. He wanted to meet Stewart, he told one of his counselors.

By accident, by design, or by a fortuitous mixture of both, he got that chance before long. One day he beat up another kid and went into a rage. It took several guards to subdue him. Bob Stewart recalls the first time he saw Tyson, two of the biggest guards at Tryon were escorting him over to Elmwood, the "bad cottage." It happened to be during Stewart's shift. Tyson was placed in a "secure room" with people assigned to watch him. "Be careful of this kid," one of the guards who had brought Tyson over said. "He's trouble. He beats the kids up; he'll attack anybody."

Immediately, Tyson told those assigned to watch him that he wanted to talk to Bobby Stewart, but Stewart decided to let him cool down for a while and see what happened. The next day, Tyson's overseers reported to Stewart. For a complete animal, such as they had been warned he was, he had been amazingly well behaved; he had not caused any trouble. So Stewart ordered that Tyson be shifted from his secure room into the general living area of Elmwood, though he was still kept isolated from the other boys. Tyson kept asking to speak to Stewart. Another day passed. All three shifts reported back to Stewart that Tyson had been well behaved, had done everything they'd asked, had caused no trouble. Stewart was satisfied—to a point. He decided to bypass the standard procedure in his first encounter with Tyson. To establish his dominance, to test Tyson's motives, he would skip the psychologically approved, kid-gloves approach. Instead, he went up to Tyson's window and startled the boy by banging on it and shouting, "I'm Stewart. What the fuck do you want?" Tyson responded, "I want to talk to you. I want to be a fighter." "So do the rest of these assholes around here," Stewart screamed back, "but they can't even clean up their own act. You keep your act straight, and maybe in a week or two we'll see what happens."

From that day on, Tyson was a model inmate. Stewart was astonished by the radical change in his behavior, considering the reports he'd received about the boy's constant flare-ups prior to coming to Elmwood. Finally, Stewart told him, "I'll work with you, teach you to box, if you behave yourself in school. Don't fool with the teachers, don't mess with the other students. I want you to try. I don't care if you flunk every subject, but you pay attention and you try."

Stewart still had a lesson to teach Tyson. The first time he boxed with the youngster, he wanted to make a point, to give the young bully a taste of his own medicine. With the other boys watching, "He tried to humiliate me so the other kids would see I was nothing," Tyson recalled. "He hit me in the body and I went down. My air stopped. I thought I was dead." Stewart had made his point. There would be no need to repeat it.

Stewart began to work with Tyson in the afternoons, teaching him some moves, some footwork, and beginning to win the boy's confidence. Tyson had come from an environment where the only white people he had interacted with were those he was in conflict with: school authorities, police, court officers and judges, detention-home officials. He mistrusted them. He was withdrawn, sullen, branded by the school authorities as having a violent personality. Stewart could sense that Mike was embarrassed because he could not read or write. He was a boy in a man's body, 5'8", 190 pounds, yet mentally still a child. Stewart could nevertheless sense there was a spark there, an intelligence, that just needed to be nurtured. He went to another kid at Elmwood and asked him for a favor. This boy, also black, was pretty clever, and Stewart asked him to work with Mike to help him with his reading skills.

One day, Stewart went to the school psychiatrist to read Tyson's file. He saw that Mike was classified as "borderline retarded." Mike was very slow mentally, the psychiatrist told him. "He's not very slow at all," Stewart said. "How did they determine he's borderline retarded?" "We tested him, reading and writing tests," was the response. Stewart exploded. "He can't read and write! How can you determine he's retarded if he can't read and write?" He stormed out.

Stewart continued his work with Mike in his own way, and the results quickly became apparent. After about a month, he got a call from Tyson's teacher. "Whatever happened to this kid?" the teacher asked. "He has no more problems, he's trying hard, his behavior has completely changed." In three months, Tyson had improved his reading abilities by three grade levels.

Physically, as well as mentally, Tyson continued to grow over those final months of 1979. He was up over 200 pounds, all solid muscle packed on a frame still just 5'8" tall. The first time Stewart put him on a weight bench, Mike bench-pressed 250 pounds ten times, something most men can't do once in a lifetime. Stewart spoke by phone periodically to Lorna Tyson in Brooklyn. "Mrs. Tyson," he would tell her, "this kid is changing himself." She would just laugh, only half believing him. "She sounded like a nice woman," Stewart would later recall. She did care about the kid. She tried to keep him in line. According to records, she was a registered nurse, had gone to school. But when the old man took off, she couldn't raise the kids and work, so she went on welfare."

1979 turned to 1980. Mike Tyson was thirteen and a half years old. By now, Stewart had realized that Tyson's interest in boxing was not a passing phase. He saw real talent emerging, talent that he had neither the time nor the skills to continue developing. He'd seen a dramatic change in the boy over the months. "The thing that impressed me the most," Stewart recalls, "was not the physical part, but his ability to give up all the bullshit he'd done for thirteen years to devote himself to something else. The physical stuff impressed me, but the mental stuff shocked the shit out of me." Stewart brought Tyson down to Matt Baranski's gym in Albany and showed him to Baranski. Later, Baranski would work as Tyson's cut-man from the outset of his pro career all the way through his heavyweight title matches. Both Baranski and Stewart knew there was one person who could assess this burgeoning phenomenon: the legendary—and controversial—boxing manager Cus D'Amato, who was then, at the age of seventy-two, living in semiretirement in the little town of Catskill, New York, where he ran a gym for amateur kids to train. Stewart knew about the program he ran for the kids, knew that some of them actually lived in the big white Victorian house overlooking the Hudson River that Cus shared with Camille Ewald. If one seriously wanted to learn and toed the line, he could live with Cus, go to school in town, learn how to box.

It was a Monday when Stewart phoned D'Amato in Catskill and asked him for the favor. "Cus, I've got a kid up here I'd like you to look at. He's pretty good."

That night, Stewart sat Tyson down and told him where they were going the next evening. "Mike," he said, "Cus is the guy who made Floyd Patterson the heavyweight champ of the world. When I was a fighter I was able to fight on international teams. I traveled all over the United States. I went to South America, to Canada, all for free, man, because I was a fighter. Mike, you can do the same if you want to. Maybe you can better yourself through boxing. You're good, you've got talent." Tyson listened, a little dubious about the whole thing, yet at the same time, excited. Maybe he could really become a fighter. Maybe he could.

Stewart knew that the boy was good—at least, that he had potential—but Tyson would have to make an impression on D'Amato that first night they went to Catskill. There were a few moves he knew would impress Cus if Mike was able to perform them the next night, a few tricks, a few smart maneuvers in the ring that a veteran fighter would know, moves that D'Amato was sure to notice in a thirteen-year-old kid. Some of the moves, such as how to slip out of a corner a certain way, were techniques Stewart knew Cus taught, so they were sure to catch the eye of the old man. He spent the evening showing them to Mike, then making him repeat them over and over until it was time for lights out and for Stewart to head home.

All was quiet that night until about 3:30 in the morning, when the silence was broken by noises coming from Tyson's room. A couple of counselors headed down the hall to see what was the matter. From inside the room came grunting, snorting sounds. When they opened the door, the counselors found Mike in the pitch dark, shadow-boxing, rehearsing, practicing the moves Bobby Stewart had shown him hour earlier. Mike Tyson was ready to impress Cus D'Amato.

On a March night in 1980, Stewart and Tyson made their

fateful drive from Johnstown to Catskill, a journey of about 75 miles. They stopped at the house to pick up Cus, and Tyson had never seen anything quite like it. "What am I gonna do here?" he asked Stewart, "sweep the floors?" "No Mike. You can live here if you want to," said Stewart. "If you behave yourself."

They went over to the small gym above the police station that was the Catskill Boxing Club. With D'Amato was his young trainer, Teddy Atlas, and the one professional fighter under his wing, Kevin Rooney, both of whom lived in the house that had become a sort of fighters' dormitory. The three men were immediately skeptical of Tyson's age: How could those 210 pounds of rippling muscle compressed into that stocky frame belong to a thirteen-year-old? In any case, it was one thing for a young fighter to show off his physique, to look good hitting the bag or shadow-boxing; Mike Tyson had to be tested under fire. If he passed the test, it would be a long time before D'Amato would put him in a ring again to box; before then, a long teaching and conditioning process would have to take place. But a new fighter must first be tested mentally, in the ring, much as a young bull is tested on the farm to see if he has what it takes to fight on a Sunday afternoon in the Plaza de Toros in Madrid. Both must demonstrate that they at least have the potential in their character not to falter later on, when hundreds or thousands are watching, and the moment of truth arrives.

D'Amato decided that Tyson should box with Stewart, who at twenty-seven was still in his physical prime. His active ring career had ended recently enough for him still to be able to perform at a professional level, yet he was mature enough to know that his job was to allow Tyson to show what he was capable of without egotistically trying to outdo this raw, green kid in order to make himself look good. At 180 pounds, Stewart was outweighed by Tyson by some 30 pounds. But his experience as a national amateur champion and in the professional ring, as well as the fact that he was facing a kid literally half his age, should easily overcome the weight advantage Tyson possessed.

When the bell rang, Tyson came at Stewart very aggressively. Certainly he was trying to impress his select audience, but it was immediately apparent that there was a resolve, a determination in this young boy that was somewhat unique. And then there was that power—the power that in a few years would intimidate opponents before they even entered the ring to face him. It was obvious that first night. Tyson fired shots to Stewart's ribs. Stewart was too experienced to show it, but later he told them it felt as though his ribs were breaking. And there was a quickness, a catlike speed of reflex that was also unusual in an untrained, unschooled fighter. Tyson refused to take a backward step. He kept coming forward with such raw power, such grit and determination, that Stewart was forced to do something they all thought his ring generalship would make unnecessary— he was compelled for his own preservation to open up with force on Tyson to keep the young fighter off him. One of the shots Stewart fired in aggressive defense caught Tyson flush on the nose, and he began to bleed. By the second round, the nose was bleeding badly, and Tyson's face was smeared red. Yet still he kept coming, punching, absorbing blows, coming, coming, unrelenting, until the bell rang.

Teddy Atlas wiped the blood from Tyson's face in the corner and said he'd seen enough. "One more round," Tyson said. "No, that's all, I don't have to see any more," replied Atlas. Tyson appealed to Stewart: "No, no, we always box three rounds." D'Amato glanced over at Stewart in a manner which said, "Holy Christ, look at this kid." Tyson had, indeed, impressed.

Cus and Atlas recognized that a good part of the tenacity, the persistence, the strength of mind that Tyson had demonstrated was bravado, put on by the youngster because he was in strange surroundings and knew well that he was on display, being tested. Inside he might not have felt as confident as he looked. Most likely he didn't, but he nevertheless forced himself past his doubts and insecurities and made himself perform this way. And this was of vital importance in a fighter if he were to transcend the level of the ordinary. Untrained eyes would simply have seen a brave, tough kid. But D'Amato and his disciples, Atlas and Rooney, understood the psychology of what they had just witnessed. "I figured," says Atlas, "that we could mature that, nurture that, and with that ability—not just his physical attributes, but that mental ability—he would do what we wanted him to do."

Bobby Stewart, breathing heavily, climbed out of the

ring. He walked over to D'Amato and said, "Well, Cus, what do you think? Is he a pretty good kid?" He was totally unprepared for D'Amato's reply. "Pretty good kid?" D'Amato said incredulously. "That's the heavyweight champion of the world. If he wants it, and can avoid outside distractions, Bobby, you're looking at the future heavyweight champion of the world."

"I had told Mike," Stewart reminisced, "I'll bring you down three or four times. Maybe if Cus likes you he'll take an interest in you." Now, when he heard D'Amato's words, he was so stunned he felt like crying. "When we were going out, I said, 'You know what—he said you're going to be a champ,' and Mike hugged me. It was a really nice deal."

In the weeks that followed, Tyson and Stewart returned frequently to Catskill, where D'Amato or Atlas would work with the youngster, showing him moves or combinations that Stewart would then make him practice over and over until they returned to the gym for the next lesson. Tyson picked things up so naturally that even Stewart was impressed by the way he could adapt and incorporate each new move and rapidly make himself look like an experienced fighter.

When Tyson was allowed weekend furloughs away from Tryon, he spent them in Catskill with D'Amato and Atlas. It was arranged that Tyson, still a ward of the state, would be released in D'Amato's custody. He would live in Camille Ewald's home with Cus, Atlas, Rooney and the other boys; he would go to school in Catskill; and he would learn under the supervision of the master to be a lethally efficient machine in the boxing ring. The school term began in September. In order to settle him in to his new home, new surroundings, with new people, he was released a few months early from Tryon and moved to Catskill in the summer of 1980.

With his knowledgeable boxing eye and his compassion for a sullen youngster who needed a break, Bobby Stewart had discovered the fighter the world would come to know as one of the greatest heavyweight champions and the richest, the highest-paid athlete in history. And yet, the discoverer would become a footnote, the first of several people who would be swept away and forgotten when they had outlived their usefulness to Team Tyson. There were rumors that, in gratitude, Tyson's people had set Stewart up in an automobile livery business, but he just chuckles when asked about these reports. No one set him up in any business, he says. After leaving the Tryon School, he went to work as a chauffeur for a doctor. He does not own the car he chauffeurs. It belongs to his employer. The only recognition he got for bringing Mike Tyson to Cus D'Amato was an afterthought. Six years after that fateful first trip to Catskill and a year after D'Amato died, after Tyson won the heavyweight title, Kevin Rooney (by then Tyson's trainer) asked Stewart if he had been taken care of. Taken care of? Stewart didn't know what he was talking about. Rooney was angry. He went to Tyson's manager, Jim Jacobs, and confronted him about the matter. Jacobs summoned Stewart to his New York office and handed him a check for $10,000. He told him Cus had wanted him to have it, but he was not to tell anyone. It wasn't even given tax free. Stewart ended up with only $7,800. "When Cus passed on, they sort of forgot me, I guess. Believe me, I'm not crying or anything like that," says Stewart. "It just irks me, their playing games over stuff like that . . . I wish they didn't give me nothing, to be honest with you. It belittled me in my own mind. Money can ruin people. I liked the kid. I did it because I liked doing it. I really cared about the kid."

Chapter 4

Cus

All idealism is falsehood in the face of necessity.
—Friedrich Nietzsche

When Mike Tyson arrived in Catskill to live with and learn from Cus D'Amato, it is certain that the thirteen-year-old unschooled youngster had only a vague notion of who this man was. After all, D'Amato had fought his battles and made his mark long before Michael Tyson came on the scene. D'Amato had come to Catskill (population: 5,000) in the 1960s with the aim of establishing a gym in the small town located some thirty miles from the state capital of Albany. Situated on the west bank of the Hudson River, Catskill is connected to the town of Hudson, New York, on the east side of the river by the Rip Van Winkle Bridge.

D'Amato's idea was to run an amateur club where he would train local youngsters, take in some young fighters to live in his house, boys who had trouble of one kind of another. The house and gym would also serve as a camp for professional fighters who made the pilgrimage to Catskill to seek the old master's advice. Economically depressed and located in Greene County, the poorest in New York state, the town needed a recreational outlet for its boys, especially one run by a man with the knowledge and experience of Cus D'Amato. His proposal that the town give him the small hall above the police station and Fire Company No. 5 on Main Street was accepted, and thus was established the Catskill Boxing Club, which nearly two decades later would spawn the young phenomenon dubbed by TV commentator Randy Gordon "Catskill Thunder"—Mike Tyson.

If D'Amato had a special warmth, an empathy, for troubled youngsters, his own background might well explain it. He was born on January 17, 1908, in the Classon Point section of the Bronx. His given name was Constantine, but he soon became just Cus on the streets. When Cus was five years old, his mother died. In later years, he would say, "I don't remember my mother and I was fortunate, because I was self-reliant at a very young age. I was not confused by the ideas, the thoughts of mothers and fathers who, well-meaning though they may be, mess up the minds of their children.''

It was a rough, tough neighborhood, and the five D'Amato brothers found out quickly they had to be tough to survive. Brother Tony had a reputation for being able to take on four or five cops by himself in the street and lay them all out. Later, when Tony owned a bar, he was closing up one night, alone, when two bruisers entered. When Tony informed them he was closing, they told him they were going to drink for a while and that he was staying open whether he liked it or not. Tony went to the door, but instead of fleeing as they had expected him to, he locked it so they couldn't get out and then beat the living daylights out of them both. When the police arrived, the two were laid out on the floor of the bar, barely conscious. Tony's wife says things like that happened "quite often" in those days. All Tony says is, "I didn't let nobody step on me."

In 1925, Cus's oldest brother, Jerry, got tough with a cop on the street. Jerry was drunk. When the cop poked him a little too hard, perhaps, with his nightstick to move him along, Jerry responded by striking back and grabbing the nightstick. An altercation followed. When it was over, Jerry D'Amato lay dead, shot by the cop. Cus was then seventeen years old.

At the same time that Babe Ruth was slugging home runs on the other side of the Bronx in the new Yankee Stadium, the young Cus D'Amato was learning valuable lessons about fear and cowardice, toughness and courage and survival on the streets, lessons he would later incorporate in the unique philosophy of life and boxing which he imparted to his fighters. One lesson that became familiar to his disciples was that the fear of something is usually worse than the reality, a lesson he expounded using an example from his own life. He would describe how a guy from another neighborhood, who had a reputation as one of the best knife fighters on the streets of the Bronx, was swaggering around Cus's own patch and intimidating his pals. One day the hoodlum challenged each of them to a knife fight. Everyone was afraid and no one would accept the challenge. Once his dominance was established, the challenger began insulting and humiliating them until he'd had his fill, and then left. Word of this reached Cus that evening. He was so angered that he sought out the antagonist and challenged him to a fist fight. The reply was no; instead, D'Amato was offered the opportunity to avenge the honor of his friends in a knife fight. The foolhardy Cus accepted. It was agreed the two would meet at an abandoned building at seven the next morning, alone. There would be no witnesses in case one of them ended up dead. On his way home, Cus couldn't help but think it was most likely to be him. Fear gripped him as it never had before. He hadn't the slightest idea how to wield a knife in a fight, yet here he was about to face an expert. When he was finally able to control his fear, he thought up an idea that would at least give him a chance. Maybe he didn't know about knife fighting, but he did know about boxing, about using his fists. He found an ice pick, carved the handle down so it would fit in his closed palm, with the blade extending out between his middle and ring fingers. He then practiced as if he were boxing, only now, at the end of his fist, was a deadly blade as he jabbed the air.

In the few hours that remained until dawn, he tried unsuccessfully to sleep. He then headed for the empty warehouse where the fight was to take place, getting there early in order to check out the surroundings and prepare himself for his adversary. He taped the ice pick inside his fist, made sure the blade protruded far enough and wrapped a jacket around his forearm for protection. Then he waited. When the fear built up too much and threatened to overwhelm him, he danced around, practicing his technique. He learned that motion relieves tension. The minutes passed. Seven o'clock came and went, and the knife fighter had still not appeared. D'Amato felt relieved, but then checked himself. If he began to wind down and his opponent suddenly materialized, he knew his resolve to fight might be weakened. Finally, when more than an hour had passed, Cus realized that fear must have got the better of the knife fighter. He wasn't going to appear. Cus went home, a hero to his friends. The knife fighter never showed himself again. Cus knew he had won a victory, not only over his adversary, but over himself. He had faced his fear and refused to allow it to get the better of him.

Another time, when he was a young boy, long before the challenge of the knife fight, he found himself alone, in a deserted lot at nightfall. It was common knowledge among the kids that a monster roamed this lot, and no one ever went there at night, especially alone. But it was late and Cus had to get home, and the lot was a short cut. He forced himself to carry on although he was afraid. When he had gone too far to turn back, he saw it: a shadow looming, large and menacing, against the night sky ahead. There was nothing for it but to go forward, to see if he could somehow slip past this horrible thing unnoticed or maybe outrun it to the safety of the tenements a short distance away. As he kept walking, it got larger and more terrifying, and the stories his friends had told him about this monster raced through his head. Then, suddenly, he saw what it was. A tree. A large, dead tree, standing in the middle of the lot, its branches moving in the wind. That was the monster he had seen against the sky. What his imagination had conjured up was far more horrible than the reality. Cus never forgot those lessons about fear and imagination, courage and reality. He would teach them over and over to the fighters he would eventually train.

As a young man, Cus "wasn't the type that wanted to work," according to his brother Tony. "My father used to support him." By the time he was thirty-one, other than an occasional job, his one major achievement had been running a fusion political club in his neighborhood and carrying the heavily Democratic district for Fiorello La Guardia in his successful mayoral campaign. Jerry D'Amato had done some boxing, as had another brother, Nick, and so Cus started to learn a little about the sport.

In 1939, along with two friends who eventually dropped out, Cus opened a gym, the Gramercy, at 116 East 14th Street in Manhattan, and began to handle some fighters, interrupted by a spell in the Army during World War II. Nick and Tony (when he could get time away from his bar) helped Cus, who started to build a stable of good fighters that included Jimmy Anest, a deaf mute, Johnny Brown, Joe Juliano and Artie Diamond.

In 1945, when he returned from the Army, he met the only woman in his life: Camille Ewald, a Ukranian girl who had grown up in western Canada before moving to New

York. They began a relationship that ended forty years later at D'Amato's death. When the stories about Mike Tyson began to emerge in newspapers and magazines in the mid-1980s, Camille's name came to public attention for the first time, because she ran the big Victorian house in Catskill where the young fighters lived and Tyson would refer to her as his "mother" or his "white mother." She was described as the sister of the wife of D'Amato's brother Rocco, although Rocco actually married her sister long after Cus and Camille began their relationship. Though they never married, the two shared a cabin hideaway in New Jersey for many years before buying the house in Catskill where Camille did the cooking and cleaning, and supervised and mothered the boys.

During the 1940s, Cus was learning the boxing business, sometimes the hard way. He had a young tough at his gym who he thought would be his fighter when he turned pro, a kid named Rocky Graziano. But Graziano went with different management, including a "silent" partner named Eddie Coco, a "connected" hoodlum whose resume listed more than a dozen arrests for rape, robbery and felonious assault and who eventually went to prison for life on a murder rap. Graziano went on to win the Middleweight Championship of the World in 1947, and Cus, having tasted sour grapes, spent the rest of his life knocking Graziano as a gutless guy who couldn't fight.

Another mistake that Cus D'Amato made, besides losing Graziano, was to get involved with the International Boxing Guild, the so-called "manager's guild," a large group of boxing managers who had organized themselves ostensibly to present a united front and gain better purses for those of their fighters who fought on the fledgling medium of television. At the time—the early 1950s—boxing could be seen on television three or four nights a week. The guild filled its coffers by demanding payment from the manager of any fighter who appeared on TV, whether a guild member or not. In those days, main event fighters on TV earned between $2,100 to $4,000. The customary tribute demanded by the guild was $100. D'Amato, at a salary of $35 a week, become a "collector" for the guild, dunning managers at the various arenas around the city for their payments.

The guild, controlled by mob-connected managers like

"Honest" Bill Daly, was less than a shining light. In 1953, the highly regarded trainer Ray Arcel and two partners went into boxing promotion with a contract for a weekly card of televised bouts. But for the first month of the venture, they were forced to cancel their weekly shows when one or another of the main event fighters pulled out for various reasons. Arcel would subsequently testify before the New York State Athletic Commission that when he and his group agreed to pay a tribute of $500 a week to the Guild, by some strange coincidence the health of the fighters suddenly improved and they were able to proceed with their matches without any further hitch.

When Joe Louis retired in 1949, an organization known as the International Boxing Club, through a complicated web of collusion, chicanery and quasi-legal maneuvering, had gained a virtual monopoly on professional boxing in the United States. The head of the IBC was Jim Norris, a multimillionaire in his forties who, with his father, James, and their partner, Arthur Wirtz, owned the Chicago Stadium, the Detroit Olympia Stadium, the St. Louis Arena, and held the leases on the Omaha Coliseum and Indianapolis Coliseum. In addition, Norris owned the Detroit Red-Wings of the National Hockey League and a substantial amount of stock in Madison Square Garden (eventually that amount would come to nearly 40 percent). His other holdings, outside the world of sport, were equally formidable.

To all intents and purposes, Norris was a legitimate businessman, but in his burning desire to monopolize boxing, he fell in with a good many people not so legitimate, chief among them a mobster named Frankie Carbo, who would become the real, underworld power behind the IBC, while Norris would become essentially a figurehead without the power to control Carbo. Paul John Carbo, alias Frankie, was born two years before Jim Norris, in 1904. By the time he was forty-five years old, when the IBC was formed, he had quite an impressive rap sheet, beginning as a juvenile hoodlum and progressing to felonious assault, grand larceny, robbery and five arrests for murder. He served time in Sing Sing for manslaughter, but never actually did time for murder. Perhaps the following scenario explains why.

In 1939, a gentleman named Harry Shachter, aka Harry Greenberg, was shot down outside his house in Hollywood,

California. Greenberg himself was no sweetheart, being a henchman of underworld figure Waxey Gordon and a member of the gang with the colorful and notorious name of Murder, Inc. Frankie Carbo was indicted for the killing. Indicted with him was a who's who of crime that included "Lepke" Louie Buchalter, "Bugsy" Seigel, "Mendy" Weiss and "Champ" Segal. At the trial, a member of Murder, Inc., testified that Carbo did, indeed, along with "Bugsy" Seigel, kill Greenberg. The witness, Al Tannenbaum, said that Seigel drove the getaway car, but it was Carbo who actually fired the five bullets that ended the less than exemplary life of Greenberg.

Nevertheless, the trial resulted in a hung jury. A retrial was set, for which the police had another witness against Carbo, a witness so valuable that he was held under police guard in an upstairs room at the Half Moon Hotel in Coney Island. The witness was Abe "Kid Twist" Reles. But shortly before the second trial of Carbo was to begin, Abe Reles went flying from the window of the Half Moon Hotel. His crushed and lifeless body was found on the street near the Coney Island boardwalk. It was never established whether Reles committed suicide or whether he was pushed from the safe haven of his hotel room while the police who were supposed to be guarding him conveniently looked the other way. Whatever happened to Reles, without him, there was no way Carbo could be successfully prosecuted. The trial was not held, and Carbo was freed. As Barney Nagler wrote in his marvelous exposé of this era, *James Norris and the Decline of Boxing*, "By 1947 . . . [Frankie Carbo] had achieved widespread notoriety as the underworld's commissioner of boxing."

An associate of Carbo's was a Philadelphia mobster named Frank "Blinky" Palermo, with a dossier that included assault, auto theft, violation of Pennsylvania's liquor laws and operating a lottery, which meant, in reality, that Palermo ran the numbers rackets in Philadelphia. Palermo managed fighters like Ike Williams, legitimately one of the great champions of that era, and fighters like Billy Fox, whose careers were built on fixed fights, the most publicized of those being a bout in which Fox scored an upset TKO over the seemingly invincible "Raging Bull," Jake LaMotta. It later came to light that LaMotta was forced to throw the fight in exchange for a chance at the Middleweight Championship, a chance he got and a title he won.

In 1952, the United States Department of Justice filed suit against the IBC and its front Madison Square Garden, accusing the organization of "conspiring to restrain and monopolize the promotion and broadcasting of professional championship boxing in the United States. As Nagler states in his book, "Undaunted by the shadow of federal law, Norris went right on with his business. He held all the weapons and appeared impregnable to assault by writ or competition. He controlled the activities of every champion. Those fighters that he did not control by contract he held in financial bondage, because the IBC alone was in a position to promote important matches. And, through the International Boxing Guild, he controlled the managers." The government's lawsuit was dismissed, and the IBC and Madison Square Garden, which Norris by now controlled, continued to roll merrily along.

This was the unsavory background to boxing in the post-World War II era when Cus D'Amato, a relative newcomer to the game, fell in with the guild, a tie he would eventually sever long before the guild was ordered to disband by Julius Helfand, Chairman of the New York State Athletic Commission, in 1955. Perhaps D'Amato knew no better at the time; possibly, as is most likely, he knew that as a small-time manager, he had no alternative but to join the guild; and maybe he learned from what he saw going on around him. Whatever his reasons for joining, D'Amato eventually became one of the most vocal critics of those who controlled the guild, especially of Jim Norris and the IBC. In carving his own course, independent of the IBC, Cus D'Amato would himself become a central figure in boxing surrounded by controversy. The ace-in-the-hole that permitted D'Amato to defy the powerful Norris emerged in 1952. His name was Floyd Patterson.

Like so many of the kids who eventually gravitated to D'Amato, Floyd Patterson came to him as a troubled youth who had spent time at the Wiltwyck School for Boys in upstate New York. Like Tyson three decades later, Patterson grew up in Brooklyn, where he was "discovered" by a boxing coach named Frank LaVelle, who trained amateur kids at a local YMCA. All three Patterson brothers started under LaVelle, who then brought them to D'Amato's Gramercy Gym. All LaVelle's better fighters—those with potential—moved on to the Gramercy, where they could receive better training.

D'Amato, meanwhile, having apparently learned his lesson from the Graziano experience, now had an understanding with his fighters. Any boy could come to his gym and train for free. He would teach them, with no obligation on their part if they never fought or if they only went to the level of amateur competition. But if they turned pro, they signed with Cus. "I'm like a prospector," he would say, "and here is where I look for gold." Patterson had an outstanding amateur career, which he capped in 1952 by winning a gold medal as a middleweight in the Olympics. When he turned pro, he went with Cus. LaVelle helped train Floyd and worked his corner in many of his early fights. (Later, the relationship between LaVelle and D'Amato soured, LaVelle claiming that Patterson had been his fighter.)

D'Amato professed strong objections to the iron-fisted control of boxing by the IBC. As he began to develop Patterson into a contender, he endeavored to chart his own independent course. Many of Floyd's early fights were at the Eastern Parkway Arena in Brooklyn, where promoter Emil Lence and matchmaker Teddy Brenner had no ties with the IBC. By fighting there, and later in places like Canada, California and even Kansas City, Cus was able to have the final say over Floyd's opponents. With the IBC he would have been forced to take fighters too tough for Patterson in his developing years, fighters who might have derailed him long before he could become a contender for the title. D'Amato ignored the frequent criticism that he matched Floyd too carefully, that he was too selective in handpicking his opponents. He knew a lot better than his critics how to develop his fighter into championship material. During this period of Patterson's development, the heavyweight champion of the world was Rocky Marciano, who was controlled by Al Weill. At that time, Weill had become the matchmaker for the IBC at Madison Square Garden. By law, he could not also function as a manager. He got around this rule simply enough by listing his son, Marty, as Rocky's manager. It was, however, an open secret in boxing that Al Weill controlled Marciano.

Because of Weill's duality as the IBC/Madison Square Garden matchmaker and as Marciano's shadow manager, he controlled the heavyweight championship and the road to it just about 100 percent. Therefore, in the fall of 1954, D'Amato was forced to deal with the IBC when he arranged matches against Joe Gannon and Jimmy Slade. After Patterson beat Gannon, D'Amato accepted Slade, then ranked number 4 in the world, as an opponent only after consulting with his fighter. It has long been a myth that D'Amato himself always decided whom his fighters would box, that their job was to do the fighting. In reality, if he felt Floyd's delicate psyche would come into play, D'Amato consulted more than once with Patterson before making a fight with a particular opponent. In a terrible fight, with Slade running to survive, Patterson won a decision. In a rematch the next year in Los Angeles, Slade ran even more until Patterson stopped him in the seventh round.

Meanwhile, the government had appealed the 1954 decision in favor of the IBC and in early 1955 the Supreme Court decided in favor of the Justice Department in its suit against Norris and the IBC. In 1956, Norris, Wirtz and the IBC were facing charges in the federal courts that they had conspired to monopolize championship boxing in the United States for four years beginning in mid-1949. While the trial was in progress, Marciano announced his retirement. This left Norris and the IBC vulnerable. Under the public and legal scrutiny of the trial, they could not move as aggressively to control the now vacant Heavyweight Championship.

The leading contenders for the title were Archie Moore, Floyd Patterson, and "Hurricane" Jackson, an IBC-connected fighter. D'Amato agreed to have Patterson meet Jackson in an elimination bout promoted by the IBC—if he got his price. He wanted $50,000 for Patterson, an unheard of amount at the time. The winner was to move on to a bout for the vacant World Championship. By all accounts, D'Amato got his $50,000 (or, at the least, $40,000). "I do not especially want to fight for the IBC," he said, "but such is the power of the IBC that independent promoters can't compete with it." At his retirement press conference, Marciano had named Patterson as one of the top three contenders for the title, and D'Amato stated that the public knew that Patterson was the best and would demand that he get a crack at the title. D'Amato knew he had the weakened IBC on the ropes.

On June 8, 1956, at Madison Square Garden, Patterson administered a one-sided, twelve-round beating to Jackson. Six months later, a broken bone in his hand suffered in the Jackson fight having healed, Patterson met Archie Moore for the Heavyweight Championship on November 30, 1956, at Chicago Stadium. Moore was thirty-nine years old, ancient by boxing standards. Patterson was twenty-one. Moore went into the fight, nevertheless, as an 8 to 5 favorite. A professional only four years, Patterson was asked in one prefight interview how he expected to overcome the experience of a man who had been fighting for twenty years. Patterson, by no means a braggart but, nonetheless, confident of his abilities, answered, "Well, maybe I learned as much in four years as it took him twenty years to learn." Norris was quite certain that Moore would win, but he also felt sure, having dealt with D'Amato in the Jackson fight, that Cus would fall in line and support the IBC should Patterson take the title. Patterson knocked out Archie Moore in the sixth round to become the youngest heavyweight champion in history, an honor he would hold until D'Amato's next heavyweight protégé, Mike Tyson, supplanted him thirty years later almost to the day. When Patterson knocked out Moore he also knocked Jim Norris and the IBC out of the Heavyweight Championship picture. The IBC would never promote another heavyweight title match, because despite whatever implied or hoped-for understanding Norris had with D'Amato, Cus was going his own independent way with Floyd Patterson. As the manager of the world heavyweight champion, he was now, suddenly, one of the most powerful men in the sport.

In 1956, before Patterson won the title, D'Amato had approached the IBC for two loans. He had already made up his mind never to do business with the IBC once Patterson won the title, but he was not above borrowing money from them, knowing they would not refuse since Norris was very interested in Patterson as a future attraction. On June 7, saying he needed the money to pay tax debts, D'Amato took a $15,000 loan from the International Boxing Club. Two months later he requested an additional $5,000. The

IOU's for $20,000 in unsecured cash loans signed by Cus D'Amato from the IBC. The loans were taken shortly before Patterson won the heavyweight title, when D'Amato knew full well he intended to sever his relations with the IBC. Despite frequent demands, D'Amato steadfastly refused to ever repay these loans.

total of $20,000, for which he signed two IOUs, represented a considerable amount of cash by the standards of the 1950s.

Once Patterson had won the title and D'Amato had severed his ties with the IBC, he refused to pay the loans. When the money was demanded, Cus said he was keeping it for "services rendered." He was reminded that he and Patterson had been paid for their services rendered, and that the money was a personal loan to him, asked for and granted in good faith. Cus, in later years painted as a bastion of incorruptibility and honesty, refused to budge. He never returned the money to the IBC.

Harry Markson, who was eventually president of the Madison Square Garden Boxing Department in the post-IBC era, was an executive with the Garden during the reign of Jim Norris. Despite many Athletic Commission and grand jury investigations, Markson emerged completely clean. He had always refused to do business with Carbo and his mobster friends, yet somehow had managed to survive in the IBC hierachy. Norris said he liked to keep Markson around as his conscience. Markson had many dealings over the years with D'Amato. "The picture of Mr. Clean is false," he says. "Cus just wasn't that kind of a guy and did involve himself or allow himself to get involved, for what suited his purposes, with the bad guys of the business."

Finally, in 1957, the courts ruled against Norris and the IBC, saying they had acted as a monopoly in restraint of trade, and several months later Norris and Wirtz were ordered to divest themselves of all stock they owned in Madison Square Garden, to resign as officers and directors of the Garden, and to not promote more than two world championship fights a year for the next five years. In addition, Madison Square Garden was enjoined for five years from promoting more than two title fights a year. The judge further ordered that the IBC corporations be dissolved. Norris subsequently suffered a heart attack, and in the spring of 1958 he resigned as president of the IBC, although he remained president of the Garden, which controlled the IBC. During all this time, the federal court decision ordering divestiture was under appeal, so it was business as usual.

Patterson, meanwhile, following a KO over "Hurricane" Jackson in a rematch for the first defense of his title, was fighting an odd assortment of contenders. D'Amato maintained the IBC had a blacklist and wouldn't let top contenders fight Patterson. He tried to arrange a fight between Patterson and Willie Pastrano. The challenger's managers accepted the fight, then, a short while later, when word got around, they called back and said Pastrano couldn't fight Patterson. The IBC was calling in its chits. So instead, D'Amato signed with Pete Rademacher, the 1956 Olympic champion, who, in a promotion unique in boxing history, fought Patterson for the heavyweight title in his first professional bout. Patterson stopped him in six rounds, then didn't fight for another year. When he did, it was against Roy Harris, a fringe contender from Cut 'N Shoot, Texas. Floyd stopped him in twelve rounds in his only fight of 1958. The promoter of that fight was to have been, ironically, Al Weill, despite his former association with the IBC and despite the fact that D'Amato was well aware of his close association with Frankie Carbo. The California Athletic Commission turned down Weill as a promoter, however. With the bout uncertain, a young executive with TelePrompTer Corporation named Bill Rosensohn approached D'Amato and asked him if he could promote the fight. Assured that Rosensohn had the money, D'Amato agreed, despite the fact that the young man had never promoted a bout before. But TelePrompTer was the company handling the new medium of closed-circuit theater telecasts of fights. Rosensohn did better than expected with the venture, which was held at Wrigley Field in Los Angeles and it was very successful as a theater-TV attraction. He then asked D'Amato if he could promote another fight. D'Amato agreed, provided Rosensohn could come up with a viable contender who was free of any IBC entanglements. Rosensohn went to Sweden and saw Ingemar Johansson become the number one European contender by knocking out the highly regarded Eddie Machen in one round. Having determined that the Swedish heavyweight had no association with Norris or the IBC, he signed a forty-day option with Johansson and his management for $10,000 that gave Rosensohn exclusive rights during that time to make a match for the title between Patterson and Johansson.

Back in the United States, the days passed as D'Amato hedged on signing with Rosensohn. The young promoter became increasingly worried. In a few more days, his option would expire and he would lose his $10,000. D'Amato only shrugged and told him he had signed the option on his own, that it was his problem if he lost the money, not D'Amato's.

Rosensohn did not know what to do, and so he consulted Charlie Antonucci, aka Charlie Black, a convicted small-time bookmaker and business associate of D'Amato's. Rosensohn, who had previously dealt with Black on the Roy Harris fight, explained his predicament, and Black suggested that the promoter might find it beneficial to meet with Tony Salerno. At this point, D'Amato was still refusing to sign the promotional agreement with Rosensohn. Salerno, who was a Mafia mobster known in the underworld as "Fat Tony," told Rosensohn at their meeting that he was interested in investing in the promotion. For a one-third partnership, Salerno would put up all the money to back the promotion. There were strings attached to his offer, however. Salerno wanted his and Cus's buddy, Charlie Black, also cut in for a third. Rosensohn had no choice. It was either sign over two-thirds of the promotion to Salerno and Black or lose the fight completely, and the $10,000 he had paid to Johansson. He explained to Salerno that he didn't have an agreement with D'Amato for the fight and that his option was expiring in a few days. Fat Tony told him not to worry. Rosensohn agreed to the deal, and within a day, as if by magic, Rosensohn had D'Amato's signature.

Before fighting Johansson, Patterson took a warm-up fight, a title defense against the British contender, Brian London. That fight was held amid a welter of suspicious circumstances. The fight, set for Las Vegas, was suddenly switched to Indianapolis. The original promoter, Cecil Rhodes, Jr., a Harvard-educated attorney and businessman, was apparently dumped by D'Amato, who had Rosensohn step in to help run the promotion. D'Amato later explained to Patterson that agreements he had signed with Rhodes for the London fight and subsequent bouts were not what he had thought they were and that Floyd wasn't going to get as much money for the bout with Brian London as originally envisaged. When the British fighter arrived in New York, he was met at the airport by a D'Amato associate and was immediately put under wraps so he could not talk to the press about the business aspects of the bout. He trained at D'Amato's Gramercy Gym and used the same sparring partners as Patterson. D'Amato also installed one of his associates, veteran boxing man Nick Baffi, as London's trainer, which created further suspicion. Patterson took eleven rounds to knock out the mediocre but durable London, who added more fuel to the fire by subsequently charging that he had been promised a second shot at Floyd if he agreed to let D'Amato take over his management. D'Amato denied this. Patterson would later write, "I was terribly embarrassed by that fight and all the circumstances surrounding it."

On June 26, 1959, under the promotional banner of Rosensohn enterprises, Inc (of which Bill Rosensohn was, by now, a minority owner, holding just 33 percent), Floyd defended his title against Johansson. In a major upset, Johansson knocked Patterson down seven times in the third round to win the World Heavyweight Championship. Patterson lost his title and the promotion lost $70,000 because D'Amato, in the driver's seat, contractually gave the promoters half of the net gate profits only, of which there were none. He kept all the closed-circuit TV revenue, of which there was plenty, for Patterson, himself, and TelePrompTer.

Rosensohn still looked forward to promoting the Patterson-Johansson rematch, to which he held the rights. He was in for a rude awakening when he was informed by Vincent Velella, the attorney for Tony Salerno that he, Velella, was in control of the 67 percent of Rosensohn Enterprises given over to Salerno and Charlie Black. Rosensohn sold out his share to a newly formed promotional group headed by the New York power broker and attorney Roy Cohn, Cohn's law partner, Tom Bolan, and travel agency owner, Bill Fugazy. Also forced to sell to the new promoters was Velella. Rosensohn had gone to the District Attorney's office in New York and told all about Salerno, Black and Velella taking over Rosensohn Enterprises. As a result, Velella was indicted for perjury, and though eventually cleared, he was in an untenable position regarding the running of Rosensohn Enterprises. Roy Cohn and his associates, under the banner of Feature Sports, Inc, now owned the contract to promote the return match in 1960.

D'Amato had made many enemies in the press during his long campaign against the IBC and his feud with Jim Norris. Some of the press's criticism of him was justified. But, in fairness to D'Amato, many of the journalists were on the IBC payroll, being paid off under the table by Norris in return for giving the IBC a "good press." Other newspapermen, though not "on the take," just didn't like the oddball and unorthodox D'Amato. Typical of the latter was the noted sports columnist Jimmy Cannon, who constantly attacked D'Amato in his widely read column. One example read: "The manager of Floyd Patterson is as phony as snow on a Hollywood Christmas tree and his methods are as dirty as a coal miner's fingernails. . . . Cus D'Amato belongs in the fight racket because it has long been the sanctuary of the persuasive rogue. Seldom has deceit been practiced with the suave hypocrisy of Cus the Mus, who is still Patterson's boss in all matters. In a foul business which has produced more fakers than all the quiz shows put together, the Mus is a spectacular blackguard. But the beneficiary of his surreptitious propositions has been Patterson, who is regarded as a decent kid mesmerized into a stupor of innocent acquiescence by the Mus' con."

The esteemed Pulitzer Prize–winning columnist Red Smith also criticized D'Amato, writing "Who knows anything about Floyd Patterson? . . . Hardly anybody, as a matter of fact, except Cus D'Amato, and whatever became of Cus? Every now and then, something . . . serves as a reminder that there is a man named Floyd Patterson and that he really is the heavyweight champion—the most widely unknown, the least active, the most superbly concealed heavyweight champion since the birth of Jim Figg."

A 1961 *Sports Illustrated* story by Robert Boyle referred to D'Amato as a "tragic figure." The press often reviles [him] as a crook. A crook he is not; a kook he may be. He fought the gangster-dominated IBC alone for such a long spell that he wound up with a deep and permanent persecution complex. . . . He spends most of his time in his cluttered two-room apartment at Broadway and 53rd Street, his main companion a boxer dog. . . . He has a bed in the apartment, [but] he never sleeps there. He stays with friends, and he rarely spends two nights in the same place. "I don't like my comings and going to be predictable," he says. He is wary of what he says over the phone because, he says, it may be being tapped. . . . He stays out of bars for fear an enemy agent might stuff marijuana cigarettes into his pockets, then whistle for the police."

Jimmy Cannon, continuing his attack on D'Amato, wrote: "Loyalty is a glorious trait and an uncommon one in the fight racket where integrity is considered a defect. But Patterson has been disgraced by his association with the Mus because he hasn't repudiated any of the alliances which protected him from such as Pete Rademacher and Brian London. The impression Patterson originally made on me must be altered unless he expresses his independence and renovates his views of the man who has provoked a national disgust with the fight racket which may cause it to be voted a criminal act instead of a sport." One might well ask why Cannon chose to accuse D'Amato of provoking "a national disgust" with boxing when he might better have directed his accusations at Frankie Carbo, Jim Norris and others of their ilk.

Certainly, D'Amato was no innocent. He himself was involved with numerous shady characters and underworld figures having an interest in boxing, such as Weill, Salerno, Black and so on. He was a sharp, veteran operator who had his eyes wide open, and it suited his purpose very well to project the image of a crusader against corrupt influences in the boxing world. His crusade against the IBC provided a convenient means to accomplish one of his main goals: to keep Patterson from fighting the legitimate top contenders for the title who deserved but never got their chances against Patterson. Despite his rhetoric to the press about Patterson's greatness, D'Amato knew that his man was very limited as a heavyweight. He was a good middleweight, a good light-heavyweight, but when the top heavyweight contenders were men like Zora Folley, Eddie Machen and Sonny Liston, D'Amato knew there was a good chance of Patterson losing to any one of them. What better way to shield his fighter than under the pretext of keeping him away from IBC-controlled challengers? It was a brilliant strategy: While adding to the legend of the honest, crusading Cus D'Amato, it kept Patterson in the ring for years against safe opponents like Roy Harris, Tom McNeeley, Peter Rademacher and Brian London.

However, with his behind-the-scenes maneuvering in the making of the first Patterson-Johansson fight, his involvement in the promotion while at the same time being a manager, and with the involvement of people like "Fat Tony" Salerno in the promotion, D'Amato had made himself vulnerable. The press was eager to attack, and he had given them good cause.

Johansson fanned the flames by charging that in order to get his fight with Patterson he had had to agree to sign with Harry Davidow as his manager. Davidow was an old crony of D'Amato's and had been one of Cus's original partners in the Gramercy Gym. He had dropped out to open a candy store in Brooklyn from which he ran a bookmaking operation. He had been out of boxing for fifteen years, yet here was his buddy Cus D'Amato securing a deal that would give him 10 percent of Johansson's purses for the next five years. However, the deal went sour when the New York State Athletic Commission in response to Johansson's allegations denied Davidow a manager's license a month before the first scheduled fight.

On September 4, 1959, the State Athletic Commission began an inquiry into the matter of the Patterson-Johansson fight. D'Amato was accused of being the decisionmaker behind Rosensohn Enterprises who had "cut in" his colleague and friend, Charlie Black, "a convicted gambler and associate of bookmakers," for a piece of the promotion, as well as attempting to force Davidow on Johansson and his Swedish manager. He was also accused of violating the rule that prevents a manager from being involved in the promotion of a fight. The commission reached the following conclusions:

"D'Amato put Rosensohn in as a promoter of the [Patterson-Roy Harris] fight after Rosensohn had agreed to give Charlie Black, D'Amato's friend, 50 percent of the profits. Charlie Black was also designated by D'Amato as the manager of Roy Harris, in the event of a return bout, and was to receive 10 percent of Harris's purse of said match. This was a clear attempt by D'Amato to control the future heavyweight champion in the event that Harris succeeded in winning the title.

"Charlie Black, also known as Charles Antonucci, is D'Amato's trusted adviser and go-between. He has known D'Amato twenty-five years. Whenever there is a Patterson fight, Black appears on the scene either with a part in the promotion or in the boxer management. Black apparently has no occupation. He is friendly with Tony Salerno and . . . "Trigger" Mike Coppola for twenty-five years . . ." He, Black, does not appear to be the type of personality whose presence would inure to the best interest of boxing.

"In connection with the Patterson-Johansson fight, the commission denied an application for a license to one Harry Davidow as manager of Ingemar Johansson. The record in that proceeding . . . supports the conclusion that D'Amato dictated the naming of Davidow as Johansson's manager. This was another instance of D'Amato's attempt to control the heavyweight title.

"This commission cannot accept the fact that Salerno was an innocent bystander at these meetings [involving the promotion of the Patterson-Johansson fight] and it believes that the $10,000 loan was made by Salerno to Rosensohn in Velella's office and that Salerno was a part of the promotion."

D'Amato did not help his own cause by boycotting the hearings. The commission decision stated: "Mr. D'Amato was directed . . . to appear at a hearing on September 14, 1959. . . . He failed to appear and was therefore suspended by the commission. Hearings were conducted until September 21 with no appearance by him. . . . The record amply sustains the fact that D'Amato's failure to appear, pursuant to the direction of the commission, was deliberate."

D'Amato's license to manage was revoked late in 1959. He eventually took his case to the U.S. Supreme Court, where he won a minor victory on a technicality. It seems that his manager's license had expired before the commission issued the order to revoke it, so, technically, his license had not been taken away. But it was a Pyrric victory. Afraid that if he did apply for and obtain another license, it would then be taken away, he never again held a license as a manager.

Why D'Amato had acted in this manner will probably never be known for sure. In view of his battle against the IBC and his loathing for the gangsters who exercised influence over the sport, it doesn't seem credible that he would knowingly have joined up with another band of mobsters. Yet he certainly knew the backgrounds and reputations of Davidow and Black, long-time friends, and of Salerno. Perhaps he acted out of loyalty to old friends, perhaps it was because his pathological dislike of the IBC closed many doors to him that might otherwise have opened to offer lucrative bouts for Patterson. One thing is almost certain: Money was not D'Amato's incentive, as anyone who knew him over the years will testify. He had no interest in it. He enjoyed being a power in boxing, enjoyed being the manager of the heavyweight champion, but money was generally the last thing on his mind.

All the revelations that followed the London and Johansson bouts served to create a strain between Patterson and Cus. Floyd had certainly benefited financially from the fights. His gross purse was over $600,000. But he was made to feel a fool when, with each new revelation, he realized how much had gone on without his knowledge. He would later write, "I didn't mistrust Cus . . . but I did begin to develop a mistrust of the people around him, for whom Cus always did favors." He described himself as "horrified" when Salerno's name surfaced. In *Victory Over Myself*, written while he was still at the peak of his career as a fighter, Floyd said, "I made up my mind to one . . . thing. Nobody went down with me those seven times that I went down to the canvas [against Johansson]. A fighter walks alone and fights alone. If I could be successful the next time, I promised myself I'd be my own man. The mistakes would be mine, the decisions mine. . . . Nominally, at least, Cus continued to be what he always was, but actually I tried to show him that too many things had happened for me to allow myself ever to be completely in anyone's control again. I was Cus's boy, but in defeat and confusion I became my own man. I was hurt, very badly, and maybe inadvertently by him, but whatever he did, I know he thought he was doing it solely for my benefit."

Roy Cohn went ahead and promoted the Patterson-Johansson rematch on June 20, 1960, at the Polo Grounds in New York. It was a historic fight, because in the fifth round, Floyd knocked out Ingemar with one of the most devastating left hooks ever thrown. By virtue of that punch, he was now not only the youngest man ever to win the title, but the first fighter in history to regain the Heavyweight Championship.

There's an old saying that just because someone is paranoid doesn't necessarily mean someone isn't out to get them. This was possibly the case when it came to D'Amato and Roy Cohn. Cus's attorney, Julius November, also handled Patterson's affairs. D'Amato now felt that Roy Cohn was using November as a wedge to get Patterson away from him and into his own clutches. Knowing Cohn's propensity for deviousness, it is likely that D'Amato had grounds for his accusations. Without a written contract with Patterson (it had expired and was never formally renewed), and without a license to manage in New York, Cus was vulnerable. November moved in at this point to gain Floyd's trust. Fugazy, Cohn's partner in Feature Sports, called D'Amato "mentally ill." D'Amato countered by telling *Sports Illustrated*, "This man [Fugazy] has definite psychopathic leanings. The man has no principles. This man lies to your face, and he believes his own lies. A respectable racketeer. . . . Compared to Fugazy, Norris is like a diamond in a coal pile." There is little doubt that Cohn and Fugazy maneuvered to win over Patterson. In this atmosphere, Patterson fought Johansson a third time, knocking him out to retain his title in 1961. Floyd had stated in his autobiography, ". . . my manager has been a suspicious man. Undoubtedly he had some reason to be, but over the years Cus allowed his suspicions about the IBC and his fight against its president, Jim Norris, to warp his thinking. Without question, it also warped my career. . . . Let me say here, too, so that nobody gets any other ideas, that as long as I keep fighting Cus will continue to be my manager." But shortly after the third Johansson fight, Floyd broke with Cus, and was not to be reconciled with him for the duration of his fighting career.

In 1962 Floyd defended his title without the guidance of D'Amato against Charles "Sonny" Liston, a sullen, one-time union thug and enforcer who had served "hard time" in prison, and who was controlled in his climb up the boxing ladder by shadow managers (surprise, surprise!) Frankie Carbo and his associate, a Philadelphia mobster named Frank "Blinky" Palermo. Patterson was knocked out in round one, losing his title to Liston, who stopped Floyd again in the first round a year later. Patterson would continue his career, losing a bid for the heavyweight title by TKO to Muhammad Ali and failing in an attempt to win the WBA Heavyweight Championship against Jimmy Ellis in Sweden in a fight most observers thought Patterson had won, but, in one of the awful decisions sometimes seen in boxing, the only official under Swedish rules, American referee Harold Valan, raised Ellis's hand in victory. Patterson retired in 1972 after losing a second time to Ali in a bout at Madison Square Garden. He had never fought there in his days as champion, but, after leaving D'Amato, he fought there several times, long after its association with the IBC ended. He went on to become a member of the New York State Athletic Commission and now, much as his mentor, Cus D'Amato did, he trains a stable of amateurs and professionals in a gym on his farm in upstate New York, not far from Catskill. Eventually, he became reconciled with Cus, and in the book *In This Corner* . . . he admitted that, if he had his career to do all over again, "The only thing I would change in my whole entire life, I would never have gotten rid of Cus. . . . I don't think that there'll be another, in my opinion, man as Cus, with his witty ways, his cleverness, his shrewdness, how he was able to outmaneuver a whole organization, the IBC. You've got to have tremendous respect for a man like this."

As for Norris, Carbo, Palermo and the IBC, on January 12, 1959, the United States Supreme Court upheld the decision ordering Norris and Wirtz to resign from their controlling positions at Madison Square Garden and divest themselves of all Garden stock. Within a month they had made a deal to sell the controlling interest in the Garden to the Graham-Paige Corporation, headed by Rear Admiral (Ret.) John Bergen, for just under $4 million.

Determined to stay in big-time boxing, Norris then organized National Boxing Enterprise. The Garden, free of its entanglements with him, formed Madison Square Garden Boxing, Inc. By the spring of 1959, the California Athletic Commission was investigating the attempt of Carbo and Palermo to strong-arm themselves into the management of world welterweight champion Don Jordan. Then, in September, Carbo, Palermo and three of their associates were indicted by a federal grand jury in California on ten counts of extortion and conspiracy to violate federal antiracketeering laws. The FBI arrested them the same day. Simultaneously, Carbo was under indictment in New York for conspiracy involving charges that he functioned as an unlicensed manager and matchmaker, and he was facing separate federal charges in connection with $750,000 in income taxes he had failed to pay.

Carbo switched his plea from not guilty to guilty in the New York case. Before he was sentenced, on November 30, 1959, Assistant D.A. Scotti said, in his statement to the court, "The evil influence of this man has for many years permeated virtually the entire professional sport of boxing. I believe it is fair to say that the name of Frank Carbo today symbolizes the degeneration of professional boxing into a racket. This man is beyond redemption. He is completely impervious to public opinion." Carbo was sentenced to two years in prison. When he was released, he went on trial in Los Angeles in 1961, along with Palermo and their three associates, on the conspiracy and racketeering charges. All five were found guilty. Carbo received a twenty-five-year sentence and a $10,000 fine. He was sent to the notorious Alcatraz Federal Penitentiary in San Francisco Bay.

In 1960, between Carbo's two trials, the so-called Kefauver Committee (actually the U.S. Senate's Subcommittee on Antitrust and Monopoly) conducted its own investigation into underworld influence in boxing in the United States. Jake LaMotta testified that he had been forced to take a dive in his fight with Billy Fox (whose manager was Blinky Palermo) in 1947. Jim Norris testified that he was hurt and embarrassed tremendously by his association with Frank Carbo, which he said he discovered was a necessary evil if he were to be able to function as a major promoter of boxing. The Kefauver Committee heard a great deal more interesting testimony about mob influence in boxing. But by now, that underworld control had been broken, and was virtually a thing of the past. In the 1980s, justice finally caught up with Mafia "Don" Salerno. "Fat Tony," one of those indicted by the federal government in the highly publicized Pizza Connection case, was sent away to prison for life.

Meanwhile, Cus D'Amato, sans license, continued to manage and train fighters. Most notable was Jose Torres, a Puerto Rican fighter who won a silver medal as a middleweight in the 1956 Olympics. After his split with Patterson, D'Amato developed Torres to a point where he won the World Light-Heavyweight Championship in 1963 by knocking out Willie Pastrano. But while Patterson was essentially a Spartan, Torres did not like the rigors of training, his tastes running more to the sweet life and chasing women. Cus's brother Tony said, "Torres was a lazy guy, plenty of talent, but lazy." Finally, Cus sent Tony to training camp to drum some discipline and obedience into Torres. "I made him knuckle down," recalls Tony. "I put the screws on him. I had to stay practically night and day in order to watch the bum." It paid off when Torres went on to capture the title, but within two years he lost it to Dick Tiger. An intelligent man who gained additional insight from his association with D'Amato, Torres matured following his boxing career and became a successful newspaper columnist. Eventually, he was named Chairman of the New York State Athletic Commission, becoming a highly visible boxing administrator. But his close association with Tyson through his friendship with D'Amato and Jim Jacobs would eventually land him in hot water and force his resignation as chairman.

By the late 1960s, D'Amato was in financial trouble. He owed the government a quarter of a million dollars in back taxes, and he was eventually forced to declare bankruptcy. How he ended up with nothing after managing two world champions is something of a mystery, especially since he was hardly a spendthrift, having few, if any, worldly pleasures. Jim Jacobs suggested that it had to do with D'Amato being held liable by Internal Revenue for taxes on fights from which he never actually received payment. Others have said that D'Amato's battle against the IBC cost him a great deal, although there is no firm documentation to substantiate this. True, he didn't deal with Norris, the IBC, or Madison Square Garden, but by virtue of his control over the Heavyweight Championship and his brilliant exploitation of the new medium of closed-circuit theater TV, he made Floyd Patterson a rich man. From the first Johansson fight alone, D'Amato's cut should have been $200,000, a sizable amount even after taxes in 1959. The court battles against Carbo and the IBC were prosecuted by the government, not D'Amato. He incurred court costs when he took the case of his license suspension to the Supreme Court. His brother Tony insists that it was Cus who paid for the house in Catskill, although the purchase was in Camille Ewald's name. But these expenditures still would not explain the evaporation of all the money he should have accumulated, with no family to support and living an extremely modest lifestyle.

It must be stressed that D'Amato was unique in boxing in that he was without avarice. Money meant nothing to him. Jose Torres maintains that D'Amato never took a cut of his purses, since he was making peanuts on the way up the ladder compared to Patterson's earnings as heavyweight champion. In his autobiography, Patterson stated, at the time of his second fight in 1960 with Johansson, ". . . during many years of our relationship there were no formal agreements between us. We still don't have a contract, but Cus gets, as he's always gotten, his 33⅓ percent from the purses after all the expenses are taken off the top." But British boxing manager and promoter Mickey Duff, a long-time friend and associate of Jim Jacobs and D'Amato, offers this opinion: "There's a myth that I hate to explode, but I have to be honest. Mike Tyson wasn't the first fighter to shit on Cus D'Amato. [Cus] was always prepared to compromise himself for material success. Not financial success, necessarily. Material success. He compromised himself with Floyd Patterson. He took a lot of shit and took virtually no money off him. Most of the time he didn't have the guts to take it off Patterson in case it offended him. That was his way of showing Patterson that he was honest, by not taking any money off him, which he fully deserved. And when he managed Jose Torres he was stone broke, and still took no money off him. How could a guy manage two world champions and never have five thousand dollars of his own money to count?"

Whatever the reasons, D'Amato, legally bankrupt and in debt to the government, wound up, in the late 1960s, in the upstate New York town of New Paltz. He was there to train heavyweight contender Buster Mathis for the Iselin family, wealthy business people heavily involved in sports. Mathis was a massive heavyweight who had defeated Joe Frazier in the 1964 Olympic trials, but suffered a broken hand against Frazier and so was unable to compete in the Olympics. Instead, Frazier, the alternate, fought for the United States and won the gold medal. In 1968, With Muhammad Ali stripped of his title and his license to box for refusing induction into the Armed Forces, Frazier and Mathis met for the New York version of the World Heavyweight Championship. Frazier KO'd Mathis to win his first recognition as champion, recognition he would widen with eventual victories over WBA champion Jimmy Ellis and Ali when he made his comeback. D'Amato's relationship with the Iselins soured, and Cus, always seeing conspiracies and plots, became convinced that they were going to have him killed because they believed he was trying to steal Mathis from them. He ended up barricading himself in his room at their New Paltz fight camp, refusing to come out. His fear and paranoia were so extreme that when his brother Tony came to see him, Cus refused to open the door. "Cus, it's me, Tony. It's all right to unlock the door," Tony assured him. "Yeah, I know it's you, Tony," came the reply. "But how do I know you're not telling me to open the door because they're holding a gun to your head?"

After his association with Mathis and the Iselins came to an end, Cus moved to Catskill, where he opened the small gym over the police station, dividing his time between there and New York City, 120 miles to the south. But even in Catskill, his reputation as a master teacher of ring technique, as well as his deep understanding of the psychological elements that go into making a successful fighter—a critical aspect of boxing overlooked or ignored by many so-called trainers who never develop the perceptive qualities that made D'Amato unique—led many to seek his help and advice. Muhammad Ali invited Cus to his camp in Deer Lake, Pennsylvania, hoping that he would agree to stay on as a trainer. Ali told D'Amato he would pay him while continuing to retain his long-time trainer, Angelo Dundee, as well. But D'Amato refused, telling Ali that such an arrangement would be unfair to Dundee. However, he did work with Ali at his camp as an adviser. Some years later, Gerry Cooney was brought to Catskill and spent time there being advised and assessed by D'Amato. Cooney's managers, Mike Jones and Dennis Rappaport, were anxious to have D'Amato join them as Cooney's trainer. But D'Amato explained that he was a manager, not a trainer, and that in order to guide a fighter's career the way he thought it should go, he could not simply function as a trainer while leaving the crucial managerial decisions to others. Instead, he recommended Victor Valle, who became Cooney's trainer for his entire career, earning a small fortune along the way.

In general, life was comparatively quiet for Cus D'Amato. He had sold his Gramercy Gym. Norris, Carbo and the IBC were long gone. Forgotten, too, in the public's mind, were D'Amato's crusades against them. Patterson and Torres were retired. Cus was slipping, perhaps not so gently, into old age. He had his little gym, his club of amateur boys where legend has it that he helped troubled and underprivileged kids straighten out their lives and build character in the hope that they would leave there better people than when they arrived. However, there is another side to the story. D'Amato was not a trained psychologist, and sometimes his methods could be brutal. Often, if boys didn't have an interest in or an aptitude for boxing, they came and went quickly. One particularly sad case was that of Russ D'Amico, a stubborn fifteen-year-old who came to live with D'Amato, the alternative for him being reform school. D'Amico didn't like the way Cus was treating him, while Cus felt the boy was bad and had no character. When the boy took it into his head to leave, D'Amato refused to take him back. Only the intercession of Teddy Atlas finally made him relent.

Unfortunately, as soon as D'Amico returned, Cus began to harass and badger him, often calling him a liar, a weasel. After two weeks, the youngster couldn't take it anymore.

He told Teddy he would rather be in prison than taking the constant harassment from Cus. He left, and the courts sent him to reform school. Soon after, Russ D'Amico committed suicide.

Another myth was that none of the boys who stayed at the house paid, whereas in fact nearly *all* of them paid to stay there. D'Amato was very good at finding out whether their parents could afford to pay something. The other boys were sent out to get part-time jobs locally. They all contributed financially toward their keep.

Along with his amateur boys, D'Amato was developing his young trainer, Teddy Atlas, and his young welterweight prospect, Kevin Rooney. Rooney and Atlas were best friends who had grown up together on Staten Island in New York City. Like so many of the young men who gravitated to D'Amato, they came from troubled backgrounds. In 1975, Rooney had won the 147-pound New York Golden Gloves Novice Championship. A boxer with promise, he was nevertheless at loose ends. He had had several run-ins with the law for brawling and knew he was heading for trouble and, eventually, prison.

The product of a broken, alcoholic home, Rooney would even brawl on occasion with his father and spent many nights drinking and partying in bars. He was not yet twenty years old when a friend led him to D'Amato, who explained the arrangement: Rooney could come and live in the house and train at the gym for free, doing the yard work and other chores around the house in exchange for his room and board. Rooney recognized the opportunity, and grabbed it. "Cus took a personal interest in me," he says. "I was, like, his boy. He was like a father. Cus was my friend. He made me go back to college, get a two-year degree. He showed what I knew inside me, that I was smart, but he brought it out. He'd tell me you're lucky if you have one true friend who'll stand by you no matter what, and I knew I had that in Cus."

Like many of those who came before and after him, Rooney was somewhat baffled by this strange old man who took such a deep interest in developing him not only as a fighter but as a person as well. "Here was this guy so smart, a genius, he knew about anything and everything, but, I said, this guy doesn't care about money. At the time [I was] nineteen years old, everything was about a buck. Here's this guy who'd had the heavyweight champ, the light-heavyweight champ of the world, but he didn't care about money. . . . He just cared about principle, which is very important. What's right and wrong is what mattered to him. . . . He was a great man."

About four months after Rooney arrived at Catskill, Teddy Atlas got into serious trouble with the police in Staten Island. Although his father was a physician, Atlas was a rough and wild kid who had been an amateur fighter in the same Police Athletic League gym as Kevin Rooney. When Rooney heard about it, he asked D'Amato to go out on a limb and appear before the judge on Atlas's behalf. Cus did so, offering to take Atlas into his home in Catskill and help him develop his boxing skills if the court would consider it. The judge agreed to place the boy on five years probation provided D'Amato took responsibility for him. As he had done before, and as he would do in the future with Mike Tyson, Cus D'Amato became a substitute father to both Rooney and Atlas and played a major part in helping them to turn their lives around.

Under D'Amato's tutelage, the young men blossomed as amateur fighters and showed great promise of a future professional career. But Cus soon noticed that when Teddy fought and trained, he would wince with pain. He discovered that the young fighter had a serious congenital problem with his spine that caused him great pain, although he had tried to conceal it because he was so keen to succeed as a fighter. Cus knew then that Teddy could never pursue a professional career in the ring, but he had another idea. He saw something in Atlas that made him believe he could teach him to become a good trainer, to work with other youngsters and in that way develop a career in boxing even though he himself couldn't fight. The idea did not sit well with Teddy at first. "I was selfish and not ready or directed enough and not sure what I wanted to do. I had gone there to become a fighter, and I wasn't prepared to dedicate myself to helping other people." D'Amato later told filmmaker Michael Marton: "I tried to make him [Atlas] see, and I think I succeeded, that even if you're not a fighter yourself, you can become a success through your fighter, because if you take a boy and teach him how to fight from beginning to end, part of you is in him, too, so that when he fights, part of you is in that ring. And suddenly I discovered [Teddy] had a real talent for teaching, a born teacher. He's the type of person that wants to help people, especially kids, and they come to depend on him and rely on him a great deal, so they became very close that way.''

Between the time his boxing career ended and he decided to take up D'Amato's offer to become a trainer, there was a year of aimlessness and confusion for Atlas. He left Catskill and returned to Staten Island. He was twenty years old and floundering. He got in a street altercation that nearly cost him his life. He was slashed by a knife down the side of his face nearly to his jugular vein. He spent eight days in the hospital and thought about his future, finally realizing he had to make a decision on what direction the rest of his life would take. "I made a phone call to Cus and said I'm ready now to take you up on your offer. I was prepared now, I was settled in my mind to do it. Cus was happy about it."

D'Amato realized that Teddy had a very low sense of self-esteem and decided to boost his morale by giving him more and more responsibility for the day-to-day running of the gym, as well as allowing him to take on much of the actual training of the boys. Teddy developed a rapport with the youngsters and they, in turn, responded very positively to him. D'Amato taught Atlas his own methods of training fighters. D'Amato had innovated what came to be known as the peek-a-boo style: both fists held high, tucked in alongside each cheek, elbows and arms tight to the ribs. From this defensive stance, peering over the tops of the gloves, a fighter was well protected. He also developed a punch-by-numbers system. Each punch, each part of the opponent's body, had a number assigned to it. The bags in the gym had the numbers written on them, and fighters had to land the right punches in the right place as the numbers were called out.

But the most important lessons were not learned in the gym. They were learned at the dinner table or in the evenings after the day's work was done. Sitting and talking with Cus, his young disciples learned the old man's philosophy of life as he applied it to life in the ring. "I never teach until I've spoken to the fighter," D'Amato would say. "I have to first determine his emotional state, get his background, to find out what I have to do, how many layers I have to keep peeling off so that I get to the core of the person so that he can recognize, as well as I, what is there." The crucial lesson he taught, one he felt was generally ignored by other trainers, was the recognition of an acknowledgment of fear.

"Fear is the greatest obstacle to learning in any area, but particularly in boxing," he said. "For example, boxing is something you learn through repetition. You do it over and over and suddenly you've got it. . . . However, in the course of trying to learn, if you get hit and get hurt, this makes you cautious, and when you're cautious you can't repeat it, and when you can't repeat it, it's going to delay the learning process. . . . When they . . . come up to the gym and say I want to be a fighter, the first thing I'd do was talk to them about fear. . . . I would always use . . . the same example of the deer crossing an open field and upon approaching the clearing suddenly instinct tells him danger is there, and nature begins the survival process, which involves the body releasing adrenalin into the bloodstream, causing the heart to beat faster and enabling the deer to perform extraordinary feats of agility and strength. . . . It enables the deer to get out of range of the danger, helps him escape to the safety of the forest across the clearing . . . an example in which fear is your friend.

"The thing a kid in the street fears the most is to be called yellow or chicken, and sometimes a kid will do the most stupid, wild, crazy things just to hide how scared he is. I often tell them that while fear is such an obnoxious thing, an embarrassing thing . . . nevertheless it is your best friend, because anytime anyone saves your life perhaps a dozen times a day, no matter how obnoxious he is, you've got to look upon him as a friend and this is what fear is. Since nature gave us fear in order to help us survive, we cannot look upon it as an enemy. Just think how many times a day a person would die if he had no fear. He'd walk in front of cars, he'd die a dozen times a day. Fear is a protective mechanism. . . . By talking to the fighters about fear I cut the learning time maybe as much as half, sometimes more, depending on the individual.

"The next thing I do, I get them in excellent condition. . . . Knowing how the mind is and the tricks it plays on a person and how an individual will always look to avoid a confrontation with something that's intimidating, I remove all the possible excuses they're going to have before they get in there. By getting them in excellent condition, they can't say when they get tired that they're not in shape. When they're in excellent shape I put them into the ring to box for the first time, usually with an experienced fighter who won't take advantage of them. When the novice throws punches and nothing happens, and his opponent keeps coming at him . . . the new fighter becomes panicky. When he gets panicky he wants to quit, but he can't quit because his whole psychology from the time he's first been in the streets is to condemn a person who's yellow. So what does he do? He gets tired. This is what happens to fighters in the ring. They get tired, because they're getting afraid . . . Now that he gets tired, people can't call him yellow. He's just too "tired" to go on. But let that same fighter strike back wildly with a visible effect on the opponent and suddenly that tired, exhausted guy becomes a tiger. . . . It's a psychological fatigue, that's all it is, but people in boxing don't understand that."

By 1979, Kevin Rooney had developed to the point where D'Amato decided to turn him professional. D'Amato was unlicensed, so he could not work Rooney's corner. He would be managed by Bill Cayton, an astute businessman and D'Amato's long-time friend Jim Jacobs, with Cus making all the boxing decisions. He entrusted Rooney's training to Teddy Atlas. It was not unusual for D'Amato to have another trainer handling the day-to-day routine with his fighters, even though he himself masterminded the overall strategy. Floyd Patterson had had Frank LaVelle, Buster Watson and Dan Florio training him. Jose Torres had had Joe Fariello, Tony D'Amato and Johnny Manzanet working with him. As for Atlas, D'Amato felt that working not just with kids but with a professional fighter would help center him even more, since the young man was now determined to make a career for himself as a trainer.

When Mike Tyson burst upon the scene in 1980, Kevin Rooney had progressed through half a dozen fights. He and Tyson, along with the other boys, trained side by side, ate at the same table, and slept in the same house. Rooney, too, saw Tyson's potential from the very beginning: "He had that power. Not too many guys have that one-punch knock-out power. . . . I knew this guy can't miss if he really wants it. . . ."

Chapter 5

The Catskill Years

A boy comes to me with a spark of interest. I feed the spark and it becomes a flame. I feed the flame and it becomes a fire. I feed the fire and it becomes a roaring blaze.

—Cus D'Amato

The relatively calm and quiet life in the country surroundings of Catskill were totally alien to Mike Tyson, as well as the fact that for the first time in his life most of those around this black kid from the city streets were white. It would require a big adjustment, one that at times proved very difficult for him. By his own admission, he was suspicious of this "crazy old white dude," who kept telling him he could be the heavyweight champion of the world, and of his motives.

When Mike made his permanent move to Catskill, he had just passed his fourteenth birthday. "I didn't want to be there," he would later recall. "I was a city boy. I wasn't used to that environment, [but] I had nowhere else to go." There were house rules that all the boys had to follow, and Mike often chafed at having to live in a voluntary, cooperative arrangement with others, especially when those others were mostly white. But he knew his only alternative was to return to reform school.

Another thing that caused Mike to chomp at the bit was the matter of his education. As a minor and a ward of the state, he was required to attend school. While running the streets of Brooklyn, he had been a truant; so, despite Bobby Stewart's brief and successful effort to get him to knuckle down and learn, he had had relatively little formal education for a boy of fourteen. In September of 1980, when he arrived in Catskill, Cus enrolled Mike in the Catskill Junior High School, in the eighth grade. In the following two years, Mike created many problems at the school, although at least some of the trouble was provoked by other students. Before his arrival in Catskill, the local schools had experienced several racial incidents and flare-ups. The black school population in this rural environment was less than 10 percent, and so perceived itself with some justification as the underdog in any problems that occurred. As a result of the racial conflict prior to Mike's enrollment, specific guidelines had been drafted by school administrators to deal with any matters of discipline "by the book," so that all students, black or white, would receive identical treatment. These regulations meant that Cus D'Amato could expect no special treatment for Mike, despite his concern that the teachers and administrators be made aware of the boy's unique situation. He was coming there, with no family, from a city childhood and reform school background; he was physically much more mature than the other kids of his age; and he was sorely lacking school experience.

The heightened racial awareness among students and teachers, together with Mike's imposing physical presence and the knowledge that he came from a tough institutionalized background, marked him out for more than his share of attention from the day he enrolled. In 1980 there were no special or alternative educational options available to administrators in the Catskill community as there are now, so Mike was mainstreamed into the normal school environment. Owing to his age and his physical size (he was 5'8" and a hulking 200 pounds), he was placed in the eighth grade, although his academic skills hardly warranted such a placement. However, it was felt that to place him with smaller and younger children in a lower grade would have been more psychologically debilitating. Also, although he did not have, say, the required knowledge of social studies or science or history, he was assessed by Lee Bordick, the junior high school principal at the time, as being "shrewd, very verbal, a con artist to some degree" and someone who "had a special quality about him that he was driven to be successful . . . and those involved in education for many years recognized that this was a special person, there was something unique about him." Bordick and other teachers who took an interest in Mike during that first school year in Catskill felt he had the native intelligence to catch on and catch up. Still, he had to get used to some very basic things for the first time in his life, such as sitting at a desk for an entire forty-minute period until the bell rang and it was time to move on to the next class.

Mike had several quarrels during the eighth grade, but not with other boys. Oddly enough, it was the black girls who tended to taunt him. They were "country," he was "city," essentially a new and mysterious and unknown quantity to them, a sudden, unexpected intrusion on their little town. And because he went to the gym every day after school, as well as on weekends, they knew he was a boxer. He no doubt presented a paradox in being, in some vague way, a threat, someone to be kept at arm's length, and yet, in another way, an irresistible attraction. Their way of dealing with their own confused feelings was to taunt him with jeering insults for no apparent reason about his mother, about whom they knew absolutely nothing. This would send Mike into rages, since he was particularly sensitive about his mother, whom he cared for and realized he had caused much worry and grief. And while he never retaliated physically against the girls, his rage would cause him to become disobedient, resulting in a suspension for a day or two until he cooled off.

In addition, though more because of his imposing physical presence than any actual threat he made to them, several of the teachers were intimidated by Mike, worried about the consequences to themselves if he ever directed his rage at them. But Mike was on what was for him good behavior. He didn't want to cross the line that would bring about the end of this new relationship with Cus and send him back to Tryon or the hopelessness of the streets, so he kept his temper in check for the most part.

One day, three black girls were harassing him once again about his mother, and Mike responded by chasing after them. They took refuge in the girls' lavatory, but Mike went right in after them. Lee Bordick, the principal, was summoned. As he was taking the boy outside to have a talk with him, one of the girls kicked Mike hard as he was walking past her. Mike spun round, his nostrils flaring, and glared at her, but then kept walking. Such was his strength at that age that if he had chosen to go after her, one or even two teachers would have been powerless to stop him without placing themselves at risk of physical injury. This occurrence came on the heels of several other disciplinary incidents involving Mike over a period of several weeks, and Mike stormed off, ignoring the principal. Bordick went after him, determined to assert his authority. He could see Mike snorting with rage when he caught up with him. "Mike," he told him, "I want you to run around the school campus until you calm down, and then we'll talk." Mike obeyed, and a few minutes later he and Bordick talked things out. Under such provocation, any kid might be forgiven for responding as Mike Tyson did.

Early in 1981, the school administered its annual New York State competency exam to students. It was a fairly tough test with perhaps an overall 10 percent failure rate, but Mike passed it, albeit narrowly, which was a good indication of his natural intelligence and how quickly he had managed to improve his reading and other academic skills in his few months at Catskill. Thanks to the interest taken in him by several teachers, Bordick's assessment was that "Mike overall had a very successful eighth grade year. There were some problems, but they were certainly not the worst on the list. It was a matter of adjustment. Overall, one would have to be impressed with his incredible self-discipline and focus." Bordick felt that because Mike had a rigid routine of school, followed by the rigors of his training in the gym every afternoon, plus weekends, he was more disciplined than most of the kids his age in the school. He also appreciated Cus's influence on Mike: "Cus became the consummate teacher, and I was very impressed with someone who was relatively uneducated but was fairly well read and was able to inculcate in a young fellow the things that we were trying to do with students in general, [which Cus] did very naturally."

Cus also remembered Mike's early days in Catskill: "Things were rather difficult, because there was a lack of communication and I think he was a little apprehensive that we wouldn't get along. . . . He was accustomed to being in the company of different types of people, and as a result he didn't know how I would accept or be receptive to him because of that. He was coming there to be helped in every way. As a fighter, particularly, but in order to be helped as a fighter he had to be helped in every other way. His character had to be developed and strengthened, he had to learn discipline, and he had to learn to face his problems and not avoid them, which is an essential part of the charac-

ter of any competitive athlete. The strengthening of character has been a slow process because the rules he had learned
to live by were not those generally accepted by society. His
life was a dog-eat-dog affair. But I can relate to someone of
any age because I lived through all these periods. I grew up
in a very tough neighborhood. . . . People are people and
boys are boys, and I know exactly how he feels. I know
when to put a little pressure down to make him aware,
perhaps to influence him in a particular direction. I also
know when to lay off, because pressure at the wrong time
may cause a certain amount of resentment in him to arise,
which will delay the development." Differences over when
to "lay off," and whether Tyson's character was being suffi-
ciently "developed and strengthened" would eventually lead
to a growing rift between the young trainer, Teddy Atlas,
and the old master.

D'Amato's methods for tutoring Tyson were those he had
evolved and used over the years. "I tell them the first time
they're going to fight, the night before they probably won't
sleep. I can't offer them any consolation other than the fact
that the other guy went through the same thing, and when
they get down to the fight and enter the dressing room,
especially if they're in an amateur fight, the room is full of
possible opponents, because they don't know who they're
going to fight, and everybody looks calm, confident and
smiling and all the new boy is aware of is that terrible thump
in his chest, and he's intimidated by their attitude and their
confidence. What he doesn't realize is that they look at him
and they see the same thing in him as he sees in them,
because by an exercise of discipline he also puts on a super-
ficial appearance of confidence. . . . We go on now to go
into the ring. Half the time they're walking when they go
down to the ring as though they're going to the gallows. So
when they climb those stairs, I never call a fighter yellow.
Knowing what he goes through, the very act of climbing into
that ring stamps him a person of courage and discipline.

"So now they get into the ring. . . . The other guy probably looks bigger and stronger and better conditioned and
real muscular, and when he starts to loosen up he looks
more experienced. This is the novice fighter's mind and
imagination exaggerating everything, which is what the mind
does. Nothing is ever as bad as the imagination makes it,

not even death. A person doesn't realize what's making him nervous unless he understands why he's getting scared, which is the natural, normal thing. When he understands it he accepts it as such. Then it doesn't become as intimidating, which is the reason why I take the boy step by step until actually the bell rings to fight. I take them that way so that hopefully by the time they get to fight they've experienced these different feelings which are often intimidating by themselves. 'Cus said it was going to be like this,' so that they don't feel they are inferior or less prepared than their opponent.

"Now, when they go in and face the opponent and the bell rings, for the first time . . . they're facing reality, and suddenly a relative calmness comes over them. Relative. They're still scared but it isn't that terrible intimidating unknown thing. . . . But the moment the blows start to be thrown, the effort to throw punches has begun, he gets calm, because now this is something he's been prepared to cope with. . . . However, I should add, that at no time does fear disappear. It's just as bad in the hundredth fight as it was in the first, except by the time he reaches a hundred fights or long before that he's developed enough discipline where he can learn to live with it, which is the object, to learn to live with it. . . .

"Every fighter that ever lived had fear. A boy comes to me and tells me that he's not afraid; if I believed him I'd say he's a liar or there's something wrong with him. I'd send him to a doctor to find out what the hell's the matter with him, because this is not a normal reaction. The fighter that's gone into the ring and hasn't experienced fear is either a liar or a psychopath."

Before Mike would be allowed to step into the ring for an actual fight, he would be prepared fully under D'Amato's guidance. D'Amato prepared those of his fighters who had the potential to become successful professionals just one way from the start: as professionals. In the short run, this would cause the fighter to suffer somewhat in his amateur career. He would win several national titles as an amateur, but never gain the wide public recognition of a Sugar Ray Leonard, a Mark Breland, a Henry Tillman or a Tyrell Biggs. They all captured Olympic gold; Breland won a record five consecutive New York Golden Gloves Championships.

D'Amato was probably not especially interested in Tyson achieving greatness as an amateur. He knew that Mike's style was more suited to professional boxing, and schooling him too well as an amateur could adversely affect his adjustment to professional fighting later on. It's accepted truth in boxing circles that fighters who spend too long in the amateur ranks don't achieve the same success in the professional arena. The theories vary: They burn themselves out with too many amateur bouts, they become too conditioned to being "three-round fighters," the length of all amateur fights. But the main reason long conditioning as an amateur can stunt professional growth is the marked contrast between the rules amateur boxing is governed by as compared with professional boxing.

In any other major sports, the rules of the game and the way it is played remain virtually the same from high school and college to the minor leagues and on into the big-time professional competition. Boxing is the only major sport where the rules in the "minor leagues," the amateur ranks, differ vastly from the professional side of the sport. In amateur boxing, with its convoluted scoring systems, the primary objective is to score points. In theory, a good jab counts as much in a round as a knockdown blow. So if a fighter is knocked down by a tremendous punch, he can get up at the count of nine, land three soft jabs, and he's scored more points toward victory than his opponent! The front, or fist, portion of amateur gloves are painted white, and only punches that land on the white part of the glove count. Any others will not only not count in the scoring, but will usually result in the referee stopping the action to issue a warning to the fighter. Bending at the waist, bobbing and weaving, all effective defensive techniques for professionals, are frowned upon in amateur boxing. There are so many rules and regulations that it is rare to see amateur or Olympic fights where the action is not stopped numerous times in the course of just three rounds by the referee to issue warnings to the fighters that completely break up the flow of the action and, consequently, the excitement of the fight. The use of headgear in amateur boxing was also an aspect which did not meet with D'Amato's approval. He felt—and with good reason—that headgear gave fighters a false sense of security.

Headgear is perhaps the worst innovation introduced into amateur boxing by well-meaning but misguided amateur federation administrators. The casual boxing fan may think that headgear protects young fighters from damaging blows to the head, blows that critics of the sport are always quick to point to as the cause of injury. But nothing could be further from the truth. Headgear does not provide that kind of protection, nor was it ever intended to do so. The concussive force of a blow to the head is not lessened one bit by a piece of padded leather around the skull, because it is the impact of the blow and the resulting motion of the head that causes a knockout. Nor do gloves, which the uninformed may feel are also intended to soften the force of punches, serve any such purpose. Gloves are designed to protect the hand of the man throwing the punches, not the head of the man receiving them. The acceleration of the punch and the acceleration of the brain inside the skull are what cause damage in a fight, and padded hands or heads do not reduce that acceleration one iota. All headgear does, and all it was designed to do, is to protect the fighter from being cut, and this advantage is probably more than offset by the reduction in his peripheral vision which, ironically, makes him more vulnerable, since it can take him longer to see and therefore to avoid any punches heading his way. D'Amato believed that the fighter's restricted vision forced him to keep his head higher in order to see better, thus exposing his chin and making him even more vulnerable. From the beginning, Tyson was taught to train in the gym without headgear, and to this day, in his sparring sessions, no headgear is worn.

D'Amato insisted that the primary weapon, even for such a powerfully destructive machine as Tyson, was defense, and Tyson spent many hours in the ring during his early training not throwing a punch at sparring partners. D'Amato and Atlas just had him move, duck, bob, weave and practice lateral motion to avoid being hit. He paid for his lessons by catching punches every time he failed to make the proper defensive move, and he was not allowed to retaliate by throwing punches back at his opponents, who often were fast, smaller welterweights or middleweights.

Mickey Duff recalls seeing Tyson for the first time in a junior tournament in New York City: "He paced up and down like a caged tiger and I thought at that time that he looked menacing. He looked a strong kid with not a lot of sophisticated talent yet. Natural talent, yes, but he didn't look to have any fine skills. He looked strong and awesome for his age. As I remember, he fought a kid about two years older than him. Knocked him out."

D'Amato certainly knew how to turn a situation to his own advantage and help build his young fighter's confidence. Duff remembers one such occasion, when he had come to the United States with a young British heavyweight of his own, twenty-two years old, just in the early stages of a professional career. His name was Frank Bruno. Seven years later, when Tyson was heavyweight champion, he and Bruno would meet in the ring amidst the glamour and glitter of Las Vegas with millions of dollars and the world title at stake. But in 1981 no one could foresee that, when Duff brought Bruno to box with the sixteen-year-old Tyson— except maybe D'Amato, who perhaps even then intended to build his protégé's confidence by outsmarting Duff. "Cus called me to ask if Tyson could box with Bruno. I said yes. Bruno was told twenty times before they started sparring, this is only a kid, don't go and hurt him. So Bruno went out mentally to just spar and suddenly finds this guy swarming all over him. The result was that Tyson had a good round, and when it was over, Cus said, 'That was all I wanted him to box.' He only let Mike box one round, [*note:* it was actually two rounds] and he pounced out and jumped all over Bruno." It must have given Tyson a boost of confidence then, and it certainly did when he was signed to fight Bruno in 1988, because he talked about how easily he had handled Bruno as an amateur those many years before.

At one point, the quiet house in Catskill suffered an invasion that no one who was there at the time will ever forget. Wilfred Benitez came to train in Catskill. Benitez was managed by D'Amato's close friend, Jim Jacobs, and Bill Cayton, the first world champion Jacobs would handle. The Puerto Rican native was a boxing prodigy. He won his first world title at the age of seventeen, making him the youngest professional champion in history. (Even Mike Tyson, who would become the youngest heavyweight champion ever, was still an amateur when he was seventeen years old.) Benitez would go on to win two more titles in his career, making him one of a handful of men to hold championships in three different weight divisions. He did it all on natural talent, because his training habits and overall discipline were severely lacking. Benitez had the reputation in boxing circles of being a "head case," a wacky, strutting, macho kid not playing with a full deck.

He began his career at age fourteen, managed by his father, Gregorio, who was heavily into horses and gambling. Predictably, within a few years, Gregorio was in debt and was forced to sell his son's contract to raise cash. Teddy Brenner, the matchmaker at the old Eastern Parkway Arena in Brooklyn who had started out Floyd Patterson, put Gregorio together with Jacobs and Cayton, whom he knew had the money. Financially it was a steal. They grabbed Benitez's contract for $75,000. Guided by them, the fighter would earn several million dollars over the next few years, and their cut earned back their investment many times over. But handling Wilfred Benitez took its toll in aggravation, since the fighter's father insisted that he remain involved in his son's career as the boy's trainer. Father and son would prove to be their own worst enemies. Neither knew how to handle their new-found wealth, perhaps thinking those million-dollar purses would pour in forever. Eventually, a victim of his own profligate ways and milked by his father's continued gambling, Benitez would burn out while still in his twenties, his career over and with virtually all his money gone.

When he and his entourage arrived in Catskill he was at the peak of his fighting powers, preparing to challenge Carlos Palomino for the welterweight title. It was Jacob's hope that the two men might gain some insight by training under the watchful eye of Cus. Apparently unfamiliar—or unconcerned—with the conventions of civilized society, the Puerto Ricans turned things upside down at the house. One member of the group would wake up between four and five every morning and begin to practice his martial arts, complete with loud screams and whoops, waking everyone up. He also had the charming habit of blowing snot from his nose right onto the floor and leaving it there.

Wilfred himself would spit on the floor around his bed. He would also gorge himself on his favorite diet of chicken, beans and rice to the point where he would sometimes throw up or get stomach cramps and shit all over the toilet, leaving his mess unflushed until someone would discover it the next morning.

Benitez also began a hot pursuit of a thirteen-year-old girl in town, until Cus put a halt to it by explaining that although this might be acceptable behavior in the islands, in a small country town it could land him in jail for statutory rape, or perhaps provoke the girl's family to come after him with shotguns.

At dinnertime the Benitez entourage did not bother with utensils: They used their hands for everything. When the other boys in the house complained about this behavior that was turning the place into a shambles, Cus tried to explain to them that these people came from a different culture. As Cus put it, all these people knew how to cut sugar cane all day and screw their women at night.

However, the final straw came one day when Camille was trying to clean up. She had noticed that her expensive, monogrammed towels had been disappearing. While cleaning in Wilfred's room, she found a pile of them, along with a stench. When she examined more closely, she was repulsed. It seems that Wilfred had been using them as toilet paper and just dumped the excrement-covered towels in his room. Camille was enraged, and it was not long before Benitez and his merry men were sent packing.

When D'Amato came to the gym every few days, his professional eye watched and he tutored Tyson as he boxed. However, day to day, it was Teddy Atlas who was in the gym, delivering the same object lessons to Tyson and Rooney that he'd learned from Cus, week in and week out. As D'Amato told the documentary producer, Michael Marton: "Teddy always comes to me when he has some doubts or something important. Otherwise I let him do it because I know he can do it. I wouldn't let him do it if I didn't know he could do it. I'm the one that makes the final decision. Teddy and I are together. We're synonomous. I'm Teddy, Teddy's me."

"I'm not a creator," Cus would often tell people. "What I do is discover and uncover. My job is, take the spark and fan it. When it starts to become a little flame, I feed it. I feed the fire until it becomes a roaring blaze, and then when it becomes a roaring blaze, I pour huge logs on it, and then you really get a fire going. That's what I do with these boys, that's what I try to do."

During these early months in Catskill, Tyson fought in a few small tournaments, and also in "smokers," amateur fight cards often held in small gyms that were not sanctioned by any official amateur organization, but a good place for kids to get experience in the ring, even though the fights would not go down on their official amateur records. Mike won impressively every time.

Every fighter comes to a crossroads in the ring, a test which he must pass if he is to progress up the ladder. Sometimes that test is met in the gym, and many fighters have given up without progressing beyond that point. Some fighters may meet their first real challenge when it's too late, when they are ill-prepared to cope with it, as happened with Gerry Cooney when he met Larry Holmes for the Heavyweight Championship and found he had not been properly prepared by facing tough opponents on the way up, even though his managers had done a brilliant job on the business side by maneuvering him into a title fight and a $10 million purse.

For Mike Tyson, the first test of his character—the first test not of his natural ability but of his resolve and determination—came on a forgotten night on a forgotten boxing show against a forgotten opponent in Scranton, Pennsylvania. But it was a test that proved crucial to his development, although only the inner circle of Teddy, Gus and Mike himself would know it. They had gone to Scranton because Kevin Rooney was booked to fight a professional bout on a small card. Because of the realities of promoting small-town boxing, the undercard would be made up of amateur bouts, which served to give the local boys some experience, while relieving the promoter of the burden of having to pay purses to pros in the prelims. Cus and Teddy brought a couple of their amateurs along. Mike was one of them. He was fourteen years old and had not arrived at the point where he could overcome his fear. Up till then he'd never had to, since things had always gone his way in the few fights he'd had.

His opponent was a local white kid, not very skilled, but tough. In the first round, Mike overwhelmed him, knocking him down twice. But something unusual happened, something that Mike was not used to. The kid got back on his feet both times and instead of giving up, fought back hard. Mike came back to his corner at the end of the first round, flopped on the stool, and told Teddy he was very tired. Cus was watching him from ringside and saw the fatigue Tyson was showing. But Cus and Teddy knew that Mike was in great shape and that physically it was impossible for him to be tired after just three minutes of boxing. "Mike," Teddy said as he sponged him off, "you're not tired. You're letting your feelings get the better of you. You're better than this guy. You've got to concentrate, just be steady, do the things we've worked on. If you knock him down and the guy gets up, knock him down again. And don't let your imagination get the better of you."

The bell rang for the second round, and Tyson went out confidently. He put his opponent down for a third time, but again he got up. Mike was dominating the round, and if the kid hadn't been a local boy, the referee might even have stepped in and stopped the fight. When the bell sounded, Mike came back to the corner and dropped to his stool again, completely exhausted. "Teddy, my hand is broken," he told his trainer. Atlas knew better. His experience and judgment told him it was Mike's will that was faltering. He had less than a minute to pull his fighter together. It was critical. If Tyson came apart here, the future they had anticipated for him would be in question. At the very least, he would suffer a psychological setback that would delay his development. In the corner, Mike was glazed, drifting off, unfocused. His mind was out of control. The seconds were ticking away. Teddy had to be sure his assessment was right. He grabbed Tyson's gloved hand and squeezed it as hard as he could. Mike didn't even notice. The hand was obviously not broken. Teddy twisted Mike's face toward his. He was nose to nose with the panting fighter. He had to make his words count, make Mike listen. "Mike, there's nothing wrong with your hand," Teddy told him. "What's broken is your spirit. All this crap about how you want to become heavyweight champ of the world, here's your heavyweight title. Go out and win the damn thing. Be a man, damn it. This guy's falling down. If I was in the other corner I would have stopped the damn fight already. Here's your first test and you want to fail it. You want to quit. Now get out there, damn it, and keep doing what you been doing, which is knocking this guy down. If he gets up, you knock him down again. Otherwise all this work and all these dreams, it ends right here. You gotta want it. With all your skill, you just gotta want it. Now go out there and win the fight." It was all the time Teddy had. He stuffed the mouthpiece between Mike's teeth and literally shoved him off the stool and into the center of the ring.

Both fighters were spent, so neither was doing very much, groping and clinching, throwing harmless punches. Mike's mind was still not straight, despite Teddy's lecture. The white boy threw a few punches. Mike countered and hurt him again. They grabbed each other and staggered toward Tyson's corner. Cus had once told Teddy that when you get experienced enough as a trainer, you get to a point where you can almost see what's going on in the fighter's mind. Teddy suddenly knew what Mike was about to do. Although he wasn't being hit, Teddy knew that Mike was going to go down. He was going to quit, take the count on the canvas. His psychological exhaustion had got the better of him, his last ounce of resolve was gone. The crowd was going wild, rooting for their local boy. Teddy didn't have time to think. He had to react like a fighter, instinctively. He knew that in a more formal structure what he was about to do would result in the disqualification of his fighter, but something in that split second told him that here, in a small arena, with the crowd screaming, he might possibly get away with it. By now, Mike was backed into the corner just above Teddy. His knees were beginning to buckle, and Teddy knew if he went down he wasn't going to get up. In an instant, Teddy jumped up on the ring apron, outside the ropes. He leaned in and shouted, "Don't do it! Don't do it, goddamn it!" Hearing him, Tyson grabbed his opponent and fell into a clinch. The two fighters staggered out of the corner, mauling and wrestling until the bell rang some thirty seconds later to end the fight. Teddy jumped into the ring, and Mike stumbled into his arms, hugging his trainer and mumbling, "Thank you, thank you," to him, again and again. Teddy knew what Mike meant. Without saying it, Mike understood that Teddy had saved him from himself, something much more important than the decision the judges awarded him after the final bell.

D'Amato, too, watching from ringside, knew that he had just witnessed a mental fight inside his young protégé much tougher than the outward, physical battle. One of D'Amato's main axioms concerned the paramount importance of the will: "When two men are fighting, what you're watching is more a contest of wills than of skills, with the stronger will usually overcoming the skill. The skill will prevail only when it is so superior to the other man's skill that the will is not tested. . . . As many times as you see a fellow get tired in the course of a fight, note that he gets tired when pressure builds up, after he gets hurt or he's been in some kind of doubtful situation, not being able to control the situation. That's when he starts getting tired. That's why when two good fighters get to fight, they're head to head, so to speak, they won't give an inch and they're using all their skill and ability, until maybe about the seventh or eighth or ninth round, one fighter starts to visibly weaken. It only means he's reached a point where he no longer can stand the pressure. He's now become dominated, because when two people fight it's very much like two armies. They seek to impose their will on one another."

Back in the dressing room in Scranton, Teddy didn't have much time. He had to get Kevin taped and gloved for his fight, but he pulled Mike aside to talk with him briefly, while the experience was fresh in their minds. Mike was still experiencing his postfight euphoria, still hugging and kissing and thanking Ted, who calmed him down before telling him, "Mike, look, I'm only gonna say this once because it's not a thing I'm gonna keep banging you over the head with, bringing up all the time. . . . You were gonna give up out there . . . but you didn't. For the first time you felt the feeling of a person when he felt he couldn't control something and the only thing you could go on wasn't your skill any more, it was your will. This is the first time you were tested. . . . The weakness would have been if you had given in and actually given up. You didn't. You felt it, so you know you're human, you know like anyone else it's possible to be vulnerable, and it's also possible to fight that vulnerability off and overcome it. . . . In the future you can avoid getting that close because you won't allow your imagination and the unknown to get the better of you. You didn't quit. That's the most important thing!" Mike acknowledged that he understood what Teddy was telling him. Kevin went out and won his fight, after which they all drove back to Catskill. Teddy never spoke to Mike again about that night. He didn't have to. The lesson had been learned.

A few months later, Tyson took his first big step up. He was entered in the National Junior Olympics Tournament held at the USAF Academy in Colorado Springs, Colorado. This was a showcase for the best young fighters in the nation under the age of sixteen, and so not yet eligible to compete in senior amateur events. D'Amato sent Teddy Atlas alone with Mike to Colorado. Mike was not yet fifteen, but it was at this tournament that the "Tyson mystique" truly began. It started even before Mike had his first fight. He stood out from all the other boys waiting in line to take their physical exams. Most of the other fourteen- and fifteen-year-olds still had baby fat. Their bodies were not fully formed yet, their muscles did not have the definition they would get as they matured. Mike, by contrast, looked as if he were sculpted out of rock. And his demeanor only added to his mystique. Schooled by Cus that the fighter does the fighting and the manager does the talking, Mike remained aloof, refusing to join in casual conversation with the other boys. If any of them asked him anything, he would just point to Teddy. He was scoring psychological points over the others before they even saw him with a glove on.

Even so, although a fighter can build up a forbidding image, he has to be able to back it up when he steps in the ring or else it serves little purpose. That night, Mike's first opponent was a hulking boy from Hawaii. He weighed 265 pounds, big but soft. Mike was small by comparison, barely 5'9" and under 200 pounds, but solid as a rock. In the first round, he hit the Hawaiian with a tremendous left hook to the liver. All 265 pounds of the youngster quivered, and he went down in a massive heap on the canvas. The arena, filled not only with spectators but coaches, officials and other fighters, was electrified. Everything they had feared and imagined about this unknown kid from back east was true.

The next night, Mike won his second fight, also by knockout. Suddenly he was larger than life. Yet he still refused to talk to anyone, trying to project an attitude of sullen invincibility. Out of earshot of Mike, the fighters were talking: "See that Tyson who's knocking everyone out, he's Sonny Liston's nephew." The rumor spread like wildfire, further intimidating the other heavyweights in the tournament: Mike Tyson was Sonny Liston's nephew, at least in their minds. The day before the finals, a black kid who had lost in the semis the night before was talking to the boy who'd beaten him. "Man, you didn't beat me," he said. "I was just smarter than you. My momma didn't raise no fool. I knew if I won I'd have to fight that animal Tyson in the finals, so I quit. I *let* you beat me. Now what are you gonna do tomorrow night, man? You gotta fight Tyson!" The next night, Mike scored another knockout. He became the national junior olympics heavyweight champion, his first national amateur title, and as the word spread in amateur boxing circles about this fourteen-year-old destroyer, the Tyson legend was born.

Mike continued to develop as a fighter, knocking out virtually all of his opponents. In the fall of 1981, he entered Catskill High School. During the course of the next year, a widening conflict would develop between Cus and Teddy, fueled largely by their differences concerning Mike's education and his overall discipline.

According to a former school administrator, racial tensions had caused the school to be closed down for several days in September of 1981 as Tyson entered to begin ninth grade. Subsequently, some of the black students were concerned about where Mike stood vis à vis the situation, because of his close affiliation with whites at home and in the gym. Now that he was a national boxing champion and had featured in the local newspapers, he was more and more the center of attention at school, where he was still at a disadvantage academically, although the principal, Richard Stickles, feels that he did pretty well considering the circumstances of his background.

However, the disciplinary incidents kept mounting, sometimes because Mike was provoked into fighting. The black kids would taunt him, calling him "whitey" because he lived with Cus, Camille, Teddy and Kevin. Mike's rage would sometimes reach flash-point. One black boy in particular, a school tough nicknamed "God" because of his dominance over the other black kids, kept baiting Mike. One day he pushed him too far, and Mike pounced. Incredulously, one of the young blacks ran into the principal's office shouting, "There's a fight outside—Mike's beatin' up God!"

There were also more serious incidents involving confrontations with teachers, as well as displays of temper such as the occasion when Mike entered the school cafeteria before lunchtime, saying he was hungry. When he was told the cafeteria wasn't open yet, he angrily grabbed several milk containers and splattered them against the walls. Some of the stories of his misbehavior may have been overblown, but there is no doubt that he was a disciplinary problem to the school. On numerous occasions he was suspended for brief periods, and several times he was the subject of superintendent's hearings.

After one such hearing, Teddy Atlas said, "Cus was heard leaving the school saying to Mike, 'If they expel you, I'll get Jimmy [Jacobs] to get you a tutor.' Then I went and confronted Cus with this and we had an argument because I said, 'Cus, this is like giving him carte blanche to act any way he wants to with anybody, and I don't think it's healthy.' To me, it was tantamount to saying, every time Mike threw his left jab and he was dropping his right hand, not to correct him. We would never let that happen. God forbid! He would have been jumped on by me and Cus. . . . I didn't think that we were giving him the same kind of time and direction and help in developing him personally as we were in the ring. We had a young man who had a background that wasn't the greatest, I know that. But still, there are certain standards and rules of discipline that we all have to adhere by." Teddy believed that Mike needed a tighter rein than Cus was willing to give. "Mike was learning," says Teddy, "there were certain things the didn't have to control in his temper, in his emotions outside the ring, and I thought he better learn that if he's going to be successful in a true sense. I even said to Cus, in a real self-serving way, 'It's going to hurt us, because if we don't discipline him and guide him properly now, we're going to have problems with this guy after we've put in all our work . . . when we're supposed to be enjoying the fruits of this success financially and personally and professionally, we won't be able to. So if you just want to do it for selfish reasons, we have to give him the discipline, but I also think we have an obligation to do it. . . . He's learning to control himself quite good in the ring, but he's not learning to deal with his emotions outside the ring.' " In the years that were to follow, Teddy's words would have a prophetic ring.

Eventually, Teddy felt he had to take matters into his own hands. If other youngsters had bad report cards, he would suspend them from the gym. He felt that to be consistent he had to deal with Mike in the same manner. He suspended him from the gym for two weeks and told him he couldn't attend any boxing shows the other kids were fighting on during that time. But a couple of nights later, at an amateur show across the river in Hudson, Cus appeared with Mike in tow. And although for the most part Cus only came to the gym every week or so, relying on Teddy to run the daily training activities and getting reports from him over the dinner table, things suddenly changed. During Mike's suspension from the gym, Cus began bringing him there in the mornings, on his own, to train him. Again, it served as a definite signal to Mike that he need not abide by the rules so long as he kept up his progress in the boxing ring.

During Mike's freshman year in high school, he and Teddy returned to Colorado Springs for the 1982 National Junior Olympics Tournament, where Mike was to defend his title. Teddy told him, "Just keep your mind where it's supposed to be and you'll be champ of the world some day." In the days before departing for Colorado, Teddy intensified his physical and psychological work with Mike, understanding the fear that was inside his fighter. As Mike sparred, Teddy kept up a constant banter: "That's it . . . bad intentions . . . who's the last guy to stop punching? . . . don't drop it, even half an inch . . . let it come in the same height as your shoulder . . . straight across . . . throw it with bad intentions, like you're hitting someone you want to hurt . . . throw it like you don't like somebody . . . that's it . . . throw it hard . . . that's better, see the difference? . . . It's in you all the time, it's just gotta come out . . . you better throw it with bad intentions . . . when you're in the ring you're not playing Ping Pong with the guy . . . that's it . . . good . . . now you gotta slip."

Teddy told Michael Marton, who was traveling to Colorado with them in the course of producing a documentary: "He's not as tough or hard as people think he is. Everyone that sees me, they say, 'Oh, boy, you got that Tyson, you're lucky, he's an animal, he just loves to fight, he just loves to hurt people, he's not afraid of nothin'.' Well, when we're done with him he won't look like he is, anyway. He's got the potential to go down as one of the greatest fighters ever, but he'll only reach that potential if he keeps his head screwed on straight."

Marton observed, "Whenever they traveled, Teddy would always do this amazingly unending psychological job on Mike. He would always be with him, he always slept in the same room. He would give Mike some space to be with the kids and play pinball and stuff like that, but he would always be around him. And at that point Mike really needed that. Teddy carried that guy because that fear thing was so terrific. He was a very fragile guy."

All eyes were on Tyson in this tournament because of his spectacular first appearance in it a year earlier. Mike did not disappoint. He won his first four bouts by knockout. Before his final bout, Teddy could tell Mike was nervous. They went outside the arena to get some fresh air, away from all the tumult and noise in the dressing room. "Loosen up," Teddy told Mike, "especially when you feel the tension mount. Motion relieves tension. You're the champ; they're the ones who gotta worry. If you weren't nervous, there'd be something wrong with ya. That nervous feeling is a sign you're gonna win, a sign you're ready, ready to win." They returned to the arena. Teddy's pep talk was longer than the fight. With the first punch Mike landed, a tremendous shot to the head, he flattened his opponent. The referee didn't even bother to count. The boy was unconscious. Mike had won by knockout in an amazing eight seconds of the first round. It was the fastest knockout ever recorded in the history of the Junior Olympics Tournament.

The next night, inside the arena waiting for the finals, Mike should have been the picture of confidence. He'd won all five of his bouts by KO, and he was the defending champion. But he wasn't. "They want to take my title, but they're not gettin' it," he kept muttering. He was tight and tense. Teddy coached him to "box smart, like a hungry tiger, smart and calm. Once you get inside, set up those body punches, then switch up. Left jab, move your head, and cover. Win this title, then we'll go home to our friends."

Again, Teddy took him outside so he could walk and relieve the tension. "Just relax, Mike, just relax," Teddy told him. Then, suddenly, it all came out. Out of sight of all the fans and coaches and boxers who thought he was an indestructible fighting machine, Mike's body began heaving, and he broke down in uncontrollable sobs. Teddy comforted him, knowing he had to remain calm, yet also realizing he only had a few minutes to bring Mike back under control. "All it is is another boxing match. You done it already twenty times, you done it in the gym with better fighters than you're ever gonna fight here. It's always hard . . ." Mike kept crying. In between sobs, he was muttering, "I'm Mike Tyson . . . everyone likes me. . . ." What Mike was saying was that he was afraid, afraid that if he lost, everything he had would be taken away—the respect of Cus and the others back in Catskill, everything he had, which was wrapped up in his success in the ring. "That's right," Teddy assured him. "You have a reason to be proud, and you'll continue to do it, as long as you don't let anything mess you up, as long as you don't let yourself mess you up, you'll continue to have people like you. Always remember, don't let your feelings get the better of you. Don't let things mix you up." That was all he could say. He knew it was time. "Now let's go get ready for a fight," he said, and they went back into the crowded arena.

Mike's opponent, a 6'7" well-built youngster named Kelton Brown, was already in the ring. The TV commentators were telling their audience about Mike: "There's a lot of noise being made about this young man as a possible Olympic prospect and a possible professional champion in years to come." In the corner, Teddy was giving his last words of instruction to Mike, "Fight smart, and like a tiger, and calm." Mike kissed Ted on the cheek, and the bell rang. Mike swarmed over Kelton Brown, throwing punches from all angles; just seconds into the bout, Brown was taking a standing eight-count. A moment later, Tyson had Brown pinned in the corner, and Brown's trainer threw in the towel to spare his fighter any more serious punishment. In less than one minute it was over, and Mike was the national junior champion for the second straight year.

Back in Catskill, Mike displayed yet more bravado than he had outside the arena in Colorado Springs. He told Michael Marton, "I don't need nobody. I don't give a shit, anybody can train me." Marton was incredulous. "Mike," he said, "I was there, remember? I saw Teddy Atlas carrying you through that fight in Colorado. You were hanging over the railing crying like a baby. How could you talk like that?"

The question of Mike's education was coming to a head. "Mike didn't want to go to school," Camille Ewald acknowledges. Cus told Bobby Stewart, "Look, the only time he gets in trouble down here is in school." But Stewart agreed with Teddy Atlas, that disciplining himself to finish school was as important to Mike as learning to fight, that Mike would need a high school diploma if he didn't make it in boxing and wanted to take an exam some day for a civil service job. Cus told him, "This kid is going to be the heavyweight champion of the world. Forget the high school diploma. He's going to make so much money some day he won't have to worry about getting a job."

According to Richard Stickles, the principal, Mike was "becoming restive. He wanted out. . . . At this point, it was clear that the objective of a high school graduation was not going to be attained within the time frame Cus wanted." And perhaps there were more ominous indications, which Stickles only alluded to: "If Michael was to have any small problems . . . these continual things eventually could lead to a hearing . . . a major thing, which would not be in his best interests." At last, Stickles and Cus met, and it was decided that it would be in the best interests of all concerned if Mike continued his education outside the school environment. A program of home study, with a tutor coming to the house, was arranged for him. Thus his formal schooling ended after his freshman year in high school.

As a school official, Stickles has to temper his words carefully. But a Catskill town official, able to speak more candidly, says, "I'm telling you, Mike Tyson was a major problem in that high school . . . and the fact that he was not thrown out of school was simply because Cus pulled him out under an ultimatum—'Get him out of here or we're going to take things in our own hands.' . . . Cus's big concern was having that kid pulled back by the state. And once that happened, good-bye heavyweight champion. That was his major concern. . . . They had tremendous problems with Tyson in the local school system, with the local police, he was constantly in a jam."

Before very long, Cus allowed the tutoring to lapse, and Mike's education became a thing of the past. Now Cus could concentrate full-time on his primary goal, which was to turn Mike Tyson into the heavyweight champion of the world. But even outside the school environment, Mike's troubles continued. Sometimes he would stay out all night, and often he was disrespectful to both Cus and Camille.

Despite the provocations, however, Cus's attitude continued to be surprisingly ambivalent. One night when Mike arrived home very late, Cus confronted him and browbeat him to the point where he had the boy crying. But more often Cus would let things slide. One day when Mike was leaving the house, Cus asked him when he'd be home. "I'll be home when I feel like it," was the reply. Teddy Atlas grabbed Mike. "What the hell are you talking to the man like that for? Talk to him respectfully!" Atlas ordered. Mike put his head down, embarrassed and contrite, but Teddy noticed that Cus did not appear to be angry. Later, he asked Cus how he could allow Mike to talk to him that way, but Cus couldn't—or wouldn't—give him an answer. Teddy knew that Cus was wrestling with his own conscience, realizing perhaps that if he disciplined Mike too harshly, he might open a Pandora's box and risk losing Mike back to the state reform school system or to the streets of Brooklyn.

Another incident clearly illustrates Mike's growing abrasiveness and Cus's reluctance to discipline him. Mike had a habit of not bathing. Often he would come home from the gym and not change his sweaty workout clothes. One day Camille told him to take a bath. Mike tore into the 78-year-old woman: "Fuck you, you piece of shit," he told her. "*You* take a bath." Teddy chased after him, but Cus intervened and said he'd handle things his way. Nothing was done of any significance, and once again Mike Tyson's behavior was conveniently overlooked.

"For the years I was there before Tyson came," says Teddy, "I developed a lot of these kids. There was an atmosphere of discipline. We had harmony, and there was a set of rules that was consistent for everybody. Now there were two sets of rules, one for everybody else and one for Mike Tyson. I didn't think that was healthy for Tyson or the rest of the fighters or for us. . . . I'm sure Cus's judgment was a lot more experienced than mine. He helped a lot of kids, and he obviously knew that Mike still needed development as a person. He was just afraid maybe he wouldn't keep him as a fighter."

Around this time, during the summer and fall of 1982, several significant events occurred. Teddy married a local girl, Elaine, over the objections of Cus D'Amato and moved out of the house. At the same time, Mike's mother, still living in Brooklyn, died of cancer. For whatever their reasons, the people in Catskill who said they cared about Mike dumped him on a train alone and sent him back to Brooklyn by himself to attend his mother's funeral.

With Mike's mother dead, Cus began proceedings to become his legal guardian. The story, effectively fed to the press over the years to the point where it became part of the myth, was that the kindly old man adopted the poor young black boy because he had been left an orphan. While it is true that Cus did care very much for Michael, he may have had less altruistic motives in quickly moving in to gain custody of the boy.

During the two years he had lived in Catskill, Tyson was still a ward of the state and therefore subject to the authority and possible whims of the state. Since Mike's arrival, D'Amato had done an effective job of keeping the state's interference to a minimum. As one person close to the situation put it, "There were a couple of caseworkers that were supposed to be keeping tabs on [Mike's] progress. They used to come around once in a while, but Cus was a pretty persuasive man. . . . He went to work on these caseworkers in his charming way, sincerely, and he won their confidence, so they didn't feel they had to come around. So visits became phone calls. The only one to inform them of any misbehavior . . . was Cus. Obviously they got sent clippings on [Mike's] success in winning tournaments, when he knocked somebody out, but they didn't get sent the reports from the dean's office. And of course, once he was out of school there was no contact with anyone official anymore. The state never knew that he was out of school. If they knew, it's very possible they would have taken action because it was their responsibility. The state was paying Cus for Mike's boarding and his rooming and his clothing. They didn't know he was out of school or about any of the problems and his aggressive behavior, rude remarks to girls, physically putting his hands [on them], being forceable with girls, taking kids' lunch money, threatening kids, things like that. The state was paying his freight. And there were certain responsibilities that had to go along with that. His behavior had to be in line, and his education had to come first."

Cus knew that if he became Mike's legal guardian, he could then control the boy and his future in the manner he thought best, a way which did not necessarily coincide with what the state youth authorities might think were Mike's own best interests.

Cus D'Amato had brought Mike a long way. From the outset he had recognized the boy's potential, and he did not want to risk losing everything now. He had developed two world champions, had seen the boxing game pass him by. Now, suddenly, in the December of his life, he had found a youngster who could be one of the best of all time, a fighter who would allow him to go out in a final burst of glory, his self-perpetuated reputation as a genius assured. Teddy Atlas observed that "Cus had a hunger to get another champion at an increasing age. Because he knew he was against the clock, Cus felt that exceptions had to be made with Mike, where otherwise he would have taken the time and made sure that the guy was also proceeding along the right way socially and personally. But Cus needed a champion."

There was another reason why D'Amato wanted legal custody of Mike. Cus's friends and business associates, Jim Jacobs and Bill Cayton, had been paying the taxes and fuel bills for the house and financing D'Amato in other ways. They were experienced in boxing and in negotiating business deals. Above all, they were honest. They had already managed several world-class fighters, as well as three-times world champion Wilfred Benitez (with D'Amato calling the shots as a behind-the-scenes adviser). The understanding was that Mike's future would be in their hands once he turned pro, and Cus had to protect him from the scum of boxing that was already beginning to sniff around the young phenomenon. With his lifelong paranoia that everyone was constantly out to steal his fighters, D'Amato believed he would be under siege for eventual control of Tyson.

As events following his death would prove, his fears may have been well founded. Bobby Stewart, who remained in close touch with Cus, said, "Mike was drawing a lot of attention in national tournaments, and guys like Don King were already taking notice. Cus told me that 'Jimmy [Jim Jacobs] has a lot of money invested in this kid, I'm going to adopt the kid legally.' He loved the kid, but he was doing it for financial reasons also. Why see Jimmy or any of them get screwed because a scumbag like Don King comes in and robs them of the fighter?"

If one were still looking for a purely altruistic motive in D'Amato's behavior, one need simply ask: In the previous seventy-five years of his life, how many other needy kids did he adopt? The answer, of course, is none. The bottom line is, Cus D'Amato wanted to adopt Mike Tyson because Mike Tyson could hit like a mule and he was going to be heavyweight champion some day.

In short, Mike gave Cus a reason to live. D'Amato himself explained it this way: "I often say to Mike, 'You know, I owe you a lot,' and he doesn't know what I mean. . . . If he weren't here, I probably wouldn't be alive today. . . . Nature is smarter than people think. Little by little we lose our friends that we care about and little by little we lose our interest, until finally we say what the devil am I doing around here if I have no reason to go on? You get used to everything. Even the idea of dying is something a person gets used to, and he accepts it. I believe that people die because they no longer want to live, they have no motivation to stay alive. But I have a reason with Mike here; he gives me the motivation. I will stay alive and I will watch him become a success, because I will not leave until that happens, because when I leave he not only will know how to fight, he'll be able to take care of himself. I don't succeed when I help make a guy become champion of the world. I succeed when I make that fellow become champion of the world and independent of me. . . ."

*   *   *

One evening, when Bill Hagan, the Greene County (Catskill) Supervisor, and a friend of Cus D'Amato's, was dining with friends in a restaurant, the waitress came to tell him that an old man was asking to see him right away. Hagan was surprised to find it was D'Amato, in a state of some agitation. "Bill," he said, "I have a problem. The wise guys just gave their telephone numbers to Tyson. They're trying to get to him. I've got to get guardianship of him." Hagan told Cus to go home, that he would call him in twenty minutes. One of those dining with Hagan happened to be his attorney. Hagan explained the problem, and the lawyer told him to have Cus in his office the next morning at ten o'clock. In a small town, local powers can pull together and close ranks quickly if need be. At 10:00 A.M. the following day, D'Amato was in the offices of Pulver and Stiefel, Attorneys. By 10:30, they were in the local court offices, the papers were presented, the judge banged down his gavel and Cus had been granted guardianship of Mike Tyson.

It was not the first favor Bill Hagan had done for Cus. Earlier he had cut through Washington red tape and approached a friend of his, a former congressman, who was the Deputy Director of the Community Services Administration. As Hagan himself puts it, "In the waning days of the Carter Administration, we played a little shenanigans with the CSA and got a grant . . . which essentially put $25,000 bucks in Cus's pocket to run his boxing club." Unfortunately, there is no evidence to show that the money was ever used for its intended purpose. A few new pieces of equipment were purchased for the gym, and a used van to transport the boys to and from amateur tournaments was obtained for about $2,000. The bulk of the money has never been accounted for, and evidence points to the fact that a large part of it may well have been misappropriated by D'Amato.

The proposal for the grant said that part of the funds were needed to pay the gym's one full-time trainer, Teddy Atlas, a salary, but Teddy never saw a dime of the money. County Supervisor Hagan confirms this is true. Atlas was told by one of D'Amato's associates that since the grant had been obtained under the pretence of paying him a salary, it would have to appear as such. He was asked to sign tax papers showing he was receiving a salary and told that at the end of the year he would have to file an income tax return. As he was not actually receiving payments, they assured him, he would be indemnified against any actual tax liability. Since his concern was taking care of the boys in the gym, not financial gain, Atlas did as he was asked. It didn't matter to him at the time whether he was paid for the work he was doing or not. He trusted Cus, and believed Cus would do the right thing.

D'Amato used at least $2,000 of the government grant funds to make an illegal loan to a friend of his in New York City. There is also evidence to support the contention that two or three of his most trusted cronies in Catskill were handed cash payments by D'Amato for their loyalty to him and for services rendered, payments he may well have believed were legitimate because they helped further his goals concerning the Catskill Boxing Club and Mike Tyson but which nevertheless are decidedly suspect.

When D'Amato received the periodic $3,000 checks from the Community Services Administration, he would immediately go to the bank and cash them rather than deposit them. Perhaps his paranoia extended to banks, too—or perhaps cash rather than checks, which are traceable, made it a lot easier for him to use the money without being accountable to anyone.

One of Cus's rules was that no one should ever enter his room when he wasn't there, or without knocking and waiting to be asked in when he was. But one evening Camille opened the door unannounced. D'Amato was sitting on the bed, together with one of his local cronies, with about $10,000 spread out over the mattress. It was the government grant money, which, unbeknown to anyone, he kept stashed under his mattress. Frantically, he tried to gather up the bills, scooping them in his arms, while launching a tirade at the woman who had shared his life for forty years for having the nerve to come into the room without knocking. Camille made a hasty exit and so was unable to determine whether the money was simply being counted or whether Cus's buddy was there to receive a payment for "services rendered."

Some of the funds may well have been used to support Tyson, which in Cus's mind was justifiable; after all, wasn't Tyson part of the Catskill Boxing Club, even the major part of it? It soon became clear that if Tyson was not involved in a project, any expenditure of money from the grant was deemed not worthy in D'Amato's judgment. For example, when the federal grant money came through, Cus allotted $2,000 of it for a trip to the Ohio State Fair where, each summer, one of the most important national amateur boxing tournaments takes place, with top amateur fighters from throughout the United States taking part. D'Amato arranged for Teddy Atlas to take five fighters from Catskill. To eke out the $2,000 for six people for a week to ten days, it was determined they would drive to Ohio and stay in the dorms at Ohio State University rather than pay air fares and motel costs. One of the five fighters was Mike Tyson, but shortly before they were due to leave a chronic wrist problem flared up, rendering him unable to compete. D'Amato immediately canceled the trip, despite the disappointment of the four other boys.

Around this time, Kevin Rooney was preparing to fight three-times world champion, Alexis Arguello. Although no title was at stake, a victory for Rooney would be a tremendous boost and propel him to the top of the division and into big-money welterweight bouts. But Teddy Atlas, both his friend and trainer, detected that Rooney was not ready for the fight. Rooney had to make weight according to the contract and was forced to lose the excess by daily sessions in a steam bath, which weakened him. Teddy brought him to a doctor who knew both young men very well. After examining Rooney, the physician told Atlas that there was no way Rooney should be allowed to step into the ring in his condition. Teddy confronted Cus, but the old man would not budge. The fight was in a couple of days, it would be on national TV, Rooney would earn his best purse, and there was no way Cus was going to pull him out. The result was not surprising. Arguello knocked Rooney out cold with one of the most powerful punches ever landed by a welterweight. To all intents and purposes, it ended Kevin Rooney's career as a viable contender, and it served to trouble Atlas further and alienate him from the man whose opinions and principles he had previously so admired.

The final split between Cus and Teddy Atlas came in November 1982. Teddy had again banned Mike from the gym until he learned to accept the same rules of behavior the others were required to live by. As before, Cus overrode Teddy's ban and started bringing Mike to the gym and training him on his own. Teddy and Cus began avoiding each other at the gym. In the morning, Cus would bring Tyson there and work with him. Later in the day, when they were gone, Teddy would work there with the other boys. To Tyson, Teddy had become the bad guy, the enforcer, the only one demanding that he abide by the rules of society. Cus wanted the title; therefore, he sided with Mike.

Atlas maintains that it had come to the point where Mike had become more and more bold with his actions, and had gotten bold to where it was becoming dangerous. "Up to that point, I was giving Mike a fair mixture of support, emotional support and backing, and discipline at the right time," Atlas recalls. "Then Cus started bringing Mike to the gym. He went against me. It was obvious to me that I was going to have to make a decision. I obviously couldn't stay involved in a situation like that. I wasn't going to compromise myself and be in an uncomfortable position. Tyson started getting out of hand, and it would come to my attention that he was being abusive to people; it was getting to a point where he was getting completely disrespectful, unrefined in his choices of what he was doing. . . . I felt betrayed; I felt that the situation was brought on by Cus not being loyal to our partnership. We were partners in the gym with the dream of developing fighters, and we had been doing this for six years together. I felt that Cus walked out on me."

Surprisingly, Atlas got no support from Kevin Rooney, who felt that Teddy was being disloyal and had no right to question the old man's methods or motives. As Rooney continued to follow D'Amato blindly, a rift developed between Atlas and his Staten Island street pal, a rift that eventually grew bitter and irrevocable.

The parents of those youngsters with whom Teddy worked and who put great trust in him, began to come to him with their complaints about Tyson's antisocial behavior. Although Cus always said he'd handle it his own way, Tyson did not mend his ways.

"Mike was a ghetto kid, and so his behavior was not unusual," observes Fred Chetti, an influential citizen in Catskill who was friends with both D'Amato and Atlas, and whose sons were part of the boxing club. "That's what you expect from a kid from Bedford-Stuyvesant and Tryon. The behavior was not unusual for him, but it was unacceptable for the society he was living in. The things he's doing today (as champion) and paying his way out of is what he did then."

Finally, all the pressure and tension came to a head when Teddy found out one evening that Mike had made lewd suggestions to a twelve-year-old girl. The previous year, Teddy had turned a blind eye when the mother of a thirteen-year-old girl complained to Camille that Mike was having sex with her daughter. Since the girl was a willing partner and the situation did not involve coercion, Teddy decided the affair was a part of growing up and was best left to take its own course. But this time it was different. No doubt part of Teddy's enraged reaction came from his being on emotional overload stemming from his feelings of rejection and betrayal. However, the incident became the proverbial last straw, and Teddy ran from his house, looking for Mike.

He found Tyson and took him to the gym. All Teddy will say of the incident is that "Cus allowed a situation to get to where a guy was really getting very dangerous and very abusive to more than himself, to other people's well-being. . . . It came to a head through letting Mike get away with these things, and it came to a showdown, so to speak, where finally he abused someone, some of it verbal abuse, along with physical, and I had to go and confront him." Tyson himself has never spoken about the incident, turning away all questions about it. But what happened was that Teddy pulled a gun on Mike Tyson, put it to his head, and threatened to blow his brains out if he didn't change his behavior toward people. Tyson panicked. He bolted from the back of the gym and ran full speed down the hill and home to Cus.

That incident ended things once and for all between Cus D'Amato, Mike Tyson and Teddy Atlas. According to Jay Bright, who was living at the house then, and indeed still does, Mike planned to get his revenge on the trainer he was once devoted to. Tyson confided to Bright that he was going to kill Teddy: "Teddy should thank God he's alive. . . . Michael wanted to go and in no uncertain terms get rid of the guy, really, and Cus talked him out of doing what he wanted to do. . . . I know exactly what Michael was going to do, and no one would be able to trace it back to Michael. No one would have known."

What D'Amato did do was get Tyson out of Catskill for a couple of weeks until the volatile situation was defused and Teddy had gone. He called Bobby Stewart and asked him to take Mike back up to Johnstown to the Tryon School, a procedure Cus had followed several times in the past when Mike had had problems in Catskill.

Under Teddy's guidance, Mike had had more than twenty sanctioned fights, plus numerous "bootleg" bouts. He lost just once and that was a disputed decision to an amateur named Ernie Bennett in Rhode Island. At the time, Bennett had close to two hundred fights and was twenty years old. Mike was fifteen and had engaged in fewer than fifteen bouts. The old newspaper clippings from the two years that Mike spent with Teddy in Catskill, testify to the bond between the two:

"Tyson works out two hours a day in D'Amato's downtown Catskill gym. His trainer is Ted Atlas, a former fighter. 'Teddy has taught me everything I know,' Tyson said. . . . 'Back when I was in New York, nobody encouraged me. . . . If I stayed in New York I might have become a fighter but it wouldn't have been the Mike Tyson you see now. I learn more here in one month than some guys do in two years.' "

"The people I train with are good people and Teddy, he's great. I love him to death."

And there are the other images: Teddy saving Mike from giving up and quitting in the ring in Scranton; Teddy pulling Mike together when he broke down minutes before his championship bout in the Junior Olympics; Teddy and Mike hugging and kissing after victories; Teddy giving Mike his last $50 so he could buy a clean warm-up suit to wear to his mother's funeral. Yet today, Teddy Atlas is a forbidden subject in the presence of Mike Tyson, who will go so far as to deny that Atlas was ever even his trainer, despite the proof that exists on film and video tape.

It may be that Mike Tyson is afraid of Teddy Atlas, afraid to look his ex-trainer and teacher in the eye when their paths have occasionally and accidentally crossed in the years since 1982, afraid of the 145-pound ex-amateur fighter with the bad back—not in a physical way, but for a much deeper, more significant reason. Perhaps Teddy Atlas, the one person who would not bow to expediency, represents a portion of whatever conscience Mike Tyson may have. Perhaps the easiest way for Mike Tyson to deal with his uncomfortable feelings is to make Teddy, once and for all, a non-person, since he knows his first trainer was the one person who would not compromise what he expected of Mike as a person for the sake of expediency.

Today, Atlas's friends joke with him about how he has become the invisible man in the Tyson saga. "Hey, Teddy," they tease him, "when they make the Mike Tyson movie, who's going to play you? Claude Rains?"

On the other side, the D'Amato loyalists, who had formed an almost cultish devotion to the late trainer, dismiss Atlas's contribution to the development of Mike Tyson. Jay Bright says, "Everything was orchestrated by Cus 100 percent. Cus was the genius behind the whole thing."

Then there are others with perhaps a more objective view who feel differently. Mickey Duff maintains that D'Amato was forced to choose where his loyalties would go, to Mike or Teddy. "Cus wrongly chased [out] Teddy. Cus had a decision to make whether he was going to have this world heavyweight champion or stay loyal to Teddy, and he had no choice really."

At the time of the break-up, D'Amato did not yet have legal custody of Mike. That would come a few weeks later. In the meantime, concerned that problems might arise if any of the news of Mike's behavior or the resulting showdown with Teddy got out, he sent an intermediary to Teddy with an offer: If Teddy left quietly and made no waves, he had Cus's word that he would receive 5 percent of Tyson's earnings for the rest of Mike's career once he turned pro. Atlas, mixed up, confused, hurt by his parting with Cus, wasn't interested. The fact that his relationship with D'Amato had ended meant more to him than the offer of money. He left quietly out of loyalty and respect for what he and Cus had built together and never said anything which might have brought the state youth authorities back to Catskill. Subsequently, when Tyson turned pro, the promise made to Atlas was conveniently forgotten, and he never received a penny from the fighter he had helped develop.

The end of the story, however, had not quite yet been written. Soon after he left, many of the boys involved at the boxing club and their parents came to Teddy and said they wanted to go with him. If he could open another gym in town, they'd leave the Catskill Club and join him there. It was Teddy who had won their respect and affection, not Cus. If the boys had problems outside the gym, at home, in school, Teddy was always ready to help them. If the poorer ones couldn't afford groceries, he would buy a bag of staples for their family. But Teddy told them that it was Cus's gym, his club, and it would be disloyal of them—and him—to leave and start another gym. Stay with Cus, that's the right thing, Teddy told them.

The parents then called a meeting with Cus. And here D'Amato made a mistake. He told them the reason Teddy had left was to take a job in New York for pay as a pro trainer and there was nothing he could to do persuade him to stay on. But the boys knew what Cus didn't—that Teddy was still in town, that he had never left—and they confronted D'Amato with the truth. They also knew Teddy was willing to stay in Catskill if given the chance.

D'Amato was shaken by being caught in a lie. Perceiving that Teddy presented a threat, fearing that his authority was being eroded and that "his fighters" (except Mike, of course) wanted to leave him, he took vindictive action against Teddy. Insidious and untrue rumors began to circulate: Teddy was a psychopath, Teddy was involved with drugs, Teddy was involved with the Mafia. Atlas, completely unaware that these rumors were going around, was befuddled when he kept running into dead ends at gyms and with boxing managers in New York City. One night, speaking with Fred Chetti on a return visit to Catskill, Teddy expressed his confusion as to why he couldn't land any fighters to train. Chetti, an IBM executive and a member of the Catskill Town Recreation Board, had been instrumental in D'Amato's getting the gym twelve years earlier. He had become a friend of Cus's, spending evenings at the house talking boxing and watching fight films with D'Amato. He had also become friendly with Teddy and so was undecided whose side he was on. Until now, he had remained friendly with both.

Chetti went to Cus's house one evening to ask him about

the break. Cus spent the entire evening telling Chetti all the negative things in Teddy's past. D'Amato filibustered, Chetti hardly getting a word in for two hours. True, Teddy in his earlier years had had personal problems, problems with the law. But so did every boy who had come there, and hadn't Teddy turned his life around? He was now twenty-six years old. What did his youthful past have to do with the present? "I had difficulty deciding who was right," Chetti acknowledges, "but the one thing I didn't like was the fact that Cus was trying to convince me he was right by telling me all the bad things Teddy did when he was a teenager. That wasn't the way to convince me." Chetti did not like the rumors that were circulating about Teddy, and he was convinced it was D'Amato who was floating them. He decided to run a test.

He told a fighter in the D'Amato's club that he was going to use his political influence in town to have the gym closed down. Chetti knew this youngster was a talker and that word would spread. "I wasn't serious. I was just trying to scare Cus," Chetti admits.

Sure enough, word got back to D'Amato, because the very next day, one of his emissaries phoned Chetti and said he wanted to come over and talk to him. He was Joe Colangelo, President of the Catskill Boxing Club, a title D'Amato had bestowed on him. Colangelo's son was a member of the club. He had been nurtured by Teddy Atlas. Yet when Colangelo got to Chetti's house, it was obvious he was speaking for D'Amato. He told Chetti how important the gym was to the kids, how much his son had been helped there, how Teddy was a bad influence and that it was best for him to be gone. Chetti became enraged over the convenient lapse of memory Colangelo was displaying. But at last Chetti's patience snapped. "Joe," he said, anger boiling over in his voice, "I've heard enough. It's time for you to leave. You go back and tell Cus that sending you here to convince me to keep hands off the gym is not going to work." Colangelo protested that Cus hadn't sent him. "Bullshit," Chetti told him. "I told the kid yesterday I'd have the gym closed down, and today you're here. Who are you kidding! You tell Cus one thing: If he doesn't leave Teddy Atlas alone, stop spreading lies about him and just let him get on with his life, that goddamn gym is gone!" Atlas, who was unaware of all that was taking place, phoned Chetti several days later, completely confused. He told Chetti he had no idea what was going on, but suddenly, as if out of the blue, people were calling him to talk about his working with their fighters. Fred Chetti knew why.

Today, Teddy Atlas is one of the most respected trainers in boxing. Jim Jacobs himself had recommended him to friends, saying, "Forget about everyone else, Ted Atlas is the best trainer in boxing." Working out of the famed Gleason's Gym in Brooklyn, New York, his stable of top-notch pros have included contenders Chris Reid, Felix Santiago, Tyrone Jackson, Art Tucker, plus world champions Donny Lalonde and Simon Brown. He played an instrumental role in Ireland's Barry McGuigan winning the World Featherweight Championship, and he will no doubt develop many more contenders and champions in the years ahead.

All the same, the break with D'Amato was painful for Teddy, and it still hurts. "When I first went up there I was fighting, having problems, getting in trouble," he says. "Cus did help me. Nobody ever denied that. That had nothing to do with our falling out. I'm the first one to say I'm grateful to Cus for being a friend and for being a helpful person at that time in my life. . . . When it came to a head with me and Tyson, Cus, of course, was in the middle of it. Cus had to make a decision, either me or Tyson. Because of what Tyson could be, because of Cus's needs at that point, it was natural it would be Mike. I left out to some degree of what I owed Cus, loyalty to the things we have together. . . . It was never a part of why I left that I got what I needed and no longer had a need for Cus or that I was ungrateful and I walked out on him. It had nothing to do with it. It was a falling out. I didn't even want to leave at that time. It was an unhappy break."

Chapter 6

Turning Pro

There is no such thing as a natural puncher.
There is a natural aptitude for punching and
that is different. Nobody is born the best.
You have to practice and train to become the best.
— Cus D'Amato

With the departure of Ted Atlas, Cus needed someone to step in and undertake the day-to-day chores of training Mike. He turned to Kevin Rooney, who had remained intensely loyal to him during the turmoil of the previous weeks. Rooney's career had reached a crossroads. He had climbed the welterweight rankings until his crushing knockout loss to Alexis Arguello caused a major setback to his career. Although he continued to fight for a while longer ("We'd fight on the same card," Tyson would recall. "He'd train me, then fight himself"), he agreed to help Cus train Mike, since it was apparent to everyone at this point that Mike's career potential was much brighter than his own. "Mike was fifteen when I started working with him," notes Rooney. "I had him for all his senior fights as an amateur." And Rooney, with the advantage of having been a fighter, began to learn the nuances of training from D'Amato. "You cannot be around a man like Cus D'Amato, with his genius, and not learn something," he points out today. "I was Cus's eyes and hands and Cus was the mind." When Tyson had first come to Catskill, Rooney was a bit suspicious. "I figured he just wanted to come out of the can and go home. Then he started winning fights and I said, this kid is gonna make it. He was so fast, and he had that punch. I saw the potential. He was fourteen, but he was so big and strong. He picked things up so quickly." (This quickness was what had impressed Bobby Stewart when he or Cus would show Mike techniques while he was still at Tryon.) Kevin and Mike were close, having lived together for more than two years, and Kevin had been doing some training all along, helping Cus in the gym and working with the boys when

Teddy Atlas took Mike or the others to tournaments out of town.

Perhaps, however, the adjustment to a new trainer was too abrupt for Mike, who was now sixteen. He was stepping into the seniors bracket now, and Cus entered him in the 1982 United States Championships. The fighters he would meet there were much more seasoned than those he had faced in the juniors. Before going to the U.S. Championships, Mike did not get a lot of good, tough sparring in the gym, and he had just emerged from the emotional upheaval of the break with Atlas, which may well have had an unsettling effect on him. He paid the price at the tournament. He faced an experienced heavyweight named Al Evans, a mature man ten years older than himself. In the third round, Evans pulled a shocker. He dropped Tyson three times, scoring a knockout victory.

The loss was a temporary setback. Cus, with Kevin, continued the teaching process, determined to instill in Mike a professional attitude. To Cus D'Amato, being a professional had nothing to do with whether or not an athlete was paid. He believed that what set the true professional apart from the amateur was the way the professional thinks. "I believe a man is a professional," he would often say, "when he can do what needs to be done no matter how he feels within. An amateur is an amateur in his attitude emotionally. A professional is a professional in the way he thinks and feels and in his ability to execute under the most trying conditions. The ability to do what needs to be done regardless of the pressure and do it with poise, with no reflection of his inner feeling or conflict if it exists, is what makes a professional. It has nothing to do with their knowledge. I'll show you many amateurs with far superior knowledge and ability than top professionals."

"When you get hit," Cus would drill into Mike, "that's when you've got to be calm. A professional fighter has got to learn how to hit and not get hit, and at the same time be exciting. That's what professional boxing is about. You've got to be clever, you've got to be smart, and not get hit; and when you're able to do this, you're a fighter."

Another rule was, "If you can hit your opponent with two punches, you don't hit him with one. Get off with some bad intentions in there. Believe in yourself. A guy can feel it if you don't believe in yourself. Set your mind to make yourself do it."

Over the years, Cus would use the example of the hero and the coward in teaching all his fighters how to perform even under adverse circumstances. It was a lesson so indelibly drilled into Mike's conscious and subconscious mind that he can repeat it by rote to this day. Here's how Cus would explain it: "I tell my kids, what is the difference between a hero and a coward? What is the difference between being yellow and being brave? No difference. Only what you do. They both feel the same. They both fear dying and getting hurt. The man who is yellow refuses to face up to what he's got to face. The hero is more disciplined and he fights those feelings off and he does what he has to do. But they both feel the same, the hero and the coward. People who watch you judge you on what you do, not how you feel."

In 1983, Mike continued his sweep through the amateur ranks, losing only in the finals of the National Golden Gloves Tournament, where, according to Kevin Rooney, he was "robbed" by the amateur rules to which Mike's style, by Cus's design, had never adapted. In a nine-day period, he swept through two tournaments a thousand miles apart, mowing down every opponent he faced and capturing two national titles.

Beginning on August 12, 1983, with a first-round KO that took him just forty-four seconds, Mike began his march through the Ohio State Fair National Tournament. In his next bout, on August 13, he met Jerry Goff, a veteran of some 150 fights. He knocked Goff out in the second round with a combination so devastating that Goff lost two front teeth and was unconscious for close to ten minutes. In the finals, on August 14, Mike was set to face national golden gloves champion Olian Alexander, but Alexander did not turn up for the bout, claiming he had a bad hand. Many fighters along the way suddenly found they had bad hands or sore shoulders when they discovered they had to tangle with Tyson. By default, Mike won the Ohio State Fair crown.

The next day, Mike and Kevin Rooney flew to Colorado for the 1983 U.S. National Championships, which began on August 16. When Mike arrived, four of the six other fighters entered in the heavyweight division withdrew. Mike automatically advanced to the semifinals, where he met 250-pound Dave Yonko. He knocked out Yonko at 1:38 of the first round. In the finals he didn't waste as much time. He stopped Mark Scott at 0:54 of round one, returning to Catskill with the Ohio State Fair and U.S. National Championship titles.

Cus was extremely pleased with Mike's progress in such a short time. Though Tyson was still an amateur, Cus offered this appraisal of him. "The boy can do everything a champion is required to do, and if he does everything that he's capable of doing, I tell you he may go down as one of the greatest fighters of all time. . . . As a professional my judgments of a fighter are detached. I never allow my personal feelings to get involved, no matter how much affection I may have for him, and I can honestly say I have a very deep affection for him, and an admiration, having watched him come from where he was to what he is, because I know what it takes to do what he's done and what he's doing. I feel I was a part of it. It's almost like watching yourself. You never know how much you contributed to it, but the result is there and you like to think you had something to do with it."

Mike, too, had a deep feeling for Cus. He knew just how much this man had helped him. "People think I was born this way," he said. "They don't know what it took to get this way. The training, when you have to do things over and over again until you're sore. Deep in your mind you say, God, I don't want to do this no more, and then you push. I always used to think I was a coward because of the way I felt. Cus was there when I needed him . . . he was the one. Cus would always explain you should always do things to build your character and make you a better individual. He was different than anyone I'd ever met, because principle meant more than anything to him, more than money, more than health, more than his life. He would sacrifice anything for principle, for what he believed was right."

But there was still much of the streets, much of the uncontrolled wildness in Mike, and often he would lapse from the lofty principles that Cus strove to inculcate in him. He continued to have difficulty in showing respect for those in authority, including Cus. One member of the household said Tyson even spat on Cus. Another acknowledged that there were many times Cus got so angry he wanted to toss

Mike out and be done with him. "Give him enough time," D'Amato said to an intimate, "and the nigger will come out in him."

There were other problems as well. One person, who requested anonymity, recalled: "I overhead Cus talking to Jimmy on the phone. I know that Cus and Jimmy paid off a woman five or ten thousand dollars, a poor woman in the Catskill area, because Mike knocked up her daughter when he as living up there, and they decided it wouldn't look good because he was going to be heavyweight champ some day. I'm not sure if the girl had the baby or had an abortion. But Tyson may have a kid out there somewhere. And then they deny payoffs were made to cover things up that Mike did!"

Mickey Duff, the British promoter, was very aware of the situation with Tyson from the beginning because of his close friendship with Jim Jacobs: "Mike Tyson has been nothing but a pain in the ass since day one, in my opinion. And Mike Tyson has been a far more sophisticated user of people than anybody ever gave him credit for until recently. He has that habit of putting his head on your shoulder like a little boy. I think that Jim Jacobs and Bill Cayton genuinely hoped that success would lead to making him a nicer person, a better person, a more responsible person. They also hoped and believed that success would introduce him to a nicer group of people and disassociate him from some of the people they felt he shouldn't associate with."

In the summer of 1984, after winning the National Golden Gloves Championship, Mike was entered in the United States Olympic trials. It was, for some reason, a time of tension between D'Amato and Tyson. Sitting with two friends at the trials in Las Vegas, Cus turned to them and said, "If Jimmy and Bill didn't have so much money invested in this kid, I'd get rid of the son of a bitch right now." But now, no matter what his personal feelings at that moment, there was no turning back. The commitment had been made—to Mike, to Jacobs and Cayton, and mostly to himself. After four years of blood and sweat, drilling and teaching, anguish and frustration, it was almost time. Mike would go to the Olympics in Los Angeles. Without the Cubans and East Germans and Soviets there (they were boycotting the Games), Tyson would sweep through the heavyweight division and win a gold medal, watched by millions of his countrymen and millions of others around the world on television. It would make Mike Tyson a household name and provide the ideal launch pad for the professional career that was to come.

But it was not to be. In the trials, Tyson was beaten by Henry Tillman, who repeated his victory over him a week later in the Olympic box-off. There was griping by D'Amato after Tillman won the decision that kept Mike out of the Olympics. It was a close fight, but Mike was not effectual against the 6'3", 195-pound Tillman, who, he said, "kept pushing me and trying to stick his thumbs in my eye." Tillman said Tyson was just jumping at him and jabbing with his feet in the air instead of being solidly planted on the canvas. Tillman's trainer acknowledged that Tyson was strong, but called him excitable and mechanical, "a doer, not a thinker. . . . There's more to boxing than being able to bang." Tyson certainly did not fight with his mind and physical skills together, and Tillman took advantage of his own weight and reach to outbox him.

Tillman went on to win the Olympic gold medal in the 201-pound heavyweight division. Mike went as a spectator to Los Angeles, where, frustrated at not making the Olympic team, he managed to stir up a little unpublicized trouble by pouring a can of beer over security guards at the Athletes' Village, then taunting them and shouting, "Go fuck yourselves, white boys."

In the long run, his failure to make the Olympic team would not matter. Tillman, after winning the gold medal, was knocked out in his only important fights, including a cruiserweight title bout against friend and fellow Olympic gold medalist Evander Holyfield. Tillman soon faded from the scene, talk of an eventual professional title showdown against Tyson forgotten. While there is no doubt that the publicity attendant upon an Olympic appearance is tremendously valuable, if a fighter can fight, it is not of paramount importance. Some of the greatest fighters of the past two decades, including Roberto Duran, Alexis Arguello, Thomas Hearns, Marvin Hagler, Michael Nunn, Larry Holmes and Julio Caesar Chavez, have not been Olympic champions.

In the short run, however, it changed the strategy of how to market Mike Tyson. Without the Olympic fanfare behind

The very first application for a professional boxer's license, signed by eighteen-year-old Mike Tyson in 1984. It was approved by then-New York Athletic Commissioner Jose Torres, who was a friend of Tyson, Jacobs and D'Amato. Tyson, as a matter of fact, thoughtlessly entered Torres's name as a reference. That was crossed out, and the name of writer Pete Hamill substituted.

him, it was decided that Tyson would turn pro quietly, almost unnoticed. D'Amato was the architect of these plans; but Jim Jacobs and Bill Cayton now moved to the forefront. They became Mike Tyson's co-managers, and their brilliant maneuvering on behalf of their fighter on all fronts would make him, in less than two years, the heavyweight champion of the world, and in just over three years the best-known and most financially successful athlete in the world.

Jim Jacobs was born in 1930 in St. Louis. When he was five years old, his family moved to Los Angeles, where Jim entered Los Angeles High School during World War II. As a boy, he had an avid interest in comic books. During the war, he worked as a volunteer on paper-collection drives. In sorting through the old newspapers and magazines donated to aid the war effort, he would take home discarded comic books that caught his interest. These finds, along with purchases and trades he made as a youngster, helped form the nucleus of a comic book collection that contained duplicates of many rare first and early editions, including Superman and Batman. Jacobs maintained and built the collection for more than forty years. At the time of his death in 1988 it was probably the largest and most valuable collection of its kind anywhere, containing some 800,000 comic books with a value of perhaps $2 million.

During his adolescent years, Jim lived somewhat in a fantasy world with his comic books. "I always pretended that I was Robin, the Boy Wonder," he said. "Superman I admired, but Batman and Robin were human; and everything athletic that Robin did, I tried to do. He threw a boomerang, I learned how to throw a boomerang. Robin was an excellent tumbler, and so I would run off diving boards to practice double flips. Robin swam underwater for two minutes . . . [so] I learned how to hold my breath underwater. Before long I could swim underwater for two minutes. I didn't want to admit that Robin could do something I couldn't do. Being Robin, the Boy Wonder, was a tremendous help to me in sports. All of us are susceptible to our emotions when under stress, and when I was younger I would think: What would Robin do? Instead of succumbing to nervous apprehension, I would transform myself into this other character who was emotionally unaffected." It's interesting how, through the device of using Robin, Jacobs arrived at a means of controlling his emotions and "performing in a professional manner" so close to the theory of Cus D'Amato, whom he was not to meet for many years.

Jacobs was a natural athlete. Tales of his exploits in high school still survive. He was a standout basketball player, reportedly good enough to be invited to try out for the Olympic team. He excelled in track, running the 100-yard dash in 9.8, second in the city among high schoolers at the time. He was also a top-notch baseball, football, tennis and table tennis player. As an adult, he shot in the low 70s in golf.

A friend of his related a story once about Jim that gives a clue to his natural athletic talents and his incredible hand-eye coordination. According to his friend, Jim, strictly as a challenge, decided to see if he could take up and master the sport of skeet shooting. Within a relatively short time, he became so proficient that he was able to win a major skeet shooting championship, after which he put his shotguns aside, satisfied that he had mastered his own challenge, and never pursued the sport again.

Jacobs, along with his sister, Dorothy, was raised by his mother after his parents divorced. He remained extremely close and devoted to his mother, often visiting her in Los Angeles following his move to New York in the early sixties, until her death in December, 1986. Although an excellent athlete, he was less than devoted to the academic rigors of school and was close to flunking out of Los Angeles High School when he apparently dropped out. He never completed his high school education, although he went on to become a tremendous success in life.

In the late 1940s when he left school, Jacobs had developed two consuming passions that would lead, respectively, to his putting his own name in the sports record books and to building his own fortune. They were handball and collecting boxing films. He began playing four-wall handball at the Hollywood YMCA. His climb to the top of that sport was interrupted by the Korean War. He was drafted, served two years in the infantry with the First Cavalry Division and earned a Purple Heart, although he said that he wasn't a very good soldier. In 1953, representing the Los Angeles Athletic Club, he competed in his first national championship, finishing fifth, an excellent showing. The following year he finished third. In 1955, he was matched in the finals of the United States Championships with his idol, Vic Hershkowitz, one of the legendary names in the sport but who was thirty-seven years old at the time and whose skill was declining. Jacobs defeated Hershkowitz to win his first national singles title. It was the beginning of a run which would match Joe Louis's reign as heavyweight champion in both dominance and duration. The Guinness Book of World Sports Records, under a photograph of Jim Jacobs in action on the handball court with the caption "Handball Master," lists Jacobs as the record-holder for titles won. He captured six United States Handball Association National Four-Wall Championships from 1955 to 1965. In addition, from 1960 to 1968 he won six doubles titles, most of those with playing partner and friend Marty Decatur. Jacobs is considered the greatest player in the history of the sport, and he became known as "The Babe Ruth of Handball." He also won the three-wall championship three times, the AAU four-wall title twice and was one-wall singles champion six times. He was inducted into the Jewish Sports Hall of Fame in Israel and the Helms Hall of Fame in Los Angeles.

In a story published in 1966 in *Sports Illustrated* magazine, Robert Boyle wrote: "There is no athlete in the world who dominates his sport with the supremacy that Jimmy Jacobs of Los Angeles and New York enjoys in four-wall handball. . . . Jacobs is generally hailed as the finest player of all time. Indeed, there are those who say Jacobs is the best athlete, regardless of sport, in the country." Many years later, Jacobs would acknowledge that "my partner, Bill Cayton, and Cus D'Amato . . . took those energies that I had given to handball and redirected them to business."

While still a teenager, Jacobs became equally obsessed with boxing films. He had heard about the controversial decision in the December 5, 1947, bout between Joe Louis and Jersey Joe Walcott, and he set out to obtain a copy of the film so he could judge for himself. After that, he was hooked. He began seeking out and buying whatever old and rare boxing films he could find, often spending his free time while playing handball exhibitions overseas in this pursuit. He amassed an impressive collection, which was no small feat. During the reign of the controversial first black world heavyweight champion, Jack Johnson, from 1908 to 1915, several of his victories over white opponents had touched off race riots in American cities. So as not to inflame the passions of fans both black and white who viewed the films of these fights in movie theaters, the federal government passed a law banning the interstate transport of boxing motion pictures. This law remained on the books for decades, and so hundreds and hundreds of old fight films lay for years unused and uncared for in vaults and archives and storage rooms. Jacobs rescued most of these films from decaying to the point where they would have been lost forever. In later years, he and his partner, Bill Cayton, would invest much money in restoring these brittle old nitrate negatives so that the rich legacy of the sport could be preserved forever. For this, boxing historians, journalists and fans owe these two men an eternal debt of gratitude, for without their efforts no one now would be able to see many of the films of Jack Johnson, Jack Dempsey, even nineteenth-century champions like Bob Fitzsimmons and Gentleman Jim Corbett, plus scores of other great champions, in action. Jim's consuming passion was to build the world's greatest archive of boxing films. In 1970, a young writer set out to do a book on boxing history. It involved traveling around the United States to interview champions of the past. Jacobs advanced the writer the money for a major swing around the country. He asked just one thing in return: that the writer ask all the champions he interviewed if they had any old films of themselves boxing which he could borrow to reproduce prints. The writer turned up two gems: One was a brief film of the world flyweight champion, Corporal Izzy Schwartz, in Paris in 1928, training and boxing a humorous sparring session with a giant heavyweight for the benefit of the newsreel cameras. The heavyweight was a young and still unknown Primo Carnera, who was just beginning his professional career. It provided a first look at Carnera, long before he became heavyweight champion, as well as the only film that exists of Schwartz. The film had been gathering dust for more than forty years in a closet in Schwartz's Bronx apartment, just twelve miles from the offices of Cayton and Jacobs in Manhattan. The other find was a complete print of the 1913 World Lightweight Championship fight between Willie Ritchie and challenger "Mexican" Joe Rivers. Until then, Jacobs had no film of Ritchie in his library. Now he not only had one, but it was Ritchie in top form, defending his crown against a great challenger by knockout. Jacobs was ecstatic. It was all he wanted.

"I always wanted to have the greatest collection of fight films in the world," Jacobs said. "I wanted to own the most comic books. I wanted to be the greatest handball player in the world. I wanted to be a millionaire. . . . I've always been very compulsive about everything . . . I can't explain why."

Jacobs, in many ways, presented an enigma. He was very loyal to friends, accessible, helpful, friendly. Yet he kept a good part of him closed off from the outside world. Long-time friend and associate Mickey Duff says, "Jim was a very private person, and it was very difficult to get through to him." His sister, Dorothy, with whom he did not have a particularly tight relationship, termed him "close to the vest." Perhaps the biggest conundrum was the story that Jim came from a wealthy family. Over the years he himself carefully and deliberately spread the word that he had inherited a considerable fortune from his father. At the time of his death, one New York sportswriter wrote that Jacobs "inherited hundreds of millions from his family, St. Louis department store moguls and Los Angeles real estate giants." Nat Loubet, long-time editor of *Ring* magazine who had known Jim since the 1940s said that when he talked to Jim about the expense of buying boxing films, "Jim would say, 'Don't worry about it. Mom's loaded.' " Top Rank matchmaker Teddy Brenner, who also knew Jim for years, remembers the time he asked him, "Jimmy, is it true, they tell me that when your father died he left you $9 million? He said to me, 'Not only is it true, but what you didn't know is when my grandfather died, he left me $20 million!' " Another source said Jacobs's family had owned a chain of St. Louis-based stores named Stix, Baer and Fuller, but that the estate left by his father was at most "two or three million dollars."

In tracing Jacob's life, however, the evidence does not support the lifestyle of someone who had money, at least until he made his own fortune as an adult. For one thing, Jacobs attended public schools in Los Angeles. Even when he was in academic trouble, he was not moved to a private school or academy. When he began playing handball at the Hollywood YMCA as a teenager, he often played against the television personality Art Linkletter, who beat Jacobs quite often in those early days. Jacobs, determined to improve, practiced for hours in front of a mirror until his weaker left arm was virtually as good as his right. In a short time he was able to beat Linkletter and just about everyone else. Seeing Jim as a prodigy, Linkletter got together with several other backers and put up the money that financed Jim's first trip to a major tournament, the Junior Nationals in Bremerton, Washington. There, he won the junior singles championship. If his family had had money, he would not have needed the financial backing of Linkletter to travel from Los Angeles to Bremerton.

In 1950, Jacobs, then twenty, went to Chicago. While there, he was able to arrange a game against former national champion Gus Lewis. To say the least, Lewis was impressed. He telephoned Robert Kendler and told him, "I just played a kid who doesn't know what he's doing, and for a kid who doesn't know what he's doing, he's a hell of a handball player." Kendler asked to meet Jacobs. Kendler was a multimillionaire businessman who had a passion for handball. He had gathered up twelve or thirteen of the country's best players and given them jobs in his home remodeling business. He then built the Town Club of Chicago so his "team" would have a place to practice and play. He offered Jacobs the chance to do the same. Jacobs went to work for Kendler as a home remodeling salesman, practicing his handball in his off-hours. He stayed in Chicago for a year and a half with Kendler until he was drafted. Again, one might question the need to work as a salesman to support himself during his stay in Chicago if there was great wealth in the family.

After his service in Korea, Jacobs returned to Los Angeles and went to work as a salesman for a business machine company. He said it was his father he worked for, that his father owned a business machine and supplies company. But his business partner of twenty-eight years, Bill Cayton, who knew Jim perhaps better than anyone, told Phil Berger of the *New York Times:* "I know Jim said that, but it wasn't so."

One of Jacobs's oldest and most trusted friends and business associates, a member of his small inner circle who admired Jim and was truly devoted to him over the course of their nearly thirty-year friendship, nevertheless had this observation: "[One thing] I've tried to find the answer to with Jim, and I can't, that completely astounds me. He lived in this world of make-believe. And it turned out to be bullshit. He'd have you believe that he came from very wealthy parents. The funny thing is, he did it to everybody. I [believed it] and it's totally untrue. . . . He told me that when his mother died, from the time she died until the time they settled her estate that the interest on the money was six million dollars. We were talking one day and I said, 'Everything is for sale. There's not a thing in this world that's not for sale for the right price. Do you want to sell your fight film business?' He said that's not for sale. I said, 'If somebody came along and gave you 100 million dollars it would be for sale.' He said, 'No it wouldn't, because I already have $100 million.' He told me that when his father died he was left a chain of stores, for him and his sister, but he had total control, and he couldn't stand the sight of the stores, so he sold them to the manager and the manager paid him back the money over a period of years. And he said that when his parents divorced they were both independently so rich that they didn't even have a settlement. He said his mother came from rich people. It's all bullshit. . . ."

In an interview with United Press some years ago concerning his success, Jim said, "I always wanted to be a millionaire." That is not the aspiration of someone who has already inherited millions. Possibly the most revealing comment came from his sister, Dorothy, to Phil Berger in the *New York Times* on June 28, 1988: "My father was a salesman for Alfred Hart distilleries, a liquor salesman," she told Berger. "Before we came to L.A., he had been in ladies' ready-to-wear in St. Louis. When my father was old and retired and had nothing, Jim sent him a check every month." Berger went on to write: "Whatever his reasons, Jacobs was uneasy about what his father did for a living."

It was a lack of finances that resulted in Jacobs meeting and eventually forming a business partnership with Bill Cayton. In 1959, Jacobs found out that a collector in Australia had the only known copy of Jess Willard's knockout over Jack Johnson in Havana in 1915, a copy that included the actual sequence of the knockout. For years, controversy had swirled around this fight, Johnson claiming that he was pressured by financial problems and legal persecution to "throw" his heavyweight title to Willard. Jacobs felt the film could help solve this mystery, and he had to have it. The price was $5,000. Jim needed the money, so he called Bill Cayton, knowing that Cayton had a sizable library of boxing films and had been the producer of the fight film series "Greatest Fights of the Century." Cayton agreed to advance the money. Jacobs went to Australia and obtained the Johnson-Willard film.

In 1960, Jim Jacobs combined his library and went into partnership with Bill Cayton, a partnership that would last for twenty-eight years until Jacobs's death. During that time they would build a successful boxing film syndication throughout the world, their boxing documentaries would win numerous awards, including two Academy Award nominations, they would manage a stable of top contenders and world champions, and they would develop Mike Tyson into the most financially successful athlete of all time, growing rich themselves along the way.

Bill Cayton was a dozen years older than Jim Jacobs. He was forty-two years old when they began their partnership in 1960. Cayton was in many ways different from Jacobs, which made for an effective symbiotic relationship between the two over the years of their association. Never having any athletic prowess to speak of, Cayton was, on the other hand, a good student. He grew up in Brooklyn, the son of a stockbroker, and graduated from the University of Maryland with a degree in chemical engineering. He then went to work as a technical report writer for the Du Pont chemical company for $35 a week in the Depression years of the late 1930s. From Du Pont, he went to work for an advertising agency, and by the end of World War II he had his own ad agency in Manhattan, Cayton, Inc. Television was then in its infancy, and one of his clients wanted to sponsor some sort of sports show on TV. Cayton thought boxing would be ideal, and in 1948 he began obtaining the rights to vintage boxing films, and launched the TV program, "Greatest Fights of the Century," which followed the Gillette Friday Night Fights. The program, often giving viewers their first glimpses of legendary champions on film, proved to be immensely popular. When he and Jacobs joined forces they combined their respective fight film libraries and went on to purchase the vast collection of boxing and other sports films that belonged to Madison Square Garden. They eventually built a library of nearly 20,000 boxing films. Over the years, Jacobs carved out a reputation as a boxing historian and was the "up front" man, the spokesman for the company, the manager-of-record for their eventual stable of fighters. Jim enjoyed this role, guesting on boxing broadcasts, being sought out for his opinions on upcoming bouts or the great fighters of the past. Cayton, meanwhile, enjoyed functioning in relative anonymity, handling the nuts-and-bolts detail work of their companies. Cayton handled matters concerning contracts and negotiations, although Jacobs, of course, was always involved as well. "Jim knew nothing about contracts. I'm an expert," Cayton told an interviewer. And Jim agreed. "Bill is an excellent contract man," he would say.

In the early 1960s, Jim Jacobs met the other man who would have a profound influence on his life. That was Cus D'Amato. They met one night when Cus attended a screening of old boxing films that Jim was presenting. Afterward, they began talking about the merits of various past champions, and the two hit it off. Jacobs was just beginning his business association with Bill Cayton and was relocating permanently in New York. Jim and Cus quickly developed an extremely close bond. D'Amato admired not only Jim's serious interest in and knowledge of boxing, but he admired Jim because he excelled at everything he did, especially pursuits involving athletic prowess. Jim on the other hand was fascinated with the complex man that was Cus D'Amato. He saw that this was a unique individual, a man he regarded as brilliant and someone to be admired for his principles. At this time, D'Amato was in the midst of his battle against the IBC. Jacobs became convinced that Cus, despite some detours he might have taken, was on the side of right.

Cus D'Amato may have served another purpose in Jim Jacobs's life as well. D'Amato was in his early fifties when they met; Jacobs was barely thirty years old. Because Jacobs came from a broken home and had been raised by his mother, he lacked a strong father figure in his life. D'Amato may have filled that psychological and emotional void. He became Jacobs's mentor, and not only in matters pertaining to boxing. For a while, Jacobs even moved in with D'Amato, and the two—despite differences in age, upbringing, ethnic background and just about every other surface consideration—shared something much deeper, a sympatico. They were kindred spirits, and Jacobs in large part formed his life-view through the eyes of Cus D'Amato. Over the years, many people who knew both of them would remark that to listen to Jimmy was to really hear Cus. It was an observation that no doubt pleased Jim Jacobs. Eventually, D'Amato relocated in Catskill and Jim, after dating a variety of women over the years, settled down and married Lorraine Atter, a New York businesswoman.

When it was time for Mike Tyson to turn pro, perhaps the best team in the history of boxing was standing by and ready—Cayton the negotiator, Jacobs the publicity and boxing strategist, and D'Amato, the trainer, teacher and boxing mastermind. Combined with Tyson's fierce and visceral determination and ability, it was as near to a sure thing as it is possible to be.

Meanwhile, Cus was still concerned about Mike's behavior. He knew the boy still had a "street" mentality. Cus confided in one friend that every time Mike was out of the house and the phone rang, he worried that the call might mean trouble of one sort or another. At the end of 1984, as preparations were being made to turn Mike pro, Cus told Alex Wallau of ABC Sports, "Many people who have been around boxing all those years never had a champion, certainly a heavyweight champion. . . . for that to happen in one's lifetime is so improbable. I got Floyd Patterson; then, here at the age of seventy-six, I was fortunate to come in contact with this young man who has, in my opinion, all the requirements to be the great champion that I believe he's going to be, maybe the best that ever lived." D'Amato realized that if he were to fulfill his dream of masterminding another heavyweight champion to the top, he had to move with cautious haste to achieve the agenda. He and Jacobs mapped out a strategy unique in modern-day boxing. Tyson, while being carefully matched, would fight every two to three weeks. In other eras, this would not have been unusual. In the 1980s, however, no contender climbing to the top maintained such an active schedule. However, apart from enabling D'Amato to move Tyson up the ladder quickly, keeping him in the ring would serve another important purpose. It would use up Mike's time and energies, leaving him less of either to get into trouble. Certainly if a fighter engaged in grueling, bruising fights every two or three weeks over a long period, he would burn himself out quickly. But Team Tyson did not plan to put Mike in with anyone who was likely to give him a hard time or last very long, so the fights themselves would be much easier and quicker than the long, tiring sessions in the gym. The fights would present Mike with opponents who had differing styles; they would get him used to performing under pressure in the professional arena; and then build him up in the public's eyes as an invincible destroyer.

For Jim Jacobs, like D'Amato, the success of Mike Tyson would fulfill a dream. In the late 1960s, when he had reached the heights in the handball world, and his career on the court was winding down, and when he had achieved his goal of being independently wealthy (by then his film partnership with Bill Cayton was thriving), he told a friend that he now had one driving ambition: He wanted someday to manage the heavyweight champion of the world. This ambition perhaps predated this conversation, since his friendship with D'Amato may have ignited that spark a decade earlier. There is even a story that at one point Jacobs, with his bull-like strength, tenacity and natural athletic ability, under D'Amato's guidance, would take a crack at becoming a fighter himself. The scenario was that Jim would be taught by D'Amato, would practice in closed-door gymnasium "bouts," and then would put up $100,000 to challenge Archie Moore for the Light-Heavyweight Championship in his first professional fight, much as Rademacher had done in his pro debut against Floyd Patterson. Only in this case, D'Amato felt Jacobs could defeat the clever but aging Moore. For some reason—if indeed the story was true—it never happened.

In the late 1970s, when he was already a fight manager, Jacobs became the international booking agent for highly rated South African heavyweight, Kallie Knoetze. He was optimistic that with D'Amato's behind-the-scenes help in tutoring Knoetze, he would achieve his goal. "He reminds me of Rocky Marciano," Jacobs said, perhaps a little overenthusiastically, ". . . there is no question that Knoetze will be the heavyweight champion of the world before the end of 1978." However, Knoetze was knocked out by John Tate and then, in rapid succession, by journeymen Mike Koranicki and Jimmy Abbott, and Jacobs's hope of finding a second Marciano was gone. Now, the better part of a decade later, he had the genuine article in Tyson; now, his goal was not only to manage the heavyweight champion, but to make him the most financially successful champion in the history of boxing in all weight divisions.

As a first step to put their plans for Mike Tyson into action, D'Amato approached Bob and Loraine Miller, a local husband-and-wife team who promoted small boxing shows around Albany. Raising a house full of kids, working as a receptionist near their home in Troy, New York, Loraine Miller got involved in the sport through her husband, who had fought while in the service, then trained her brother, who was a fighter for a while. Developing local amateur kids, Bob bought an old, decrepit building, gutted it and turned it into a gym. He also managed local pros. Loraine took out a promoter's license to keep the business in the family, and they began running shows in their spare time, since Bob also had a full-time job in the local high school. D'Amato told them, "I've watched you . . . for a number of years running shows. I like the way you do things. You're honest, you try and keep things running smoothly, you watch out for the fighters. I'd like to turn Mike Tyson pro. I've had a lot of offers, but I want him to go with you. I feel that Mike will be champ of the world one day, and I'd like you people to promote him. I'm not saying that along the line I won't have other promoters, but if Mike makes it to the top, we all make it to the top. There'll be other people involved, but we'll all make money." They shook hands, Cus kissed Loraine and everything was set. Cus had what he wanted—local promoters who could build Mike as a local attraction while keeping him away out of the limelight until the time was right.

Mike's first fight was fought on the undercard of a Miller promotion on March 6, 1985. His opponent was a harmless trialhorse named Hector Mercedes. Mike attacked him as he would all his early opponents, with a vengeance. Digging right uppercuts, he pinned Mercedes on the ropes, then pounded left uppercuts to his ribs. Mercedes went down from this relentless barrage and took the ten-count on his knee, getting up immediately after he heard "ten" when he knew he was safe from any further onslaught. At the age of eighteen years and nine months, Mike Tyson had successfully made his debut as a professional.

The deal with the Millers was that they would not lose any money promoting Mike Tyson. If they made money on their shows, fine. If not, their losses would be covered by Jacobs and Cayton. After the Mercedes fight, there was no profit, so the Millers could not pay Tyson a purse. Jacobs and Cayton chipped in and covered a $500 purse for Mike. The money went to D'Amato, so that Mike wouldn't blow it all at once. Kevin Rooney got his traditional trainer's cut of ten percent. Cus gave Mike $100, and Tyson was thrilled. The rest of the money was put aside for him.

A month later, again on a Miller-promoted show, Tyson did away with Trent Singleton. A furious flurry dropped Singleton barely more than ten seconds into the bout, and when he rose, a winging left hand ended things a few seconds later, less than one minute into the first round. On May 23, Don Halpin gave Tyson a longer fight than any he had ever been in outside his gym sparring sessions. Halpin lasted into the fourth round, until a crushing right to the face put him down, followed by a smashing left-right combination when he arose that put him into the ropes and ended matters.

At this point, Team Tyson was ready to reveal their tiger a little more to the world. Despite a previous conflict with Bob Arum stemming from a contractual battle over control of Wilfred Benitez, they were willing to let bygones be bygones for the sake of advancing Tyson's career. Arum had a valuable outlet for exposing Mike Tyson. His organization presented a weekly series of live bouts called "Top Rank Boxing" on the ESPN national cable-TV network. Arum was being given the chance to get in on the ground floor where Mike Tyson's promotion was concerned, an opportunity he would take but later fail to follow through and capitalize on. (While no one will ever have to throw any benefits for Arum—who grew rich promoting major fights

with Tommy Hearns, Marvin Hagler and Sugar Ray Leonard—
it nevertheless cost him financially as well as lost him the
high profile he would have had in promoting Tyson once
Mike reached the top.)

Arum agreed to use Tyson on his cable-TV shows. Mike's
first fight before a television audience was set for the undercard of Arum's show at Resorts International in Atlantic City
on June 20, 1985, against Rick Spain, who was 33 pounds lighter
than Tyson. Mike overwhelmed Spain from the opening bell,
dropping him with a right hand. Spain beat the count, only to
be flattened by the first left hand that hit him after he arose.
The fight was over at 0:38 of the first round. Three weeks
later, on another Arum promotion in Atlantic City, Tyson met
a big, awkward white opponent named John Alderson, who, at
6'4" and 226 pounds, towered over him. Alderson managed
to last two rounds before Tyson stopped him. Just eight days
later, Tyson was back in the ring, this time on his familiar
turf in upstate New York, where he knocked out Larry Sims in
three rounds. Four weeks after that it, it was back with Top
Rank in Atlantic City, where Lorenzo Canaday was his next
victim, going down just ten seconds into the first round from an
overhand left, and finished by Tyson less than a minute later.

Despite the strategy of keeping him busy, Mike managed
to find the time to seek out trouble. D'Amato knew well that
Mike had a lot of "street" still in him, along with a volatile
temper. Cus had once confided to an intimate "Give him enough
time and the nigger will come out in him again." D'Amato's
apprehensions were well founded. Though now a professional fighter in the early stages of his career, Tyson re-
verted to the behavior that had landed him in the Tryon
School as a twelve-year-old. He and a former street buddy
of his, who later told this story, were back in their old
neighborhood in Brooklyn, where Mike frequently went
after fights to alleviate the boredom and routine of Catskill.
On this particular day, the boys had about $10 between
them, but Mike got it into his head that he had to have a
radio. The two were riding in the elevator of an apartment
building when another man got in. According to Tyson's
friend, Mike "yoked" the guy around the neck, grabbing
him in a stranglehold. The pair then went through the
victim's pockets, coming up with about $80. Instead of let-
ting the man go, Tyson's mean streak emerged, and he

began banging his face into the elevator wall. Mike's buddy, incredulous, intervened. Mike stopped, the two made off, and later that day, Mike bought his radio.

There were two more fights in Atlantic City for Top Rank, and one for a new promoter, Jeff Levine. Tyson scored two knockdowns in rapid succession, the first with a devastating left to the ribs and the second with a right hand that left Michael Jack Johnson prone on the canvas for several minutes. That fight lasted thirty-nine seconds. A month later, Tyson was matched with a solid veteran of eighteen fights, Donnie Long. Teddy Brenner, Arum's matchmaker, had been dubious about Tyson's abilities. In Long, he felt Mike would meet his match. Long had gone ten rounds with both James Broad and John Tate, ranked heavyweights. He was 6'2" and weighed 215 pounds, the same as Tyson. Tyson destroyed Long in less than a minute and a half, knocking him down three times in that short span of time.

It was around this time that Arum allowed Mike Tyson, the biggest fish in the shark-infested waters of boxing, to get off the hook. Bill Cayton maintains that he and Jim were prepared to continue to do business with Arum because of the help he was giving them in exposing Mike Tyson on the ESPN network. "We would have stayed with Arum," insists Cayton, "but it would have been fight by fight. We don't make any long-range commitments." However, a snag developed. For some reason, Arum's matchmakers were not cooperating in making available opportunities for Mike to fight as often as Team Tyson wanted him to. Cayton went to Arum and said, in effect, "You're the Chairman of the Board [of Top Rank], it's your decision." But Arum protested that his matchmakers ran that end of the business, that it was up to them. As a result, after six appearances on "Top Rank Boxing," Jacobs and Cayton met with Jeff Levine, who was then affiliated with the Houston Boxing Association, and made a deal with him to become Tyson's promoter. Years later, after the Tyson-Spinks fight that grossed some $70 million, Arum, in an interview with sportscaster Bill Mazer on WFAN Radio in New York, lamented the loss of Tyson to Top Rank, blaming his matchmakers for underestimating Tyson's potential. He told Mazer that Teddy Brenner and Bruce Trampler, Top Rank's matchmakers, didn't think much of Tyson as a fighter. They said his style was "too wide open," that he was a marginal talent who didn't warrant the amount of on-air exposure Cayton, Jacobs and D'Amato were asking for. So Arum, on their advice, let Tyson slip through his fingers.

Less than three weeks after disposing of Donnie Long, Tyson was back in the ring at the Atlantis Hotel in Atlantic City to face Robert Colay, a 14 and 5 fighter, under Jeff Levine's promotional banner. Tyson made Levine's debut as his promoter a brief one. The first clean punch Tyson landed, a pulverizing left hand, sent Colay down. He barely beat the count, but was so helpless that the referee quickly jumped in and waved the fight over. It had lasted thirty-nine seconds.

Mike Tyson was now a perfect 10 and 0 as a pro, with ten knockouts in just eight months. Seven of his ten KO's had come in the first round, although, as with any fighter being properly advanced, none of the ten opponents presented any real threat to Tyson. Perhaps a little defensively, Cayton, while acknowledging that Mike's opponents were "very carefully selected," nevertheless maintains, "There was never a "tomato can" in the whole group. . . . We always wanted a fighter who Mike would beat [but] that Mike could learn something from." However, Jacobs privately conceded that some of Mike's early opponents were "embarrassing" in their lack of boxing ability. Despite the fact that they had the best talent in the heavyweight division to come along in years, one whom they were moving along with great speed, they were extremely cautious in their matchmaking, following D'Amato's advice.

Each day, as he had done for the previous twenty-five years, Jacobs would start the morning over coffee in Bill Cayton's Manhattan office. In the past, it was their film business or boxing that they would talk about. Now the sole topic was Mike Tyson. They would consult a variety of trainers and promoters around the country about the merits of prospective opponents. Whenever possible, they would obtain video cassettes of those fighters, send copies to D'Amato and study their various styles. While many of the opponents chosen for Mike did not have a lot of ability, most were selected for a particular reason, to expose Mike to fighters with different styles or abilities. Many of the opponents were obtained through Johnny Bos, a booking agent with the reputation for providing any type of opponent needed in any weight division. Jacobs had tremendous respect for the job Bos performed, saying, "There are people who are geniuses in different areas. Johnny Bos is a genius when it comes to shit." And Jacobs meant it as a strong compliment and endorsement of Bos, recommending Bos to any manager who needed help in building his fighter's ability and record. Bos could deliver just the right type of mediocre opponent.

Opponents in boxing are a highly sought-after commodity. For every much-vaunted new boxer who appears on the scene with a 22 and 0 record, or eighteen straight knockouts, you can bet there's a trail of nonentity opponents with unrecognizable names in his wake. Any manager or promoter developing a kid with potential will stress how important opponents are, especially in the heavyweight division, where there seems to be a scarcity of fighters upon whom aspiring champions can fatten their records. In the case of Mike Tyson, it quickly became difficult to find opponents willing to step into the ring with him. When a willing fighter was located, he or his manager wanted more than $1,000, even for undercard prelim fights, to risk life and limb with a monster like Tyson. Jacobs and Cayton soon learned they would have to foot the bill for these purses. Fortunately, they had the financial means to do so, ensuring that the Mike Tyson bandwagon would keep rolling along. Jacobs handled the actual procuring of opponents on behalf of D'Amato and Cayton, and he could be a stern taskmaster when it came to his fighter. Nothing was left to chance. Loraine Miller recalls hours spent phoning around the country, trying to locate someone to face Mike in one of her upstate shows, restricted in terms of the type of opponent Jacobs had specified for that particular fight. When she found a fighter, she would call Jacobs and Cayton. "I would say, I have a kid. I think his record is seven and five." Jim would then demand more precise information. "You don't 'think,' with Jimmy. You 'know.' Everything had to be just perfect."

The development of Mike Tyson was brilliantly orchestrated not only in the ring, but outside it as well by Jacobs and Cayton. They scheduled his fights early enough in the evening for sportscasters to have highlights in plenty of time for their 11:00 P.M. newscasts. They compiled a list of the top sports writers and sportscasters in the country and began sending them video tapes of each of Tyson's knockouts to view or use on their news programs. Stills of Mike in action were also supplied to the newspapers and magazines. And, always, the story of "Mike and Cus" was played to the hilt: how the brilliant, aging guru had found this troubled but talented black youth; how they had developed a father and son relationship that rescued him from reform school; and how D'Amato had taken this rough diamond and not only developed him as a fighter on the verge of greatness, but had instilled in him a sense of values and loyalty as well. It was a great public relations job, and it paid off.

For a quarter of a century, as purveyors of boxing films, as packagers of billiards tournaments on network television, as managers of world champions and contenders who often fought on network TV, Jacobs and Cayton had made many friends and developed many valuable business and press contacts. As a result, Mike was featured on the covers or in major stories in over a hundred sports and general-interest magazines, extraordinary for any fighter, specially one who had not won an Olympic medal. "They've done the best marketing job ever done on a fighter," says Mickey Duff. "The fighter was good enough to stand up to it, but they saw it very early and they got him all this publicity well before he deserved it." At a time when the heavyweight division was weak in terms of viable contenders, when Larry Holmes was reaching the end of his long and distinguished reign as champion, when the title was divided among three champions, each recognized by a different sanctioning group, and when most people didn't really care who was the champion anyway, Mike Tyson was sold and quickly adopted by the media and fans as the savior of the heavyweight division, the fighter who would bring excitement and magic back to what had traditionally been considered boxing's most glamorous division. Everything was going right for Mike Tyson. Then tragedy struck.

Cus D'Amato was attending a boxing convention in upstate New York. He was ill, but had insisted upon going despite Camille's objections. While there, he collapsed and was taken to a hospital in Albany, where he spent a week. He was diagnosed as having a form of pneumonia, and his condition did not improve. At the insistence of Jacobs, he was transferred to Mount Sinai Hospital in New York, but he continued to deteriorate. Tyson went to visit him in the hospital, where they had an emotional scene. Mike told Cus that without him he couldn't go on, that there would be no purpose in his continuing to fight. "It would be tough fighting without you," Mike said, "tough remembering the things you taught me, tough not having you to stay on my back. I can't fight if you're not around." D'Amato told him that was nonsense. "If you don't continue fighting when I'm gone," he said, "we're going to find out if people can come back from the dead, because if I can, I'm going to come back and get you if you give up, or if you do anything wrong." A few days later, on November 1, in Latham, New York, Mike won his eleventh fight, destroying Sterling Benjamin in the first round in under a minute, knocking him down with a left to the face and then finishing him with a dazzling flurry of a dozen punches, crunching body shots sending him down for a second, and final, knockdown. It was the first time D'Amato was not at one of Mike's fights, sitting at ringside, supporting the three-man corner of Kevin Rooney, Steve Lott and cut-man Matt Baranski.

D'Amato continued to weaken, but he resisted all efforts to put an oxygen mask on him. He fought off three hospital attendants with a final burst of strength, and they had to sedate him. Cus then lapsed into a coma from which he never emerged. On November 4, 1985, two months short of his seventy-eighth birthday, Cus D'Amato died of interstitial pulmonary fibrosis, just a few miles from where he had drawn his first breath nearly eight decades earlier. Both Tyson and Jacobs were distraught. Each had lost a man who had had a profound influence on his life. At Cus's funeral, on a crisp autumn day in Catskill, Tyson stood alongside Jim Jacobs and Kevin Rooney, Jay Bright and Tom Patti, another of Cus's boys, Floyd Patterson and Jose Torres. Each was lost in his own private thoughts. It's certain that each in his own way felt diminished by the loss of this man. Miles away, in New York City, Teddy Atlas's thoughts also dwelled this day on Cus D'Amato and on what might have been.

* * *

Mike's next fight was scheduled for just a week after Cus's funeral. Of course, he had the opportunity to cancel it, but he didn't. Continuing his training and going through with the fight was his way—and Kevin Rooney's—of working through their grief. Mike knew that it was Cus's wish that he continue. The old man had said he would live to see Mike become a success, and he had. Mike was 11 and 0. He was on the threshold. Cus hadn't quite made it all the way with him, but Mike could repay him by fulfilling his dream, so he would fight on. He and his team went to Houston to meet Eddie Richardson. Now it was up to Mike to apply the lessons he had been taught. What's the difference between an amateur and a professional? A professional can perform no matter what he's feeling inside. Eight seconds after the opening bell, Eddie Richardson was on the canvas. For the better part of the next minute, Mike was all over him, a left hand finally sending Richardson's 6'6" body toppling like a felled tree. And it was over at 1:17.

Nine days later, back home in upstate New York, Conroy Nelson became ring victim number thirteen, going down in the second round from a right-left combination after absorbing a brutal body beating throughout most of the first round. By now, Tyson was playing to full houses in such upstate arenas as the Latham Coliseum and the Rensselaer Polytechnic Institute stadium. Although the rest of the country and the world had not quite caught on yet, Tyson-mania was rampant in the Albany-Troy area. The fans wore T-shirts that proclaimed "Mike Tyson—Future Heavyweight Champion." It was a far cry from the previous spring when Mike was just turning pro and Loraine and Bob Miller had to hustle tickets for the shows featuring Tyson and the undercard and Kevin Rooney in the main event, the days when a local sportscaster told Loraine that Mike Tyson was a nobody, but be sure to call him if he ever got anywhere. Tyson had now been featured on CBS's "Sunday Morning," with a profile of himself and D'Amato. The networks and magazines were clamoring to set up stories about him. Suddenly, the sportscaster from the Albany TV station was calling the Millers. Tyson was hot, and he wanted to be in on the story. The Millers were only too pleased to oblige, because they had been given a promise. If Mike Tyson made it to the title, he would come back home to defend the crown at least once in the Albany area, and the Millers would be given the chance to promote a World Heavyweight Championship bout. After scraping by all these years with club shows, they would at last get a piece of the big-time pie.

Now it was time for another step for Tyson. He would make his New York City debut, at Madison Square Garden, with all the New York sports media on hand. His New York "coming out" party was a spectacular one. On December 6, against huge and ponderous Sammy Scaff, a journeyman opponent, Tyson drew blood in the first twenty seconds of the bout, rocking Scaff with a left hook to the nose. The fury of his attack overwhelmed the lumbering Scaff, who was pounded relentlessly until his face was a bloody mess. Mercifully, it ended quickly with a final left hook at just 1:15 of the first round.

Next, it was back to Latham, New York, to close out 1985. Two days after Christmas, Tyson was presented with a foe who showed no fear of him. Short, compact Mark Young, at 207 pounds, was built in much the same way as Tyson, but there the similarity ended. To his credit, Young came right at Tyson and at least tried to challenge him. However, he just didn't have the tools required, and a right uppercut sent him flying across the ring. He was counted out fifty seconds into round one, raising Tyson's record to 15 and 0, all by KO. The demand for stories about Tyson increased every day. NBC's "Today" program and ABC's "Good Morning America" interviewed him at breakfasttime, and the "CBS Evening News" profiled him at dinnertime. *Sports Illustrated* hit the stands in the new year with a cover that featured Tyson under the banner, "Kid Dynamite." Mike Tyson, who had still not defeated a ranked fighter and who had been fighting professionally for less than a year, was being touted as the hottest attraction to come down the boxing pipe since Sugar Ray Leonard.

On January 11, 1986, in Albany, David Jaco was the opponent. A lanky, frail-looking white kid, Jaco proved to be amazingly resilient during his brief time in the ring with Mike. Less than a minute into the bout, he dropped like a strand of wet spaghetti when Tyson nailed him with a left, but he rose, took an eight-count, and came back at Mike. Just seconds later, another left toppled him face forward, and it seemed certain that the evening was over.

Surprisingly, Jaco got to his feet a second time and still attempted to fight back. Only when a right hand sent him down a third time did the fight finally end, with the three-knockdown rule forcing a mandatory finis at 2:14 into the opening round. Two weeks later, Mike got a few rounds of work in at Trump Plaza in Atlantic City. Mike Jameson survived a fourth-round knockdown, then was blasted out by Tyson in round five. It was the furthest Tyson had ever been extended by any opponent.

Mike's next fight would give the entire country its first chance to see him. Until now, his bouts had been seen on cable-TV, but a good portion of the U.S. was not yet cabled, and even in those regions that were, many people did not subscribe to the service. However, late in 1985, ABC-TV Sports approached Cayton and Jacobs about a deal for Tyson to fight on the network. They made a solid offer, but Cayton felt his fighter was worth more, even though he was not yet ranked in the top ten. Cayton knew that TV was starved for an exciting new boxing face. Until that time, ABC had made long-term deals almost exclusively with fighters who had the glamour of Olympic gold attached to them, such as Sugar Ray Leonard, or the 1984 U.S. Olympic crop that included Meldrick Taylor, Evander Holyfield, Tyrell Biggs and the most celebrated amateur of all time, Mark Breland. Yet Cayton's clever bargaining enabled him to make a deal for Tyson's services that doubled what ABC had paid to get Breland. For five fights, with Jeff Levine as the promoter, Mike Tyson would be paid $1 million by ABC, on a graduated scale, as the level of his opposition increased. It was a sensational deal on behalf of a fighter who, though attracting a lot of publicity, was essentially unproven against any opposition of note.

Tyson's first fight for ABC was set for February 16, 1986, a Saturday, and would be broadcast on ABC's "Wide World of Sports." The opponent, while not top-ten ranked, was placed among the twenty or so best heavyweights in the world and would certainly be a step up for Tyson. His name was Jesse Ferguson. Both ABC and Team Tyson wanted the fight away from the bland casino setting in Atlantic City that had become so familiar for the staging of fights. To show off Tyson to full advantage and exploit the excitement he was generating among his growing army of fans, as well to promote a "small town" atmosphere, the location selected was the Rensselaer Polytechnic Institute fieldhouse in Troy. Tyson's fans would pour in from Albany, Catskill, Rotterdam, Schenectady, Watervliet, Cohoes and all the other nearby upstate New York cities and towns. The Millers would run the local promotion in cooperation with Jeff Levine.

On the day of the fight, the fieldhouse was packed to the rafters with a 7,600-strong crowd. Several million more people around the country were tuned in at home. Outside, the weather was freezing, but in the fieldhouse things were hot. When Tyson entered the arena, the crowd erupted with deafening cheers, which were repeated when the ring announcer introduced him a few minutes later. Ferguson must have felt as though he were in the lion's den, but he proved to be a game opponent, fighting back through the first four rounds as Tyson piled up the points and pursued him around the ring. In the fifth round, one of the patented Tyson combinations finally connected solidly, a right to the ribs and then immediately a right uppercut with the worst of bad intentions that sent Ferguson sprawling on the canvas. He barely beat the count, rising as the referee, Luis Rivera, reached nine. For the rest of the round, it was bombs away, as Ferguson absorbed a terrific pounding that took away any desire to fight that might have been left in him. When he answered the bell for the sixth round, his only thought was to survive. He grabbed Tyson and would not let go. When Rivera tried to break the clinches, he had to struggle time and again as Ferguson refused to release his grip. Finally, after Rivera had battled to pull Ferguson off Tyson one final time, he waved his arms in the air, pointing at Ferguson, and indicated the fight was over. ABC's commentator, Alex Wallau, quickly shouted, "He's disqualified him!" and pointed out that this would end Tyson's run of consecutive knockouts at seventeen. However, Rivera, perhaps suddenly aware that a highly visible heavyweight did have a knockout streak at stake explained that he was awarding the fight to Tyson on a technical knockout, not a disqualification. In his judgment, Ferguson was hurt and therefore refusing to fight. It was a close judgment call, but that is how it went down in the record books, and Tyson had stopped his eighteenth opponent in as many bouts.

The victory was almost overshadowed by Mike's postfight interview with the press, where he made a statement that shocked most of those who heard it. Speaking of Ferguson, he said, "I tried to punch him and drive the bone of his nose back into his brain." The admission of such murderous intent provoked reactions ranging from raised eyebrows to out-and-out incredulity, and over the next few days, Jacobs had his work cut out trying to limit the damage, explaining to reporters who called his office that it was an unfortunate statement, that Mike had not meant it literally, and so on. Nevertheless, it was widely reported and it certainly stuck in people's minds. Long after the Ferguson fight, the "nose bone into the brain" statement would continually resurface in stories written about Tyson.

Mike Cohen, one of the best liked and most respected sports publicists in the country, was handling press relations for Tyson at this time. Jacobs felt Cohen was responsible for touting the "bone through the nose" remark to the press, however, and Cohen was fired as Tyson's publicity representative for this mistake.

The morning after the fight, Tyson headed to New York City to appear on a couple of local TV shows. An Albany station wanted him for their show. No, Jacobs said. After a couple of days off in New York City, Mike would be returning to Catskill to resume training; his strict rules would not permit Mike to break his routine. The producer was persistent, assuring Jacobs that Mike could be finished and on his way back to Catskill by eight in the morning. Jacobs was polite but adamant. Mike's routine could not be interrupted. The media blitz was on in full force, and Jacobs was determined to control it as best he could so that Mike's concentration remained on track.

Four days after Mike's defeat of Jesse Ferguson, the concern D'Amato had always felt about Mike's activities and whereabouts when he was away from the house once again proved well founded. Tyson and a friend were in the Crossgates Mall in Albany. After creating a disturbance, they were asked to leave the shopping mall. Word got out, and a reporter from Albany's *Knickerbocker News* investigated, reporting in the paper's February 23 edition that a mall security officer said Tyson "made lewd and obscene comments to female customers and was throwing clothes around." The details (not reported in the paper) according to another reporter covering the story were that Tyson allegedly propositioned a young white salesgirl in Filene's department store in blunt language rife with four-letter words. She, in turn, told him just what she thought of him, sending the fighter into a rage. He reportedly grabbed a rack of clothing and threw it toward her, scattering garments around the store, and exploding in a torrent of filthy gutter language directed at the girl and whatever customers happened to be in his vicinity. Mall security responded to a call for help, and when they arrived Tyson and his friend were ordered off the premises. Everyone was well aware of who he was, having been a local celebrity for several years and having fought on national TV the previous weekend.

Crossgates Mall personnel did not press charges, anxious to just let the incident die and avoid adverse publicity. Team Tyson quickly closed ranks, trying to protect their fighter's well-guarded image. Jim Jacobs said Mike had done nothing wrong. *Albany Times-Union* reporter Paul Grondahl went to the mall several days later to dig a little further into the story. Kevin Rooney had denied to Grondahl that Tyson caused a problem, instead placing blame for the disturbance on Tyson's friend according to what Rooney said the fighter had told him. At the mall, reporter Grondahl found that Team Tyson had apparently beaten him there. He ran up against a stone wall. All he got were either denials or people suddenly unwilling to talk. He located a Filene's security manager who refused to give her name, but who termed the incident "a very minor thing." Grondahl pressed her for details, but she told him that if she spoke to him about what had taken place with Tyson, she risked losing her job. Obviously, someone had gotten to her superiors and succeeded in squelching the story. Grondahl then asked her if the original account in the *Knickerbocker News* was accurate. Nervously, she looked around and then nodded at him. Another Mike Tyson cover-up had succeeded. It would not be the last—not by a long shot.

On March 10, at the Nassau Coliseum outside New York City, Mike completed his first year as a professional. Steve Zouski had a solid 25 and 9 record and claimed he had never been knocked down in his entire career: however, he had lost eight of his previous ten fights and was definitely on the downslide. After absorbing a nonstop pounding, Zouski went down and out in round three. It was Mike's nineteenth straight knockout. He had averaged one fight almost every three weeks, right on target with the schedule D'Amato, Jacobs and Cayton had hoped to maintain for him. He was now poised for an assault on the top-ten rankings.

Chapter 7

Contender

First, to the Fight, advanc'd the Charioteer,
High Hopes of Glory on his Brow appear;
Terror vindictive flashes from his Eye;
(To one the Fates the visual Ray deny)
Fierce glow'd his Looks, which spoke his inward rage,
He leaps the Bar, and bounds upon the Stage.

—"Gymnasiad"
Paul Whitehead

The Tyson express slowed down slightly, as the fighter suffered an ear infection that landed him in the hospital early in the spring of 1986 and kept him out of the ring for two months, his longest stretch of inactivity since turning pro. While Tyson convalesced, the people looking out for his best interests were busy at work. When Cayton had negotiated their million-dollar deal with ABC, the network had wanted Mike's services on an exclusive basis for the seven figures they were paying. Cayton and Jacobs demurred. They wanted to be free to expose Mike elsewhere, as long as it did not adversely affect ABC, with whom they had had a long relationship leasing boxing films. Many meetings took place over a period of weeks, and shortly before the Ferguson fight they arrived at an agreement. Tyson would fight three times for the Home Box Office cable network, while ABC would have exclusive use of his services on noncable, over-the-air TV.

Once that problem was resolved, Cayton went to work. Tyson had not made it yet into the top-ten world rankings, yet the deal Cayton negotiated with HBO called for him to receive half a million dollars a fight. The purse for the opponent—$50,000 in each case—would come out of that, leaving Tyson a gross of $450,000 for each of the bouts in the three-fight HBO package. He had earned $150,000 for the Ferguson fight from ABC, along with a percentage of the live gate of $170,000. Few champions earned these kinds of

NEW YORK STATE ATHLETIC COMMISSION
BOXER-MANAGER CONTRACT

AGREEMENT made this ....5th........ day of ......November...... 19 84

between ..Michael Gerard Tyson.................... (hereinafter referred to as the "Boxer") residing at

RD 3 Box 242 Catskill N.Y. 12414 and ......Jim Jacobs......

(hereinafter referred to as the "Manager") residing at 9 East 40th St. New York, N.Y. 10016

In consideration of the covenants, conditions, and mutual promises contained herein, the parties hereto agree as follows:

FIRST: This agreement shall be binding on all parties for a period of .... years (not to exceed four years) from the date hereof.

SECOND: At any time during the period of this agreement, the New York State Athletic Commission (hereinafter referred to as the "Commission") may, declare this entire agreement, or any portion thereof, void or cancelled, for any reason the Commission, in its sole discretion, shall deem reasonable, including, but not limited to: the failure of either party to obtain at any time, or to hold, a valid New York State "Boxer" or "Manager" license, as shall be appropriate; the suspension of such license; or the failure to comply with the terms of this agreement. Or of any rules or regulations of said commission.

THIRD: The Boxer hereby agrees to render boxing services, including training, sparring, and boxing in exhibitions and contests at such times and places as designated by the Manager.

FOURTH: The Manager hereby agrees to use his best efforts to provide adequate training for the Boxer, and to secure for the Boxer, reasonably remunerative boxing contests and exhibitions against fighters of similar qualifications or skill.

FIFTH: The Boxer hereby agrees not to actively participate in any sparring or boxing exhibitions, contests, or training exercises, except as specifically approved or required by the Manager.

SIXTH: Any and all purses, prizes, fees, or other remuneration earned by, or in behalf of, the Boxer for, or in direct relation to, boxing, sparring or training services rendered, or to be rendered, by the Boxer shall be divided and distributed as follows:

(a) payment or repayment for all reasonable and necessary training and transporation expenses incurred by, or on behalf of, the Boxer; and, of the remaining sum,

(b) 33 1/3 .... % (not to exceed 33⅓%) to the Manager;

(c) 66 2/3 .... % to the Boxer; and

(d) .... % to ....(Name)......................., the Trainer, pursuant to a separate agreement filed herewith. (Note: It is not necessary that a Boxer have an agreement with a Trainer.)

All distributions shall be made within 10 days of the receipt of same by the Boxer or Manager.

The Manager guarantees that in no contract year shall the monies paid to the Boxer, pursuant to clause (c) above, be less than .... Dollars.

SEVENTH: The Boxer and Manager each agree to use their best efforts to perform their obligations under this agreement and shall perform any ancillary services, including, but not limited to, traveling to a specified location for training or a bout, or executing documents approved by and filed with the Athletic commission, as may be required.

EIGHT: It is understood and agreed by both parties that the services of the Boxer as provided herein are extraordinary and unique.

NINTH: Neither the Boxer nor the Manager may assign, pledge, transfer, or in any way encumber, all or any portion of his rights, interests, or obligations hereunder. Both the Boxer and Manager certify and warrant that no person or party, other than the parties hereto, in any way, directly or indirectly, has an interest or shares, or participates in any purses, prizes, fees, or other remuneration earned by, or in behalf of, the Boxer, or as a result of his rendering services hereunder, except pursuant to agreements on file with the Commission.

TENTH: Both the Boxer and Manager certify and warrant that there are no other written or oral agreements between the parties, or with any other person or party, regarding: the training of the Boxer; the services he is to render hereunder; the division of fees or remuneration earned; the length of, or renewal of, this agreement; or any matter in relation, directly or indirectly, to boxing services rendered, or to be rendered by, the Boxer, except as are filed herewith with the Commission.

ELEVENTH: In the event of an unresolved dispute between the aforestated boxer-manager, the Commission may, at its discretion and option intercede in said dispute by notifying both aggrieved parties in writing as to its intention to mediate the dispute and that the decision rendered by said Commission shall be binding on both parties.

The parties further specifically certify, warrant, agree, and understand that no such agreement, whether oral or written, shall be binding unless specifically approved by and filed with the Athletic Commission.

The undersigned have read and understand this agreement, and have received a copy of it.

Witnessed by:

_____
A Representative of the Commission

_____
Boxer

Approved by:

_____
Chairman

_____
Manager

The first contract between Jim Jacobs and Mike Tyson, executed in November 1984. Four months later, the eighteen-year-old Tyson had his first pro fight.

paydays, let alone fighters in the top ten. For a fighter still not even number 10 in the world, the deals Cayton and Jacobs were making were unprecedented. The matchmaker Teddy Brenner, known as a tough negotiator himself, said the trouble with Bill was, "When Cayton made a deal it was always 99 to 1 in his favor." Brenner may not have meant it as a compliment, but when it came to serving Tyson's interests, Cayton could not have been paid a better one. And ABC, and HBO certainly never complained that they did not get their money's worth.

Mike was far from polished, but his lethal punching power and his tremendous will to win overcame any possible lack of technical skills. Although he'd won nineteen fights, the cumulative time he had spent in the ring added up to less than an hour and a half of actual combat. He was still learning, although to the public he was already an indestructible fighting machine. His victims added to his reputation by the comments they made to the press. Sammy Scaff said he'd boxed with world champions Tim Witherspoon and Greg Page, but Tyson had hit him harder than anyone in his entire life. Eddie Richardson, whose fight with Tyson lasted 0:02 longer than Scaff's, was asked if he'd ever been hit as hard as Mike hit him. "Yeah," he said, "about a year ago. I was hit by a truck." Someone asked one of Mike's sparring partners if he'd ever really tried to open up on Mike and get the best of him in the ring. "I'm no fool," the man replied. "I'm paid to survive, not to commit suicide."

Jacobs and Cayton—especially Jacobs—were sensitive to criticism in the press. When it was written on more than one occasion that Tyson's opponents were a bunch of hand-picked nobodies, Jacobs reacted defensively by referring writers to the record books to look up the caliber of Joe Louis's or Sugar Ray Robinson's first nineteen opponents. When they were criticized for putting Tyson in the ring so often he might burn out, Jacobs was stung into responding that regardless of whether a person is a boxer, a brain surgeon or a plumber, the more often he practices his trade, the better he gets at it; to rest is to rust. Tyson was criticized as being too small to make it to the top as a heavyweight. Jacobs maintained that Tyson's size was actually an advantage, not a disadvantage. By punching upwards at most of his opponents, with the force generated by his tree-trunk thighs, he was able to hit with much more power. Jacobs took much of the criticism personally and felt obliged to reply to it whenever it caught his eye. Journalists and reporters began to refer to him and Cayton as "arrogant," "condescending," "stuffed shirts."

There may have been some strategy behind Jacobs's behavior. D'Amato had always felt it was his job to shield his fighter, to deflect criticism from his boxer to himself, to make himself out to be the "bad guy" to the press. Jacobs may well have decided to adopt the same strategy. The bottom line was, *he* managed Tyson, not the press, and *he* would make the decisions that affected his fighter's future, not the newspapermen. Significantly, no one criticized the way Jacobs and Cayton were managing their charge. Everyone, either admiringly or begrudgingly, admitted they were doing the most efficient and effective job of building a heavyweight champion, both in the ring and in the bank account, that anyone had ever done. Tyson was becoming a serious contender for the Heavyweight Championship, and he was still just nineteen years old. Now it was time for the next step, and it would be a big one.

Tyson's ear infection (the result of an injury he suffered to the cartilage on his right ear when he banged it accidentally on one of his pigeon coops) had cleared up. He was now scheduled to fight the shrewd veteran James "Quick" Tillis, once a legitimate contender for the heavyweight title, who though now twenty-eight years old and somewhat past his prime was still top-ten caliber. Tillis's wars with Carl Williams, Ernie Shavers, and former champions Mike Weaver, Pinklon Thomas and Gerrie Coetzee had gained him invaluable experience, and he and manager Beau Williford knew that an upset over Tyson on national TV would catapult Tillis back into the title picture and into big paydays.

The Tillis fight had originally been set for March, three weeks after Mike had demolished Zouski, but Mike's ear injury and infection had forced a five-week delay. The bout was rescheduled for May 3, 1986, in the Glens Falls Civic Center in upstate New York, 50 miles north of Albany. Tyson Territory. During his convalescence, when the monotony of his enforced idleness got too much, Tyson had done some unscheduled traveling, disappearing down to Brooklyn without Kevin Rooney's knowledge in pursuit of girls and the smell of the streets. When he returned to Catskill, it was time to knuckle down and do some serious work. Tillis was tricky, and Rooney knew he would be no walkover like Dave Jaco or Steve Zouski. Rooney had also seen things during the Ferguson fight that he did not like. After digging Ferguson to the body in the first round to the point where he was wincing, Mike had let up in the second round, and he and Ferguson had ended up clinching, mauling and holding. Mike had had no spark, he had forgotten about his lateral movements and his sharp combinations. Later, he had become careless and had been on the receiving end of a few good shots to the head by Ferguson. They hadn't done any harm, but Rooney was not happy, and he applied pressure to Mike during their training for Tillis. Tyson responded by getting mean. He knocked several teeth loose on one sparring partner, knocked another down twice and knocked a third unconscious.

One day, Tyson did another disappearing act, chasing girls somewhere in Albany while Rooney waited, impatient and embarrassed, at the gym—embarrassed because Mike's no-show was being documented by an NBC-TV crew and a reporter for the New York *Daily News*. Rooney's discomfort was compounded by the fact that when the reporters asked him where Mike was and when he would be there, he had absolutely no idea.

In a jam-packed Civic Center in Glens Falls and in front of millions of ABC viewers, "Quick" Tillis managed to do during the first four rounds what none of Tyson's previous opponents had been able to. He made Mike back up. He confused him. He threw off Tyson's timing with his own well-timed jabs, which Mike ate as he fell behind on the scorecards. Then, with fifteen seconds left in the fourth round, Tillis decided the time was right to take a shot and test Tyson's chin. He fired a big left hook, but it missed, carrying him off balance and leaving his face momentarily unprotected. Instinctively, Tyson seized the moment. He shot a short left hook to Tillis's jaw, and Tillis went down hard. He was hurt, but not enough to stay down, and luckily the bell rang before Tyson could follow up. For the rest of the fight, Tillis adopted a more cautious demeanor, making sure he was safe before firing combinations at Tyson. Tillis continued to have his moments, but they were fewer and further between. Tyson kept the pressure on and piled up points, drawing even on the scorecards. But Tillis still had the tools of the trade, and he knew how to use them to survive, how to tie Tyson up on the inside. When the bell rang ending the tenth round, Tillis was still standing, still fighting back. He had never been in serious danger after the fourth round knockdown, and Tyson's KO streak ended at nineteen. The decision was unanimous, but very narrow, for Tyson. He had just pulled away from Tillis with a strong finish. If one round had been different on the scorecards, Tillis would have held him to a draw. Instead, Mike had his twentieth victory, but for the first time he had been forced to go the distance. He had failed to impress the national audience except for his brief flash of power early in the bout. His shortcomings were still apparent to observers, his trainer and his managers. Jacobs had admittedly underestimated Tillis. He would later confide to a friend, " 'Quick' Tillis was a mistake, a big mistake. And it was my mistake as the manager."

Mike's next fight was set for May 20, just seventeen days after the Tillis bout. His bout against Sammy Scaff had taken place in the Felt Forum, Madison Square Garden's small auxiliary arena. Now he would appear for the first time in the main 22,000-seat arena of the Garden, for decades the fabled "Mecca of Boxing", and he would be fighting the main event which Home Box Office would televise live. His opponent was Mitch "Blood" Green, a talented fighter but a "head case" who had some trouble with the law. Green was ranked number 7 in the world by the World Boxing Council. He had a solid record of 16-1-1, with ten of his victories by knockout. Before the fight, Green talked long and loud about what he would do to Tyson. But in the ring the name of his game boiled down to one word—survival. Green took no chances with Tyson. He was big enough and experienced enough to avoid Mike's power, and Tyson allowed himself once again to be frustrated by a big, durable opponent. However, unlike Tillis, Green was unable or unwilling to mount any kind of effective attack. The fight was less than a pleasing aesthetic experience, but at the final bell there was no doubt this time about the winner. Tyson had achieved a near walkover. The three judges, scoring by rounds, had the bout 8–2, 9–1, and 9–1. Tyson had won a total of twenty-six out of a possible thirty rounds on the three scorecards, easily handling the man the WBC considered the seventh-best contender in the world. Two years later, Tyson and Green would meet in an unscheduled fight on a Harlem street that would earn them both headlines far outstripping the ones that followed their meeting in the ring at the Garden.

Three weeks later Mike returned to the Garden's main arena, this time on the undercard, facing Reggie Gross. Tyson's wins over Tillis and Green had catapulted him to the number 4 position in the WBC ratings. He was determined to get back on the KO track. Gross was a solid pro, a spoiler, with an 18 and 4 record. The fight was exciting while it lasted. Gross came out winging, unleashing a rapid-fire flurry at Tyson, an offensive that had the crowd screaming encouragement to the lopsided underdog. What many failed to notice as they cheered a rare display of courage by an opponent against Tyson was that Gross failed to land solidly a single punch from his entire barrage. Tyson's great upper-body movement, his vastly underrated defensive abilities, took over, and he bobbed and weaved away from Gross's fists. Biding his time, not getting rattled, he waited for an opportunity. Suddenly, as Gross persevered with his volley of punches, Mike unleashed a solitary, lightning left hand seemingly from nowhere, and Gross was sent sprawling onto the canvas, in serious trouble. When the referee completed the count, Tyson closed in for the kill. It came at the end of another left hand, and the evening had ended for Tyson—and Gross—at 2:36 of the first round. The crowd was awed at this first-hand look at Tyson's power. Mike showered and dressed and then returned to the ringside to cheer on his stablemate, Edwin Rosario, who was challenging Hector "Macho" Camacho in the main event for the World Lightweight Championship. Rosario lost a hotly contested and controversial decision to the "Macho Man," after which he and Mike and Team Tyson left the arena. It was Tyson's last fight at Madison Square Garden. A few more appearances in the upstate arenas, and then it would be on to the big fights in the gambling capitals of Atlantic City and Las Vegas.

The next venue was a return to Troy two weeks after the Reggie Gross fight, for a quick dispatching of William Hosea, who decided discretion was the better part of valor after tasting Tyson's fists. He listened intently on one knee while the referee counted him out, then got up the instant he heard that comforting word, "ten," which came exactly 2:03 after the opening bell. Thirteen days later, at the Stevensville Hotel in the resort region of the Catskill Mountains, with the summer vacation crowd eager for an evening's entertainment, Tyson was booked to fight Lorenzo Boyd. Strolling on the road outside the hotel grounds on the warm summer evening several hours before the fight, Tyson and Rooney encountered one of the judges assigned to the bouts that night. They knew each other, and after exchanging a greeting the judge ribbed Tyson, "You know, I'm judging your fight tonight, so I shouldn't be talking to you. People might get the wrong idea." Tyson smiled, and turned to Rooney. "Hey, Kevin, look who's here. Maybe if we give him something . . ." he joked. "Mike," said the judge, "if you need to rely on my scorecard tonight to win this fight, I've got the biggest sports story of the year." The judge was right. Mike celebrated his elevation to the number 2 slot in the WBC rankings by taking Boyd out in the second round with a lightning-fast 6-4 combination—right to the ribs, and then the right immediately whipped to the chin.

Joe Frazier was a brave warrior who feared no man during his days in the ring. He still feared no man in 1986, long after his career was over. Unfortunately for his son, Marvis, whose boxing career he was now managing, this fearless attitude led him to accept the offer of a chance for Marvis to fight Tyson on July 26 at the Glens Falls Civic Center. It was a bad move. Nearly three years earlier, Marvis had been knocked out in one round by Larry Holmes in a bid for Holmes's title. True, it was Frazier's only loss in seventeen fights, but Holmes did not have the same reputation as a puncher of "bad intentions" as Tyson did, and if Holmes could polish Marvis off in one round, it did not bode well for Marvis's chances against Tyson. Joe was training his son and tried to mold Marvis after himself, which was a mistake, because Marvis had neither the grit nor the firepower that his father had possessed. The strategy they devised was to bob and weave and slip, the way Joe had fought, but Tyson and Rooney had worked out an effective plan to counter any bobbing and weaving Marvis Frazier might do. In the locker room shortly before the fight, Tyson told Jacobs exactly what was going to happen. "When you jab him," Tyson said, "he bends forward at the waist, like he's bowin', just bends straight over. He doesn't bend his knees. When I jab and he bends over, I'm gonna catch him with the right uppercut."

ABC's cameras were on hand to televise the bout live to the nation. This fight, under the terms negotiated by Cayton, would earn Tyson $250,000 from the TV network. True to form, Mike entered the ring without robe, without socks, just black trunks and black leather shoes. He paced the ring like a caged animal after he had climbed through the ropes. His mouth curved in a snarling sneer. When the bell rang, he moved quickly at Frazier and immediately backed him against the ropes. In a lightning burst of controlled fury and power, Tyson pinned him in a neutral corner with a series of jabs. Sure enough, as Tyson had predicted, Frazier bent forward. Planting his massive legs for optimum leverage, Tyson fired a right uppercut that caught his opponent flush on the jaw and effectively ended the fight then and there. Frazier was stunned and in the corner with no place to retreat, a bad situation to be in with Tyson. Instinctively, he tried to bob and weave away from Tyson's fists, but was caught by a second right uppercut. Frazier was now semiconscious, although still standing. He was in that in-between world where, as Muhammad Ali told author Thomas Hauser, "You see black lights, the black lights of unconsciousness." Tyson shoved Frazier's gloves away to get another clear shot at the helpless fighter, and for a third time in a matter of seconds, Tyson's right fist crashed into Frazier's head. As he started to topple, a left hook provided the unnecessary finishing punch. Frazier went down in a sitting position, his legs folded underneath him, his upper body propped up by the two lower ring ropes. Referee Joe Cortez jumped in and began his count. Seeing it was pointless to continue, he waved the fight over. Just thirty seconds had elapsed from the opening bell to the end of the fight, Tyson's quickest and most impressive outing in twenty-five fights. Mike moved across the ring to Joe Frazier and, concerned about Marvis, asked him to check his son. "I'm sorry it had to happen like this," he said to the former great heavyweight champion.

The Marvis Frazier fight marked the end of two promotional relationships. First was Jeff Levine. For reasons that had nothing to do with Tyson, or the Frazier fight, Jacobs had felt that Levine had crossed him and vowed never to do business with him again. Levine had obtained promotional rights to Hector Camacho and intervened when a match was about to be made between Camacho and Jacobs's and Cayton's other fighter, Edwin Rosario, for Camacho's lightweight title, killing the match. "Jim never forgave him," says Cayton. "Jim laid it out, he said Jeff had done the wrong thing, that he was interested in a few bucks instead of a relationship with us. . . . I never felt that way about Jeff. I didn't think he should have done it, but I rationalized, I understood, while I did not like it." Jacobs's extreme displeasure was enough to shut Levine out of any future dealings concerning Mike Tyson.

Levine has, naturally, his own view of what transpired between himself and Jacobs: "I promoted Mike's early fights. Jim assured me, 'As long as we have no problems working together, you'll be with Mike Tyson for his entire career.' With all the things written about Jim's integrity, 'his handshake was his bond, he never broke his word,' Jim's memory could conveniently lapse when it suited his purposes. When he needed Don King to join the HBO tournament [which Tyson entered and in which he won the heavyweight title] he dropped me. I understood his reasons, because this business is like this. But they were in the driver's seat with Tyson. All they would have had to say was, 'Jeff Levine is our promoter, so he has to be in for a $25,000 fee for each fight.' Jim didn't." Subsequently, Levine says, Jacobs asked him not to get involved with Camacho in jeopardizing the fight he was trying to make for his lightweight Rosario. "If I'd been in still with Tyson, OK," says Levine. "But I had nothing else to fall back on. I'm a promoter. Camacho came to me to do business. I have a mortgage to pay, kids to feed. I'm not a millionaire like Jim. Later, Jim didn't want Tyson to fight Tony Tucker because I stood to profit from the promotion. But he finally relented because he wanted Tyson desperately to have all three title belts." Jacobs also told his friend Judd Maze that Carl "The Truth" Williams would never get a title fight with Tyson as long as Jeff Levine was involved with him.

Just as surprising was Team Tyson's parting with Loraine Miller. She had done her job in the belief that she would share in the big time when Tyson made it. Instead, she found herself shut out. She says that she received payments to cover her losses on Tyson shows she promoted upstate, as per their agreement. But when she informed them in the summer of 1986 that the combined losses on the Hosea-Rensselaer and Boyd-Stevensville shows were $22,000, she received a check for only $4,000. She called Jacobs for an explanation. "He said, 'You can just consider that a gift,' " Miller recalls of their conversation. "I said, 'But that wasn't our agreement.' And he said, 'Well, Loraine, you're a promoter. That's the chance a promoter takes.' I trust people in general, I try to stay honest with people, and I just figured that's the way everything is in return. I didn't realize they had gotten TV money from [those shows]. They're cheap . . . I felt they did wrong to me. . . . When Mike got a chance to fight for the title, Bob and I never so much as got a phone call to say, look, you have to buy your own seats, pay your own fare, but we'll save you two seats if you'd like to come down. Not even as much as a thought. . . ."

Jacobs may have grown disenchanted with the Millers after Loraine made a mistake with the seating arrangements for his wife and some friends at one of Mike's fights, inconsequential as that may seem. "We got back back to the Holiday Inn in Latham [New York]," Loraine Miller recalls, "and Jimmy said, 'Loraine, I'd like to speak to you.' We went over to one of the corners and Jimmy said, 'I want you to remember something. Who is the most important person in the world?'. . . . I just looked at him, and he said, 'I am, and I never want you to forget that. I am the most important person in the world, and my loved ones, and that means my wife. . . . Don't you ever mess up those [tickets].' Don't forget, Bob and I aren't a Don King . . . my twins were two years old, my little girl was three, plus my other three kids, so it was like a zoo. My phone is ringing, I had people coming in my front door to buy tickets. . . . It's only

Bob and me doing this, it's not a Don King promotion. . . . With them, it wasn't feelings. It was strictly business."

Bill Cayton acknowledges that "Jim was a little hard on her," but is nevertheless surprised to hear of Loraine Miller's dissatisfaction. "I thought we treated them extremely well. . . . When they were short, Jim and I put the money out of our own pockets. . . . They were on a fee basis on most of the fights [*note:* when Jeff Levine joined Team Tyson as a promoter, he paid the Millers for several of the ABC-TV fights on a flat fee basis, rather than working on a profit basis from the live gates], where she got a very substantial fee and she was very happy."

One of the things the Millers had been promised for their promotional work when Tyson was climbing the ladder was the chance to promote a Heavyweight Championship fight in the Albany area when he became champion. That promise was never fulfilled.

Three weeks after his dramatic disposal of Marvis Frazier, it was time for Tyson to fulfill the second part of his three-fight commitment to HBO, by taking on Jose Ribalta, a Cuban-born, Miami-based, 6′6″ fighter with a top-ten ranking and a solid 23-3 record. The fight was held at Trump Plaza in Atlantic City. Tyson floored Ribalta for the first of three knockdowns in round 2 with his now-familiar rapid-fire combination of a right to the ribs and a right uppercut to the jaw. Ribalta was up quickly at the count of two. Later, in round 8, Tyson dropped him for the second time, but his opponent was game and was still there to answer the bell for the tenth and final round. A left hook to the head dropped him for the third time in the fight. Again, he arose quickly, and said, "Hell, yes," when the referee asked him if he wanted to continue. Tyson quickly backed him up against the ropes and landed a right-left-right combination to the head, all the punches landing on target, unanswered by Ribalta. At that point the referee jumped in and stopped the fight over Ribalta's strong protests that he was all right and wanted to continue. Tyson now had his twenty-fourth KO in twenty-six fights. He was the number one contender in the world, ready to challenge for the heavyweight title.

Chapter 8

The Youngest
Heavyweight Champion

A little man against a big one, and the chances are in favour of the little one. The cat has the best of it with a dog. Goliaths are always vanquished by Davids.
—The Man Who Laughs
Victo Hugo

When Mike Tyson came on the scene, the heavyweight division had fallen on hard times due to the activities of promoter Don King, who controlled most of the top heavyweights, and due to the activities of the three sanctioning bodies—the World Boxing Council, the World Boxing Association and the International Boxing Federation—that effectively ran the sport on the championship level. Nearly a decade earlier, in 1978 when, after upsetting Muhammad Ali, Leon Spinks refused to fight the WBC's top contender, signing instead for a more lucrative rematch with Ali, the title had been fragmented, leading to confusion and apathy among much of the public. That same year, Larry Holmes won recognition as the WBC champion by defeating Ken Norton. Ali regained the title by a decision over Spinks on September 15, 1978, although by then it was only the WBA version of the crown that he regained. However, the following year, without fighting again, Ali announced he was retiring, leaving the WBA title vacant. Over the next half dozen years, a motley assortment of relative unknowns played musical chairs with the WBA belt, winning it and then, inevitably, losing it, often in their first defense, months later. To say that any of them failed to capture the imagination of the public would be an understatement. Among the WBA heavyweight champions were such names as John Tate, Mike Weaver, Michael Dokes, Tony Tubbs, Greg Page and Gerrie Coetzee.

Holmes, meanwhile, gained wide public acceptance as "the real" heavyweight champion. He defeated Ali when, a mere shell of his former magnificent self, he attempted a comeback. Holmes then polished off a succession of top contenders including Leon Spinks, Earnie Shavers, Renaldo Snipes, Carl Williams, Mike Weaver, Trevor Berbick and Gerry Cooney. During this period, the International Boxing Federation, with its base in America, was formed to counterbalance the strong influence of the WBA and WBC, which were controlled by Mexican and Latin-American interests and often acted in ways prejudicial to U.S. interests in boxing.

When Holmes defied a WBC dictum on which opponent he should fight, the WBC withdrew recognition from him, leaving their title vacant. The IBF, which needed a recognized champion to give its organization instant credibility, jumped into the void, and accorded Holmes recognition as champion. The WBC then filled its vacant title with a succession of champions that, like the WBA, the public could not have cared less about, champions such as Pinklon Thomas, Tim Witherspoon and Trevor Berbick. By overwhelming public consensus, Larry Holmes, by virtue of his performances in the ring and the continuity of his reign, was the true champion. After ruling the division for more than seven years, Holmes was upset by Michael Spinks late in 1985, losing his title by decision to the former Olympic champion. Spinks became the first light-heavyweight champion to successfully challenge for the heavyweight title.

Thus, as 1985 was drawing to a close, the heavyweight division was in some confusion. Michael Spinks was the IBF champion, the man who had defeated the true champion, Larry Holmes, in the ring, and so many felt he had a legitimate claim to the title. However, he held only one-third of it. The WBA champion was Tim Witherspoon (who had previously held the WBC title briefly). The WBC championship belonged to Pinklon Thomas at this time.

Seth Abraham, a thirty-nine-year-old one-time Brooklyn street kid who had risen to become head of sports programming at the HBO cable-TV network, conceived the idea of a tournament to crown one undisputed heavyweight champion. Abraham had become a friendly adversary of Don King's, buying scores of fights for HBO from the promoter. In 1985, when King was visiting Abraham's apartment to see his new baby daughter, Abraham made his pitch. They stayed up until 2:30 A.M. discussing it. As Abraham recalls, "With King, I appealed to his sense of history, believe it or not. Don really wants to be, when he's all done, recognized as the greatest promoter of all time. Just saying to Don, 'This can't be done, this can't be done—can it?' appealed to Don's sense of the impossible, and for him it was, in a sense, his Mount Everest. That's not to say he was philanthropic about it, but it was not money that drove King. He loved the challenge. . . . To Butch Lewis [promoter of Michael Spinks, the IBF champion] it had nothing to do with history. Butch was new . . . to wealth after Michael beat Larry Holmes in September of '85. For him, [it was] strictly money. As we put the deal together, I was able to show them . . . fight by fight what they could amass, and it became dollars and cents."

After a succession of marathon meetings, the deal was made. Then it was up to Don King to deal with the WBA and WBC, and Butch Lewis to bring the IBF into the fold. HBO did not get involved directly in negotiations with the sanctioning organizations, but King and Lewis did their jobs. Now everything was in place. Home Box Office would put up $16 million for the rights to televise the eighteen-month long series of round-robin bouts that would lead to the unification of the heavyweight title. It was a major coup for HBO, since King and Lewis usually wouldn't even set foot in the same room together, much less work cooperatively as co-promoters, and the WBA, WBC and IBF were constantly at each others' throats.

In 1920, in the United States, the National Boxing Association was formed. Like most attempts at organization within the sport of boxing, it was less than a cohesive, well-oiled cooperative effort involving various state and local boxing commissions and officials. In 1962, the NBA, which sanctioned title fights and recognized dozens of its own NBA "world" champions over the years, changed its name to the World Boxing Association. In those years, despite its new, global monicker, the WBA was firmly centered and rooted in the United States, which was, in fact, the world center of boxing. In 1962, the heavyweight champions were Floyd Patterson and Sonny Liston; the light-heavyweight champions were Archie Moore and Harold Johnson; portions of the Middleweight Championship belonged to Gene Fullmer and Paul Pender; the junior middleweight champion was Denny Moyer; the welterweight champion was Emile Griffith; the lightweight champions were Joe Brown and Carlos Ortiz; and the featherweight champion was Davey Moore. All were Americans. Only a portion of the Middleweight Championship (won by Dick Tiger, a Nigerian, who was under American management and was based in the United States for much of his career), the Bantamweight Championship, the Flyweight Championship, and a couple of junior championships in the lighter weight divisions were held by foreign fighters. The United States was the dominant power in boxing.

In 1963, the rival World Boxing Council was organized, in large part by George Parnassus, a leading boxing promoter in California. Parnassus, a Greek immigrant, promoted shows in the lighter weight divisions dominated by Mexican, Latin-American and other non-USA fighters. He became fed up with the pro-American bias he perceived in the actions of the NBA/WBA. The WBC, which was Mexican-run, virtually excluded the United States from any position of power. It was divided up into seven geographic regions. Each region had two votes. The United States was part of the North American region. But because that region, or "federation," as the WBC termed it, also included Mexico and Canada, the United States wound up with two-thirds of one vote! This while in point of fact the United States generates an estimated 80 percent of worldwide boxing revenue.

In 1974, control of the WBA was also removed from the hands of American interests, as a cabal of Panamanians were voted in. They accomplished their bloodless coup through a clever manipulation of the organization's very own rules. One rule in particular. It said, basically, that the athletic commission or any other duly authorized body that existed for the purpose of regulating boxing in any country, *territorial or political subdivision, province or city* is eligible for membership in the WBA and is *entitled to one vote*. Another key portion of the rules stated that only delegates who were actually in attendance at the annual convention were eligible to a vote. Utilizing this rule, dozens of newly discovered delegates from Latin-America and the Caribbean showed up, and because of the clause allowing a vote not only to a country, but to any "territorial or political subdivision, province or city," small countries like Panama, Venezuela and even the Virgin Islands showed up with three, four, five or even six delegates each, every one of them entitled to vote. In a well-documented 1981 exposé by Pat Putnam in *Sports Illustrated,* it was stated outright that "many of the WBA's delegates since 1974 have been shipped in [to annual conventions] prepaid, or have been outright phonies. . . . At the 1979 convention in Miami Beach, as an example, there were three delegates from the Virgin Islands. . . . If the credentials committee had bothered to check, it would have discovered that there has never been an official boxing commission in the Virgin Islands." With technicalities conveniently cast aside, the WBA has been controlled lock, stock and barrel ever since by a succession of Latin-American interests.

In the years since, these organizations have been run with a banana-republic mentality in keeping with the geographic makeup of their top leaderships. World rankings and lucrative title fights go to those managers and fighters with the right friends or connections, whether deserved or not; plum "junket" assignments have frequently gone to officials, it's been alleged numerous times, who score bouts the "right" way for the "house" fighter. The WBA and WBC have watered-down the sport by adding, collectively, a dozen new and unnecessary in-between weight divisions such as straw-weight, super-bantamweight, junior-lightweight and super-middleweight. This demeans the sport but is all important to the sanctioning groups since more weight divisions means more champions, more title fights, and thus more sanctioning fees to fill the WBA and WBC coffers, with fees of 2½ percent of the gross purse of each fighter in a championship bout. Allegations of wrongdoing or strange coincidences are legend. Some examples:

According to promoter Bob Arum, he had to agree to pay Pepe Cordero, a boxing manager and henchman for the WBA leadership, $85,000 to obtain a crack at the WBA Lightweight Championship for Ray Mancini; in addition, when Mancini won the title, Arum had to give Ernesto Espana, an over-the-hill, shot fighter, a title bout with Mancini and a quarter-of-a-million-dollar purse. Espana was managed by Cordero, and the manager collects one-third of his fighter's earnings. "There's one bagman in the WBA," Arum has stated, "and that's Pepe Cordero. Anytime you want a fix in the WBA, you bribe Cordero and he takes care of it. When I want something done, I have to pay off Cordero. We shouldn't really call it a bribe, because you can't bribe a person who's not in a position of authority. Cordero has no office at all in the WBA. . . . But anyone who wants anything done in the WBA has to pay Cordero."

An American boxing judge who used to officiate at WBA bouts told *Sports Illustrated*'s Pat Putnam: "I was officiating a fight in Puerto Rico, and Dr. Elias Cordova [then the most powerful figure in the WBA] came over to me just before round one, touched my arm and said, 'Remember who you are working for. We want to keep the championship here.' The fight was between a Latin American and a U.S. fighter. Later at another fight that year, Dr. Cordova told me that the reason I wasn't used much was because I wasn't a house referee. I had just voted against one of their fighters. The WBA has never called me to work again."

In 1979, a mediocre club fighter, "Irish" Mike Baker, was suddenly ranked number 7 in the world by the WBC in the junior middleweight division and given a title fight with world champion Maurice Hope of Great Britain. Baker in no way belonged in the same ring with Hope. He was beaten badly and stopped in the seventh round. Baker's manager was the powerful Washington, DC attorney Edward Bennett Williams. Coincidentally, Williams represented in his law practice both Don King and the WBC's president, Jose Sulaiman.

Bob Busse, who has served as president of the North American Boxing Federation and chairman of the WBC Ratings Committee, has said, "One of the WBC's problems is that it refuses to recognize that the United States represents the heart of professional boxing. Jose [Sulaiman] will say time and time again that the United States is only one of 104 countries, but that's ridiculous. You can't compare boxing in the United States with boxing in Barbados, and, too often, American fights are treated unfairly by the WBC as the price of appeasing other countries." Busse said that while he was chairman of the WBC ratings committee, 90 percent of the ratings were done by Sulaiman, without any consultation with Busse or the committee. "How some of the people get into our ratings I couldn't tell you," Busse told *Sports Illustrated.* "Promoters call me and ask about fighters they say we have ranked, and I didn't even know they were ranked."

The WBA rules state that a champion must defend his title once every six months against the leading available contender. Yet, from 1977 to 1979, Ayub Kalule was the top contender for the Junior Middleweight Championship, and the WBA did everything in its power to keep Kalule from getting a title opportunity, in direct violation of its own rules. Their apparent purpose was to protect mediocre Latin-American fighter, Eddie Gazo, from having to risk his title against Kalule, an African fighter living in and fighting out of Denmark. Finally, only after pressure on the WBA mounted to the point where Kalule could no longer be avoided, and long after Gazo had lost his title to a Japanese fighter, Masashi Kudo, did Kalule get his long-overdue title shot. He easily defeated Kudo to win the World Championship.

As recounted by Pat Putnam in his *Sports Illustrated* exposé, in 1977, Dr. Elia Cordova, the WBA President, told a Japanese promoter of a world title fight that the WBA would not sanction the fight unless the organization was provided with seven round-trip airline tickets to Tokyo, along with first-class hotel and dining accommodations. Included in the WBA party that arrived in Tokyo, all expenses paid, were two wives, including Cordova's, and Pepe Cordero, who held no official position with the WBA. The day after the party arrived, the Japanese promoter took them all to a shop in Tokyo where they picked out pearls, silks, and other gifts, all of which were paid for in cash by the Japanese "host."

In Colombia, a fight manager wanted very much to have his boxer rated, but did not have the cash necessary. A WBA official told him, not very subtly, his daughter liked emerald earrings. In Colombia, emeralds are relatively inexpensive. The official's daughter got a set of beautiful earrings. The fighter got rated.

When Mandry Galindez replaced Cordova as president of the WBA, he traveled to Korea, where he was surprised to find managers and promoters trying to give him money. He didn't know what they were doing, until one of them asked him, "Are you the man we now pay for the ratings?"

In the WBC Welterweight Championship fight in Montreal in 1980 between Roberto Duran and Sugar Ray Leonard, one official assigned scored the fight 3 rounds Duran, 2 rounds Leonard, 10 rounds even! Despite this unprecedented monument to indecision in a major title match, the official continued to be given world title matches to judge, along with travel, hotel and meal allowances, and $1,200 fee that goes along with such assignments.

In 1988, when Sugar Ray Leonard decided to once again come out of retirement and challenge Donny Lalonde for the WBC Light-Heavyweight Championship, the WBC created a new 168-pound super-middleweight division and declared that this new title, as well as Lalonde's 175-pound Light-Heavyweight title, would be on the line in the fight. This virtually handed to Leonard the opportunity to become the first boxer to win titles in five different weight divisions, even though it violated WBC rules which stated that a fighter could only hold one title at a time.

These examples, plus numerous others documented by Pat Putnam, Thomas Hauser and other journalists over the years, point to an obvious pattern of rules violations, incompetence and, in some cases, outright corruption. Putnam concluded in 1981 that "the WBC and WBA are failures," yet they continue to flourish today, with the WBC the dominant organization.

Don King aligned himself closely with the WBC and its president, Jose Sulaiman, while also maintaining ties with the WBA. Sulaiman, eager to please, became little more than an errand boy for King. British promoter Mickey Duff said, "My complaint is that Jose Sulaiman is not happy his friend Don King is the biggest promoter in boxing. Sulaiman will only be happy when Don King is the *only* promoter in boxing." *Ring* magazine termed Sulaiman King's "personal lap dog." But because King has controlled many of the fighters over the years who were WBC champions or challengers and therefore has emerged as the promoter of many lucrative WBC title bouts, the organization relies heavily on him for its economic survival. It is a perfect symbiotic relationship.

As there seemed no chance of things changing, Bob Lee, at that time the Boxing Commissioner in the state of New Jersey, and president of the United States Boxing Association, began in 1983 to set up a third global sanctioning organization: the International Boxing Federation. Seeing this as a potential threat to Latin-American and third-world dominance in controlling boxing, the WBC and WBA, traditional rivals, have, in recent years, begun a rapprochement in the hope that some degree of unity will limit the power and influence of the IBF, with its strong American bias.

All three independent organizations continue to exist because of the demand for world championship matches by the American television networks. For years, boxing reformers have proposed the simplest of solutions for doing away with the undue influence of these organizations, a solution that would relegate the WBC and WBA to the backwaters of boxing beyond the U.S. borders, and eventually to virtual extinction. The proposal calls for the establishment of a federal boxing commissioner with the power to appoint qualified officials; to control boxing in all fifty states and U.S. territories, such as Puerto Rico, under one uniform set of rules; to institute strict licensing and medical procedures in order to ensure the caliber and safety of fighters, as well as the competence of trainers, managers and promoters; and to sanction U.S.-recognized world championship bouts. With 80 percent of boxing revenues originating in the United States, such a move would quickly bring government-regulated control of the sport back into American hands. Whatever its reasons, Congress has failed to act on such a proposal, however, and so boxing continues on its merry, laissez-faire way, with the IBF, the WBC, the WBA, Don King and Bob Arum at the controls. It was against this backdrop that Home Box Office brought all parties together (except for Arum, who did not figure in the heavyweight picture) to create the Heavyweight Championship Unification Tournament.

The Heavyweight Unification Tournament began in the early spring of 1986. Mike Tyson was not included at that time for several reasons. First, Don King was not interested in having him in it: King controlled the WBC champion, Pinklon Thomas; he controlled the WBA champion, Tim Witherspoon; but mostly, King did not exercise any control over Tyson. Jacobs and Cayton were running an independent course with Tyson, and this made King uncomfortable.

If he can help it, King promotes only fighters he can control. Second, Tyson had been fighting for only a year, and he wasn't quite ready to face the mental pressure of fighting for the title, his toughest opponent to date having been Jesse Ferguson. Third, Jacobs and Cayton knew they had the hottest property in the heavyweight division, and if they continued to bring him along slowly and successfully, they could step in and challenge for the title when their fighter was ready and when it suited their schedule.

On March 22, 1986, in the first bout of the HBO tournament, Trevor Berbick upset Pinklon Thomas to win the WBC Heavyweight Championship. Both fighters were controlled by Don King. Berbick had been the Canadian heavyweight champion. In 1980 he knocked out a washed-up John Tate. In 1981, he won a decision over a washed-up Muhammed Ali in what was to be Ali's last fight. Subsequently, he'd gone fifteen rounds with Larry Holmes in a title bid, losing the decision. Now he was the new WBC world champion.

A month later, on April 19, Michael Spinks defended the IBF version of the title on a narrow, controversial decision over Larry Holmes, the man he had taken it from the previous September. Next on the list was the WBA title. On July 19, in London, a less than well-conditioned Tim Witherspoon, trailing on points, came back to knock out British challenger Frank Bruno late in the fight to retain his crown. On September 6, Michael Spinks defended his IBF title in a walk-over, knocking out Scandinavian challenger Steffen Tangstad, in four rounds. The fight drew little interest. Most people had never heard of Tangstad, and those who had knew he didn't belong in the same ring with Spinks. What did attract interest was the presence of Mike Tyson on the same card. HBO, knowing that the Spinks-Tangstad match alone could not sustain their national telecast, added Tyson to the card. Before his name was added, a little over $200,000 in tickets had been sold at the Las Vegas Hilton. Once Tyson was on the show, the live gate came to a near sellout of $1.1 million.

Tyson's opponent was Alfonzo Ratliff, the former WBC cruiserweight champion. Ratliff tried to run, but, as they say, he couldn't hide. In the second round, Tyson's left hook dropped him. He was up at the count of nine, but

Mike pinned him on the ropes and a right hand sent him careening, only the ropes holding him up. A combination with a right-hand coup de grace ended the fight. A few weeks earlier, Jim Jacobs had said there was no pressing need to put Tyson into the Heavyweight Tournament. "Mike can make a lot of money while a unified champion is determined," he reasoned. "If Mike continues as he has, he will be the number one contender in all three organizations by then. There are a lot of big fights for Mike without going after the title—Holmes, Tyrell Biggs, Gerry Cooney," although Jacobs was also quick to point out that Mike would have no trouble fighting the reigning champions if he were to enter the tournament. "After all," he added, "we are not talking about Jack Dempsey and Joe Louis." Jacobs invited critics to look at films from his vast library to see for themselves if Tyson didn't surpass them all at the same stage of development. However, they realized that keeping Mike out of the tournament was not the right way to go. As Seth Abraham of HBO said, "Jimmy and Bill . . . were very, very practical . . . and practically speaking, it would have taken Mike Tyson years to get all three belts."

HBO wanted Tyson in the tournament because, as Abraham frankly acknowledges, "Tyson out of the series really jeopardized the credibility of the series because Jimmy and Bill had done such a remarkable job in marketing him. He had already been on HBO twice, and every boxing writer was writing that this man indeed may be the real champion, and if you want credibility, so that people believe this is legitimate, that it's not a 'Don King series,' let's go out and get this man in. It was something we turned our attention to in earnest in June [1986]."

Of course, nothing is simple, and protracted negotiations took place throughout the summer. Abraham spent much of his time at Wimbledon in July in trans-Atlantic telephone conversations with Jacobs, Cayton, King and Lewis, including one with Cayton and Jacobs that lasted for five hours. On his return from Wimbledon (which HBO televises in the U.S.) Abraham went on vacation to Fire Island, from where the negotiations continued. HBO offered to sweeten the pot, adding additional millions to the $16 million they had already invested in order to lure Tyson into the tournament. There was yet another marathon meeting at the Home

Box Office headquarters in Manhattan. This one lasted fourteen hours, with the two promoters Don King and Butch Lewis, Jacobs and Cayton and their respective attorneys present. According to Abraham, King was anxious to have Tyson in the HBO series, seeing it as a way to legitimize his involvement as Tyson's promoter in the future. Lewis was opposed to Tyson's inclusion, which he saw as a block to his man, Spinks, eventually unifying the title. Finally, an agreement was reached. A meeting was set for August 20, 1986, at Cayton and Jacobs's office at which all parties involved were to sign a memorandum of agreement. At the very last moment, Butch Lewis balked, and only a stern talking to by Abraham, who pulled him aside, caused him to relent. But Abraham is convinced that the seeds that eventually led to Lewis pulling Spinks out of the tournament were sown that day, when Mike Tyson came into it.

D'Amato had predicted that Mike would be ready to fight for the Heavyweight Championship by the end of 1986. Jacobs had often said, when asked when Tyson would be ready to fight for the title, "The aim is not for Mike to fight for the title. The aim is for Mike to win the title." Now Team Tyson believed he was ready. His fighting skills were not fully polished yet, but he was mentally tough, physically the most powerful of the heavyweights, and what he lacked in experience he made up with what might be termed his intimidation factor. Tyson's image, backed by his impressive performances in the ring, had been carefully cultivated to the point where there was an aura of invincibility around him that had his opponents psyched-out before they even set foot in the ring against him. Jacobs used to describe it as the "Joe Louis syndrome," since Louis had the same effect on many of his opponents. However, by the time Tyson had moved to the top of the heavyweight division, Jacobs had renamed it "Tysonitis." And Tysonitis was racing like an epidemic through the heavyweight ranks.

Mike Tyson was now in the Heavyweight Elimination Tournament. On November 22, 1986, he would step into the ring at the Las Vegas Hilton to challenge Trevor Berbick for the WBC Heavyweight Championship. Tyson would be twenty years and five months of age. It would be only the twenty-first month of his professional career. He had boxed only seventy-five rounds in his twenty-seven fights, and twenty-five of those rounds were only partial rounds because knockouts brought them to an end before their three-minute duration. He had two and a half months to prepare, following his KO of Ratliff. Some of that time would be spent in isolation, working in the quiet confines of Catskill with Kevin Rooney. Then, about a month before the fight, they would move more into the spotlight, shifting their base of operations to Las Vegas where he could become acclimated to the desert conditions and where, although it did not please Tyson, the media would have easier access to both him, and Berbick as well.

Away from that spotlight, yet with Tyson every day in the weeks leading up to the fight was a member of his entourage somewhat unique to the training camp of a fighter. His name is John Halpin. He remained quietly in the background, out of reach to the curious and inquiring press, which is always looking for a story or an "angle." John Halpin, nevertheless, had been with Mike Tyson since his very first fight as a professional, brought in by Cus D'Amato, who had been using Halpin's expertise for his fighters for nearly twenty years. John Halpin is a hypnotherapist. From his office on West 72nd Street in Manhattan, just off Central Park West, Halpin spent most of his time working with patients who used his services to help them lose weight or quit smoking through hypnotic suggestion. D'Amato believed in the value of hypnosis to help his fighters more quickly overcome doubts, fears and lack of confidence. He would often bring boys down from Catskill, three or four at a time, to have Halpin work with them in his office. Along with D'Amato's fighters, D'Amato disciples such as Joey Fariello and Teddy Atlas have brought their boxers to Halpin as well, and he has worked with Canada's Hilton brothers, heavyweight Art Tucker, Canadian champion Donny Poole, light-heavyweight champion Donny Lalonde and welterweight champion Mark Breland.

Hypnosis is as old as recorded time, dating back to the "sleep temples" of ancient Egypt, where women went to give birth after being placed in hypnotic trances. But hypnosis has suffered from a lack of understanding by those unfamiliar with its sound therapeutic foundation, in large part due to the false image presented in the Boris Karloff genre of

Hollywood horror and melodrama films in the 1930s and 40s. There is really nothing mysterious, supernatural or occult about hypnotism. It is simply a means of placing a subject in an altered state, resembling sleep but not really sleep. Under hypnosis, an individual's awareness can be dealt with on a subconscious level, usually more effectively than when the subject is conscious, because in a hypnotic state the subject is focused and free from distraction. Hypnotism is actually an effective and perfectly plausible means of achieving certain theraputic results, although it has also failed often enough so that it has not gained universal scientific and medical acceptance.

John Halpin has been a successful practitioner of hypnotherapy for years. A distinguished-looking man of middle age with a penchant for conservative gray suits, white shirts and tailored topcoats, with a clear and resonant speaking voice, he is quick to point out that "The person under hypnosis is not the pawn of the hypnotist. The person under hypnosis has his mind moved to a different, altered state, other than the active, conscious state. In that state, where he is so suggestible, he is not without his protections of self. He has his morals, his ethics, his principles, his understandings of legality"—meaning, basically, a person under hypnosis cannot be made to do anything he or she would not ordinarily do while fully conscious.

Halpin first worked with Tyson when D'Amato brought him down from Catskill to the hypnotist's Manhattan office when Mike was sixteen years old. But his regular work with Mike began when Tyson turned pro in 1985. Except for a few of the easy fights, Halpin has worked with Mike for every important fight along the way. "Cus believed in the hypnotist's ability to reinforce the lessons of the trainer. . . . Usually a man is brought to me who does have great basic mechanics but has fears that are overwhelming and are handicapping him. Unless a man has the mechanics, I can't help him. I can [only] help him overcome his psychological obstacles so that he can develop the mechanics much more quickly," says Halpin.

D'Amato would often be present at the sessions, and when Halpin had Tyson under hypnosis he would get D'Amato to talk directly to the fighter, to reassure him that whatever doubts he had were unfounded. "You have a wonderful right hand," he would say. "You haven't believed in it, but now you're going to."

Now, as the fight approached, Halpin was constantly working with Tyson, as often as twice a day. His procedure was always the same. He would get Mike in a relaxed, comfortable position, lying on a bed or perhaps on the floor. He would then place him under hypnosis and proceed to talk to him about his fears, about how his doubts and concerns were unfounded, emphasizing how good, how talented he was, perhaps talking him through how he was going to perform in the fight. After the session, he would generally leave Mike in a deep sleep, telling him how refreshed he was going to feel when he awoke.

"Every fighter has fear. That's part of the reason why I see a fighter a lot in the weeks before a fight. I want to work with him two times a day for four or five days while he's in training. Then I want to work with him four or five days right before the fight. The reason for all of my activity on that level is because of the incredible emotional level a fighter experiences even two weeks before the fight, then a week before the fight, then the days leading up to the fight, whether he knows it or not. He can be walking around in a daze. It may not hit him as a big, fearful emotion, but rather as an underlying uneasiness, and that's why he needs me. It is ever-building toward the climax. It isn't on an even keel." That is why, Halpin says, it requires more intense work as the fight draws closer. He has worked with inducing a hypnotic trance in Tyson as close as two hours before a fight, but he is quick to point out that Mike never fights while under hypnosis. At fight time, Halpin would be in his seat at ringside, near Cayton and Jacobs. Like the managers, once it is fight time, he can do nothing. Their jobs are done, and all they can do is watch. The only difference is that Jacobs and Cayton are known, are recognized, are greeted, interviewed, photographed. John Halpin remains anonymous. The public watches the invincible Mike Tyson, unaware that a hypnotist has been constantly at his side helping him to prepare for his fights. It's one of the things Jacobs and Cayton did not make public, feeling, perhaps, that it had no part in the Tyson myth.

*   *   *

As November 22 drew near, opinion was divided. Many were giving Berbick a good chance to beat Tyson, reasoning that Berbick was durable; he had gone fifteen tough rounds with Larry Holmes; he had the edge in experience, and was used to the pressure; he'd been in big fights besides Holmes— his KO of Tate, his win over Ali, his title victory against Pinklon Thomas, all proved he could stand up to the pressure of a big fight, he had the stamina and mental toughness to go the distance. Tyson had fought nobodies or over-the-hill fighters. The two best fighters he'd fought, Green and Tillis, had extended him the full distance and had negated the power with which he had dominated lesser fighters. Berbick had an awkward style that could keep Tyson off balance, frustrate him and perhaps take away his punching power. This was going to be Tyson's toughest test, with the new and added pressure of a championship fight weighing heavily on his mind.

The flighty Berbick made one strategic move not to his advantage. When he had defeated Pinklon Thomas and won the title eight months earlier, he had had the great trainer Eddie Futch, considered a master, working with him and making him toe the line. Berbick needed this, since he had proved to be an in-and-out fighter, depending on where his mind was. He had shown well in losing to Holmes, he had beaten Tate, Ali, Greg Page and Thomas in an upset for the title, but he had lost decisions to Renaldo Snipes, a good and unorthodox heavyweight, and to S.T. Gordon, a cruiserweight, and had been knocked out by hard-punching but mediocre Bernardo Mercado. Now, in the most important fight of his life, his biggest payday (he was getting $2.1 million to fight Tyson and would be a star with more million-dollar purses on the horizon if he could beat him), he stubbornly refused to come to a financial agreement with Futch and so did not have the venerable trainer with him as he prepared for Tyson. Although he brought in another top trainer, Angelo Dundee, he did so only two and a half weeks before the fight, and so Dundee's contribution was severely limited by time.

Futch, now an impartial outside observer, told *Sports Illustrated:* "Tyson has wonderful attacking abilities. His hands are tremendously fast for a man with that kind of upper body and he can really punch with either hand. God, he can punch. His right uppercut especially will take your head off. But so far he has had a big psychological edge. He has intimidated his opponents, made them freeze and wait to be slaughtered. I think you have to go to him, back him up, never let him take you into the corners or onto the ropes, keep him in the middle of the ring where you can use mobility against him. I believe Berbick has the nerve and the equipment to make a good attempt at all that, to have a real chance of pulling it off. But Trevor is never sure to be the same fighter twice in a row. You never know how he will be."

Dundee talked up his man, saying Tyson was only a kid about to fight the most important fight of his life against the best heavyweight he'd met in his career. "Berbick has the style to do a number on him. . . . Tyson won't find Berbick running, like all those guys he's been knocking over." Dundee predicted Berbick would stop Tyson late in the fight. Jacobs simply said he had no worries: "Mike Tyson is the best heavyweight in the world, and he is about to prove it." Tyson volunteered that while he did not think D'Amato would be there in the ring with him, he would go into the fight taking with him everything he had been taught by his late mentor.

Tyson's routine in Las Vegas was laid back. He lived in a private house with his small entourage, which included trainer Kevin Rooney and assistant manager Steve Lott. The house belonged to a friend of Jim Jacobs. In it, Mike could keep himself isolated from the press and the public, both of which he found irksome.

His days began with roadwork early in the morning. In the afternoon, he trained in closed sessions at Johnny Tocco's Gym. The rest of the time, apart from sessions with his hypnotherapist, he spent relaxing, killing time by watching television and video cassettes, preferably cartoons and kung fu movies. Steve Lott, Tyson's assistant manager, had the most difficult job in camp. It was up to him to see that everything functioned smoothly, that Mike had all his creature comforts taken care of, that he had all the training equipment he needed, that he got to his training sessions and anywhere else he needed to be, that press interviews were duly scheduled, that good sparring partners were hired, that plane reservations, accommodations and meals were properly arranged, and that whatever Mike needed or wanted in order to keep him happy and focus his mind on preparing for the fight, free of worries, was done. His was the least noticed, yet the most taxing job in camp. Jacobs and Cayton arrived a week before fight time, but Lott was there right through, from beginning to end, coping in a professional manner with the vagaries of Tyson's childish and often nasty mood swings.

Berbick, a native of Jamaica, spent part of his time off in Las Vegas at the Moments of Miracles Church. An ordained minister who described himself as a "soldier of the cross," Berbick would preach the gospel there in his lilting island accent. Another part of his time off from his training was spent in responding to legal depositions just when he did not need such a distraction. Five days before the fight he was in court, being sued by a Texas promoter named Tom Prendergast who claimed that Berbick (and heavyweight Randy "Tex" Cobb) had pulled out of a fight show he was promoting four years earlier. Possibly due to the emotional overload of the forthcoming fight and his legal entanglements, Berbick experienced some respiratory problems the day after his court appearance and ran around town all day going to doctors trying to get medicine that would alleviate his condition. His quest was made more difficult because of the necessity of obtaining a medicine that the Nevada Boxing Commission would allow him to have in his system when he fought. Berbick's mental state must have been further adversely affected two days before the fight when he learned that the district court judge had attached his purse to the tune of nearly half a million dollars until the lawsuit with Prendergast was resolved at some future date.

On fight night, Tyson was the 3 to 1 favorite on the betting boards. While still pretty strong odds, they were down considerably from their original high of 6 to 1 for the challenger. Tyson would be earning his largest purse to date, a million and a half dollars. The celebrities were out in force at ringside. From Hollywood there was Kirk Douglas, Eddie Murphy, Tony Danza, Rob Lowe, Sylvester Stallone. The world of boxing was represented by Hector Camacho, Tommy Hearns, Archie Moore, and heavyweight champions Michael Spinks, Larry Holmes and Muhammad Ali. All were there, fenced off in the $1,000-a-seat VIP section, to witness, as one of the TV commentators put it, "a corona-tion." Berbick wore the crown, but at 10:20 P.M. Eastern time, it was the crown prince, Mike Tyson, who made his way to the ring first, with Kevin Rooney leading the way. Tyson wore a terrycloth towel over his chest and shoulders. A hole had been cut in the middle of it so he could slip it over his head like a poncho, a concession to the chilly November night air of the desert, since he customarily entered robeless. Steve Lott and cut-man Matt Baranski followed Mike up the ring steps. Already in the ring were a host of officials and the adversarial dynamic duo of Don King and Butch Lewis. (The only reason Lewis was involved in the Heavyweight Elimination Tournament was because he controlled Michael Spinks, and Spinks's participation was necessary to make it a true attempt at unifying the title. To King, Lewis was simply a thorn in his side.) Meanwhile, Tyson moved around, getting the feel of the ring.

Moments later, Dundee brought the champion into the ring. The crowd was amazingly silent and indifferent. There was no cheering for Berbick, who was dressed all in black, including a black satin robe with a hood that covered his head. Also with Berbick was his nominal manager, Carl King, the promoter's son. Both fighters wore black trunks, different only in that Berbick's carried the symbol of his religion, a small red cross. Traditionally, the champion has the choice of trunks. Knowing Tyson always wears black, Dundee had Berbick wear black. Under the rules, Tyson was obliged to select a different color. Instead, he opted for his customary black. It cost him a $5,000 fine from the Nevada Athletic Commission, but that mattered little to Jacobs and Cayton. Mike had worn black prior to this fight, and he would wear black this night as well, fine or no fine. Berbick, variously stated to be thirty-two, thirty-three or thirty-four years old, had weighed in at 218 pounds. At 6'2½" he was half a head taller than Tyson, who claimed to be 5'11½" but looked closer to 5'10". After giving both men their instructions in the center of the ring, Mills Lane, a veteran Nevada referee who had handled many world title fights, uttered his traditional "Let's get it on," to both men. They returned to their corners. Dundee reminded Berbick not to get in a slugging match with Tyson. "Box him, move side to side," were his final words, while across the ring, in what had become an odd tradition in the Tyson corner, Mike and Rooney kissed on the lips. Kevin then hugged him, and the bell rang.

Tyson moved out fast, bobbing. Both men were tight, and a right by Berbick drove a slightly off-balance Tyson back. Tyson answered with a left hook that landed. Berbick was trying to keep the young bull off him, but Tyson kept coming forward. Berbick threw a quick flurry of half a dozen punches, digging an uppercut to Tyson's body. A right and left by Tyson landed solidly to Berbick's head and then, 1:15 into the round, Tyson was on target with a clubbing right to Berbick's skull. The fighters clinched, Berbick holding on to clear his head. When they broke, Tyson shot a left hook to Berbick's jaw. They then fought on the inside, but with just under thirty seconds left in the first round, a quick right-left-right-left combination by Tyson sent Berbick stumbling backward. He was groggy and hurt. A final left hand shortly before the bell sent Berbick back to his corner stunned, although, in a show of bravado, he stuck his chin out in the direction of Tyson's corner as he made his way back to his stool.

Dundee was more agitated than he usually had reason to be after just one round, screaming at his cornermen for the sponge, then spending what remained of the one minute rest trying to revive and advise his champion, who was in serious trouble. In Tyson's corner, Rooney was calm. "You're head hunting," he told Mike. "Use the jab, stay calm. Body shots first, then the head." The bell sounded for round two, Berbick's last as a world champion.

Just seconds after the bell, a big right to Berbick's head rocked him back on his heels, and he stumbled off balance. Two more rights followed, and Berbick was down, just eight seconds into the round. He jumped to his feet immediately, but his legs were unsteady. A left-right combination by Tyson forced him to hold, and he spent most of the next minute clinching and holding, trying to regroup his senses and figure out a battle plan to counteract this relentless young warrior, the likes of which he had never encountered before. Halfway through the round, Tyson buried a right hand to the champion's ribs, then shot a right to his jaw and a clubbing, hurting right hand to his head, forcing Berbick once again to grab the smaller man he had boldly said would not beat him. Lying on Berbick's chest, Tyson blasted his opponent's body with a right, then bounced a short left hook to the top of his head. The force of that punch rearranged Berbick's equilibrium in a way that most viewers had never before seen. The champion toppled onto his back like a tree. At the count of three, he tried to get up, but stumbled on ankles that bent like rubber tubes, and tumbled back down, for a second time, into the lower strand of ropes. Again he tried to rise, and did make it to his feet momentarily, but the liquids in his inner ear must have been swirling like a whirlpool, and his legs would not—could not—follow the commands his brain was issuing. He buckled at the knees and stumbled forward, across the ring, falling and rolling over on his back. It was the third time he had hit the canvas in less than ten seconds, all from the pulverizing force of just one punch. Those who witnessed it will never forget the sight of Berbick stumbling helplessly out of control around the ring. By sheer force of will, he managed to rise at the count of nine, but Mills Lane was there to referee a fight, not be party to a murder, and so he wisely draped his arms around Berbick's neck to help support and steady the big man from Jamaica, and waved the evening's proceedings over. At 2:35 seconds into the second round, Mike Tyson had become the new—and youngest—heavyweight champion of the world. Mike raised a gloved fist and pointed out into the crowd, then shrugged his shoulders as if to say, "No fuss, no bother. I did what I came here to do. End of story." Tyson, as he had seen Jack Dempsey and others do in the hours of films he had watched over the years, went to help Berbick back to his corner, a courtesy to the fallen ex-champion. Jimmy Jacobs entered the ring, and Mike kissed him. Also there, inexplicably, was Jose Torres, who blatantly disregarded the impartiality he was duty-bound to exercise as chairman of the New York State Athletic Commission and openly rooted for Tyson at all his fights. Now, he was here in Las Vegas to see "his fighter" crowned champion, and he was in the ring as a member of Tyson's entourage. Tyson posed for the ringside photographers while Berbick sat on his stool, being checked by the ringside physician. The new champion was flanked by Rooney and Lott and Jacobs, and, of course, a beaming Don King. The goal had been achieved, but at what price.

For now Don King was in the picture. The octopus of the boxing world had been, of necessity, permitted to wind his tentacles gently around Mike Tyson, and when events less than a year and a half later afforded him the opportunity he was waiting for, King would tighten those tentacles around the most valuable athlete in the world until his grip could not be loosened.

His victory achieved, Tyson opened the floodgates of emotion as he talked with reporters. "This is the moment I waited for all my life since I started boxing. . . . Berbick was very strong . . . I never expected him to be as strong as me . . . every punch I threw with bad intentions to a vital area . . . I aimed for his ear . . . I wanted to bust his eardrum . . . Every punch had bad intentions. . . . My record will last for immortality, it'll never be broken . . . I want to live forever . . . I refused to lose . . . I would have had to be carried out dead to lose . . . I was coming to destroy and win the Heavyweight Championship of the World, which I done. . . . I'd like to dedicate my fight to my great guardian Cus D'Amato. I'm sure he's up there and he's looking down and he's talking to all the great fighters and he's saying his boy did it . . . I thought he was a crazy white dude . . . he was a genius . . . everything he said would happen happened."

The comments and observations from the opposing side were more restrained. Berbick acknowledged he'd made a "silly mistake" by trying to punch with Tyson. "I tried to prove my manhood," he said. However, Angelo Dundee expressed awe: "He [Tyson] throws combinations I never saw before. I was stunned. Nothing is supposed to bother me. I've worked with Ali and Sugar Ray Leonard, but I'm seeing [from Tyson] a three-punch combination second to none. When have you seen a guy throw a right hand to the kidney, come up the middle with an uppercut, then throw a left hook?"

What amazed many who were seeing Tyson for the first time was his remarkable defensive ability. The impression given by reports of his exploits in the ring was that he was a slugger and nothing else. In reality, he has tremendous defensive skills every bit as good as his power of attack. It is extremely difficult to hit Mike Tyson with a clean shot. "From thirteen to eighteen," Jim Jacobs said, "Mike was taught by Cus D'Amato that the object was not to get hit. He learned nothing but how to avoid getting hit." Jacobs explained that because of his height and reach disadvantages, Mike had to expose himself to potential danger by getting closer to his opponents in order to land his shots. Therefore, "when he fights, he gets down in a crouch. People have to punch down, which makes their punches ineffective."

Mike Tyson was the heavyweight champion of the world (at least according to the WBC), and a full-fledged millionaire. No matinee idol when it came to looks, uneducated and unread, for the most part unpolished and uncomfortable in the presence of others, Tyson nevertheless, owing to his new-found fame and fortune, suddenly had access to the attractive and desirable women with whom he had always been obsessed, but who, until now, had not been available to him. The world was at his feet. The task ahead of him in the ring was to unify the Heavyweight Championship in the coming year of 1987 and become the first undisputed heavyweight champion in nearly a decade.

Chapter 9

Unification . . . and Robin Givens

Boxing is much more a battle of wills than of skills. Given fighters with equal skills, the one with the stronger will inevitably wins.

—Cus D'Amato

Three weeks after Tyson took the WBC crown, the stage was set for the next fight in the Unification Tournament. The scene shifted to Madison Square Garden, where, on December 5, 1986, Tim Witherspoon was scheduled to defend his WBA title against Tony Tubbs. But Tubbs withdrew from the bout, claiming an injured shoulder, and King, against the will of Witherspoon whom he controlled, forced the WBA champion to accept James "Bonecrusher" Smith as a substitute opponent. (More on the questionable circum-King later.) Witherspoon had previously defeated Smith and did not want to fight him again at such short notice because he had prepared physically and psychologically to do battle with Tubbs. But Witherspoon had nowhere to turn. When disputing with a promoter, a fighter usually has the backing of his manager. In this case, Witherspoon's promoter was Don King and his manager was Carl King, Don King's son. With no one, including the New York State Athletic Commission, willing to take his side, Witherspoon had no choice to capitulate. The fight was postponed one week, and reset for the night of December 12 at the Garden.

"Bonecrusher" Smith got his chance of a lifetime for two reasons. First, he was actually in training to fight Mitch Green for a $35,000 purse, so he had the advantage of being ready and in shape and did possess the requisite top-ten ranking, which qualified him for a title fight. But most important, Smith got the fight because he and his manager, Alan Kornberg, were willing to do "business" with Don King. In other words, to no one's surprise, it was announced shortly before Smith was signed to meet Witherspoon that Smith had signed over 50 percent of his contract to the promoter's son. Presto! Smith had the title shot and a $230,000 purse. On the night of the fight, there was an audience of barely 5,000, leaving 17,000 empty seats. After all, it was winter; fans could stay at home and see the fight for free if they subscribed to the HBO cable-TV service. In any case, who cared about Tim Witherspoon vs. "Bonecrusher" Smith? Whether there were 5,000 or 500 or 50,000 people present didn't matter one jot to Smith. He was earning a lot more money than he would have received fighting Mitch Green in Fayetteville, North Carolina, and he had the chance to win the world title. He made the most of it. He went out at the opening bell and took his best shots, and they landed. Witherspoon, his mind distracted by his dispute with the Kings, was a listless and uninterested participant. Unfortunately for him, his title was on the line. Smith blasted Witherspoon with right hand bombs to the head. Witherspoon was knocked down four times in less than three minutes, and, having struck like lightning, "Bonecrusher" Smith was the new WBA heavyweight champion of the world at the advanced age of thirty-three, with his next fight a WBC-WBA unification bout against Mike Tyson with a million-dollar purse.

The Kings were in a no-lose situation in this fight, since they controlled not only Witherspoon, but now Smith as well. They were winners no matter who won. The only loser was Witherspoon. He was fed up with the games he said the Kings had played with his purse monies over the years. "I been heavyweight champion of the world twice, and I live in an apartment in Philadelphia I'd be embarrassed for you to see. I got nothing to show for it," he told a friend from the media just after the fight with Smith. He then handed the same person a souvenir of the fight that had ended less than an hour ago. It was one of his front teeth, complete with root, that had been knocked out by one of Smith's punches. Witherspoon, his trainer, "Slim" Jim Robinson, and his small group of friends and family then stepped on to the Garden's service elevator, rode downstairs to the street level, and stepped out into the cold night.

*　　*　　*

What nearly everyone hoped for was that Tyson and Spinks would eventually meet in the final bout of the tournament. Spinks had name value, as well as a legitimate claim to the title since he had won it from Holmes. While Tyson was next to meet Smith, Spinks was due to meet the IBF's number one contender, Tony Tucker. It was here, in the early weeks of 1987, that the Unification Tournament went topsy-turvy. Butch Lewis, Spinks's promoter and de facto manager, decided that instead of making the mandatory defense against Tucker, which would have been televised by HBO as part of the tournament, he would take Spinks out of the tournament for a more lucrative and possibly safer match against the unranked Gerry Cooney who was making a comeback. Lewis maintained his contract allowed him to take his fighter out of the tournament for one bout and then rejoin it. He might have negotiated a financial settlement with Tucker and his people to step aside temporarily from their mandatory fight with Spinks, but Tucker demanded a ridiculously huge amount of money and they were unable to work out an agreement. Lewis still felt that Bob Lee, president of the IBF, could grant Spinks an extension on his obligation to fight Tucker. However, Lee refused; and when Lewis went ahead with his arrangements for Spinks to meet Cooney in June, Lee directed the IBF to strip Spinks of his IBF heavyweight title. Spinks would now earn $4 million in the fight against Cooney, but he was out of the Elimination Tournament and no longer held any official recognition as champion. This would eventually bring Spinks and Lewis a financial windfall far beyond what they might have earned had they remained in the tournament. It would also bring down on Lewis's head several lawsuits that would be contested through 1989, as well as the wrath of HBO, King, and Jacobs and Cayton. By lifting his fighter out of the tournament, it seemed that Lewis was taking a tremendous amount of glamour and prestige away from it and losing the hoped-for Tyson-Spinks showdown for the undisputed title in 1987.

The fight to unify two-thirds of the title was set for March 7, 1987, at the Las Vegas Hilton. While the IBF maneuvered to arrange a fight to fill its vacant title, Mike Tyson and "Bonecrusher" Smith would face off with two title belts at stake. Smith was a 7 to 1 underdog in the posted odds, but it mattered little to him, for overcoming odds had become a way of life to this most unlikely of heavyweight champions. He was born, and still lived, in the small town of Magnolia, North Carolina. His parents were poor sharecroppers who believed that education would provide the road out of the fields for their children. Smith's younger sister became a doctor, while he himself graduated in business administration. When he upset Witherspoon to win the WBA crown, he became the first and only college graduate in boxing history to win the Heavyweight Championship.

Smith never laced on a boxing glove until he was serving a hitch in the military and did not have a pro fight until the age of twenty-eight, when, in 1981, ill-prepared, facing an experienced fighter, he was knocked out by James Broad in four rounds. Ready to quit, Smith reconsidered, put together a string of victories and, after joining up with manager Kornberg, took on the respected trainer and former world champion Emile Griffith who taught him how to refine his style. Ready to face Tyson, Smith had compiled an unimpressive record of 19-5 in his five-year pro career. On May 13, 1984, trailing on the scorecards in London, he came back with his great equalizer, his knockout punch, to stop Frank Bruno. That same year he fought Larry Holmes for the heavyweight title. He was stopped by Holmes in the twelfth round of a fifteen-round fight. He lost a decision to Witherspoon; then, in 1986, he knocked out ex-WBA heavyweight Champion, Mike Weaver, in one round.

His fight with Tyson was a major disappointment. Instead of taking his best shot and going for broke, Smith played it cautiously. He was in there to survive, to avoid being knocked out. It was twelve rounds of driving a standard-shift car—clutch, clutch, clutch all night. Smith spent the evening grabbing and holding. Tyson did nothing to overcome Smith's survival tactics. He allowed himself to be grabbed and held, did not fight his way out of the clinches and did not punch inside to Smith's body when he was being held. While Smith was intent on survival, Tyson was lackluster. There was no sign of the hand speed, the devastating body punches, the combinations to the head. Tyson plodded through the twelve rounds, building up points on his attempts at aggression and for the punches he was able to land, which was more than Smith was doing. Actually, the best punch of the fight was thrown by Smith. It momentarily stunned Tyson, but unfortunately for those spectators struggling to stay awake during the forty-eight boring minutes the fight lasted, the punch came in the final ten seconds of the last round, when it was too late to make a difference. Tyson was declared the winner on a unanimous decision, the scores being 120-106, 119-107, 119-107 (the maximum each judge could award Tyson was 120) but his reputation had suffered. He did not look invincible. Jacobs put the blame on Smith for fighting the way he did and making Tyson look bad. To punish the "Bonecrusher," Jacobs had him banned from a subsequent Tyson undercard, telling Don King that he had damaged Tyson's ring reputation and so he did not want him appearing in the future on any Tyson cards.

Mike Tyson was now the heavyweight champion of the world, recognized by the WBA and the WBC. As a matter of fact, with the IBF title vacant, he was the only heavyweight champion. He had the trappings of success: an apartment in an exclusive building on Manhattan's chic East Side, the same building in which Jim Jacobs, assistant manager Steve Lott, and British promoter Mickey Duff lived; a bachelor pad in Albany, near Catskill; gold and diamond jewelry galore; more automobiles than he needed, including a Rolls-Royce, Jaguar, Corvette and Mercedes-Benz. He was also bored. Winning the title wasn't the thrill he had thought it would be. "I was happy to win the title," he said early in 1987, "but it wasn't a big anything because I knew I was going to win the championship as soon as I stepped in the ring." He described himself as "moody" and "grumpy." He didn't like too many people around him and was ill at ease in public. Whereas Larry Holmes stood joking with fans and admirers, signing autographs while attending a fight one night at Madison Square Garden, Tyson, in a ringside seat, began to take on the look of a caged animal when people approached him to say hello or shake his hand. Finally, he broke off a conversation with a friend and retreated to the shelter of the ringside press area, which was fenced in and beyond the reach of the public. Holmes continued to accommodate every autograph request he was presented with. Muhammed Ali has always, at least until his health began to fail, been equally accessible. Mike Tyson had not learned, and still has not, that fame and publicity entail certain responsibilities and duties.

Though saying he was reasonably content, Tyson was at loose ends. He suddenly had fame and wealth, but had never had the time, education or grooming to develop a sense of values or indeed any interests beyond watching mindless action films and satisfying himself with as many women as he could. He had always had problems relating to women; once, he had lamented to Cus that girls wouldn't pay any attention to him, wouldn't talk to him, much less go out with him. He was depressed and felt no girl would ever be interested in him. D'Amato had then gone into town and bought a baseball bat. Returning home, he gave the bat to Mike, saying it was a present. "Save the bat," he said. "Someday, when you're the heavyweight champion and you're rich, you're going to need it to beat away all the women who'll want to be with you then." Now he was the champion, and the women, indeed, were there. Mike's obsession was to have beautiful women, women recognized by the public, high profile women whom the world would see at his side, and who would make him the envy of the world. His goal was to marry a beautiful woman. He fantasized about the singer Whitney Houston. He became obsessed with the TV actress Lisa Bonet, then co-starring in "The Cosby Show," once remarking, half-jokingly, that he would give up all he had if only he could meet her. Finally, he zeroed-in on a then little-known TV actress and made conquering her his goal. Her name was Robin Givens.

Givens was part of an an ensemble cast of the ABC-TV sitcom, "Head of the Class." Tyson spotted her and was irresistibly attracted by this light-complexioned black woman a year older than himself, with her high cheekbones, pouting lips, long, flowing hair, and petite figure. He managed to arrange a meeting with her early in 1987. It took place at a Los Angeles restaurant. Mike was somewhat surprised when Robin arrived with an entourage that included her mother, her publicist and several other people. It was a portent of things to come.

Tyson and Givens began a roller-coaster relationship. Robin played hard-to-get until she could twist Tyson around her little finger. After a while, Mike didn't know if he was coming or going. The couple presented an incongruous picture. Tyson was huge, massive, hulking. Givens was small and delicate. Tyson was rough, unpolished, crude, from the streets. Givens was refined, well-spoken, educated. Tyson shunned the limelight, Givens relished it, lived for it. But each had what the other wanted. For Tyson, Givens represented everything that had been missing from his life—beauty, refinement, education. For Givens, Tyson was the means to get what she desired—fame, wealth, a ticket out of the ensemble casts and on, perhaps, to stardom. Robin Givens was an ambitious girl, with an even more ambitious mother behind her, pushing. Mike Tyson could be their passport to the big time.

When Mike arrived for the press conference to announce his title defense against former heavyweight champion Pinklon Thomas, Robin was in tow. No one in the media really knew who she was then, but it was obvious Mike was anxious to show her off. Press conferences were the bane of Mike's existence. He hated attending them, answering questions, sitting on the dais listening to Don King and Las Vegas hotel executives and closed-circuit TV entrepreneurs drone on and on. Often, Jim Jacobs had to implore Mike to attend, apprehensively urging on him the necessity of participating in these media circuses. Mike wanted to get in the ring. That he enjoyed. That he looked forward to with relish. That gave him pleasure. Attending news conferences did not. His usual demeanor was that of a bored child. He would either be fingering some trinket or reading a boxing magazine someone had handed him, totally ignoring the proceedings, or else he would fix his gaze on the ceiling. Often he would lean over and rest his head on Jim Jacobs's shoulder and close his eyes, or put his head down on his arms on the table in front of him, as if by shutting his eyes he could shut out all that was going on around him and make it disappear. All this in full view of several hundred boxing and media people, not to mention those on the dais whose combined efforts were going to pay him $3- or $8- or $10- or $22 million. Certainly they had the right to expect at least some interest on Mike's part, but that was never forthcoming. He felt they would get their money's worth from him when he stepped into the ring, and as far as he was concerned, that was all he owed them. Mike was also conspicuous by his lack of sartorial elegance. He would inevitably arrive in a sweatsuit, or rumpled slacks and a T-shirt of some sort, or jeans and a wool training-sweater. Invariably, he would look as though he had just came from a gym workout or had just fallen out of bed, while everyone else was dressed as befitted the formality of the occasion, the setting for which was usually a posh Manhattan hotel. Basically, Mike didn't give a damn. But now, with Robin, he had a new interest that sparked his enthusiasm. He wanted everyone to see her, to see him with her. The media, looking for new stories, jumped on it. The day after the news conference, the stories were full of Mike's new girlfriend, along with photos of Robin Givens, the Hollywood starlet.

Mike's first defense of his WBA-WBC titles was set for May 30, 1987, back at the Las Vegas Hilton. It would be a double-header. On that same night, the IBF would fill its vacant Heavyweight Championship so that the tournament could proceed later in the summer with its concluding unification bout. Pinklon Thomas was regarded by many as a tough, solid test for Tyson, although some boxing insiders believed that Thomas had had a relapse of a drug problem and that he was essentially a shot fighter and no real challenge for Tyson. Regardless, Mike had to show well against Thomas if he was to restore the damage done to his reputation by his lackluster performance against "Bonecrusher" Smith. "Bottom line, people pay to see Mike knock someone out," said Jacobs, and that was the truth. Angelo Dundee was training Thomas. The twenty-nine-year-old former champion was a big heavyweight at 6′3″. Despite the skills he possessed—or, perhaps, had once possessed—he was a 5 to 1 underdog, which was especially remarkable considering that he had an outstanding record of 29-1-1 with twenty-four KO's and was ranked number 1 by the WBC.

In the first of the evening's two main events, Tony Tucker, whom Michael Spinks had ducked in order to fight Gerry Cooney, won the vacant IBF Championship by knocking out James "Buster" Douglas in the tenth round. Tucker improved his record to 35-0 with twenty-nine KO's and moved into line for the finals of the Unification Tournament.

Next into the ring came Pinklon Thomas, followed moments later by Tyson. When the bell rang, Mike went right at him. In the final minute of the round, Tyson connected solidly with a left to Thomas's jaw, followed it with a right to the same spot, and Thomas sagged backward into the ropes. He was hurt, and Tyson followed up with another right and left to the jaw. At ringside, once again abandoning any appearance of impartiality, Jose Torres jumped to his feet, cupped his hands around his mouth, and shouted instructions to Tyson, calling out "five-six, five-six," D'Amato's number combinations, to the young champion. Thomas was in serious trouble, but managed to land a right hand to Tyson's head in the closing seconds and survived the round.

Back in the corner, Dundee worked furiously to revive his man. The ringside physician came up to the corner to check Thomas and see if he was badly damaged. Dundee, who had seen Berbick destroyed by Tyson six months earlier and was now experiencing déjà vu with Thomas, let rip a torrent of misplaced aggression at the doctor. "Leave him the fuck alone, get the fuck away from him," Dundee screamed, utterly frustrated at the inability of his warrior to stop the relentless onslaught of the twenty-year-old boxing monster.

Surprisingly, Thomas was able to pull himself together and began to land effective jabs, keeping Tyson a bit off balance and enabling the challenger to survive a bit longer. Basically, though, he was postponing the inevitable. At the end of round five, the customary one-minute rest was extended to two and a half minutes while a torn glove was replaced on Thomas. Veteran ringsiders chuckled. They remembered a similar incident involving Dundee in London twenty-five years earlier. A young Muhammed Ali, a.k.a. Cassius Clay, was fighting Henry Cooper. Ali, who had not yet won the Heavyweight Championship, was rolling along when suddenly Cooper landed a tremendous left hook flush on the brash young American's jaw. Ali went down hard on the seat of his pants. He was hurt badly; fortunately for him, the bell rang as he got up, saving him from a possible knockout. Dundee worked furiously over Ali, when he suddenly noticed a small split along the seam of one of his gloves—and as Dundee admits in his autobiography—stuck his finger in the split, "helping it along." It had taken several minutes to find another glove, remove the torn one, lace it up and tape it around Ali's hand. By that time, Ali had rested and recovered all his scrambled senses. The deliciously devious strategy worked. Ali came back to TKO

Cooper on cuts. Now, in Thomas's corner, history seemed to be repeating itself.

Meanwhile, in Tyson's corner, the extra rest was also giving the champion time to regain his strength. Rooney told him it was time to "start throwing punches with mean intentions." When the sixth round started, that's what Tyson did. A left drove Thomas back. As soon as Tyson saw he had staggered the ex-champion, he closed in for the kill. He fired hurting punches like a machine gun, sixteen unanswered shots to the head, finishing with a pulverizing left to Thomas's forehead and a left hook flush on the side of the face that shook Pinklon like a cannon ball and knocked him flat on his back. As Thomas struggled to his feet, attempting to beat the count, Angelo Dundee had seen enough. He jumped into the ring to rescue his fighter and spare him any more punishment. Pinklon Thomas had become victim number thirty for Mike Tyson.

The fight over with, Tyson turned his attention once again to his pursuit of Robin Givens. It blew hot and cold, as Robin turned the emotional taps on and off at will to control the flow of the affair with the emotionally immature and insecure young champion. Her mother was against the relationship. A willful woman, Ruth Roper had seen to it, by hook or by crook, that Robin and her sister went to the best schools, lived in the best neighborhoods, had the best clothes. And now she wanted the best husband for her daughter—a doctor or a lawyer, not a hardly reformed juvenile delinquent, ex-reform school inmate, high school dropout, ghetto-raised prizefighter.

Mike's next fight was to be on August 1, 1987. His opponent would be the IBF champion Tony Tucker, and the fight would be the culmination of the HBO Unification Tournament, all three titles on the line, the winner to be the undisputed heavyweight champion. The news conference to announce the fight was held in June in New York. A sullen and depressed Tyson turned up alone. The night before, Robin had broken up with him and given him back the diamond friendship ring he had given her. Now, waiting for the news conference with Tucker to start, he stood alone, fingering the ring. When a friend asked him what was wrong, he said, "I don't have a girlfriend anymore. Robin broke up with me. I was doggin' her a little bit because she wouldn't give me any pussy all this time. I kept askin' her, Robin, what's goin' on? So I dogged her a little bit, and she broke up with me." Givens was clever enough to realize that if she gave in too easily, she would just be another Tyson conquest, to be discarded, and that was not what she had in mind.

Several days later, on June 21, Tyson's rage and frustration boiled over. He was in Los Angeles, no doubt in pursuit of Robin. He attended a rap music show at the Greek Theatre in Hollywood. Afterward, in the parking lot, Tyson spotted an attractive female attendant. Without bothering to check whether his advances were welcome or not, he grabbed her around the waist, pulled her close to him and laughingly demanded a kiss. She began screaming at him to let go and leave her alone. A co-worker, twenty-year-old Jonathan Casares, seeing her struggling, gallantly but foolishly intervened. Tyson turned his rage on Casares, slapping him across the face several times, a slap from Mike Tyson being sufficient to rattle the average person's teeth. Tyson's friends stepped in and calmed him down, and the situation was defused. Jim Jacobs attempted to play the incident down, saying it was just a misunderstanding blown out of proportion. But this time the attempt to cover up another Tyson indiscretion and preserve the champion's "image" did not work. After conducting an inquiry, the Los Angeles City Attorney's office found sufficient grounds to file charges against Tyson. Early in July, the heavyweight champion of the world was charged with one count of assault with a deadly weapon (his fists) and one count of battery. Tyson was ordered to appear in court in late August to face the charges. He never did. The two parking lot attendants were bought off. For payments totaling $105,000, they withdrew their charges and Tyson's lucrative commercial marketability was not compromised by a court appearance.

Tyson and Robin were reconciled, and during a hiatus in the taping of her series she joined him in Catskill, where he had returned to begin training for the Tucker fight. But all was still not well. A friend, visiting one day, asked Mike how things were with Robin. He indicated that things weren't smooth because "her mother doesn't like me much." But even in the gym, he couldn't keep his hands off her. He would take her off to a quiet corner, lean against a wall, pull her to him, and kiss her passionately for several minutes.

Robin returned to Los Angeles to resume taping her series, and a lonely and lovesick champion continued his training in Catskill. About a month before the fight, he shifted his camp to Las Vegas, staying with Rooney and Steve Lott in the private house they customarily used to avoid the tumult and chaos and distractions at the Hilton. Tensions always built up inside Tyson in the weeks leading up to a fight until they literally got to breaking point. However, in Las Vegas, before the Tucker fight, he was especially tense, perhaps because of the turbulent state of his emotions over Robin's manipulation. This time, his temper kept exploding in confrontations with Rooney during his gym workouts in Vegas behind closed doors. In public, they kept up the facade of brotherly love, with Jacobs denying to the press there was any rift between the fighter and trainer.

Two weeks before the fight, when Mike's emotional and psychological state usually reached the lowest point, it happened. He disappeared, amid rumors that he was upset with Rooney. He turned up 2,500 miles away, in Albany, where he had an apartment. He was seen at a nightclub he sometimes frequented, a hangout for local drug dealers and users. He told friends there that he'd had it with boxing and that he was retiring. But bolting from camp was something Mike frequently did when the pressure got too much for him. After four days around Albany and Catskill, he was ready to return to Las Vegas and resume training.

On the night of August 1, both fighters weighed in at 221 pounds. That was the only similarity. Tucker, 6'5" and handsome, entered the ring in a dazzling robe of sparkling gold sequins trimmed in red over red Spartan trunks. Though he had fought in relative obscurity, his professional record was as sparkling as his robe—35 and 0. Tyson, by contrast, ever the gladiator, entered robeless in his customary black leather shoes with no socks and plain black trunks.

What no one knew was that Tucker was coming into the fight with a badly injured right hand, an injury sustained in training. His father, who managed him, foolishly kept the injury a secret instead of bringing it to the attention of the Nevada Athletic Commission physicians and requesting a postponement. In the first round, Tucker showed that he had come to fight. As Tyson charged in, a ripping left uppercut by Tucker caught him flush and sent him reeling backward, the hardest punch Tyson had received in his pro career. Tucker then bombarded him with rights to the head until the bell ended the round.

Watching the action from on high were two interested spectators, Butch Lewis and Michael Spinks. Since their withdrawal from the tournament and the stripping of the IBF crown from Spinks, he was no longer a recognized champion. But Lewis knew that down the line, although it was Tucker in the ring on this night defending the IBF title, the economics of the situation would dictate a meeting between his man and Tyson, and he was astute enough to keep Spinks's name and face in the public eye. Michael, he declared, was the "People's Champion," never defeated in the ring but stripped of his title by decree of a sanctioning organization. He therefore sat with his fighter where the common man was sitting, high in the bleachers in the cheapest $50 seats. In the months ahead, Lewis would proclaim loudly and often that Michael Spinks was the true champion who had followed the line of succession by defeating Larry Holmes and that Tyson had to prove himself by beating Spinks. By doing so, Lewis helped feed the flames and create the demand for a Tyson-Spinks showdown.

On this night, Lewis and Spinks were shown that Tyson was not invincible. Dancing, moving, boxing, holding, Tucker was able to bother Tyson enough to throw off his timing and render his power largely ineffective. Lateral movement, the observers said, would always be the key to beating Tyson eventually. Unfortunately for Tucker, one of the right hands he bounced off Tyson's skull early in the bout reinjured the hand, and after the fifth round he was reduced to fighting a battle of survival. Still, he was able to prevent Tyson from landing any effective combinations throughout most of the twelve rounds. Tyson fired hard jabs, then came in and banged to Tucker's body in the early rounds. Finding his range, he then slammed shots to Tucker's head, effectively building points on the scorecards of the three judges. In the twelfth round, Tyson banged a left hand off Tucker's head, sending a spray of sweat and water flying into the air, but

Tucker shook his head to say it didn't hurt (usually a sign that it did).

When the bell ended the bout, both men were on their feet. There had been no knockdowns and neither fighter had been in serious trouble. Tyson's relentless pressure and aggression, however, had made the difference. The scores were 119-111, 118-113, and 116-112, all in Tyson's favor. Via unanimous decision, Mike Tyson was now the undisputed heavyweight champion of the world. He had already fought four title bouts to defend and unify the championship, and at twenty-one years and one month, he was younger than Floyd Patterson had been when he had gone down in history as the youngest fighter to win the crown. Tyson earned $2.5 million for this bout (Tucker's purse had been just under $2 million), bringing his ring earnings to $14 million in just two and a half years as a professional, a remarkable tribute not only to his fighting skills, but perhaps even more to the way Jacobs and Cayton had marketed their fighter. And now the road to even greater riches lay before them, for now Tyson held universal recognition as the champion. The day following his victory, an embarrassed-looking Tyson was the focal point of a "coronation" ceremony only a Don King could stage. At the hotel, with boxing officials, press, hangers-on, and even Muhammad Ali on hand, Tyson, wrapped in a fur robe and with a jeweled scepter in his hand, was crowned the new "King of the Heavyweights."

For Tyson's next fight, his first defense of the undisputed title, the venue would change, thanks to the entrance on the scene of a new power in boxing, forty-one-year-old Donald Trump, hardly the type one would expect to find mixed up in a sport that Mike Tyson himself said attracts "scum." ("All my life," Tyson had once said, "I've been dealing with scum.") Now he would be dealing with a different player, one of America's youngest and wealthiest entrepreneurs, who would eventually make his own power play for control of the champion.

Donald John Trump is not the wealthiest billionaire in the United States. He's not even the youngest. He is, however, without a doubt, the best known and the most flamboyant.

Born in 1946 in the exclusive Jamaica Estates section of New York City, he was one of five children of Fred and Mary Trump. His father was a real estate developer who built 24,000 apartments in Brooklyn, Queens and Staten Island, amassing a fortune of $20 million. Having learned the hard realities of the real estate wars from his father, Donald then went out to see what he could do on his own.

In 1976, he persuaded the bankrupt Penn Central Railroad to sell him the aging and run-down Commodore Hotel on 42nd Street, adjoining Grand Central Terminal, for $10 million, as well as an option on their Hudson River railroad yards, a now prime piece of mid-Manhattan real estate which is currently the site of the showcase Javits Convention Center. With the option on the Commodore and using his father's powerful political and financial connections to smooth the way, he secured $80 million in loans and a $120 million tax abatement and set about renovating the Commodore. Not knowing much about hotels, he entered into partnership with the Hyatt Corporation, and in 1980 the old Commodore was reopened as the showplace Grand Hyatt Hotel with 1,347 rooms. Today it provides Trump with $30 million in profits annually. It was just his starting point.

In 1982, on Fifth Avenue, he built the skyscraper Trump Tower. Its lower floors house some of Manhattan's most exclusive and expensive shops, plus an atrium complete with an 80-foot waterfall and walls of pink marble. The apartments sold for upward of $4 million apiece to people like TV superstar Johnny Carson and film-maker Steven Spielberg. He sold out the condominiums for a total of $275 million.

Trump also owns numerous other hotels and properties in New York and Florida, including the landmark Plaza Hotel on Central Park South, together with one of the prime pieces of undeveloped real estate in the world, a 76-acre parcel stretching from 59th Street to 72nd Street along the Hudson River waterfront on Manhattan's West Side, where he plans to develop a $5-billion Trump City, a complex of luxury apartments, shops, restaurants and parks, and the world's tallest building.

His personal lifestyle is one of unimagined luxury. He dresses in $2,000 Brioni suits, $350 shirts and $100 ties. His wife, Ivana, a Czechoslovakian-born former Olympic skier and fashion model, purchases $1.5-million worth of clothing each year! He boasts that his private French Puma helicopter, capable of 180 mph speeds and with passenger space for ten, is used by the Queen of England when she visits the U.S. because of its speed and safety. For longer trips, Trump owns his own Boeing 727 jet. Several years ago, he picked up the crowning glory of his private holdings, the 282-foot long *Trump Princess* yacht, at a "bargain" $29 million from financially strapped international wheeler-dealer Adnan Khashoggi. Said to be the world's largest private ship, it contains 100 rooms, including eleven guest suites. The walls are covered in chamois leather, the baths done in gold and onyx.

On dry land, the Trumps and their three children divide their time between three homes: a forty-five-room estate on ten acres in Greenwich, Connecticut; the 118-room Mar-a-Lago landmark estate in Palm Beach, Florida, set on 17 acres with its own golf course and 400 feet of private ocean beachfront (built in the 1920s for cereal heiress Marjorie Merriweather Post); and their main residence in Trump Tower, a 50–room triplex worth between $15 and $20 million, which has among its features an 80-foot-long living room which includes a 12-foot high onyx waterfall, hand-carved marble columns, pure goldleaf-covered ceiling moldings; a bathroom with a bathtub carved from lilac onyx, and ceilings adorned with hand-painted murals.

Trump has little free time, however, to enjoy the luxuries he has amassed. He is essentially a workaholic who doesn't particularly enjoy vacations and gets his true pleasure from his business dealings. To get the jump on his competitors, he sleeps just four hours a night and is already up, planning his deals, at 4:00 A.M. Ten law firms handle his business affairs. In the 1980s he challenged the supremacy of the National Football League by helping to organize the United States Football League and luring top college prospects to sign with his team, the New Jersey Generals, with the offer of multimillion-dollar contracts. The NFL proved too big to take on, and the USFL eventually folded, but it provided an insight into Trump's fiercely competitive nature. In his spare time, Trump has dabbled in corporate raiding, moving to take over major companies, acquiring large blocks of their stock, then selling out at inflated prices. From 1986 to 1988 he earned "pocket change" profits of $137 million in this manner.

His wealth has been estimated at a low $1.3 billion by journalists on *Forbes* magazine (whom he calls "idiots"). *Business Week* puts his worth at just over $3 billion. *Fortune* magazine says it's just under $1.6 billion. Trump himself says it's all rubbish. "I know what I'm worth," he says, and puts his total net worth at $3.7 billion, including liquid cash assets of nearly $700 million, then candidly acknowledges, "Who the fuck really knows?"

So why would this fabulously wealthy and successful real estate entrepreneur become the world's unlikeliest boxing promoter? The answer lies in Trump's other holdings, those in the East Coast gambling capital of Atlantic City, New Jersey. Trump is a major player—probably *the* major player—in the Atlantic City casino sweepstakes. He owns two hotel casino complexes, Trump's Castle and the Trump Plaza, which provide him with a major source of his income, an estimated yearly profit of $100 million. In addition, in 1990, he will open the Taj Mahal, the world's largest hotel-casino complex, bigger than anything in Las Vegas, which will cost $750 million to complete.

Although Atlantic City had hosted many championship fights, all the major bouts for years had been co-opted by the casinos in Las Vegas. With his enormous holdings in Atlantic City, always looked upon as a shabby, poor cousin to the glitzy Las Vegas, Trump decided to turn the city's image around. One of the ways to do this, he decided, was to bring in the big fights. They would focus worldwide attention on Atlantic City, take the play away from Las Vegas and, not incidentally, ring up tremendously increased casino profits, as the high rollers, traditionally attracted by the glamour of the big fights, brought their money to Atlantic City instead of Vegas. Trump, who has said "I just keep pushing and pushing to get what I'm after. . . . I like beating my enemies to the ground," decided to take on Las Vegas and beat them at their own game. He did it the old-fashioned way. He opened his checkbook and outbid the Vegas interests, thereby snagging the hottest property in sport, Mike Tyson, in a glamour bout. Tyson would defend his title on October 16, 1987, for the first time in Atlantic City, against the undefeated 1984 Olympic gold medalist, Tyrell Biggs. The fight would take place in the venerable Convention Hall. But since the hall is adjacent to and connected by a walkway with Trump Plaza, to all intents and purposes it was Trump's hotel that would be the site of the fight. Don King, with an option on Tyson's services, would be the promoter.

Fighting Tyrell Biggs was something Mike Tyson looked forward to with relish. He had wanted the chance to win a gold medal at the Olympics; he had never gotten it, and he was always jealous of the attention given to those who did win gold, especially Biggs in the glamorous super-heavyweight division. Tyson was disdainful of the stand-up style of jabbing and moving that won points in the amateurs, a style he did not use and for which he felt he was unfairly penalized by the judges in the Olympic trials and box-off against Henry Tillman. The style Tyson most admired was epitomized by the contemporary fighter he most respected, Roberto Duran, a no-holds-barred, two-fisted slugger. In the past, Tyson had tried to goad Biggs into fistfights by taunting him when they had had chance encounters. Now Tyson would get his chance to show up this Olympic "pretty boy" in the ring, in front of millions of spectators. "I want to give him a good lesson. I want to hurt him real bad," Tyson said, with undisguised evil in his eye.

With fewer than twenty professional fights to his credit, Biggs was rushed into the bout with Tyson by his managers before he was ready. Theirs was a calculated business decision, nothing more. The talented Biggs was regarded by many in boxing as a "head case." He had had problems with drug abuse and, privately, Shelly Finkel and Lou and Dan Duva, who oversaw his career, didn't know how much longer they could keep his fragile psyche in one piece. Finkel, a friend of Jim Jacobs, confided that it was best to grab the payday against Tyson now while they could, while Biggs was still undefeated, while he was off drugs and before who-knows-what might happen. With Jacobs's cooperation, the favor was done, and the match was made. It was like feeding a lamb to a lion.

There was the dream, always the same dream. He was about to fight Mike Tyson, the heavyweight champion of the world, and he was afraid. Who wouldn't be? The bell rang. He was terrified. He didn't know what to do. He just went out and started throwing punches. Did he win? He never knew. He woke up. He was Mike Tyson! But in the dream, he was someone else, his mind, its deep recesses freed by the narcotic of sleep, showing him what it might be like to face himself in the ring. A fantasy about fighting himself, this was always Mike Tyson's dream.

In training, Tyson was his usual abusive self. Assistant manager Steve Lott, who, along with Rooney, was the target of most of Tyson's boorishness until he was summarily dismissed without so much as a good-bye after the Spinks fight, described Tyson's usual pattern of behavior. "The middle three weeks, especially two weeks before the fight, he got very surly; that would happen every fight. The last week when he knew the fight was getting so close, the last couple of days, he was fine. When training was over, that's when he was most relaxed. Two weeks, three weeks before the fight, that's when . . . he would treat Kevin and me like shit. That was his style. 'Mike, would you like to have some dinner with us?' He wouldn't say a word, just walk back into his room. 'Time to go to the gym'—he wouldn't say a word. He'd leave the house without telling us where he was going, take the day off all by himself. Kevin would give him instructions during the round [while sparring], Mike would ignore him completely. The round would be over, Mike would walk back to the corner, Kevin would start talking, Mike would walk away, indifferent, wouldn't listen to Kevin. The sparring would be over, Mike would start to take the gloves off himself, throw them on the floor and walk away, take the wraps off with his teeth, not let Kevin do it, walk away, not even change his clothes, just leave the place. Completely indifferent to everyone around him. . . . He's just a surly motherfucker during that time. Mike knows; he says, 'Steve, you know I'm an asshole, but that's my style.' I say, 'Hey, it's no big deal, forget about it.' He knows he's an asshole, I know it, Kevin knows it. So what? Let's just get the job done. Everyone else does their job; when they go home to go to sleep, then they're personal. But when it comes to boxing it's a job, and he does his job. He's not expected to behave himself like Sir Laurence Olivier. He's supposed to fight. I don't think [there's] anything Cus could have done or Jimmy or Kevin or anyone to help him [Tyson] rid himself of that mood he has three weeks before a fight. . . . He was too young. He hadn't experienced enough life, he hadn't been a professional long enough, he wasn't a human being with the objectivity of a thirty-year-old person knowing how he should be perceived and how he is perceived and how he should treat people. That wasn't his job. His job was to fight. As he gets older, then maybe he starts to think, 'You know, I don't want to go down in history as an asshole. I better cool it a little bit. Maybe it'll hurt my boxing, but I can't treat people like this.' . . . The only thing that matters is, what did he do in the ring? That's the bottom line. And he did okay. Now, could he have done better outside the ring? I'd take that two-week period anytime, of him being surly, if he puts on those type of performances [when he fights]."

Tyson also played psychological tricks on himself. He would deliberately slack off on his training until the fight drew close. Then, realizing the danger that his opponent was likely to be better prepared and would have the edge, he would feel challenged, threatened and would come on strong, whipping himself into fighting shape. Not being ready, in his own mind, would serve for him as self-imposed prod, forcing him to knuckle under and concentrate.

At last, on the night of October 16, 1987, with Donald Trump, his wife and family ensconced at ringside along with a host of celebrities, Mike Tyson gave them what they had all come to see, a show of controlled violence, legalized brutality, blood and, finally, the kill. Biggs began the fight moving, dancing, jabbing nicely. Tyson just applied the pressure and kept coming forward. He didn't want to finish Biggs too soon. He wanted to savor this one, torture his opponent a little before finishing him off. Biggs's number one rating was a joke. He had had just fifteen fights, none of them against any top-notch contenders. His number one ranking owed more to the ability of the Duvas duo and Shelly Finkel to pull strings and exert their influence with the sanctioning bodies than to his true abilities after just fifteen bouts. Tyson kept cutting the 6'5" Biggs down to size, methodically chopping away at him. Finally, late in the seventh round, Tyson had had enough fun. He whacked a vicious elbow into Biggs's mouth, illegal, but a customary Tyson tactic nevertheless. He then banged a left off Biggs's head. As Biggs attempted to dig a left uppercut to Tyson's body, the champion fired a left hook to Biggs's jaw, and the

Olympic champion crumpled backward through the lower ropes, his head out on the ring apron. As Biggs was going down, Tyson tried another left, which missed, and the momentum of the punch carried him off balance, stumbling into the ropes directly over the fallen Biggs. The challenger just beat the count, rising at the count of nine, a cut above his left eye pouring blood down the side of his face. He was a tired, beaten fighter. Tyson swarmed in for the coup de grace, throwing a flurry of punches from every angle, finally landing a left hand flush on the jaw of the battle-weary Biggs. He went down hard, on the seat of his pants, in a corner. His upper body was supported by the turnbuckles that held the ropes. There was no count. Referee Tony Orlando had seen enough. He dropped to his knees alongside Biggs and waved it over.

Mike Tyson, now 32 and 0, had had his revenge over the Olympic gold medal winner who had stolen all the attention three years earlier. He had also picked up some extra spending money. Cayton and Jacobs had negotiated a seven-fight deal for Tyson with HBO for $26.5 million.

Chapter 10

Hello, Robin . . .
Good-bye, Jimmy

A fairytale proposition: The heavyweight champion is the most dangerous man on earth: the most feared, the most manly. His proper mate is very likely the fairytale princess whom the mirrors declare the fairest woman on earth.

—On Boxing
Joyce Carol Oates

Steve Lott sat up in bed with a start. He thought he must be dreaming. He had heard screams. Awake now, he knew it wasn't a dream, because the screams persisted. They were coming from the next room in his Manhattan apartment, the apartment Tyson shared when he was in New York City, as he was on this night. Staying with him and sharing his bedroom was Robin Givens. Something was obviously wrong. Lott got up to investigate. He opened the door to Tyson's room and got a sinking feeling in his stomach. Robin had been screaming for help. Mike had apparently gone into a fit of rage and had been hitting her. Lott didn't know what to do. If Tyson resumed, Lott thought, he would be facing the unpleasant task of having to help her by taking on Mike Tyson in a fight. He knew the odds were not in his favor. Instead, much to his relief, Mike picked up the telephone and called for a car to come and fetch Robin. He wanted her out of his sight, out of the apartment, away from him. He saw Lott's questioning expression. "Everything's cool, Steve. No problem," Tyson said, so Lott left the room and closed the door. Lott never knew the extent of the physical attack by Mike on Robin. The next day, Mike said to him, "Steve, just remember one thing. Robin's an actress, a good actress." But the incident was definitely a portent of things to come. Tyson later confided in a friend that he hit Givens so hard that she "hit every fucking wall in the apartment."

*   *   *

Robin's mother, Ruth Roper, was a woman driven by the desire to succeed, to get on at any cost, to achieve success for both herself and her daughters. "I raised my daughters," she would say, "to be smart, beautiful and gutsy—everything that can be intimidating to a man." Ruth Roper wanted her girls to have it all. She was born Ruth Newby in October 1946. Her family was from Lexington, Kentucky, then a part of the South of segregation, the South before the 1964 Civil Rights Act. Her grandfather owned a successful garbage-carting business, and so she was spared the abject poverty that afflicted many black families in that era. After her parents divorced, Ruth was raised in New York City by her mother. As a teenager, she went to visit her father in Lexington, where she met Reuben Givens, a local high school basketball star two years her senior. The two fell in love, and Ruth stayed in Lexington, transferring into the high school there in order to be near Reuben. Not only was Givens a top athlete, he came from an athletically prominent family: His brother, Jack, was a star player for the University of Kentucky Wildcats in the 1960s and helped lead them to the NCAA basketball championship. A cousin, Lou Johnson, was a major league baseball player.

Reuben gave up any chance he might have had to play college basketball when he and Ruth got married on the day they graduated from high school, June 6, 1964. They had to. Robin was born five and a half months later, on November 27, 1964. Two years later, her sister, Stephanie, was born. A year after that, the marriage broke up, although it took an additional two years for the Givenses to obtain a divorce. Ruth was seventeen when she married Reuben. At twenty she was a single parent with two little girls.

"I told her," says Reuben Givens, "that I didn't want to have to live up to her standards. When our marriage broke up, I told Ruth to go home to her mother, because her mother kept interfering with our lives." Obviously, Ruth had goals and ambitions that Reuben could not, or would not, try to keep up with. Her own domineering mother set the pattern for her behavior.

Before the divorce, the Givenses had moved north to New York, and now Ruth was raising the two girls in the Bronx. But not for long. She went to work for Trans World Airlines, learned about travel, and opened her own travel agency. She married businessman Phil Roper, but according to Reuben Givens, the marriage lasted only a few weeks and was annuled. Ruth Roper began to move up in the world as fast as her brightening economic situation allowed her to. She left the decaying Bronx to move to the Westchester suburb of Mount Vernon. Although an improvement over The Bronx, that, too, was largely blue-collar working class, so as soon as she could, Ruth moved on to the much more affluent (and largely white) suburban town of New Rochelle. Her girls were not sent to public school. They were enrolled in the more exclusive, private New Rochelle Academy, and Ruth worked hard to pay for the Westchester County lifestyle, the private school tuition and the preppy clothes the girls needed in order to blend in. Although she had never attended college, she was a shrewd businesswoman. Armed with some knowledge of data processing, she formed her own highly successful computer consulting company.

She continued to drill into her daughters the urgent necessity to succeed. Robin's sister, Stephanie, a professional tennis player on the U.S. Tennis Association's satellite tour, told *Vanity Fair* magazine, "It was like a plan. Robin was going to be a doctor. My mother worked very hard to put her through the best schools. It was like a dream for her because she didn't have the opportunity herself. . . . Both of us have a tremendous amount of faith in our mother. We think there's nothing she can't do. But it's true she doesn't want us to grow up."

All was not complete sweetness and light as Ruth Roper climbed the ladder of success toward the American dream, however.

She was sued in New York State Supreme Court by a former business partner. An ex-husband also sued her, saying she had failed to pay him 50 percent of the proceeds of the sale of their former home. But she drew most public attention when she went to court herself to sue Dave Winfield, a superstar with the New York Yankees and one of the most famous athletes in America, with whom she had had a three-year affair during the mid-1980s and whom when the relationship ended she charged with giving her a sexually transmitted disease (believed to be herpes). The case ended when Roper and Winfield reached an out-of-court settle-

Mike Tyson, youngest heavyweight champion in boxing history. Tyson won the title at the age of twenty years, five months. (Courtesy The Big Fights, Inc.)

The country house in Catskill (Athens), New York, where Mike Tyson came to live with Cus D'Amato at the age of twelve in 1980, following his release from reform school. (Courtesy Peter Heller)

The police and fire departments of Catskill, New York. On the second floor of the building on Main Street is the Catskill Boxing Club, where Mike Tyson was nurtured, and where world-class fighters like Matthew Hilton, Frank Bruno, Wilfred Benitez and Gerry Cooney also came to train during D'Amato's fifteen years there. (Courtesy Peter Heller)

Cus D'Amato (far left) is joined by Floyd Paterson (checked shirt) and Jose Torres, the two world champions he developed in the 1950s and 1960s, after an early Tyson victory in 1985. (Courtesy The Big Fights, Inc.)

The morning after his title victory over Trevor Berbick, a smiling Mike Tyson is flanked by co-managers Bill Cayton (left) and Jim Jacobs. Tyson is wearing his newly won WBC title belt. (Courtesy The Big Fights, Inc.)

Tyson launches a furious attack to knock out former champion Pinklon Thomas in a 1987 title defense in Las Vegas. (Courtesy The Big Fights, Inc.)

Tyson's January, 1988, title defense against former champion Larry Holmes ended in a fourth-round KO in Atlantic City. (Courtesy Don King Productions)

Mike Tyson lands a left jab on the face of Trevor Berbick on his way to becoming history's youngest heavyweight champion, November 22, 1986. (Courtesy The Big Fights, Inc.)

One minute into their $70-million super-fight, Michael Spinks hits the deck for the first of two knockdowns. He got up from this one, but not from the second, and the biggest-grossing fight in boxing history was over in just ninety-one seconds. (Courtesy Lori Grinker/The Big Fights, Inc.)

Tyson works in the Catskill gym with trainer Kevin Rooney, who suceeded Teddy Atlas. (Courtesy Peter Heller)

A pensive Mike Tyson relaxes at his Catskill home after breaking his hand in an August, 1988, street brawl with former ring opponent Mitch Green. (Courtesy Peter Heller)

Mitch Green delivers a right to the face of Mike Tyson in their 1986 Madison Square Garden bout. (Courtesy George Kalinsky/Major League Graphics)

Tyson and wife, Robin Givens, strike an affectionate pose in September, 1988, at their New Jersey home. (Courtesy ABC Television)

Mike Tyson, complete with robe, sceptre and crown, at this "coronation" ceremony as "King of the Heavyweights" following his victory over Tony Tucker, which unified the three versions of the heavyweight title. (Courtesy Don King Productions)

ment, with no admission of guilt by Winfield, who, according to his attorney, categorically denied all of Roper's allegations. No more details are known, the court papers in the case having been sealed. A former employee said of Roper, "She doesn't flinch. You cross her and she'll hurt you. . . . Ruth is vindictive."

And what of Reuben Givens? Left behind by the ambitious Ruth, he remained behind. He remarried and fathered several more children. Contact with his successful daughter, Robin, has been minimal. He is a self-confessed "street person," while Robin was raised in a different world with different values and standards, far away from the run-down tenements of The Bronx. When Tyson and Givens and Ruth Roper began making the headlines almost daily in 1988, amid all the accusations, charges, innuendo, rumors, countercharges and allegations, Reuben Givens said he felt it was important to separate Robin from his ex-wife in the public's mind, to "let them know what the real deal is, who the real person who's doing the dirty work out here [is]." "Which you think is Ruth?" he was asked. "Which I *know* is Ruth," was his reply.

For Robin, a bright student in private school, the next step was to attend a top college. The best schools were actively seeking qualified minority applicants, and Robin had no problems, her grades and color both working in her favor. She was accepted at the unusually early age of fifteen by Sarah Lawrence, in Bronxville, New York, just a short drive from her home in nearby New Rochelle. Sarah Lawrence is considered one of the most prestigious colleges in America, and competition for admission is stiff. Black, aggressive and strikingly pretty, Robin made her mark quickly and became very unpopular on campus before very much time had passed. She recalls her four years there as being miserable.

Coincidentally, two classmates of hers, Lauren Holly and Holly Robinson, also went into the world of television. Neither has fond memories of her. Lauren Holly roomed with Robin before going on to prominence in the ABC-TV daytime soap opera "All My Children." She says that she and Givens were once close friends, although today they no longer speak. She told newspaper columnist Cindy Adams, "You just knew she'd make it. Nothing would stop Robin.

Robin was determined to get ahead. She has a vibrant personality. She's smart, literate and went about life with a vengeance. . . . She was focused positively. She wanted to be educated. . . . I can't say she was really popular—either with boys or girls. . . . Robin is very controlled, even emotionally. It's important to her to remain cool." When Givens and Tyson split up in the fall of 1988, Lauren Holly was not surprised. Lauren commented, "All I'll say is that, relative to the Tyson story, I'm seeing a familiar pattern in her."

Holly Robinson, who went on to become the star of the TV detective drama "21 Jump Street" and who is the daughter of Delores Robinson, a Hollywood talent agent, got to know Robin Givens soon after she entered Sarah Lawrence two years after Givens had started there. Robinson, a smart and beautiful young black woman, says it was only natural that she and Givens should become friendly, since Sarah Lawrence is a small campus with only a handful of black students. Holly's mother recalls being surprised at Ruth Roper's frankness when the two met for the first time. Roper told her that now she had gotten Robin into a good school where she was getting a good education, her next job was to find her a rich husband.

The friendship between Holly and Robin ended spectacularly after Robin was invited to spend the Christmas recess with Holly in California at her mother's home in the exclusive show business colony of Malibu. According to Holly, when they got back to college, Givens told people on campus that Holly and her mother had stolen money from her wallet in California. The two mothers, Delores Robinson and Ruth Roper, spoke on the phone about Robin's accusations, and Ruth laughed it off. "You know how Robin can be," she said. "She doesn't mean it." She suggested they all meet for lunch to sort the matter out. But Holly had different ideas. Finding Givens in the dormitory, she punched her in the face and the two wrestled to the ground, screaming and rolling around until the fight was broken up.

Mrs. Robinson minces no words in her opinion of Robin Givens: "Everybody hated Robin. She's a manipulative, scheming opportunist." On graduation day at Sarah Lawrence, her classmates let her know what they thought of her. As her name was called and she went up to receive her degree, a loud chorus of boos swelled up from the student body.

Despite her mother's wish that she pursue a career in medicine, where she could find a nice Ivy League-educated doctor or lawyer to marry, Robin had been bitten by the show business bug. She decided to try her luck in Hollywood. Once she saw Robin was determined to make it in acting, Ruth Roper headed for Hollywood with her daughter, rather than loosen her controlling grip. Robin auditioned for a small role on "The Cosby Show," and Bill Cosby was impressed with her. He made Robin's still doubtful mother an offer: If Robin didn't make it in show business, he would pay for the rest of her education when she returned to graduate school. However, the offer would not be necessary. Givens's agent at William Morris was quick to spot the nineteen-year-old's fierce desire to make it as an actress. Before long, Robin landed the part of a brilliant high school student in the ensemble cast of the ABC-TV series "Head of the Class," and her career was launched.

Supplied with information from Robin, her official studio biography read: "Robin's academic excellence was almost surpassed by her love for the theatre." Listing her work in films and television, it pointed out that she had been "one of the top young models at New York's Ford Agency." It also mentioned that she had attended the prestigious American Academy of Dramatic Arts as a youngster and, after graduating from Sarah Lawrence College, had gone on to further her education at the Harvard University Medical School, dropping out to pursue her acting career. Eileen Ford, founder and owner of the famous modeling agency which bears her name, says Givens was never a model with her company. A director of the American Academy of Dramatic Arts says Givens attended for five Saturday sessions, then dropped out. Most significantly, Harvard University's Graduate School of Medicine says Robin Givens never dropped out of its medical school, because she never attended Harvard to begin with. Other than that, the biography was accurate!

Once she settled into the Hollywood scene, Givens moved on the fast track. Run-of-the-mill successful men weren't good enough for her, apparently. Her sights were set higher. The hottest star in basketball was Michael Jordan of the

Chicago Bulls in the National Basketball Association. He is one of perhaps half a dozen superstars of American sports. A spokesman for the agency that represents Jordan acknowledges that Givens "wanted to meet him because of who he was." She sent them some photos of herself and asked that they be passed along to Jordan, along with her wishes to get together with him. Jordan's people say they met only a couple of times, and that was it. In reality, the two shared a hot and heavy relationship over a period of time longer than just two or three meetings. But Jordan quickly bailed out of the relationship.

Another of Givens's paramours was one of Hollywood's hottest box office attractions, Eddie Murphy. Givens set her sights on landing this most eligible bachelor, and Reuben Givens told a TV interviewer he thought for a while that Eddie Murphy was indeed going to be his son-in-law. Soon, however, Murphy's relationship with Givens also came to an end. Later, when Tyson and Givens got married, Murphy privately wisecracked to members of his inner circle, "Everyone in Hollywood fucked Robin, but Mike went and married her."

Tyson was certainly unaware of his girlfriend's checkered past or of her domineering mother when he became involved. Even had he known, it's doubtful the unsophisticated young man would have believed any of it or indeed cared, so obsessed was he with possessing this delicate, feminine creature.

Their relationship continued on its bumpy course for eleven months, interrupted constantly by his training schedule and fights, her television commitments in Hollywood, both necessitating long separations, and by their regular heated arguments, usually provoked by Mike's keeping a stable of girlfriends on the side while he pursued Robin. But he pursued her relentlessly, and she said she liked that, that she had never had a man so bent on "claiming her" as his own.

Tyson set out to win Robin's affection by lavishing gifts on her. Starting with a five-carat diamond ring, the jewelry and other baubles piled up, hundreds of thousands of dollars' worth. For the first time in his life, Mike was able to give expensive, material tokens of his love to someone, and he liked the feeling. So did Robin. Now, however, as 1988 loomed on the horizon, so did Tyson's biggest professional challenge to date and he had to divert his attention from Robin to face it head on. Larry Holmes, the great former champion who had dominated the division for seven years until his narrow loss to Michael Spinks in 1985, was coming out of retirement to challenge Tyson's claim to the title.

On June 9, 1978, Larry Holmes had pounded out a fifteen-round decision over Ken Norton in one of the classic toe-to-toe heavyweight slugfests of all time to win the WBC Heavyweight Championship. Over the next seven years, he had ducked no challengers. Taking on all comers, he had carved out widespread recognition as the real heavyweight champion, while the WBA belt was passed back and forth among a host of heavyweight nonentities. Holmes won forty-eight consecutive fights without a loss, and grew rich defending his title. At the age of thirty-five, he had one more goal in boxing, to surpass the record of Rocky Marciano, who retired as undefeated champion in 1956 with a perfect 49 and 0 record. Holmes aimed to have two more fights, then retire with an unblemished 50 and 0 record to oversee his varied business interests. For his forty-ninth fight, the one that would put him even with Marciano, his opponent was Michael Spinks. Either way, it would be a history-making fight, for if Spinks won, he would become the first light-heavyweight champion in history to win the heavyweight title. They met on September 22, 1985, and on that night, the years caught up with Larry Holmes. Out-hustled by Spinks, Holmes lost a close but unanimous decision in Las Vegas, and with it went his Heavyweight Championship and his hopes of wiping the great Marciano's record off the books. Afterward, a bitter and intemperate Holmes lashed out, saying that, if the truth be known, "Rocky Marciano couldn't carry my jock strap." His ill-considered remarks, directed at a dead man and an icon of the sport, caused him some unpopularity. But for someone intent on continuing his career, he made an even bigger strategic mistake: He openly criticized the Nevada boxing judges whom he felt had robbed him of his title, saying they were drunks and incompetents. The judges had long memories, and when Holmes signed to fight Spinks in a rematch at Las Vegas, his fate was essentially sealed. The second time around, on April 19,

1986, Holmes defeated Spinks fairly handily, and most independent observers acknowledged Holmes's superiority that night. When the decision was announced, however, the Nevada judges, by a 2 to 1 vote, had seen to it that the title stayed with Spinks. Always conscious of his inability to capture the public imagination the way his predecessor, Muhammad Ali, had done, Holmes was now more bitter than ever. With the boxing establishment obviously out to get him—at least in his own mind—he had no choice but to announce his retirement. Back in his home town of Easton, Pennsylvania, with his wife and children, he watched over his business investments. He had done well. He had achieved fame in the ring as "The Easton Assassin," and the fruits of his blood-and-sweat labor were apparent. He lived in a $1.5 million home and had an automobile and motorcycle collection worth a million dollars. He had invested his money in his home town and owned several properties, including a nightclub/disco, a restaurant, a $1.5 million office building and a 130-room hotel in nearby Phillipsburg, New Jersey; he was in the process of putting up a $10 million complex of offices and luxury apartments. But more and more, he was drawn to his modern gym and training facility. At first, it was just to lose weight, but increasingly Holmes felt the urge to return to the ring. Tyson had now come on the scene, and throughout 1987 Holmes played a cat-and-mouse game with Jacobs and Cayton, engaging in an on-again, off-again series of negotiations with them concerning a fight with Tyson. But each time he was about to sign on the dotted line, something inside him made him back off. Still, in the end, he wanted to do it, wanted to lance the festering boil that his two losses had become in his psyche. He told people, "I hated the way I lost against Spinks. I want to get back what was taken from me. I'm coming back to prove something."

Gene Tunney and Rocky Marciano walked away from the sport at their peaks, retiring with the title, but they were exceptions. Most fighters stay around too long for their own good, finding ways to justify to themselves their reasons for doing so. Certainly Larry Holmes must have thought back to that day in 1980 when he stood in the ring to face the faded legend that was Muhammad Ali. On that October night in Las Vegas, Holmes mercilessly pummeled perhaps the greatest heavyweight of all time. Ali had nothing, no jab, no legs, no reflexes, and suffered the first and only knockout of his career, quitting on his stool. Afterward, one wag remarked, "Ali still has a million-dollar punch. He got paid $8 million and he threw eight punches all night." Ali was thirty-eight years old on that night. Now Larry Holmes was thirty-eight years old and he was the former champion coming back to challenge the young kid. Despite all this, he had to do it or he would never be able to enjoy a peaceful retirement. For his own satisfaction, he had to try.

Holmes signed with his old nemesis Don King, and the fight was set for January 22, 1988. Once again, Donald Trump had taken the action away from Las Vegas and had put up the multimillion dollar site fee to bring the bout to Atlantic City. Holmes had to bring himself down from 250 pounds and shake off the ring rust which built up over his twenty-one months of inactivity. Yes, he was thirty-eight, just as Ali had been on the night he had humiliated the former champion, but, Holmes rationalized, he hadn't been through the battles with Frazier and Norton and Foreman and Spinks and Bonavena and all the others that Ali had. Yes, he was thirty-eight, but he was a young thirty-eight. Conveniently, Holmes chose to overlook the signs of age—the difficulty in getting up and running the miles every morning, how much harder it was to take off the pounds, the fact that his first grandchild had just been born. In his gym every day, he worked with Richie Giachetti, one of King's men, to try and get it all back, to somehow recapture the past.

For Tyson, the fight would be the first in his seven-bout, $26.5 million new contract with HBO. Specifically, his payday for this one would be $5 million, but he would also receive site fee money and foreign television rights fees that would double the HBO $5 million. The game plan laid out by Cayton and Jacobs for Tyson in 1988 would bring the twenty-one-year-old fighter a mind-boggling $50 million in gross earnings, more in one year than Dempsey, Louis, Marciano and Ali combined had earned in their entire careers! But also, a victory over Holmes would be a rite of passage for the young champion. Many experts were saying this could be his toughest test, facing a clever and experienced veteran of ring wars who had been a proud and skilled champion. So many of the great fighters had moved to the forefront with victories over once-great heroes of the past. Jack Johnson had beaten Jim Jeffries. Louis had risen with victories over Carnera, Sharkey and Baer. Marciano, in turn, had knocked out Louis. Ali had done it to Archie Moore, who was nearing his fiftieth birthday at the time; and then Holmes had done it to Ali.

Jacobs, Cayton, Rooney and Tyson knew that Holmes, despite his age, would be no pushover. They knew he was smart. They knew he was durable. They knew he had power in his sneaky right hand, behind his pulverizing jab, power enough to stop thirty-four of his fifty opponents. And echoing in the minds of Jacobs and Tyson were the words of Cus D'Amato, who had told both of them many times his theory about once-great but aging fighters: On any given night, a fighter who had known greatness could recapture that and so should never be underestimated.

During his preparation for Larry Holmes, Tyson's attention was diverted by something unexpected. Jim Jacobs, not only his manager but also his closest friend and confidant since the death of D'Amato in 1985, was taken ill and hospitalized. Although nearing his fifty-eighth birthday, Jacobs had always been vigorous, the picture of health, the supreme athlete himself. Only a few trusted friends knew that for many years, Jacobs had suffered from lymphocytic leukemia, a secret he kept even from Tyson. Previously, when he had disappeared, Jacobs had told friends he was going to Texas on business or to London to work on some film deal. In reality, he had gone into hospital for chemotherapy treatments.

He never even told his mother or other family members of his illness, not wanting to cause them grief or worry. In December of 1985, however, a month after D'Amato's death, Jacobs was in Los Angeles on one of his many visits to his mother. During that visit, perhaps made more aware of his own mortality by the recent death of his mentor, Jacobs took his lifelong friend Nick Beck aside, and told him: "I have lymphocytic cancer. The prognosis once you're diagnosed is about seven and a half years. I was diagnosed seven years ago. I'm telling you because if anything happens to me I want you to keep in touch with my mother." His mother and her welfare were one of his main concerns in life, but she was spared the knowledge of her son's illness, for the following December she passed away.

Just as Tyson's career was beginning, the illness worsened. In London on business, Jacobs had an attack in Mickey Duff's office. He grew weak and broke out in a cold sweat, telling Duff he had a blood problem and needed a doctor. Duff arranged for him to see a specialist. The next morning, Jacobs seemed fine. Duff never knew the true nature of his ailment, despite the nearly thirty-year friendship between them.

Following Tyson's victory over Pinklon Thomas in May of 1987, Jacobs suffered another attack on the trip back to New York. He started shaking at the airport in Las Vegas and grew so weak that he had to ask his wife to hold a small bag he was carrying. On the flight home, he sweated profusely but rode out the attack, and by the end of the day, once he was home, his condition had improved.

By the end of 1987, however, Jacobs could not ignore the fact that his health was now deteriorating rapidly. As the Holmes fight approached, he had developed further complications. Although he chose to keep the nature of his problem a secret once again, this time he went into the hospital for surgery to have his spleen removed. It was nip and tuck whether he'd be discharged from the hospital in time to travel to Atlantic City for the fight. His release from the hospital came only days before the fight, and when he arrived in Atlantic City two days before the bout those who knew him were shocked. He looked very ill. His skin had taken on a sallow complexion, he had lost a substantial amount of weight, and patches of hair had fallen out as a result of his chemotherapy.

On fight night, January 22, 1988, Robin Givens was among the celebrities at ringside. Inside his dressing room, Mike Tyson was ready. His gloves were on, and he wanted to do damage. Minutes before it was time to enter the arena, while warming up, he threw a right hand at the ¾-inch-thick plasterboard wall, which exploded from the force of his punch. Tyson's fist went right through it, leaving a huge, jagged hole. Mike Tyson was indeed ready to do damage.

Holmes had vowed to use "all my old tricks" in the ring against the powerful young champion. He knew he couldn't match Tyson for strength, but he felt he had a marked advantage in experience that could turn the fight in his favor. He was 226 pounds, the heaviest of his career and ten pounds heavier than Tyson.

Tyson won the first two rounds, pressing the former titleholder, landing some big punches, with Holmes holding off the charging Tyson by keeping his left hand in Mike's face or grabbing and forcing clinches. But when they clinched, Tyson twisted his way out, compelling Holmes to use extra energy to hold on to him. In the third round, Holmes landed some uppercuts and this, combined with his controlling the tempo of the round, won it for him on the scorecards of two of the judges. The final moment of glory for Holmes in a professional ring career which had spanned nearly fifteen years came in the first half-minute of the fourth round, which would prove to be the final round for Larry. He came out dancing, moving, recapturing for a moment the old footwork and the fast hands. He pumped sharp jabs into Tyson's face—one, two, three . . . six jabs landed crisply. The crowd responded with cheers for the old warrior. Sugar Ray Leonard, one of the HBO-TV commentators, was awed. "Look at the jab! Look at the jab!" he kept repeating. The two fighters fell into a clinch, during which Tyson popped an illegal but by now familiar elbow into Holmes's face. Fifty-five seconds into the round, Tyson landed a left hook to the head, forcing Holmes once again to clinch. Then, suddenly, out of nowhere, Tyson saw an opening and sent a right hand crashing off Holmes's head, clipping the ex-champion with another elbow to the face for good measure on the follow-through. Holmes toppled backward as if he had been shot. Grabbing the ring ropes, he pulled himself to his feet at the count of four, shaking his head to clear it. He was obviously hurt, and Tyson knew it. Not wanting to give the clever Holmes any chance to recover, Tyson moved in quickly. Two left hands rocked Holmes again, and when a Tyson right grazed off the top of Larry's head, he went down for the second time. His champion's heart brought him to his feet again, although the end was now inevitable. Hurt and dazed, he stumbled into the ropes and then, finding his feet, walked around the ring to try to bring the feeling back to his legs while referee Joe Cortez counted off the mandatory eight-count.

Now, it was time for the kill, and Tyson pounced like the

hungry predator he becomes in the ring, throwing a barrage of punches. Holmes was very unsteady. He tried to hold Tyson, to find some way to tie him up and somehow survive to the bell, but Tyson would not be denied. Holmes did manage to parry a good many of Tyson's punches, but caught a big right hand that wobbled him once again and sent him reeling crazily for a moment. That was followed by another crisp Tyson right to the head. Holmes tried to punch back and move, but he ran out of room. Tyson pinned him on the ropes, landing another tremendous right to Holmes's jaw. Now there were less than ten seconds remaining in the round, and it looked as though Holmes might somehow survive. If he could just land one more good shot, take the offensive for a moment, the saving bell and a much-needed minute's rest on his stool would be his reward. He reached back to launch a right uppercut to Tyson's jaw, but the unexpected happened. His right hand, on the backswing, got caught in the third strand of the ring ropes, and for an instant he was a fighter with one hand literally tied behind his back. Tyson fired a right hand at that same second at Holmes's jaw, but it missed and went sailing by. Tyson's speed and reflexes were so uncanny, however, that even as Holmes freed his arm and slid down the ropes, away from him, the young champion was back in position and ready to fire the right hand again. He had recocked his shotgun. With Holmes pulling away, Tyson's pulverizing right, with the full extension of his arm, landed flush on Holmes's jaw, and he went down hard on his back, the third knockdown of the fight. Joe Cortez had seen enough. He dropped to his knees, straddling the fallen ex-champion's body, and pulled out his mouthpiece so the semiconscious fighter could breathe more easily. The fight was over.

Larry's two cornermen, Richie Giachetti and his brother, Jake Holmes, ran across the ring to their man, as did the ring physician. "I want to get up. Please let me stand up," Holmes insisted, but referee Cortez kept him pinned to the canvas until the doctor had a chance to look at him. "Richie, get me off the goddamn floor," said Holmes, trying to regain a last moment of dignity in the ring. He was helped to his feet and went to Tyson to congratulate him. "You're a great champion," Holmes said to the younger man. "Thank you, you're a great champion, too," replied Tyson. After regaining his senses on his stool, Holmes wrapped himself in his fighter's robe for the last time and took his final climb down the ring steps. The crowd gave him a warm ovation to send him into retirement, and Larry responded by saluting them with one of his still-gloved hands. Holmes said he had no regrets: "The guy beat me legitimately. I can't make no excuses for that. I just got caught. People will say Tyson beat my ass, and he did. He beat me good. As we all go along, someone eventually gets us, and he got me tonight."

Mike's next fight was set for March 21, 1988, exactly two months away. The circumstances were extraordinary. Tyson would be fighting in Tokyo, Japan. Although he had never been to that country, the Japanese had become Tyson-crazy. Stories about him were flooding Japanese publications, his picture was on magazine covers throughout the country and the people couldn't get enough information about him. Michael Jackson, the black American entertainer, had had a similar effect on the Japanese, although their homogeneous society, isolated for centuries, otherwise harbored a strong racist attitude toward blacks, Jews and even other non-Japanese Asians. In 1987, Prime Minister Yasuhiro Nakasone had said that Japanese society was "more intelligent" than the United States because "blacks, Mexicans and Puerto Ricans lowered [the] level of intelligence" and literacy rates in the U.S. The following year, Michio Watanabe, a senior official of the ruling Liberal Democratic Party, who had apparently not learned a lesson from the furor caused by Nakasone's indiscretion, said that American blacks were irresponsible because they tended to accumulate bills on their credit cards that they could not repay and did not intend to repay. Nevertheless, the Japanese attitude, it seemed, was different when it came to black celebrities, and they had to have Mike Tyson in Tokyo no matter what the cost. Cayton and Jacobs were able to cut an almost unbelievable deal for their fighter.

Within a few months, egged on by those around him, Mike Tyson would begin making wild, irrational, unsubstantiated charges about the way Cayton and, by implication, Jacobs, had mishandled his money. In point of fact, however, they handled his fight deals, his endorsement deals, and the resulting income with impeccable scrupulousness and integrity, making him the richest athlete in history. Far from keeping Tyson in the dark where his money was concerned, shortly after the Holmes fight, Cayton sat down with Tyson in his 40th Street office in Manhattan and spelled out for him the deal they had cut in Japan. The fight would take place at a brand new, $465 million stadium in Tokyo. Cayton had tied in the stadium interests with Nippon TV, the country's largest network, along with the major advertising interests. Mike's money had been guaranteed, secured in letters of credit. When it was all counted, Mike would gross some $10 million, and the Japanese did not even care who the opponent was! It was a $10 million payday for Tyson against anybody they named! Tyson spent more than an hour listening to Cayton's patient explanation. When he returned to Catskill, he made a point of telling Camille Ewald how much he loved and respected Cayton, how patient Bill was in teaching him the business side of things.

Finished with the Larry Holmes fight, a month away from beginning serious training for his Tokyo bout, Mike was free to continue his pursuit of Robin Givens. The previous June, he had told Wally Matthews of *Newsday*, "I'm never going to get married. These women are all just after my money. If I wasn't rich and famous, they wouldn't want no part of me, and I know it." In Atlantic City that January he had essentially repeated the same words, yet he was besotted by Givens. He would phone her constantly when they were apart. Her phone might ring at three in the morning, with Mike asking her if she was ready to marry him. Minutes later he'd call back and say, "Are you ready now?"

On February 7, 1988, Mike and Robin were in Chicago to attend the National Basketball Association All-Star Game. Shots of them sitting at courtside and enjoying the game were shown on national TV periodically during the telecast. Only six or seven people were aware of what happened after the game. Mike Tyson and Robin Givens eloped. With just a few friends in attendance, they were married early that Sunday evening in a Chicago church. Afterward they went out to a local nightclub, where Mike had the band play "My Girl" in tribute to his new bride. He had acted on impulse.

When Robin had finally said yes, he had jumped. He did not even phone Steve Lott or Jim Jacobs to let them know. Had he done so, Jacobs would doubtless have counseled him not to rush out and get married that night, but to plan things more carefully. And most certainly, Jacobs would have strongly advised that the couple enter into a prenuptial agreement, so that Mike's assets would be protected.

The next day, when word of the marriage leaked out, Jacobs was astounded. All he would say publicly was that he and Mike had a great deal to talk about when Mike returned to New York. Reading between the lines, it was obvious that Jacobs was very perturbed by Tyson's impulsive and secret nuptials. Bill Cayton reportedly said, "Mike is in love, and the woman he is in love with has ideas." Both men had Givens and her mother pretty well sized up and were upset that Mike had now left himself financially vulnerable. But they were caught in a dilemma. Mike was smitten not only by Robin, but by her mother; to criticize, or even appear to question anything the two women did, might alienate Mike. And, in any event, he wouldn't want to listen to anything they, or anyone else, might have to say about them. He told *Life* magazine that Ruth and Robin "display so much class I hope it rubs off on me.' " A few weeks later in New York, Mike and Robin repeated their wedding vows in a civil ceremony, since, in their romantic fervor, they had failed to obtain a marriage license in Illinois prior to their spur-of-the-moment Chicago wedding. A couple of weeks later, it was time to head for Tokyo, but before they left, the self-willed Givens made sure she asserted herself. She phoned Bill Cayton and told him, "I'm Mrs. Mike Tyson and I'm taking over."

Tyson went off to Tokyo with Givens at his side, while his two managers went off to the hospital. Jacobs's leukemia was advancing, and more chemotherapy was needed. Cayton had suffered a relapse of endocarditis, a serious heart infection which had plagued him. Don King, the nominal promoter because of his options on Tyson's services, was having his own problems. He was being paid on a flat fee basis by Jacobs and Cayton, and so was not skimming off the millions of dollars he had been able to with previous fighters. The Japanese had made it clear that this was their show and that no interference from King would be tolerated. For a while, they were reluctant even to allow King into the country because of his unsavory background, and they clearly indicated that his role would be very limited.

Tyson's challenger would be Tony Tubbs, a notoriously overweight fighter who had held a piece of the revolving-door title for a few months before Tyson came on the scene. It was a fight that would have been hard to sell in the United States, but the Japanese, hungry for a Tyson appearance, were willing to accept Tubbs. So concerned were Cayton and Jacobs that Tubbs should not be a bloated embarrassment, that the services of Jose Ribalta, a top-ten heavyweight whom Tyson had beaten on his way to the title, were secured on a stand-by basis. Ribalta would receive a substantial payday just for waiting in the wings. If Tubbs showed he was not making an effort to get in shape, Ribalta would be substituted as the opponent and he, instead of Tubbs, would receive a $1 million purse. To give Tubbs more incentive to take off the extra poundage, a clause in his contract guaranteed him a $50,000 bonus if he weighed in at 230 pounds. At the weigh-in, he tipped the scales at 238 pounds, thus blowing his bonus money. (With the weigh-in taking place a day before the fight, it's safe to assume that by the time he stepped into the ring, Tubbs was comfortably over 240 pounds).

At ringside on the night of the fight were co-manager Bill Cayton, his wife, and Camille Ewald, who had traveled from Catskill to see her "son" defend his title. Ominously absent, however, was Jimmy Jacobs. He and Cayton had kept in touch by phone from their hospital beds in the weeks preceding the fight. They felt that Jim would be out of hospital and in sufficient health in time to travel to Tokyo, although Cayton's situation was more uncertain. As it turned out, Cayton had improved enough to make the trip, but Jacobs had taken an unexpected and serious turn for the worse. Weakened by his chemotherapy treatments, he had developed pneumonia, and so, for the first time in thirty-four outings, he would not be at ringside for a Mike Tyson fight.

Mike wanted to get the fight over with and then head home. He didn't like being away from friends and familiar surroundings. He was concerned about Jacobs. And he was bored in Japan. He wasn't there to sightsee, to observe a different culture, to enjoy the adulation of the Japanese masses. He was there to fight, to collect his $10 million, and then to go home. Except for a few carefully orchestrated excursions—to the Tokyo zoo with Robin, to visit some sumo wrestlers for a press photo opportunity, to see the film *The Last Emperor* (which put him to sleep), to attend a Tina Turner concert (which he left after twenty minutes), and to film a Suntory beer commercial (which took him two hours and for which he was paid more than $600,000)—Tyson spent most of his five weeks in Japan training and holed-up in his hotel room, watching the usual genre of action films that he enjoys. He took most of his meals in his room.

There were two more reasons why Tyson wanted to get home quickly. He had sent Robin and her mother off on a mission while in Tokyo to find a home for himself and his bride. Ruth had picked out a $4.5 million dollar estate, and Robin flew back to sign the papers on it. Mike also wanted to get home to await the birth of his first child. He boasted that Robin was pregnant, although she was evasive when asked directly about it in Tokyo and her publicist issued the curious statement that the pregnancy " 'was not official,' " whatever that meant.

For only the second time in history, Japan was hosting a heavyweight title fight, the first time in fifteen years, since George Foreman had knocked out the grossly overmatched Joe "King" Roman in the first round. Tony "TNT" Tubbs came into the ring with a number two world ranking and an impressive 24 and 1 record. For a big man—a fat man—his punches were surprisingly crisp and fast. Using his jab, he fought Tyson on even terms in the first round, but felt the champion's power, as Tyson dug rights to his flabby body. He, in turn, landed squarely with several short, punishing hooks to Tyson's head.

At the start of round two, Tubbs continued to pump his jab into Tyson's face, successfully fending off the champion's attack. Tyson then landed a solid uppercut, but Tubbs answered with a right uppercut of his own. The two men then proceeded to fight on the inside. Tubbs whipped a left hook and a right to Tyson's head. Tyson came back with a left that grazed Tubbs's head but still landed with enough power to knock the challenger off balance with one minute to go in round two. Tyson then pinned Tubbs on the ropes, and landed several clubbing shots to his head. Suddenly, a crisp left hook found the mark on the top of Tubbs's skull and he slumped back into the ropes as Tyson dug a right hand to his body. Tubbs was hurt and forced a clinch. He then shot a good left hook to Tyson's head and followed with a right to the face. Tyson blasted his familiar combination of a right to the ribs and then a right uppercut to the jaw. It landed hard and flush, hurting Tubbs again, taking the fight out of him, and Tubbs fell into another clinch, trying to earn time to recover, with less than thirty seconds remaining in the round. When referee Arthur Mercante broke the clinch, it was apparent how much that right hand combination of Tyson's had hurt Tubbs. The challenger stumbled on unsteady legs into the ropes. Tyson stepped toward him and banged a single left hook off the side of his head, opening an ugly cut over his right eye. Tubbs did a drunken dance, stumbling across the ring. He grabbed the ropes for an instant, instinctively trying to stay on his feet, but his legs collapsed and he tumbled onto his back. Tyson, in pursuit, took four quick steps toward Tubbs and threw a final left hook, which missed as Tubbs sank to the canvas. Even as Tubbs was beginning to fall, his trainer, Odell Hadley, was jumping into the ring to end the fight. Tubbs probably could have made it to his feet and survived into the third round, but to what purpose? He and Hadley had no doubt agreed before the fight that the trainer would stop it as soon as there were any signs Tubbs was hurt. He was earning the same million dollars whether he took more punishment or less, so why not opt for less, grab the money and head home? Sometimes discretion is, indeed, the better part of valor.

As Tubbs lay on the canvas, his eye dripping blood and Mercante waving the bout over, Tyson stood in the center of the ring, legs spread apart, hands on hips. It wasn't the first time he had struck this pose. He had done it two months earlier, after stopping Larry Holmes. It was Tyson's tribute to a great champion of a bygone era. Much taken with the history of his sport, Tyson enjoyed reading about and viewing films of the old-time champions. He felt a direct connection to them. He often wore his hair cropped closely around the sides and back, because that was the way Dempsey wore his. He dressed in newsboy caps and thick wool sweaters with buttons up the front, because that was how the old-time greats appeared in the still photographs and flickering motion pictures he studied. Often he helped lift his fallen opponents to their feet once a fight had ended, because he had seen Dempsey and others do it. And shortly before the Holmes fight, he had seen an old photograph that intrigued him. It showed the great lightweight champion, Battling Nelson in 1910, standing over a knockout victim, legs spread, gloved fists resting on his hips. Tyson loved it, the champion posing in triumph, and he made a conscious decision to strike the same pose.

On Tuesday, March 22, 1988, Tyson returned to the United States from Tokyo. The following day, at Mount Sinai Hospital in Manhattan, Jimmy Jacobs died at the age of fifty-eight. Having never realized how seriously ill Jimmy was, Mike was shaken and distraught. In little more than two years he had lost the two guiding, stabilizing figures in his life—first Cus D'Amato in late 1985 and now Jim Jacobs.

The tributes to Jacobs showed how highly he was regarded in the boxing world. Howard Cosell, writing in the New York *Daily News*, said, "In the dirty world of boxing Jacobs was a clean man, a man of character. He was proof that boxing and character need not be mutually exclusive. . . . And boxing is that much less a sport without his presence." Doug Krikorian, in the Los Angeles *Herald-Examiner*, wrote, "The beleaguered sport [of boxing] suffered another damaging blow the other day when it lost its most eloquent spokesman, Jimmy Jacobs. . . . He was respected and trusted by bitterly divisive factions and his sound reputation was never tainted by rumors of dishonesty—rumors that inevitably curse everyone in the sport who reaches Jacobs' lofty status." "I never heard a bad word about him," says Don Fraser, veteran fight promoter." "If there is anyone in boxing who didn't like Jimmy Jacobs, then he didn't like him because Jimmy wouldn't sell out," says Gene Kilroy, charter member of the old Muhammad Ali entourage and long-time Jacobs friend. "Jimmy was very honest and very honorable." Ali himself said, "Jimmy Jacobs has always been a good friend of mine. I will truly miss him. I not only respect him, I had great admiration, compassion and love for this man." Ali recalled that Jacobs was one of the few who stood by him in the late 1960s when he was stripped of his title for refusing to serve in the Armed Forces. Even Wally Matthews of *Newsday*, who was often critical of Jacobs's personal style, wrote: "Nobody had anything bad to say about Jacobs the manager. . . . [he] was the consummate professional manager. . . . As Jacobs liked to say, his only obligations were to his fighters, and he fulfilled those very well indeed. For the sake of the fighters, boxing could use more managers like Jim Jacobs."

Jim's funeral was set for Friday, March 25. He was to be buried alongside his mother at the Hillside Memorial Park in Los Angeles. A sobbing Mike Tyson sat in the chapel during the service. He was alone. His wife and mother-in-law had chosen not to accompany him to the funeral of the man who had played a major role in turning this kid of the streets into the most successful athlete in the world. Instead, Ruth Roper and Robin Givens spent the day in New York. Even as Jacobs was being laid to rest, Givens was storming into the offices of Merrill Lynch, where Cayton and Jacobs had established a trust account for Tyson worth several million dollars. Givens wanted access to the account although it was in her husband's name. She angrily demanded "my money" in a confrontation with Merrill Lynch officials.

Anticipating the worst, Jacobs and Cayton had taken precautions to protect themselves and their wives in the event of the death of one of the partners. On February 12, five days after Tyson's marriage to Givens and six weeks before the passing of Jacobs, the two managers and Tyson had signed a new contractual agreement in the offices of the New York State Athletic Commission. The contract stipulated that if either manager should die, his 50 percent interest in Tyson (of the manager's standard 33⅓ percent interest in the fight) would pass to his widow. The duration of the new contract was a standard four years. Tyson signed it with no reservations. He had complete faith and trust in Jacobs and Cayton, and they had never done anything to cause him to question that faith and trust. Jose Torres, acting both in his capacity as chairman of the Athletic Commission and as a friend of all the parties involved, witnessed the proceedings and affixed his signature to the new documents. The contract was watertight, and would presumably keep anyone from trying to muscle in on Mike Tyson if anything happened to Jacobs or Cayton.

Promoter Don King's options on Mike Tyson had come to an end. Jacobs and Cayton, in the weeks prior to Jim's death, had been putting together the deal for Tyson to meet Michael Spinks in a super-showdown in June. They had once anticipated making Spinks and his promoter, Butch Lewis, wait, sweat it out, until 1989, but it was The Match, the big one, the one that Jacobs wanted to see happen, and his rapidly declining health made them put Spinks on their immediate agenda. Jacobs wanted to live to see the fight that would cement Tyson's place among the great heavyweights. Don King would be part of the deal, co-promoter along with Butch Lewis and Donald Trump, but King knew that it had long been the intention of the Tyson camp eventually to move from promoter to promoter, making the best deals on the open market. That could ultimately put him on the outside looking in. He knew control of Mike Tyson was essential to his survival in big-time boxing, and he set out to gain that control any way he could.

Chapter 11

Don King . . .
Only in America

You can't believe anything anybody tells you in boxing. The business is predicated on lies. You are dealing with people who very rarely tell the truth.

—Don King
promoter

Don King is like a vulture, circling his prey, always looking for signs of weakness; waiting, never far away, until he determines it's the right time to close in. In the case of Mike Tyson, King literally did not even wait for the body to get cold. On the day of Jim Jacobs's funeral in Los Angeles, Jacobs's friends, relatives and colleagues gathered at the Beverly Hilton Hotel before proceeding to the memorial service. Among the mourners was Don King, but his mind was more on "trickeration," as he terms it, than on mourning. In the hotel lobby, he and a henchman homed in on Tyson, and King told him he did not have to go through with the Spinks fight, even though plans were being finalized. He offered an alternative: He would put together a five-fight deal for the champion at $5 million a fight. A business associate of Jacobs, noticing that King had Tyson's ear, signaled Mike that he wanted to talk to him. Mike came over, and Jacobs's friend told him, "Mike, just be aware of one thing. Now that Jim is gone, people are going to be making moves on you." Gesturing toward King across the lobby, Tyson replied, "I know it. That motherfucker is trying already." Jay Bright, one of Cus's "boys" from Catskill, also saw what was going on and warned Tyson. But Mike Tyson was fresh meat, and Don King was determined to hook his talons into him as quickly as possible. King had proved over the years that once he set his mind on something his determination was formidable.

*   *   *

Don King was born in 1932 in Cleveland, Ohio, one of six children. On December 7, 1941, the day the Japanese attacked Pearl Harbor, tragedy struck the King family in a more personal way. Don's father was killed in a horrible steel mill accident. He was incinerated by molten metal. The family received a $10,000 insurance settlement, which Mrs. King used to move her family to a better, although modest, neighborhood. She baked and sold pies as well as roasted peanuts to support her family.

Don graduated from John Adams High School in Cleveland and says he planned to attend Kent State University in Ohio. In order to earn tuition money, he began running numbers. The numbers racket, nothing more than an illegal lottery, flourishes to this day in the poor neighborhoods of virtually every city in America. As a runner, it was King's job to pick up the $1 or $2 or $5 bets from people, then deliver the money to the numbers boss. According to King, one day he did not deliver a bet and that number turned out to be the winner. He had to pay the bettor out of his own pocket, thus wiping out his college savings. That story should be taken with a grain of salt. Betting the numbers is a way of life in the inner city, and King in later years explained his involvement, with some justification, by saying that regardless of the law, black people bet the numbers the way whites are allowed to go to church or parlors legally and play bingo for money. Why shouldn't blacks, in their neighborhoods, be allowed the chance to relieve a little of their poverty by hitting on a number and maybe winning a few hundred dollars?

King rose rapidly from his days as a teenage runner. By the time he was in his mid-thirties, he was the undisputed "policy" or numbers racketeer in Cleveland. Along the way, in 1954, he had shot and killed a man who was trying to rob a numbers house operated by King. The killing was ruled a justifiable homicide.

In 1966, King hired an ex-convict named Sam Garrett to help him with his thriving numbers business. King drove around his Cleveland neighborhood in a big Cadillac, flashing huge wads of money as he paid off his winners. One day, King discovered that Garrett had not laid off some bets with other policy operators, and the number hit. It was a similar situation to the one King said he had been in as a young man. But he stopped his Cadillac and confronted Garrett in the street, accusing him of cheating him out of $350. King, weighing about 250 pounds and variously described as standing 6′1″, 6′2″, or 6′4″ tall, became involved in a brawl with the much smaller Garrett which ended with Garrett's head banging on the concrete, causing a severe brain injury. A week later, Sam Garrett died, and King was tried and convicted of second-degree murder. Subsequently, the murder conviction was reduced to manslaughter. King was sentenced to serve ten years in the Marion, Ohio, Correctional Institution. (Years later, a lame-duck governor of Ohio, in his final week in office, issued the now-successful King a full pardon.)

He used his time in prison to read and study, and he was paroled on September 30, 1971, after serving just three years and eleven months of his sentence. Exactly four years to the day after his release from prison, Don King would be the promoter of the climactic "Thrilla in Manila," the classic third meeting between Muhammad Ali and Joe Frazier for the Heavyweight Championship of the World. King's meteoric rise to the top of the boxing world is a remarkable story and was achieved through a combination of his considerable intelligence, his seemingly limitless energy, his driving ambition, his predatory nature, the clever use of his color to develop bonds with important blacks in boxing, and his instinctive ability to exploit to his advantage the laissez-faire atmosphere in the sport. "All the way through boxing I have played by the rules," he has said. The trouble is, in boxing there are few rules and fewer still that can't be bent and manipulated.

Deciding to get involved in boxing after his release from prison, King bought in on the career of rising heavyweight Earnie Shavers, who was then managed by Blackie Gennaro of Youngstown, Ohio, and former Major League pitcher Dean Chance. King bought Chance out for $8,000 then acquired the contracts of two more fighters, heavyweight Jeff Merritt, who had the potential to become a top contender but eventually fell by the wayside after developing a drug habit, and light-heavyweight contender Ray Anderson, who rose eventually to a number one world ranking and a title shot. Thus was launched the career of Don King.

In addition, King approached Muhammad Ali and asked him if he would take part in a charity boxing exhibition to benefit Forest City Hospital. Ali did not want initially to get involved with King, saying the fledgling boxing manager was a mobster. But having checked around and found out that the hospital benefit was a legitimate charity affair, Ali agreed to take part. In this way, King got to know Ali, and Ali's manager, Herbert Muhammad.

At the time, Joe Frazier was champion, and King succeeded in getting an introduction to Smokin' Joe through Ohio boxing promoter Don Elbaum, who promoted Shavers's fights. King flew to Jamaica when Frazier was to defend his title in Kingston against George Foreman. He walked to the ring with Frazier and his entourage. Less than fifteen minutes later, Frazier was an ex-champion, knocked out in the second round by Foreman. King quickly switched allegiance, turning up with a big smile on his face among the celebrants in the new champion's corner.

The following year, 1974, King became involved in a company called Video Techniques, which promoted and handled the closed-circuit TV of Foreman's title defense against Ken Norton in Caracas, Venezuela. King says he was the company's "token nigger," but said he needed the association with Video Techniques and a major fight in order to establish his credibility and make himself in the eyes of the boxing world more than just "a wild nigger from Cleveland."

King next went to Ali's manager, Herbert Muhammad, and told this son of the Black Muslim leader, Elijah Muhammad, that he wanted the chance to promote a fight between Ali and Foreman. He told Herbert, "God has put me here to do this. You must give me the chance because your father said in his holy words that if you find a black man comparable to a white man in doing his duties you must give the black man the chance, or else how will he ever get the chance?" Herbert Muhammad may have been a Black Muslim, but he was also a very practical businessman. He told King he could promote the fight if he could come up with the money.

King offered Foreman and Ali $5 million each, a vast amount of money far beyond what any fighter had ever been paid before. Not surprisingly, both fighters found the amount acceptable. Now all King had to do was to come up with the $10 million in guarantees. He went first to Britain's Hemdale Corporation and got them to back the promotion with $1 million in front money. King, always thinking, then came up with another idea. He would make this a black event, two black men fighting for the heavyweight crown, both managed by black men, in a fight promoted by a black man, so what better place to stage it than in the heart of black consciousness and black history—Africa? King took off for Zaire, and arranged an audience with President Mobutu Sese Seke. He proposed that President Mobutu back the fight with $10 million of his poverty-stricken country's money, telling him that world attention would be focused on Zaire in the months and weeks leading to the fight, which would give the new nation worldwide prestige. The name of Zaire (and, by the way, that of Mobutu) would become known throughout the globe. Mobuto agreed to put up the $10 million to bring the Foreman-Ali fight to the capital city of Kinshasa. And so, the "Rumble in the Jungle," as it was billed, had been made, and a new company, Don King Productions, was in the boxing business in a big way.

When Muhammad Ali was champion, Bob Arum promoted many of his title fights. King and Arum had had a few conflicts in the early 1970s, when Arum was the dominant promotional power in the heavyweight division and King was starting to climb the ladder. On October 30, 1974, Ali knocked out Foreman in a major upset to regain the heavyweight title, and now it was Don King, not Bob Arum, who had the inside track with Muhammad Ali and Herbert Muhammad.

King promoted Ali's title defenses against Chuck Wepner, Ron Lyle and Joe Bugner. Then, on October 1, 1975 (September 30 in the U.S., across the International Date Line) in Manila, he staged Ali-Frazier III, considered to be one of the greatest heavyweight fights of all time. As he had done in Zaire, he persuaded Filipino President Ferdinand Marcos to foot the bill for the big show in exchange for worldwide exposure for his nation and himself.

Whereas Jim Jacobs and Bill Cayton prided themselves on having concern for their fighters as people and for looking out for their financial welfare, and were respected in boxing circles for doing so, Don King treats the fighters he has been involved with simply as commodities to be used for his advantage, and to be discarded when their commercial usefulness has been sucked dry. This pattern of operating can be traced back to King's earliest days in boxing.

Ernie Butler, an elderly black man, was the first to experience Don King's methods. A small-time trainer in the small town of Easton, Pennsylvania, Butler had spent his life in boxing. In the late 1960s, he found a young boy on the streets of Easton who showed some promise. His name was Larry Holmes. Butler took the youngster and nurtured him through the amateurs, then turned him pro in 1972. Holmes began winning consistently and became a local attraction around Scranton, a hotbed of boxing in eastern Pennsylvania. One night in 1973 Don King was there and saw him in action. He liked what he saw and talked to Butler about becoming involved with Holmes. As Butler was to discover when it was too late, "All the talk he was giving me was trickery talk. He didn't do anything he agreed to do."

Butler liked Holmes to box with top heavyweights in the gym, believing it was valuable experience. He would bring Larry to New York City to spar at Gleason's Gym; he would also take him to Muhammad Ali's training camp in nearby Deer Lake, Pennsylvania, to work as a sparring partner with The Greatest. King had a chance to see Holmes spar with Ali and became more determined than ever to latch on to the young heavyweight. He asked Butler to bring Holmes to Grossinger's resort in the Catskill Mountains to spar with Earnie Shavers. Butler agreed, since it would not only be a good opportunity for Larry to learn, but King also promised them a fight on the undercard when Shavers fought Jerry Quarry at Madison Square Garden.

Butler had to leave Holmes at Grossinger's while he returned to his regular job in Easton, and this gave King his chance without Butler around to interfere. He began to sweet-talk Holmes with promises about what he could do for the young boxer's career. When Butler returned to Grossinger's, he and Larry had their first argument. Butler had a contract with Holmes, but King had found a loophole. The contract had never been executed with the Pennsylvania Athletic Commission as required. It was simply a contract between Butler and Holmes. King had the contract declared invalid and signed on Larry Holmes.

While Holmes went on to earn millions, Butler was left in the cold. When he began to make noises about the way Holmes had been taken from him, he received an anonymous threat. "I don't know who it was . . . but I got a threat over the telephone. The guy told me to lay off, or else. I got a wife, two kids, and a house. I don't want nobody to blow up my house, kill my kids, nothing like that. So, naturally, I begin to back off more then, and stop fightin'. . . . How are you going to take a sport like boxing," asks Butler, "that's supposed to be so corrupted, how you going to take a sport like that and let a man come out of prison and run it?"

Although Holmes became a multimillionaire during his seven and a half years as heavyweight champion, Richie Giachetti, who worked with King for years as Holmes's trainer, had a bitter parting with the promoter (but has since gone back to work for him), has charged that King cost him $6 million and Holmes about $20 million by skimming from the fighter's purses. During his separation from King, Giachetti said, "Don King is a crook. You've got to get burned by Don King to really know Don King. . . . Don King is a liar and a thief, the greediest bastard I've ever known. This guy wants all the money and all the fighters. He talks about fairness and equality, but he wants everything for himself and doesn't want to give anything to anybody." But Giachetti also acknowledged, "If I was a fighter and needed a promoter, who would I take? Don King. The man is the best. Don King delivers."

Holmes's attorney, Charles Spaziani, says that King would take 25 percent fees for consultation or advisory services. Spaziani told *Newsday*'s Wally Matthews, "Early in Larry's career we had to make a decision. Either you let Don King take advantage of you and make half a million dollars or stay away from Don King and get no fights that are above the $20,000 to $25,000 range, because Don had all the heavyweights tied up."

Holmes had a love-hate relationship with King throughout his career. Now that he is retired from boxing and financially secure, Holmes is more willing to talk freely, "Don would say, 'I'm going to give you $3 million for a fight,' and I'd say, 'Great.' Then Don would say, 'I got to get 25 percent of that.' That's the way Don did it. . . . The only mistake I made in my whole career was getting tied up with Don King. I was exploited, used and abused," he told Matthews. "I listened to all of King's black talk . . . he sells it to you. He tells you, "We're both brothers, let's get all the money we can together. I thought I would be protected."

Over the years, King has been nothing if not resilient. He is the Teflon Man of boxing. Nothing sticks to him. He has demonstrated a remarkable ability to slide out of jams with minimal damage to himself. Twice he was investigated by grand juries, but was never indicted. In 1983, it was reported that King was the central figure in an investigation into boxing being conducted by the U.S. Attorney's Organized Crime Strike Force unit. He was not indicted. The FBI also investigated him. Joe Spinelli, who spearheaded that operation for the FBI spent a considerable amount of time in Catskill talking with Cus D'Amato about Don King and about the involvement of organized crime in boxing, going back to the days of the IBC. D'Amato must have been convinced that the FBI was going to nail King. He confided to intimates that when King went to jail, Jimmy Jacobs would move in to fill the vacuum and become the main power in boxing. Cus would then regain his manager's license and once again move to the forefront, handling much of boxing's top talent. This was in the early 1980s, and it proved to be just a pipe dream. The FBI investigation came to nothing, and King remained firmly in control of the heavyweight division and many fighters and champions in other weight divisions as well.

On December 13, 1984, King and his assistant, Connie Harper, were indicted by a federal grand jury on twenty-three counts of income tax evasion, filing false and fraudulent income tax returns, and conspiring to conceal more than $1 million in unreported income. The case went to trial. When it was over, King walked away a free man, while Miss Harper was convicted and went to prison for several years.

Publicly, King makes light of his situations. "I'm a victim of trickeration. I think I'm destined to be investigated until I die," he says, and blames his plight on the fact that he is a black man whom the establishment is out to get. But when it comes down to brass tacks, King plays hardball when cornered. In one lawsuit filed against him, he refused to answer any questions, pleading the Fifth Amendment against self-incrimination no fewer than 364 times.

Perhaps the best example of King's ability to rise like a phoenix from the ashes occurred in 1977. He had gone to ABC Sports in 1976 and sold the television network a new concept in boxing he had dreamed up, the United States Boxing Championships. The tournament would begin in January 1977, and would eventually crown U.S. champions in eight major weight divisions. It would provide young fighters on the rise with an opportunity to move to the forefront of boxing, gain valuable national TV exposure, and earn modest but substantial purses as they progressed through the competition. ABC agreed to finance the tournament with an investment of between $1.5 and $2 million and committed twenty-three hours of national broadcast time to televising it over the course of six months. To give the tournament credibility, King had enlisted the services of "The Bible of Boxing," the prestigious *Ring* magazine, whose ratings of fighters had been widely respected for more than fifty years. *Ring* was to be paid a fee of $70,000 in exchange for providing special ratings of just U.S. fighters, from whom the tournament participants would be selected. The association of *Ring* with the tournament would insure the integrity of the U.S. Championships, which was critical to ABC.

The tournament had barely got off the ground when charges of irregularities began flying about. It was later established that as a precondition, any fighter invited to participate had to sign a contract giving Don King the option on three fights should he win the tournament. It was also established that King had paid John Ort (the editor at *Ring* magazine in charge of the ratings) $5,000 in cash. Subsequently, Ort played all sorts of games with the ratings. Two King associates, boxing managers Paddy Flood and Al Braverman, were paid $20,000 each to help administer the tournament and serve as consultants. Eight middleweights were invited to participate, but they did not include one of the best in the division, Marvin Hagler, despite Hagler's 38 and 2 record. However, three fighters Hagler had beaten were invited to take part. Hagler later charged that he was blacklisted from the tournament because he had refused an ultimatum to take Flood and Braverman as his new managers.

In December 1976, ABC's boxing consultant, Alex Wallau, sent two memos to one of the sports department's senior executives, outlining other flagrant examples of how the tournament was being rigged with fighters who did not deserve rankings but who received them because they were in some way connected with King and his cronies. Among the examples cited by Wallau were: Mike Colbert, "a Portland prospect who has been unconscionably promoted by Ort on behalf of his rumored partner Mike Morton of Seattle who manages Colbert. His number one ranking in *Ring* magazine is laughable"; Paddy Dolan, managed by Paddy Flood, and John Sullivan, "White club fighters who have never fought a main event or an opponent of any reputation . . . two disgraceful examples of King handing $15,000 to Paddy Flood and his friends"; Hilbert Stevenson, "An unknown unproven nonentity"; Juan Cantres, "[An] embarrassment . . . an unskilled club fighter'; Biff Cline, "Perhaps the greatest example of King's payoffs to Ort and Ort's lack of integrity lies in the inclusion of Donald 'Biff' Cline in the light-heavyweight division. He has never even fought as a light-heavyweight. The only reason he will collect a paycheck of $10,000 is his father, Chris Cline." (Chris Cline was a Baltimore manager rumored to be a business partner of John Ort.)

In addition to Wallau's conclusion that thirty-one of the fifty-six fighters invited to participate were not qualified, it was shown that at least eleven of them had been credited with phony victories to beef up their records. Ike Fluellen of Houston, Texas, had not fought in more than a year, yet was credited with two victories in 1976 and received an honorable mention by Ort in *Ring* for the 1976 *Ring* Progress Award! Fluellen subsequently told ABC executives that he had received a call from Chris Cline, who told the inactive fighter he could get him ranked in *Ring*'s U.S. top-ten ratings, which would earn him a place in the tournament and some good money. Fluellen therefore allowed Cline to represent him. Sure enough, the next month, Fluellen was rated number ten. Cline then told Fluellen he would be moved up in the ratings; without a fight, Fluellen was jumped to number three in the February 1977 issue of *Ring*, and was even more surprised to see that he had also been added to the world rankings, without having fought in more than a year! Fluellen was in the tournament (and, of course, the "connected" Cline would be getting a big cut out of his purse money). But when ABC made inquiries about Fluellen's charges, word got out that the fighter was causing trouble and talking too much, and he was dropped from the tournament by Don King Productions. Fluellen subsequently charged that he had received threats over the phone.

Despite these revelations, ABC began televising the tournament. King picked some very interesting locations for some of the bouts, including a U.S. aircraft carrier anchored in the waters off Florida, the U.S. Naval Academy campus, and King's own former campus, inside the walls of the Marion Correctional Institution. Not only were the locations unusual, but, coincidentally, they were on turf outside the jurisdiction of any potentially interfering state boxing commissions.

During the second telecast, on February 13 (during which, to no one's great surprise, Biff Cline was knocked out in his first bout), heavyweight Johnny Boudreaux was awarded a controversial decision over Scott LeDoux. Following the announcement of the decision, LeDoux became enraged and declared on national TV that the fight had been fixed. This served to focus more press and public attention on the charges swirling around the tournament.

Two fighters directly controlled by King, future world champions Larry Holmes and lightweight Esteban DeJesus, were in the tournament. That fact, along with the options King had extracted from every other participant, prompted *Sports Illustrated* magazine to charge, "For a promoter to control—or be in a position to gain control of—fighters in his own tournament is at best unethical. In some jurisdictions, it would be illegal." The manager of one participant came forward and alleged that he was forced to kick back 40 percent of his fighter's purse. Then ABC turned up hard evidence of faked records: Paddy Dolan, credited with four phony wins in 1975; Hilbert Stevenson, five fake wins in 1976; Anthony House, seven nonexistent wins in 1975 and 1976; plus similar examples involving at least five other fighters.

ABC persisted with the tournament telecasts until April 10.

On April 14, Nat Loubet, editor of *Ring* magazine, admitted that *Ring* had published records that were not accurate, but he put the blame on managers who had supplied false records for their fighters. He told *Sports Illustrated* that King tried to persuade him to fire John Ort. "The idea was that he could pile everything on John, use him as the scapegoat. . . . His lawyer was on the other phone. I said, 'I will not. You're just looking for a scapegoat.' All the things he's worried about in his own background, he's trying to keep covered by throwing all the attention on us," Loubet charged.

King had to do something. He announced he was dismissing his "consultants," Al Braverman and Paddy Flood. It was too late, however. ABC announced on April 16 that it was suspending telecasts of the U.S. Boxing Championships. ABC issued a statement saying, in part, "ABC believes that the very basis of the tournament has been severely compromised."

Three days later, ABC retained former prosecutor Michael Armstrong to conduct its own investigation. Armstrong, then in private practice, had considerable credentials. As a prosecutor, he had broken the New York Police Department's Serpico case. Armstrong and seventeen of his law firm's partners and associates conducted the investigation. King, meanwhile, cried race persecution once again, saying it was all an attempt "to fry this coon." Because the ABC investigation was a private one, Armstrong was at a disadvantage. He was not able to subpoena people to compel their testimony, nor could he obtain documents. Despite this handicap, he and his colleagues conducted the most thorough investigation possible. The result was a report more than 450 pages long. It conceded that many people were reluctant voluntarily to discuss their involvement in the tournament in too much detail, but the report was able to determine that King and his associates, Flood and Braverman, had a financial interest in at least fourteen fighters involved in the U.S. Championships.

Here is a summary of some of the findings contained in the Armstrong Report: The U.S. Boxing Championships included "a good deal of unethical behavior by individuals involved with the administration and organization of the tournament. . . . In a number of instances, Don King Productions failed to take even the minimal steps to secure the participation of well-qualified fighters. . . . In six cases the evidence indicates that improper payments were paid or requested, purportedly in return for getting fighters into the tournament. . . . It is clear that Flood and Braverman, both of whom had financial interests in fighters, had serious conflicts of interest in carrying out their assigned roles in the tournament. King was aware of the facts giving rise to the conflicts of interest, but failed to take appropriate steps to deal with the problems. . . . We believe that in some cases the evidence established deliberate manipulation of the process [of choosing fighters for the tournament] in order to assure the inclusion of fighters whose managers or representatives were associated with or friendly to King, Ort, Flood or Braverman at the expense of other more highly qualified fighters. . . . The most disturbing action by King for which we were able to acquire direct evidence of personal involvement was his clearly improper payment of $5,000 to John Ort, which seriously compromised the integrity of the selection process. . . . The credibility of the tournament was seriously impaired by allegations regarding King's interests in fighters." Ort denied any wrongdoing. Braverman termed the findings in the Armstrong investigation "hogwash and bullshit," but acknowledges that he and the late Paddy Flood did split with Don King at that time.

The Armstrong investigation lacked the power of the law to back it up, however, and no legally empowered body chose to pursue the matter, even though seventeen years earlier the IBC was prosecuted by a variety of different legal entities. Although King continued to make charges of racism whenever he came under attack, it might well be that because he was so visible and the first black to achieve such a high level of success in boxing, an attitude of positive discrimination was adopted when it came to dealing with him. Whatever the reasons, no one involved with the fraudulent tournament was ever prosecuted, and business at Don King Productions continued as usual. And as a result of *Ring* magazine's loss of credibility because of the part it played, the networks had no choice now but to rely on the ratings of the WBC and WBA, thus giving those groups the power base they expanded and still enjoy to this day.

King has carved out his empire by writing his own rules in a sport where he knew he could get away with it because boxing lacks a central governing body or a much-needed federal commissioner. Bob Arum is in favor of a federal boxing authority; King is opposed. Those who have done business with King over the years, including numerous disgruntled fighters, say he has established a virtual monopoly by employing the same techniques over and over again. He promises fighters a quick road to a title shot if they sign with him, then gains control over them by including option clauses in his contracts. "There's nothing wrong with options," he says. "Options are everywhere. In movies, in sports. I need to pay overhead. I invest a lot of time and money in developing a fighter and then I deserve to reap the rewards." But there is, indeed, a problem with options. It leaves a fighter under contract to King with no bargaining power. He has to accept the purse King is offering, or not fight. He cannot sell his services and talents on the open market, choosing the best deal from among the offers of a variety of different promoters.

King has also been accused by many of his fighters of having them sign blank contracts. Another frequent strategy is to cut a fighter's purse at the last minute, saying the promotion didn't do as well as expected financially and so the fighter must accept less money. And, of course, he will do whatever he can to induce a fighter to sign a contract with him. "Don King buys whoever he has to buy," said Larry Holmes. "He takes a young fighter that doesn't have any money and he puts a thousand dollars or maybe twenty thousand on the table. Boy, then you do anything. Only later do you realize he bought you, he owns you, and it wasn't the right thing to do." As Jack Newfield wrote in his 1983 *Village Voice* exposé of King entitled "Don King's Boxing Monopoly": "King's most successful promotion has been himself. His investors have lost money on most of King's major fights. . . . King makes his profit from closed-circuit franchising, subsidies from TV networks . . . and from Las Vegas casinos. . . . King is essentially a brilliant con man, who uses what he calls 'OPM'—other people's money—to make deals as a broker. . . . Three champions say King cut their purses after their fights. Larry Holmes, Thomas Hearns and Juan LaPorte all report they were paid less money by King than their prefight contracts promised them."

And then there is King's use of his stepson, Carl, to help him control fighters. Don King moved in with Carl's mother, Henrietta, in 1961 when Carl was four years old. When Carl graduated from college with a degree in marketing and management, Don promptly put his stepson in business. The business was boxing management, and Carl King got very lucky very quickly. Although many veteran boxing managers go a lifetime without ever handling a top contender or a world champion, within a few short years, while still in his twenties, Carl King miraculously ended up as the manager of world champions "Bonecrusher" Smith, Julian Jackson, Tim Witherspoon, "Irish" Leroy Haley, Carlos DeLeon, Leon Spinks, Azumah Nelson, Saoul Mamby and Michael Dokes, among others. Of course, it is not miraculous at all. Carl King works hand-in-hand with his father, since boxing commissions do not allow a promoter to manage fighters.

Saoul Mamby explained to author Thomas Hauser how he came under the promotional and management wing of the Kings. When Mamby's manager died, King asked to meet with him and proposed that the fighter sign a promotional agreement with him and a management agreement with his son. Mamby signed the promotional contract with Don but did not want to sign with Carl as his manager. King used Mamby, a world-class fighter, exactly once in nearly a year, in an undercard fight. Finally, Mamby got the message. He signed with Carl King, even though he had never met him. Immediately, he was offered two easy fights for good paydays by the Kings, and then got a fight shortly thereafter for the junior welterweight title. The bout was in South Korea. Carl King did not even go to Korea with his fighter. Nevertheless, Mamby knocked out Sang-Hyun Kim in 1980 and became a world champion. After five successful title defenses, he was matched against "Irish" Leroy Haley, a black fighter with a distinctly Celtic name, on June 26, 1982. "Just before the fight," Mamby told Hauser, "Carl King came into the dressing room and told me he couldn't work my corner. I asked why, and he mumbled something about rules and regulations or some kind of obligation. The fight went on. I lost a decision. And after the decision was announced—here I am, I've just lost my title—I look across the ring, and there's Carl King hugging Haley. I looked over there and said, 'What the fuck is going on?' Then I realized that Carl King might have been my manager, but he was also managing Haley. Why is Carl King still my manager? His daddy is the main man. Business is business."

In another King exposé by the Philadelphia *Inquirer*'s Glen Macnow, a second fighter managed by Carl King and promoted by Don King had much the same to say. Alfonso Ratliff, the former world cruiserweight champion, said, "Carl became my manager because Don King said the only way he would promote me was to have his son be my manager. I didn't want anything to do with Carl King, but I had no choice." When the Kings put Ratliff in against Mike Tyson, he says he received only $20,000 of the $75,000 he signed for. "He's like a spider who pulls you in with his money. Before you know it, you're all caught up in the web and you're at his mercy, and this man has no mercy."

In 1986, Eddie Gregg, a fringe contender under promotional contract to Don King, received a lucrative offer to fight Gerry Cooney. He was to receive $50,000, the most money by far he'd ever been offered for a fight. But the Cooney bout was not being promoted by King, and King refused to let Gregg take the offer. Gregg signed for the fight regardless, and King sued in an effort to stop the bout from taking place. Gregg and his manager, Tommy Gallagher, testified in court that King had gotten Gregg just two fights in 1985, although King's own contract with the fighter guaranteed him four fights a year. Gregg and Gallagher further testified that they had not been allowed to read the King contracts thoroughly and that the contracts they had signed with the promoter were blank. Martin Stecher, Justice of the New York State Supreme Court, had heard enough. He ruled against King, criticizing him for compelling the fighter to sign "harsh" and "one-sided" blank contracts, with King left to fill them in any way he chose. Judge Stecher also noted that in the previous year, the two fights King had provided for Gregg paid him just $12,500, one-third of which had to be paid to his manager, Tommy Gallagher. "There is no demonstration," Justice Stecher stated, "of devotion of a single dollar or a single hour to Gregg's career." Gregg fought Cooney and was stopped in the first round, but at least the $50,000 he earned gave him a little nest egg to retire on.

British promoter and manager Mickey Duff has had numerous run-ins with King. He says King stole top featherweight contender Azumah Nelson from him after Nelson looked tremendous in a narrow loss to Salvador Sanchez for the Featherweight Championship at Madison Square Garden in 1982. Nelson acquired the title after the untimely death of Sanchez in a car accident in Mexico. Duff also tells a humorous story of how Don King tried to steal Duff's top middleweight contender John "The Beast" Mugabi. Duff had Mugabi fighting in Atlantic City on a King-promoted card early in the African boxer's career when Duff wanted him to get experience fighting tough American opponents. Duff had other business in England, so reluctantly left Mugabi and trainer George Francis alone. Mugabi looked sensational knocking out tough Curtis Ramsey in one round. Duff got a transatlantic phone call after the fight. King was on the line, saying "Mickey, we got a problem. Mugabi is begging me to take over his career, but I told him no. I said you and I are friends, Mickey, so I wouldn't take him on unless he agreed to keep you as a 50 percent partner." Duff responded, "Don, I didn't know you spoke Swahili." King said he didn't. "That's very interesting," said Duff, "because Mugabi doesn't speak a word of English."

Rival promoter Butch Lewis sued Don King in 1983 for stealing a fighter from him. When Lewis left Bob Arum's Top Rank and went out on his own, he handled the careers of the two Spinks brothers and heavyweight Greg Page, who rose through the rankings to become a top contender. Lewis testified that King offered him $200,000 in cash to join Don King Productions and bring Page with him. Lewis turned down the offer. He charged that King then interfered with the exclusive promotional contract he held with Page and induced the fighter to leave him and sign with DKP. Lewis said King did it by promising to advance Page's career and by spreading about $50,000 in cash among Page's friends, and especially Page's parents, until they all began telling him that King was the man to go with. Lewis also charged that King seduced Page with $300,000 in under-the-table payments.

King's defense in Manhattan Supreme Court was nothing if not bold and frank. He said he did not interfere with Lewis's contract, but that Page came to him because he knew King was the man who held the key to the heavyweight division. To illustrate this, King proceeded to show the court how he controlled, either exclusively or in partnership, not only the champion Larry Holmes, but also all of the top-ten heavyweights in the division. Gerry Cooney, Michael Dokes, Trevor Berbick, Tex Cobb, Leon Spinks, Renaldo Snipes, Jimmy Young, Lynn Ball, Bernardo Mercado and Jim "Quick" Tillis all were under contract to Don King Productions. Therefore, King reasoned, "Greg Page must, if his career is to develop properly, fight only top-ranked opponents. I respectfully submit that, unless Greg Page can fight opponents who are under contract to DKP, his career will be at a standstill. And under DKP's promotional contracts with top contenders, they cannot fight for any other promoter without DKP's consent. In light of Butch Lewis's past and present conduct toward both me and Greg Page, such consent will not be forthcoming." In other words, to justify his co-opting of Page, King used as his defense the very fact that he already held a virtual monopoly on the heavyweight division! The jury ruled for Lewis, but Page wanted to stay with King, so Lewis accepted a $200,000 settlement. As far as King is concerned, compromise settlements are part of his business costs, just like rent or staff salaries. He went on to earn much more than $200,000 with Greg Page.

In 1982, former world featherweight champion Bobby Chacon of California, then thirty years old, was offered the chance to fight Bazooka Limon for Limon's WBC Super-Featherweight title. To get the fight, Chacon, a gutsy little scrapper, had to sign a three-fight option contract with Don King in the event he beat Limon. In what was perhaps the most sensational fight of 1982, the plucky Chacon, badly battered, rallied in the late rounds to earn a close decision and take the title.

In the spring of 1983, NBC Sports was planning to televise Chacon's first defense, against Cornelius Boza-Edwards, another of Mickey Duff's fighters. Edwards was ranked number one by the WBC, so he was a mandatory challenger. But King decided he wanted Chacon's opponent to be Hector Camacho instead. Coincidentally, King had just signed Camacho to a six-fight promotional deal. NBC said no: Boza-Edwards was the top contender, and they wanted to televise Chacon-Boza. The network did not take into account the power King wielded with his close ally, WBC president Jose Sulaiman. Even though Boza, according to the WBC's own rules, was due the title match, Sulaiman withdrew WBC sanction from the bout, and NBC no longer had a world championship match.

Independent promoters then offered Chacon $1 million to fight Camacho, but King, with his three-option contract on Chacon in hand (even though WBC rules only allowed a promoter one option) told Chacon he couldn't take either of the $1 million offers. King said he would promote the Chacon-Camacho title fight and pay Chacon $450,000. Chacon refused to accept King's much smaller offer, so Jose Sulaiman, who brags about all the gifts he's received from his friend Don King, stripped Chacon of his title. Bobby Chacon was no longer a world champion according to the WBC. Not surprisingly, King's fighter, Hector Camacho, was handed the crown in an easy fight for the vacant title which the dangerous Boza-Edwards was not invited to take part in. As Jack Newfield further pointed out in his brilliantly researched 1983 *Village Voice* exposé of King, the WBC constitution said the very multioption contract that King had trapped Chacon with was against the organization's rules in order "to promote and preserve competition and deter monopoly in the sport of boxing." And in addition, multioption contracts were illegal in California, where King signed his with Chacon but then conveniently failed to file it with the California Athletic Commission.

On November 26, 1982, a tough and durable fighter with limited talent named Randall "Tex" Cobb fought Larry Holmes for the Heavyweight Championship in Houston, Texas. Holmes took an easy, lopsided decision in a fight promoted, naturally, by Don King. Cobb's contract called for him to receive $700,000 or 30 percent of all gross revenues, whichever figure was larger. Cobb figured that the 30 percent should have earned him as much as $1.3 million. Instead, Cobb says, a week before the fight his manager, Joe Gramby, came to him and said the bout would be canceled unless he agreed to accept a flat purse of $500,000. Wanting the shot at the title, Cobb agreed and signed the new contract for the smaller amount. Cobb charges that, after the fight, Gramby received $200,000 as a "consultant's fee" from Don King Productions. Coincidentally on the same day he persuaded his fighter to sign the reduced-purse contract with King. Cobb couldn't figure out what consulting services his manager could have performed for King that would have been worth $200,000. Subsequently, a letter turned up on Don King's corporate letterhead dated November 13, 1982, which was thirteen days before the Holmes-Cobb fight. The letter is addressed to Mr. Joe Gramby, and reads: "This letter serves as an agreement between Don King Productions (DKP) and Joe Gramby for the Randy Tex Cobb vs. Larry Holmes WBC World Heavyweight Championship bout, scheduled to take place on November 26, 1982 at the Houston Astrodome in Houston, Texas. This letter will confirm our understanding that in addition to $500,000.00 (Five Hundred Thousand dollars) being paid to Randy Cobb as his purse under contract dated August 25, 1982, DKP agrees to pay $200,000.00 (Two Hundred Thousand dollars) to Joe Gramby for consultant services." The letter is signed by Don King for Don King Productions, Inc., and also signed "Accepted and agreed" by Joseph Gramby and dated November 15th, 1982 in the same handwriting.

Joe Gramby says he never received any money from Don King. He says he does not know about the letter purportedly signed by him. He says Cobb's purse was reduced by $200,000 because Cobb did not arrive in Houston two weeks before the fight, as agreed, in order to help publicize the bout. Gramby said, "It was a penalty and it was justified . . . he deserved it." This rings hollow in the light of the fact that a manager is supposed to argue on behalf of his fighter, not on behalf of the promoter, and also because the $200,000 cut would have cost Gramby about $65,000 as his one-third share, so one would think it hardly in his interest to justify the purse cut. King has changed his story several times concerning how much money Cobb was due and why his purse was cut, but he has always denied all Cobb's allegations. It will be left for a court in Texas to decide exactly what happened, because Cobb has brought suit against both King and Gramby, charging that "In return for a $200,000 payoff [Gramby] was to instruct his fighter that a new agreement was needed and that Plaintiff [Cobb] would need to accept a reduction in his compensation or the fight would be called off. . . . The agreement between Don King and Joe Gramby was not intended to be a contract for legitimate services to be rendered, rather it was designed as a payoff to Joe Gramby for his assistance in inducing Plaintiff to accept a reduction in compensation." The case was due to be heard at the time of writing (March 1989).

Playing games with fighters' purses has been a long-standing business practice of King's. Mitch Green, under promotional contract to Don King Productions, signed to fight Mike Tyson at Madison Square Garden in 1986 for $50,000. But Green says shortly before the fight, Don and Carl King told him he had to take $30,000 or there would be no fight. No reason was given. Green protested and said he wouldn't fight. King went to New York boxing commissioner Jose Torres. Torres came to Green's dressing room and, instead of looking into Green's charges, told the fighter if he didn't go through with the bout he would be suspended and Torres would see to it that he never fought again in the United States. Torres, of course, was wearing two hats: He was a boxing official, but he was also a member of Tyson's inner circle. The fight went on, since Green felt he had no alternative. He lost a ten-round decision to Tyson and claims he was given only $7,500 of the $30,000 purse.

In 1986, Green was set to fight "Bonecrusher" Smith. King was not involved in that fight. But when the promoter needed a substitute to fight Tim Witherspoon at Madison Square Garden, he obtained the services of Smith, who withdrew from his scheduled fight with Green. Mitch Green then filed a lawsuit against Don King, claiming that he had suffered financially when his fight with Smith was called off. Green, himself a 'head case,' also confronted and threatened King at a Madison Square Garden news conference. King attempted to have the lawsuit dismissed, but New York State Supreme Court Justice Beatrice Shainswit denied the motion, saying the Kings, father and son, "juggled contractual relationships when it served their economic purposes." Justice Shainswit also said the rights of Mitch Green were "mocked" as the Kings "charted their respective courses." Green's case thus remained on the court docket, but the problem with suing King, it seems, is that one has to get in line and wait his turn.

One of the biggest jokes in boxing circles for years has been the use of Carl King as a boxing manager by his father. An effective manager must function in an adversarial position with a promoter. It is a manager's job to negotiate every financial and other advantage he can for his fighter, looking out for his man's best interests and making the best deals for him. As many of King's fighters have asked over the years, how could they possibly expect Carl King to go to his father and negotiate faithfully on their behalf, when controlling those fighters was a family business? Carl King insists he operates in his fighter's best interests when he negotiates with his father. He once said, "I've gotten thrown out of his office many times," but he didn't specify whether this was for being a tough negotiator or for failing to fetch his dad's coffee fast enough.

Just how the father-and-son team operates is perhaps best illustrated by the events surrounding the WBA Heavyweight Championship fight on December 12, 1986 between Tim Witherspoon and "Bonecrusher" Smith at Madison Square Garden, part of the HBO-sponsored Heavyweight Elimination Tournament. Witherspoon had come under managerial and promotional control of the Kings in 1982 when they purchased his contract for $100,000. Owing to several disputes over money in the ensuing years, when Witherspoon felt he was grossly shortchanged by the Kings, the relationship between the promoter-manager twosome and the fighter was strained. Nevertheless, Witherspoon, as WBA champion, was part of the Elimination Tournament and was scheduled to fight another King boxer, former champion Tony Tubbs, in December of 1986. Tubbs, however, claiming he had suffered a training injury, pulled out of the fight. On short notice, the Kings needed a substitute, one who was in condition, ready to fight and ranked high enough to be a viable contender and acceptable to HBO. In reality, Tubbs was not injured but, like many fighters, was involved in a financial dispute with the Kings.

"Bonecrusher" Smith was training for a fight down south with Mitch Green, and so was ready to fight. He was approached by the Kings and offered instead what every fighter dreams of: a shot at the title. At the advanced age of thirty-three, Smith knew it would probably be his one and only opportunity to reach for the crown. Not surprisingly, he withdrew from the scheduled fight with Green, left his manager, Alan Kornberg, and signed a contract making Don King his promoter and another making Carl King his new manager. Smith said he knew if he didn't do that he'd probably never get a title shot, since the Kings controlled the division as firmly as the IBC had controlled boxing in the 1950s. Kornberg sued the Kings, who quickly settled with him by bringing him back into the fold as an equal partner with Carl King in the management of Smith. Kornberg, too, knew the reality of life among the heavyweights—and the Kings. It was better to settle than fight.

Next, Carl King went to Witherspoon and told him that Tubbs was out of the fight and instead he would be defending against Smith. Witherspoon did not want to accept Smith as an opponent just days before the fight. He had geared his training to fighting Tubbs, and Smith had a completely different style. Furthermore, he had already fought Smith and beaten him and saw no reason to fight him again. But instead of checking into Witherspoon's allegations of wrongdoing, New York Boxing Commissioner Jose Torres threatened to suspend Witherspoon if he refused to go through with the bout. Backed to the wall, much as Mitch Green had been, Witherspoon relented. Nicholas Clemente, an attorney for Witherspoon, told Glen Macnow of the Philadelphia *Inquirer*, "Torres chose to intervene solely on Don King's behalf. It's as if King said, 'Jump,' and Torres asked, 'How far?' " Witherspoon, disgusted with the Kings and all the circumstances requiring him to fight an opponent against his will, went into the ring on December 12 in a lackluster frame of mind and was knocked out in the first round by "Bonecrusher" Smith. Of course, it was a no-lose night for the Kings. Carl King collected his share of Tim Witherspoon's purse as manager. He also collected his 50 percent share (Kornberg receiving the other half) of the new WBA champion's purse as co-manager. And Don King collected his fees as promoter of the title match—making it a triple payday for the Kings!

Subsequently, Tim Witherspoon took his turn in line and

filed a lawsuit on March 5, 1987, in U.S. District Court in New York. The suit accuses the Kings of restraint of trade, fraud, antitrust violations, racketeering, unjust enrichment, breach of contract and fraudulent conversion. In it, Witherspoon charges (as have other fighters) that Carl King took 50 percent of his earnings, even though in all the states where boxing is responsibly governed, including New York, Nevada, New Jersey and California, it is illegal for a manager to receive more than 33 percent. He also says the Kings forced him to sign blank contracts and to fight when he was injured. He says he was forced to pay Carl King high management fees, even though the promoter's son did not provide him with the services due from a real manager. As an example, Witherspoon said that when he told Carl King he did not want to fight Smith, his "manager" told him, "Boy, I don't know if my father will like that. I'll have to ask him." Instead, Witherspoon contends, Carl King should have taken his side and stood firm against his fighting Smith. But as many, including Witherspoon, ex-champion Alfonzo Ratliff, and New York State Athletic Commission Chairman Randy Gordon, have asked, how can Carl King function effectively as a manager when he is completely beholden to his father and the fighters he manages are controlled promotionally by his father?

Witherspoon also charges that when he refused to accept Smith, Carl King just crossed Tony Tubbs's name off the contract and substituted Smith's name without Witherspoon's permission, which Carl King denies. In addition, Witherspoon says he was required to train at Don King's Ohio training camp, where the millionaire promoter billed the fighter for everything, including a $113 car rental, $38 medical test, and new tires for Witherspoon's car. He also billed Witherspoon $3,500 for travel expenses to a press conference for the fight, which is an expense that should be handled by the promoter, not the fighter. Witherspoon was billed over $14,000 for sparring partners' salaries. But the biggest discrepancy on the itemized expense sheet given to the fighter came under the listing "Training Camp 28 days @ $100." That comes to $2,800 for four weeks of training at King's camp. However, in the "totals" column, an extra zero was added, and Witherspoon ended up being billed $28,000 for twenty-eight days of training! The fighter's total expenses, billed by King, came to over $75,000. Such expenses are always supposed to come off the top of the purse, before the fighter and manager divide up their shares. But financial documents from the fight indicate that Carl King first took his cut off the top of the gross purse of $400,000, leaving all the expenses to be charged to Witherspoon's remaining share, which was $200,000 after Carl King had taken his 50 percent. After expenses were deducted, Witherspoon was left with $125,000. But that was not all. He then had to pay his trainer, Slim Jim Robinson, another expense which is supposed to come off the top of the gross purse. Witherspoon says he finished up with under $100,000, and after paying his taxes, he probably netted $50,000 or $60,000 for losing his WBA heavyweight title!

Witherspoon's lawsuit contains allegations going further back than the "Bonecrusher" Smith fight. In 1984, Witherspoon held the WBC version of the title. Don King put him in a fight against Pinklon Thomas, another King fighter, and told Witherspoon his $350,000 purse would have to be split 50-50 with son Carl. Witherspoon went to an attorney and got his portion of the purse increased from $175,000 to $250,000. In doing so, however, he made the Kings angry. He said Don King told him if the fight went to a decision, he would lose his title. The fight did go to a decision, a very close split decision, and the championship was awarded to Pinklon Thomas.

Witherspoon left the Kings, but had to come crawling back, unable, he says, to get any fights once he walked away from them. Back with the Kings, he got another title opportunity and won the WBA crown. In 1986 he went to London to defend against Frank Bruno, part of the HBO Elimination Tournament. Coming from behind, he rallied to knock Bruno out late in the fight. Mickey Duff, the British co-promoter of the bout, allocated $1.7 million for Witherspoon's end. Then Don King took his fees, Carl King took his cut, expenses were deducted, and Tim Witherspoon ended up with $115,000 out of the $1.7 million that had been allocated to Don King Productions! One of the expenses King deducted from Witherspoon's purse was $250,000 in "step aside" money for Tony Tubbs. This is a fairly common occurrence in boxing, paying a fighter who is next in line for a fight a fee to step aside temporarily so that a different opponent can instead fight. Tubbs had a contract to fight Witherspoon, which in itself is curious since King controlled Tubbs and presumably could have avoided that situation. Witherspoon says the promoter came to him and told him he would have to pay the $250,000 out of his end for Tubbs to agree to step aside and allow Witherspoon to fight Bruno. However, Mickey Duff says he, too, gave King the "step aside" fee for Tubbs, leaving the distinct impression that King double-dipped for an extra quarter-million dollars. King, of course, denies all allegations. The Witherspoon lawsuit is still pending and may remain so for quite some time.

Because of the stench that arose from revelations of the shenanigans surrounding the Witherspoon-Tubbs-Smith fight, New York State Governor Mario Cuomo ordered an independent investigation into the circumstances enveloping the fight. Spearheading the investigation was King's old nemesis, Joe Spinelli, who had previously and unsuccessfully tried to nail the promoter when he was with the FBI. Spinelli was now the New York State Inspector General. He found conflicts of interest in that Carl King was the manager of all three fighters involved. Spinelli recommended legislation in New York to prevent a manager from being related to a promoter he was dealing with, to outlaw long-term option contracts between promoters and fighters, and to prevent a manager from having an involvement with both fighters in the same bout.

The New York State Athletic Commission suspended Carl King's license to manage for one year for failing to notify the Commission he had two fighters on the same card, a violation of a commission rule. But that suspension did not mean much, because the Kings do most of their boxing business outside New York. Athletic Commission Chairman Torres cried mea culpa. He said the Witherspoon-Smith contract was legal because Carl King, acting as manager, had initialed the change from Tubbs to Smith. Torres said he was unaware that Carl King had an involvement with Smith as well as Witherspoon, even though it was common knowledge. Torres had, however, approved the Witherspoon-Tubbs fight, where Carl King also had dual managerial involvement. To make matters worse, the New York Athletic Commission subsequently told the press that Witherspoon had failed a postfight drug test, only to later recant and say the information was mistaken, but after harm had been done to Witherspoon's reputation. Governor Cuomo at last reached the breaking point with Torres. First it had been Torres's close, public, unrestrained involvement with Tyson while he was supposed to be an impartial boxing official. Then came his apparent siding with King and compelling Mitch Green and Tim Witherspoon to go ahead with fights they may have had valid reasons to complain about, plus his claimed ignorance of Carl King's triple involvement with Witherspoon-Tubbs-Smith. Finally, reports surfaced that Cuomo had found out that Torres had accepted tickets and travel expenses from the Tyson people to attend the Tyson-Tubbs fight in Tokyo. Before he departed, Cuomo made Torres return them. But Torres's fate was sealed. Shortly thereafter, he resigned from the Athletic Commission, amid widespread reports that Governor Cuomo had forced him to step down.

Because there are few laws governing boxing, Joe Spinelli, while labeling the activities of the Kings a "blatant conflict of interest," concluded there was no criminality involved. King is simply smart enough to be able to take advantage of the athletes in a sport that is largely unregulated. David Bey, another King-controlled heavyweight contender, said he had to split his purses 50-50 with Carl King, who would not take any action without first checking with his father. "He was just a front man," says Bey, "because Don King couldn't be a manager and a promoter at the same time." Spinelli says, "King's contracts are horrible . . . nothing more than legalized extortion. But in the world of boxing, they're legal."

Don King's oft-repeated slogan is "Only in America." On talk shows, in interviews, at news conferences, wherever he can, he is quick to point out what a great land of opportunity the United States is by bellowing "Only in America!" And he is probably right. Only in America could someone like Don King be allowed to get away

with what he has done for the last forty years, starting with his numbers running and manslaughter conviction,
and progressing to his octopuslike grip on boxing in general
and on the heavyweight division in particular.

Chapter 12

Wedded Bliss, Managerial Problems

I think obtaining me was part of Mike's "game plan" from the very beginning.
— *Robin Givens*

No sooner had Tyson returned from his title defense in Japan than a rift developed between the boxer and his surviving manager. In large part it was because Bill Cayton found himself in a Catch-22 situation. He was perceptive enough to see early on what it would take Tyson, blinded by infatuation, obsession—or love—months to realize: that the team of Ruth Roper and Robin Givens was not to be trusted. But when he tried to protect Tyson from himself, the fighter took it as an attack on his beloved wife and mother-in-law and sided with the new women (note the plural) in his life. The trouble began when Cayton learned that Tyson had given Robin power of attorney to sign checks and financial documents. He had been perturbed enough that Mike had impulsively married without executing a prenuptial agreement, and now this new development gave him further cause for concern.

Givens then said there was a problem with Tyson getting access to his money when they wanted to pay for their new mansion in Bernardsville, New Jersey—in cash, over $4 million. There was never an adequate explanation of what exactly the problem was in accessing Tyson's cash. Jacobs and Cayton had $6 million in Tyson's Merrill Lynch account, plus several million more in certificates of deposit and other annuities that would have made him financially secure for the rest of his life even if he never set foot in a boxing ring again. Perhaps the problem was that Givens, as she found out when she went to Merrill Lynch on the day of Jacobs's funeral, did not have access to the money or that the shrewd Cayton thought it would be more financially prudent of the Tysons to obtain a mortgage rather than plunk down well over $4 million in one lump. Whatever it was, egged on no doubt by her mother, Robin began sending Mike the message that things weren't right in the Tyson financial department, and when Robin spoke (as would be demonstrated many times in the months ahead) Mike listened unquestioningly, time and again turning his back on those who had faithfully served his interests over the years.

The purchase of their home finally completed, the newlyweds moved in and began improvements, renovations and furnishing estimated at a couple of million dollars. It was the house that Mike Tyson wanted, the home of his dreams, where he would live happily ever after with his beautiful wife and lots of children, the first of which was on its way, Robin had told him. Growing up in Catskill, he had gazed at photos of stately homes and castles in Britain and Ireland and vowed he would have something like that someday. Now that day had come. The house was an American castle named Kenilwood, which had been built in 1897, of stone, in the style of architecture known as Victorian Gothic Revival. It had previously been owned by Sumner Welles, Undersecretary of State for President Franklin Roosevelt, and other owners had carried the bloodlines of American "royalty," the Vanderbilts and Astors.

The massive home featured a marble-floored entry hall; a library decorated in all-white, with a white leather sofa (with zebra skin pillows), a baby grand piano, and Louis XV chairs; a formal dining room with a Baccarat chandelier and a dining table of mahogany with ebony inlay that seated sixteen people for dinner; and gold accents throughout—gilt furniture and gold leaf on the ceilings.

Mike and Robin had little time to settle in and relax in their castle. She had her TV show and a forthcoming made-for-TV movie that would keep her on a busy shooting schedule in California, and Cayton was busy finalizing plans for the fight Jacobs did not live to see, the June 27 showdown between Tyson and Michael Spinks (which would mean after April it would be time for Mike to get back to serious training). In the meantime, he and Robin shuttled between Los Angeles and New Jersey, spending what time they could together.

Meanwhile, Don King was getting nervous. He had felt demeaned by his cool treatment in Japan, by the knowledge that the Japanese looked on him as an undesirable in their country. Furthermore, he knew he had no firm deal except on a fight-by-fight basis with Cayton to work on Tyson's bouts. In the coming Spinks fight, he was to have essentially a figurehead role. He would not control the finances or the major decisionmaking. That would be in Cayton's capable hands, and the big-money worldwide TV, pay-per-view and closed circuit would be run by Shelly Finkel, a film friend and business associate of the Jacobs-Cayton team. Finkel, a rock music promoter and manager, had bought his way into the lucrative world of championship boxing in recent years and had relied on Jacobs to lead him by the hand through the unfamiliar world of pugilism. The two had become close, as Finkel, in partnership with Dan and Lou Duva, managed numerous Olympic medal winners, including Tyrell Biggs, Mark Breland and Evander Holyfield. The selling of TV rights was in Finkel's area of expertise, so there, too, King was superfluous. For the Tyson-Spinks battle, King would be paid a flat fee of $3 million. Out of that, he would have to put together the undercard at a cost of several hundred thousand dollars, and the rest was his to keep. A big payday for very little work. But King chafed at the idea of being just a "hired hand." He was uncomfortably aware that he was very expendable in the future unless he could form an unbreakable bond with Tyson. Recognizing this, and seeing the strained relations developing between the young black fighter and his elderly white manager, King did what he knew would put him on Tyson's side. He decided to ally himself with the women, and set out to win Ruth and Robin's confidence so they could stand united against Bill Cayton.

Kevin Rooney saw what was happening early on. "All the leeches are out now," he said, but he had the guts to stand up for what he knew was right. "I trust Bill Cayton. I knew what we got in Bill Cayton is good." He remembered Cayton saving him from his own weaknesses. Knowing how Rooney liked to gamble, Cayton had refused to give him his purse money from one of his last fights, held in Atlantic City, until he was safely back in Catskill and away from the temptation of the gaming tables. Over the years, Rooney had seen first hand the way Cayton negotiated deals for Tyson and the complete fiscal integrity with which he operated; he knew Bill Cayton was operating in the best interests of Mike Tyson. But Rooney was in an awkward position, for to speak out on behalf of Cayton meant, by implication, he was coming out against both the women and Don King. By taking Bill Cayton's side, Kevin Rooney effectively sealed his own fate.

In April, before beginning serious training for the Michael Spinks fight, Tyson spent some time at his Los Angeles home with Robin. Coincidentally, Don King also had a home in Los Angeles. Not surprisingly, he spent a good deal of time with Tyson, with Robin and with Ruth. King later claimed he was trying to heal the rift between Tyson and Cayton, but rumors got back to Cayton that King was actually trying to induce Tyson unilaterally to sign an exclusive promotional contract with the wild-haired huckster. Tyson professed suspicion of everyone—except his wife and mother-in-law. He constantly made such statements as: "People want to be my friend so they can get my money. . . . People are trying to steal my fuckin' money. . . . Do you think I'm gonna trust Don King? . . . You work all your life, break your fuckin' back, and a guy who doesn't have calluses on his hands wants to take your fuckin' money. . . . I'm gonna wind up rich. . . . They're stealing from me . . . I'm not gonna wind up broke. . . . We all know what Don King is, but if you keep a snake in a room with the lights on, you can control him."

In May, Tyson and Robin were back East in their New Jersey home. King let it be known that he was unhappy with his flat-fee arrangement on the Tyson-Spinks bout where he was being paid a mere $3 million on a fight expected to gross as much as $70 million worldwide. When he signed the contracts for his participation in the promotion, he added under his signature in his own hand that he was signing under "economic duress." Cayton thought this was pretty funny; picking up a quick $3 million for putting together the undercard hardly seemed to constitute economic duress. For his part, the manager did not want to create waves. He just wanted all to go as smoothly as possible in the weeks leading up to the biggest-money fight in boxing history. He established a separate corporation, Sports of the Century,

Inc., that would receive all revenues pertaining to the big fight, a move he said was made to further ensure protection for all the money due his fighter.

Ruth Roper and Robin Givens, listening to Don King's sweet nothings, continued to nurse a growing suspicion of Bill Cayton. It was obvious they were out of their depth in the unfamiliar and extraordinary world of boxing. They had Tyson retain his own attorney, Michael Winston, who happened to be Ruth Roper's attorney, too. Also working behind the scenes to secure his position in the Tyson picture was Shelly Finkel, who spent a fair amount of time cultivating a relationship with the Ruth-and-Robin team, as well as with Tyson, trying to serve as a conduit between the fighter and Cayton. However, Finkel was endeavoring to consolidate his own position. He offered to help with his show business contacts in advancing the acting career of Robin, which the family said they interpreted as a "bribe," and which annoyed Mike, who was well aware of Finkel's financial interest in the TV rights to his fights. With the tug-of-war going on around him, the fighter said it was all "bullshit" and grew increasingly annoyed at the way his wife and mother-in-law were being portrayed in the press as gold-diggers. He constantly said that if his new family wanted all his money they didn't have to steal it, he'd gladly give it to them if they asked.

Despite the love professed between Mike and Robin, things behind the scenes were anything but smooth in the marriage. On the spring afternoon of May 8, 1988, Mike was driving his $150,000 Bentley down Varick Street in lower Manhattan, near the Holland Tunnel. With him were Robin, in the front seat, as well as the world's most ubiquitous mother-in-law, Ruth Roper. An argument between the young husband and wife developed into a physical confrontation, as Robin started slapping Mike while he was driving. Trying to fend her off, he lost control of the car and smacked into a parked automobile, damaging both vehicles. Reports later surfaced that the domestic spat erupted when Robin confronted Mike with the fact that she was less than thrilled to find that he was carrying condoms, especially since he wasn't using them in their marital relationship.

Nobody was hurt in the accident, and Tyson made an impulsive gesture of foolhardy generosity that put the incident on the front pages in New York. When two Port Authority police officers who were passing by came over to investigate, Mike flipped them the keys to the Bentley and said, "I've had nothing but bad luck with this car. You guys keep it." The stunned cops were delighted with their unexpected windfall. Except for some minor damage to the bumper, the Bentley was in pristine condition. They promptly drove it across the river to New Jersey and stashed it in a garage. Unfortunately, the next morning word of the incident reached Port Authority police commanding officers, and all the two cops got instead of a luxury car was a lot of hot water. They were ordered to bring the Bentley back immediately and hand it over to the authorities. At first they refused, saying it was a gift from the heavyweight champion. They were reminded there was the little matter of rules and regulations that did not permit police to accept gifts, which in other circumstances could be construed as bribes. The car was retrieved and impounded, and eventually returned, at the behest of Bill Cayton, to the custody of Mike Tyson's corporation.

The day after the accident, Mike's new "friend," Don King, rushed out to buy him a new $175,000 Rolls Royce to replace the slightly dented Bentley. It was an obviously gratuitous gesture on King's part, designed to ingratiate himself further with the young fighter, whose trust he was trying desperately to win. When Bill Cayton learned of it, he said Mike would reimburse King for the cost of the new Rolls, making it clear that Tyson could pay his own way and did not need to accept any expensive gifts, especially from Don King.

The fireworks for that week were not yet over. In a telephone interview with sportscaster Bob McNamara of WNYT-TV in Albany, New York, McNamara said Cayton had told him he was fed up with the interference of Don King and the alliance King had formed with Givens and Roper. "There are three years and eight months to go on the contract. If they try to break it on me, I'll take it all the way to the Supreme Court," McNamara quoted Cayton. "If, after our contract runs out, Tyson wants me to manage him again, he'll have to beg me. If he doesn't, I'll walk away." Cayton further said that "King is winning Tyson with the theory that blacks should stick together. Black trainer, black manager, black promoter, black, black, black." And he remarked that "The woman [Mike] is in love with has ideas." Having spoken perhaps too hastily, Cayton tried to back off from the quotes McNamara attributed to him. He answered inquiries by saying he had been joking, and clarified his remarks to reporter Wally Matthews, telling him he had never said Tyson would have to beg him to continue as his manager in 1992. He had said he might retire at the end of the contract, when he would be nearly seventy-four years old. If not, and Mike asked—not begged—him to continue, he probably would. As for King, "He's been making moves all along," Cayton said. "I know what King is doing, wining and dining Mike. . . . But I don't think [Mike] can be swayed by it in a business sense. I think Mike has been taught better than that, through countless conversations with Cus D'Amato. Mike knows the way King operates." What Cayton did not take into account was the remarkable lack of loyalty Tyson was showing toward those who had played the major roles in helping him develop to where he was in his career, and financially, at the tender age of twenty-one. If Cayton had realized this, he would not have been surprised that Tyson was finding it extraordinarily easy to ignore all Cus D'Amato's warnings about Don King. Tyson was angered by Cayton's implications about the motives of his new family members and called him to express his displeasure. He said it was untrue that Robin had any "ideas" concerning him or his money, and he did not like his wife and mother-in-law being publicly maligned, since it was upsetting them and turning them into nervous wrecks.

Meanwhile, with Cayton in his New York office putting together all the deals and details that would earn Tyson over $20 million on the Spinks fight, what was Don King doing for his $3 million cut? He was ensconced in an Albany hotel for days, constantly at Tyson's elbow, seeking at every turn to undermine whatever confidence the fighter still retained in Cayton. More and more, Tyson's utterances sounded like the parroting of ideas he was being fed by King. He talked about Cayton and Finkel being "Jews in three-piece suits" and said that his deal when he fought in Japan had been a bad one. He claimed he had only gotten $8.7 million and not the talked-of $10 million. Ridiculously, he used as an example the Ali-Foreman fight in Zaire, saying these fighters earned $5 million each to fight in one of the poorest countries in the world, while he got less than $9 million to fight in the richest country in the world. Since the Ali-Foreman fight was a Don King promotion, it wasn't hard to figure out who planted that idea with Tyson. What Mike failed—or refused—to see was that Cayton and Jacobs had made a deal on his behalf in Japan so fabulous that the media and boxing people marveled at it. True, Ali and Foreman split $10 million, but that was for a climactic fight with worldwide interest in which Ali was seeking to regain the championship against Foreman, the reigning undisputed champion and Olympic gold medalist, undefeated and perceived by the public as an indestructible monster, in much the same way as Tyson would later come to be regarded. Each man got $5 million, watershed purses at the time (paid, Tyson failed to realize, by a frivolous dictator bent on self-aggrandizement out of the coffers of his woefully bankrupt nation's resources. Tyson got a purse nearly double that for fighting a fat and out-of-condition opponent who would not even have been accepted by the American public as a viable challenger—hardly a fight comparable with the Ali-Foreman bout.

On May 20, angry with trainer Kevin Rooney for continuing to support Cayton, Tyson moved his training camp from Catskill to Atlantic City. His fight with Michael Spinks was just five weeks away. Two days later, reportedly at the behest of his wife, he summarily fired his friend, confidant, camp coordinator and assistant manager, Steve Lott. He offered no explanation other than to say that although he liked Lott well enough, the man was employed and paid by Cayton, so he couldn't stay. One by one, Mike Tyson was severing all his ties with the past.

On that same day, May 20, on his way to Atlantic City, Tyson and the women met in Manhattan long enough for Mike to close the account at Merrill Lynch which had been established for him by Cayton and Jacobs. He transferred the nearly $5 million in assets to a new, presumably joint, account at U.S. Trust Company. He also had an additional Wall Street portfolio the two managers had set up worth another $5 million in an annuity plus negotiable securities. Mike had been spending money like water, paying out a fortune on jewelry and expensive gifts for Robin and Ruth, including, for the latter, an $80,000 BMW automobile.

In an effort to establish a truce, Cayton had dinner with Ruth Roper on Tuesday, May 24. He convinced her that any differences among all the parties concerned should be put on the back burner until after the Spinks fight, especially in order to keep Mike free of worries and on an even keel in his training for what promised to be the most difficult test of his professional career. Apparently he received some assurances from Roper, because he came away from the dinner confident they were all working, at least for the time being, toward the same goal. Cayton succeeded in having Steve Lott reinstated; nearing a momentous showdown with an undefeated champion like Spinks was not the time, he argued persuasively, to make any changes in the people and routines Mike was familiar with.

Meanwhile, Tyson continued to be bothered by the stress which he felt was affecting Robin and Ruth, and himself as well. He talked about leaving the U.S. and becoming a citizen of the tax-haven of Monaco and reportedly consulted a financial adviser about how much income his nest eggs would provide for the rest of his life if he walked away from boxing there and then.

In an interview with WNYT-TV, his "hometown" TV station in Albany, Mike stated his confidence in Bill Cayton as his manager, but said he also wanted to work with Don King as his promoter. "No one can gain control of Mike Tyson, because I'm the boss. Don King is the promoter, Bill Cayton's my manager, and that's as far as it goes. No one's my boss, no one gains control of me. See, that's what people seem to forget. 'Control of Mike Tyson,' like he doesn't have a brain, he doesn't think for himself. That's totally absurd. . . . Don King has no experience in managing," Tyson said, somewhat naively. "He never managed anybody in his life. I don't believe that he's a better manager than Bill Cayton. . . . If Bill Cayton feels like this, perhaps he's paranoid about the situation. No one's going to be my manager but Bill Cayton. As long as Bill Cayton's around, he's my manager, from the beginning to the end . . . to the end of my career, as long as I'm boxing and he's around, he's my manager."

Tyson professed a personal liking for King, saying "he's

not a bad guy." Reminded that Cus had little regard for King, Tyson responded, "This is business. . . . Because I don't like you, that don't mean I'm not going to come here and talk to you, do an interview with you. I'd be out of my mind. Business is business. If [King] can come up with the most money, you get him, he's your promoter, [Cayton's] your manager. . . . If they both have my best interests in mind, as they said, then there will be no problem, they can work together. . . . I've been with Bill for a long time and everything's been going quite well, and Don King, he got us into tournaments, got us the fights to get the champions [sic] and everything . . . but the two of them have to become trustworthy toward each other and work together. . . . If they really can't work together with each other for my best interests, then they really don't have my best interests in mind."

Chapter 13

Tyson-Spinks:
The Making of a Fight

There never were two better men, and none could be more
game,
They are both two gallant heroes of honour and of fame.
Then fill a flowing bumper, and jovially drink their health,
May the best man win and conquer, and carry off the belt.

> —The Bold Irish Yankee Benicia Boy
> (regarding the Heenan-Sayers fight)
> *Anonymous*

After stepping out of the HBO Unification Tournament early in 1987, Michael Spinks began his preparations for the fight with Gerry Cooney. Despite having failed in his only legitimate test in the ring, when he was stopped by then-champion Larry Holmes on June 11, 1982, Cooney against Spinks would, Butch Lewis knew, be an instant box-office success. In Michael Spinks, promoter Lewis knew he had one of the gamest, most talented fighters in boxing. But he also knew he had a thirty-one-year-old fighter who had been campaigning for ten years as a professional, a fighter whose knees were becoming increasingly feeble with each fight, and, most importantly, a fighter who was never a legitimate heavyweight, whose best moments in the ring as an amateur and professional had come as a middleweight and light-heavyweight. Through a scientifically planned program of nutrition, strength-conditioning and exercise, Spinks had built himself up to 200 pounds and was fortunate on September 22, 1985 to catch an aging and fading Larry Holmes on the night Holmes was ready to be taken. He had beaten Holmes closely but convincingly, yet in an April 1986 rematch, seemingly the only people in the world who thought Spinks won the fight were the judges. Everyone else was convinced Holmes had won quite clearly. So Lewis knew there was a good chance a big, legitimate heavyweight like Tucker could upset Spinks. Even if Spinks survived that test, it was an even greater certainty that a devastating puncher like Tyson could end Michael's career. And what if Spinks did stay in the heavyweight Unification Tournament and met both Tucker and Tyson? At best, he would earn perhaps $5 million for both fights. Against Cooney he would be guaranteed $4 million, and Cooney, having been inactive in the five years since his loss to Holmes except for three brief fights lasting a total of barely seven rounds, was beatable. Many in boxing had always questioned whether Gerry really had the heart of a gladiator, and he certainly would come into the fight rusty. Yes, Cooney, though much bigger than Spinks, could be beaten. With his credibility established with a win over a "name" like Cooney, what would Spinks' services be worth to step into the ring against Tyson? As a good businessman, looking out for the best interests of his fighter, Butch Lewis knew there was only one direction to go. Spinks would meet Gerry Cooney in Atlantic City on June 15, 1987. Real estate mogul Donald Trump would put up the money to draw the fight away from Las Vegas and into the gambling capital of the East Coast.

The announcement that Spinks would step outside the HBO tournament to meet Cooney set off a wave of reaction. According to his contract with HBO, Spinks did have the right to fight outside the tournament—provided the winner of such a bout, if Spinks were to be defeated, also agreed subsequently to enter the Unification Tournament. But Cooney's manager, Dennis Rappaport, wanting to keep his options open should his man win, declined to agree to put Gerry in the tournament. This, combined with his passing on the mandatory challenge of Tony Tucker, led the IBF to strip Spinks of its title. Spinks issued a statement saying he was very disappointed with the action of the IBF; he had always been a good champion for them and had always abided by their rules (except, of course, in this instance). Then, in a jibe at Tyson's claim to the title, won against acknowledged "cheese champions" Berbick and Smith, Spinks went on to say, "Had it been that I won my title from Trevor Berbick or Tim Witherspoon or James Smith, I and the public may have questioned the validity of my title. However, I beat Larry Holmes, the undefeated, universally recognized champion, who had beaten Berbick, Witherspoon and Smith, and no one can take that from me by just casting a vote." *Ring* magazine, for many years considered the bible of boxing, said it would continue to recognize Spinks as the legitimate heavyweight champion. Armed with this, the Spinks-Cooney fight was billed as being for "the heavyweight championship." Jacobs and Cayton began posturing in the media that they might now never give Spinks a shot at Tyson, no matter what happened. They criticized Lewis mercilessly, while privately acknowledging to friends that, of course, Tyson would certainly fight the winner, whoever he was.

Spinks entered the ring an 8 to 5 underdog, and even his family was afraid he would be destroyed by the bigger man. His mother, at ringside, was shouting at Butch Lewis that she was going to sue him if Michael got hurt. His six-year-old daughter, Michelle, was lying in her grandmother's lap, crying. Even his older brother Leon, the former heavyweight champion, was crying at ringside as Michael waited for the bell.

The fight itself turned out to be exciting—while it lasted. A sellout crowd of nearly 16,000 was packed into the Convention Hall on the Boardwalk. Cooney was listed at 6'7". While he might not have been quite that tall, he certainly towered half a head taller than the 6'2" Spinks. He also outweighed Spinks by 30 pounds—238 for Cooney, 208 for Spinks. The fight was billed as "The War on the Shore," but Cooney had little ammunition with which to do battle. His long spells of inactivity, along with the creampuffs he fought when he did step into the ring, had taken their toll. The first couple of rounds were uneventful, Spinks testing to see just what Cooney had to offer, while Cooney did not use his size, his jab, or his once-dangerous left hook to establish his dominance. He seemed cautious, and tentative, and couldn't corner the elusive Spinks on the ropes, where a bruiser like Cooney could do the most damage. By the third round, Spinks was beginning to find his mark almost at will, snapping his jab onto Cooney's reddening nose, following occasionally with a right hand to the face. In the fourth round, it was more of the same, as it became clear that Spinks was establishing his dominance. The jab continued to find Cooney's face like a magnet drawn to steel, and the end was inevitable. It came in the fifth round. Cooney threw the left hook that was responsible for so many of his knockout victories, but Spinks countered with an overhand right that landed solidly on Cooney's jaw. It stunned him, and he wobbled, as Spinks swarmed all over him. A left landed to start a flurry in the center of the ring, and then the punches came rapidly from all directions as the crowd rose to its feet and the shouting became deafening. A left and right to the head ended the flurry as Cooney staggered away. But Spinks would not let his fish off the hook. He followed with a succession of right hands, pounding Cooney's dazed face, until the helpless fighter toppled to the canvas. He climbed to his feet at the count of three, took the mandatory eight-count from referee Frank Cappuccino, and then met the onslaught of the charging Spinks. There was no offense for Cooney to offer, only an attempt at defense, but Spinks was determined to end it here and now. He flurried with combinations too fast to follow—left hooks, overhand rights—every punch appearing to land on target. Again Cooney fell to the canvas, climbing up slowly to take another eight-count. He nodded at Cappuccino that he was prepared to continue, but he had nothing left. With no control over his legs, he slumped back toward a neutral corner as Spinks hit him with two more overhand rights and another flurry of lefts and rights that caused Cappuccino to jump between the fighters— with Cooney still on his feet but completely helpless—and stop the fight at 2:51 of the fifth round. Michael Spinks had thrown 101 punches in the fifth round, of which eighty-four had landed. Gerry Cooney had thrown twenty-six punches in the same round and connected with only five. That convincing victory would establish Michael Spinks as a real power in the heavyweight division, the only fighter in the public's eye who could offer Tyson a legitimate challenge.

Jacobs and Cayton, however, adopted an aloof attitude toward Lewis. They felt they had been wronged by the brash young promoter, and now they were in no hurry to do business with him. They would let him squirm while Tyson went ahead and picked up a guaranteed $3 million payday knocking off Tyrell Biggs, $5 million against Larry Holmes, who was staging a comeback and then a $10 million payday in Tokyo against an out-of-shape Tony Tubbs that ended in two rounds. Spinks, meanwhile, remained inactive. Lewis knew he had a multimillion dollar commodity in Spinks, a commodity that Jacobs, Cayton and Tyson needed. There was no sense in risking overturning the applecart. He was staring the ultimate hustle in the face, and if there was one thing Butch Lewis knew, it was a good hustle.

Ronald Lewis was born on June 26, 1946, and grew up in Philadelphia. His seven-page biography enclosed in the Tyson-Spinks press kit says he was an outstanding halfback who "turned down many college scholarship offers to join his father in the family auto business." After a stint selling used cars, where (again from his official bio) "his determination, personality and respect for fairness propelled him to become the business's top producer, surpassing even his dad's output," he began hanging out around Muhammad Ali and his entourage. Using the commonality of race, he was able to convince Ali's manager, Herbert Muhammad, to give him a shot in the promotion of Ali's forgettable title defense in 1976 against Richard Dunn in West Germany. Lewis parlayed that into a job with Bob Arum's Top Rank with the title of vice-president, Arum needing a street-wise black as his conduit to the fighters he dealt with, who were light-years away culturally and socially from the Jewish, Harvard-educated attorney Arum. While with Top Rank, Lewis made the one deal on which he would eventually build his career and his fortune. He gained the friendship and confidence of two brothers from the poorest ghetto of St. Louis and, after they both won gold medals at the 1976 Olympics in Montreal, he beat off other promoters and signed them to an exclusive promotional deal with Top Rank. They were Leon and Michael Spinks. After just seven professional fights, Leon brought about the upset of the decade when he dethroned Muhammad Ali to win the heavyweight title. But seven months later, Ali regained the title from Leon, and Lewis and Arum parted ways after Arum discovered about $100,000 missing from the fight receipts and accused Lewis of being the culprit responsible. Lewis denied Arum's charges. Butch, in any event, was ready to fly on his own, so taking Leon and Michael with him, he started his own company, Butch Lewis Productions. Leon quickly faded, and Michael, who had put his own career on hold during Leon's whirlwind ascent to the top, fighting just three times in 1978 and

1979, was able to get back on track. By 1981 he had captured the WBA Light-Heavyweight Championship, and in 1983, with a victory over Dwight Braxton, he became the undisputed 175-pound champion. But there was no big money to be made in the light-heavyweight division, which sent Lewis and Spinks after bigger game in the heavyweight ranks. When he upset Holmes in 1985, Spinks became the first light-heavyweight champion in history to win the heavyweight title.

Jacobs and Cayton maintained their position for a time, saying they didn't need Spinks. On several occasions over the months, they met with Lewis, but little progress was made. They were tightening the screws on Lewis, dictating the terms to him, and, most wounding to Lewis's ego, saying that he would have no part in the promotion itself, that his name would not appear as part of the promotion and that any money he earned would be a matter between himself and Spinks. After the Tyson-Holmes fight, Bill Cayton made Lewis a take it-or-leave-it offer to meet Tyson in June: $10.8 million guaranteed against 40 percent of the profits. Lewis declined. He wanted a $15 million guarantee for his man. Negotiations broke off. But an unforeseen circumstance now entered the picture. The health of Tyson's fifty-eight-year-old co-manager, Jim Jacobs, took a sudden turn for the worse. Although he tried to keep it a secret, Jacobs knew that if this fight-of-fights were to come to fruition in his lifetime, a deal would have to be struck soon with the Spinks camp. Suddenly, Jacobs's threats that "Mike Tyson will never fight Michael Spinks" were forgotten. Also, there was the perception that the Spinks camp was creating in the public mind that Tyson was ducking a showdown against "The People's Champion." When Tyson appeared in public, people would ask him, "Hey, Mike, when you gonna fight Spinks?" During one encounter in Los Angeles, Tyson almost fought it out with a guy who wouldn't let him off the hook about not fighting Spinks. Coincidentally, Butch Lewis was in the same restaurant at the time.

As more and more people asked him why he as avoiding Spinks, Tyson grew madder and madder. Was all this orchestrated by Butch Lewis? When asked, Lewis just laughed and said, "No comment." Before Jacobs's death in March of

1988, Tyson went to his co-managers and demanded that they make peace with Lewis long enough to iron out an agreement and get the showdown with Spinks on track. He was tired of hearing the strange whispers behind his back and the heckling right to his face from fans saying he didn't have the guts to meet Spinks in the ring.

By April an agreement had been reached, and late in the month Bill Cayton and his attorney, Irving Gruber, and Butch Lewis and his attorney, Milt Chwasky, sat down to finalize details. With Jacobs gone, Tyson was being wooed by Don King and growing increasingly estranged from Cayton, but the manager had his peace, at least for the time being, in order that the agreement for what promised to be the biggest grossing fight in boxing history, should be settled without a hitch. Lewis had managed to get $13.5 million guaranteed for Spinks—and (along with Don King and the Trump organization) he would be included as one of the promoters of the fight.

When it became certain in March that Tyson and Spinks would fight, bids came in from everywhere to host the event. But from the beginning, it was apparent that only two locales vying for the rights to Tyson/Spinks were seriously in the running: Las Vegas and Atlantic City. In Las Vegas, the Hilton, which had hosted earlier Tyson title fights, thought they had the advantage. But what they didn't know was that the decision was already a fait accompli. Donald Trump had co-opted the rights to boxing's biggest event more than a year and a half earlier, before Tyson was champion, when he paid a $100,000 rights fee to bring Tyson vs. Jose Ribalta to his hotel in Atlantic City. Taking that fight away from Las Vegas (though the fight itself meant nothing to Trump) began a relationship between Trump and the Jacobs-Cayton team. Then, when Trump got the Spinks-Cooney "War on the Shore" and the subsequent Tyson title defenses against Biggs and Holmes, he had extracted first-refusal rights from both the Spinks and Tyson camps. In the boxing world of today, one of the main sources of income is the site fee, a negotiated amount of money paid in order to win the rights to host a particular fight. In the heyday of Ali's touring show in the 1970s, Don King had extracted those fees from individual nations, often impoverished, such as the Philippines, which hosted the

Ali-Frazier "Thrilla in Manila," or Zaire, which paid millions to stage the Ali-Foreman "Rumble in the Jungle." But now things had shifted to the casinos, and the big fights were almost inevitably staged in Las Vegas, until Trump came along. He quickly discovered that bringing in a big boxing event not only provided worldwide publicity for the casino hosting the fight, but paid off handsomely at the tables. On an average Monday in June, the Trump Plaza casino takes in a little over $1 million. But on the Monday the hotel hosted the Spinks-Cooney bout, gamblers dropped over $7 million. They shelled out $8.5 million at Trump's tables on a cold day in January when Tyson fought Holmes. Trump paid Don King a site fee of $3.5 million to win the rights to stage Tyson's October 1987 defense against Tyrell Biggs. He was overly generous in agreeing to pay that amount, but it won him first-refusal on the Tyson-Spinks match. Not that he didn't pay dearly for it. The Trump Organization paid a record site fee of $11 million, $4.5 million above the previous record site fee when Caesars Palace paid $6.5 million to stage the Sugar Ray Leonard-"Marvelous" Marvin Hagler Middleweight Championship fight on April 6, 1987. Some felt he had paid too much, but as Trump himself modestly said, "Any fight I've wanted to get, I've been able to get." The money didn't matter. One way or the other, he would make it up. What did matter was that he had once again taken the play away from Las Vegas. (Las Vegas Hilton chief John Giovenco, furious at what he perceived as a double-cross by Bill Cayton, could only strike back at Trump by saying, "The casino operations in Atlantic City have been an embarrassment to New Jersey.")

The foot soldier who put the fight together for Trump was Mark Grossinger Etess, of the famous Grossinger hotel family, president of the Trump Plaza. Etess had just four days to add up the numbers, consider the options and see if the $11 million site fee was viable. If he faltered, Giovenco and the Hilton were more than willing to step in and bring the fight to Las Vegas. With 2,300 ringside seats priced at $1,500 each—the highest ever for a fight ticket—Etess felt the plan could fly. He called Trump to tell him. Trump told him to go ahead and make the deal, but on one condition. He wanted a guarantee that he had the option to stage future extravaganzas between Tyson and boxing's rising young star in 1988, Evander Holyfield.

Home Box Office offered $3.1 million for the rights to show the fight on a tape-delay basis, but in the United States, the world's biggest market for spectacular events, this fight—like Leonard-Hearns, Hagler-Leonard and the Ali-Frazier fights—was too big to give away on home or cable TV. Instead, it would be offered on an admission-paying basis at 1,600 sites around the country, ranging from large theaters and sports arenas like Madison Square Garden in New York or the Coast Coliseum in Biloxi, Mississippi, to exclusive supper clubs where dinner and the fight telecast could cost as much s $200 per person. Most arenas would charge between $25 and $50 a ticket. If interest in the fight peaked as expected, those closed-circuit locations could produce an estimated $35 million in revenue.

The man who is the master at overseeing the logistics of such a huge enterprise is Lou Falcigno, the fifty-year-old president of Momentum Enterprises, headquartered in New York City. For years Falcigno has handled setting up closed-circuit telecasts for major events ranging from press conferences to the Campus Crusade for Christ, but his true calling is handling the big fights. For the Spinks-Tyson fight, he and his company would directly handle and run the closed-circuit locations in five states, including New York. But in his role as national technical coordinator, Falcigno would also be in charge of coordinating the entire hookup to all 1,600 sites. He would be responsible for seeing to it that satellite link-ups were booked and that each location had a satellite receiving dish, decoders to unscramble the telecast signal, and video projectors to beam the images onto screens.

Falcigno learned the intricacies of the technical side of television while working in American Telephone and Telegraph's TV division. He then went to work for a closed-circuit company that handled several Ali fights in the 1970s and became a believer when he worked on the 1971 super-showdown between Ali and Frazier. He saw the two fighters split a then unprecedented $5 million in purse money, knowing that what paid those purses, in large part, was the revenue generated by closed-circuit theater-TV. The Ali-Frazier fight generated intense public interest and attracted a virtual sellout audience at all locations, an audience that transcended just the hardcore boxing fan. Falcigno realized that boxing, with the right mix of fighters and publicity, could be "a happening," a glitzy event just like a big rock concert. He started Momentum Enterprises in 1975.

In January of 1988, more than three months before contracts were actually signed for the Spinks-Tyson fight, it was apparent to insiders that the fight would happen, and Falcigno began the enormous logistical planning job. Dealing with rock concert promoter and boxing manager Shelly Finkel, who was handling the closed-circuit rights for Tyson's organization, Falcigno made sure he locked up the rights to New York City for himself, for which he guaranteed a fee of $1.1 million. Falcigno would keep 45 percent of the revenue earned, handing over 55 percent to Finkel and Sports of the Century, Inc., Tyson's company which Bill Cayton ran. If the fight did well, as expected, everyone would do well, and Sports of the Century would, on its 55 percent, receive more than the money guaranteed by Falcigno. If, for some reason, it didn't do well, Falcigno's earnings from his 45 percent would be cut into sharply, since he was still obligated to meet that $1.1 million guarantee. And, if it drew very poorly, Falcigno might wind up in the red. But no one expected that to happen. Falcigno also obtained territories in New Jersey, Massachusetts, Arkansas and Mississippi, a total of about 120 locations. He kept some of the venues for himself, but had neither the manpower nor the finances to run all 120 locations. Instead, in some locations he became a co-promoter, working with local promoters and sharing the profits, and in other venues he sold the rights outright, taking a flat fee and handing over 100 percent of the inherent risk to other entrepreneurs. In addition, there were the nearly 1,500 other locations that Finkel and Sports of the Century had sold off, for which, as technical coordinator, Falcigno was still responsible in terms of seeing that facilities were in place and in working order and that each of those 1,500 box offices accounted for every dollar on every ticket sold. For handling this job, Falcigno received a fee for each location from Sports of the Century.

On the day of the fight itself, Falcigno would not leave his office, and his phone would continue to ring with last-minute questions, arrangements and problems. Outside every one of the 1,600 locations throughout the United States he positioned his own tellers, incognito, counting everyone who entered, a precaution against any local promoters selling out their, say, 800-seat theater but reporting to Momentum that only 600 seats were sold and keeping the additional revenue for themselves. Falcigno also had to see to it that a Momentum representative, accompanied by an armed guard, turned up at each box office to collect his percentage then and there, to avoid any other hanky-panky in the days following the fight.

Foreign rights—to Europe, Latin-America, the Caribbean and Africa—provided relatively modest revenues to the promotion, somewhere in the neighborhood of $2 million. Additional seating was added in the Convention Hall to increase the capacity from 16,000 to 22,000, and the house was "scaled"—from a $1,500 ringside seat to $100 for the cheapest seats up in the rafters—producing a $13 million live gate based on a sellout.

Additionally, there was a new force to be reckoned with, one that in the 1990s will, as Falcigno knows, put his closed-circuit boxing operation out of business. Called "pay-per-view," it allows viewers to obtain a fight—or any other major sporting event or concert—on TV in homes wired for cable TV simply by ordering it from their cable company and paying a fee for it. The advantages are obvious: first, convenience, and, second, cost.

While all this planning was going on, the fighters fell into their training routine. At the Concord Hotel in the mountain resort of Kiamesha Lake, New York, Spinks was under the supervision of the legendary trainer Eddie Futch, who looked, acted and sounded a dozen years younger than his actual age of seventy-seven. For more than four decades, Futch had worked with champions and top contenders, including Joe Frazier and Larry Holmes. He was a rarity: knowledgeable, intelligent, modest, gentlemanly and universally respected. Working with him was his heir apparent, Hedgemon Lewis, a top welterweight of the 1970s who fought three times for the world title and briefly held New York State recognition as welterweight champion. Lewis had retired in 1976 and now was serving his apprenticeship as a trainer. Among Spinks's sparring partners were two men who physically resembled the short, stocky Tyson—Bernard

"Bull" Benton, who had once been cruiserweight champion, and Dwight Muhammad Qawi, the former Dwight Braxton, who had been light-heavyweight champion until dethroned by Spinks. The training facility was set up in a large recreation hall behind the Concord's main building, and each day dozens of spectators from among the hotel's guests watched as Spinks went through his routine of rope-jumping, calisthenics, shadow-boxing and sparring. Also in the Spinks camp was thirty-seven year-old Mackie Shilstone, the nutritionist and conditioning coach whose methods and techniques had built Spinks up from a 175-pound light-heavyweight to the 200-pound heavyweight who won the title from Holmes. Shilstone was there to build even more muscle on to Spinks's frame, to see that he stayed away from red meat, and that he took the nutritional supplements and followed the weight-training program that Shilstone advocated. Shilstone had been a conditioning coach at Tulane University's Athletic Department after playing football while a student at Tulane (though just 5'8" and 140 pounds). With a master's degree in nutrition and another in physical education, Shilstone had worked his conditioning magic on major leaguers Ozzie Smith, Vince Coleman and Will Clark, on former middleweight champion Frank Tate and on NBA stars Ralph Sampson and Manute Bel, but he gained wider public recognition through his successful association with Spinks, although many traditionalists in the boxing business scoffed at his newfangled methods.

Across the mountains, in Catskill, Tyson went through his daily routine in solitude in the little gym above the police station on the town's main street. Only trainer Kevin Rooney was present, except possibly for a gym assistant or a friend of Tyson's or perhaps one of the amateur youngsters who also trained in the gym.

Roughly a month before the fight, both men, as they were contractually obliged to do, moved their equipment, their sparring partners, their trainers and themselves to Atlantic City, where they would be more in the media's eye, and therefore play a bigger role in helping to sell the fight. They did their part. Tyson told the *Boston Globe*, "I'll break Spinks. I'll break them all. When I fight someone I want to break his will. I want to take his manhood. I want to rip out his heart and show it to him. People say that's primitive, that I'm an animal. But then they pay $500 to see it . . . . I'm a warrior. . . . If I wasn't in boxing, I'd be breaking the law. That's my nature."

Spinks, who came from as tough a ghetto in St. Louis as Tyson did in Brooklyn, was less macho: "I'll carry some fear into the ring, at least I hope I will," he admitted. "I think fear is good for a boxer because it makes you respect the individual you're fighting. . . . I don't feel I can fight well without it." He went on to tell how he had fought without fear only once, as an amateur, and how, as a result, he had lost. He described how he had seen his brother, Leon, defeat the Soviet fighter Rufat Riskiev, and how he had not thought Riskiev much of a fighter. Several months later, he himself had faced Riskiev in Moscow. Overconfident, he underestimated his Russian opponent, was knocked down and lost the fight. Then, in the Montreal Olympics, he had to fight Riskiev in the finals for the gold medal. He entered the ring with that healthy fear and used it to his advantage to beat Riskiev and win Olympic gold. It was that same fear that he hoped would carry him through the storm that was Tyson.

Futch felt that Tyson was beatable. He had seen weaknesses in him when Tyson fought "Bonecrusher" Smith and Tony Tucker. His plan was to have Spinks exploit those weaknesses, but he also acknowledged that if Spinks made "just one mistake, you can put all of that in the ashcan."

About four weeks before the fight, Tyson skipped training one day and headed for Manhattan. Bill Cayton had negotiated a $1 million deal for Tyson to be a spokesman for Pepsi-Cola, and the champion was due in the city to film a Pepsi commercial. Tyson turned up at the filming location accompanied by his wife, mother-in-law and their attorney, Michael Winston. While agency and Pepsi executives, technical crew, producer, director, and extras all waited, Tyson balked. Besides his managerial contract with Tyson, Cayton also held a personal services contract with the fighter that covered all outside-the-ring business. Like the standard one-third–two-thirds cut that is traditonal in boxing, Cayton's personal services contract also called for him to receive 33 percent of Tyson's outside business deals (which he, in turn, split 50-50 with Lorraine Jacobs, Jim's widow). But Tyson's wife and mother-in-law persuaded Mike that this was too much to give up to Cayton. Even though Cayton had a bona fide contract, they decided that with everyone waiting around to film a national TV commercial, this would be a perfect time to put the squeeze on Cayton. Tyson and his entourage walked out. They were going to lunch. Rooney, meanwhile, was seething. The last place he wanted his fighter was 150 miles from Atlantic City filming a commercial. A day lost in the gym could not be made up. The trainer knew that Spinks was not an opponent to be taken lightly. "My fighter has the edge in speed and power and smartness," he declared. "My fighter will definitely cut the ring off . . . sooner or later Mike Tyson will hit him [and] he's never been hit by Mike Tyson." But Rooney also acknowledged that Spinks was "a cutie [who] throws punches from an angle. He's awkward." Rooney knew that Tyson would need solid preparation if he was to overcome Spinks's experience under pressure and, indeed, cut the ring off and land his bombs on the challenger.

In the past, Tyson had professed no problems with the manner in which Jim Jacobs and Bill Cayton guided his career, negotiated his deals or invested his money to make him independently wealthy by the age of twenty-one. But now, with people whispering in his ear, he sang a different tune. "I'm throwing those left hooks, I'm taking those punches. For anyone to get one-third of my outside money is totally absurd."

Cayton was in a difficult position. Unless he gave in, the whole deal would come apart at the seams. By the time the Tyson entourage returned from lunch, he had made his decision. On the spot, he agreed to revise the contract and accept a 25 percent fee instead of 33 percent. The cameras rolled, and the next day, Tyson was back to business in Atlantic City.

Tyson's wife and mother-in-law were increasingly becoming the villains in the collective mind of the public. It seemed that they were manipulating the naive fighter, and Tyson was growing more confused, more torn. One night, early in June, needing to get away from it all, he bolted to New York City. He went to the local fights at Madison Square Garden and then disappeared. Kevin Rooney was forced to make an unscheduled excursion to the city to locate him and bring him back to Atlantic City.

The fear was there. It was coming. And Tyson knew he would have to harness it, control it, in order for it to work to his advantage. He needed the fear, just as Spinks did. Sometimes he worried that he had dominated his thirty-four opponents so completely that he would become nonchalant and lose that edge the fear provided. He was actually relieved when he dreamed one night that he and Spinks had fought and that Spinks had beaten him. It was a sign the fear was still there.

After a workout one day, he was answering questions from reporters when one of them asked him about Cus D'Amato, who still casts a long shadow over Tyson. He hesitated, unable to answer, and then suddenly began crying. "When I was a little boy," he managed to say, "I didn't like fighting. But I loved Cus. I wanted to make him happy. He wanted a champ. I didn't want to let him down." On other days, he exploded in fits of temper. Assistant manager Steve Lott described the Tyson routine: "He was just very, very difficult to live with for those five weeks [before a fight]. It's a matter of having to take a lot of shit without allowing your emotions to get involved. . . . Kevin would be very vocal. He'd say to Mike, 'Fuck you.' But I couldn't do that, because I was trained by Jimmy [Jacobs] . . . no matter what Mike said, no matter how he acted, no matter how indifferent he was to what had to be done, or how mean he was or inconsiderate, I just ignored it. I said he's not doing it on purpose, it's the pressure of the fight, and I just had to forget about it. It was the pressure . . . . I knew it from the first fight, from Catskill, I knew it was his style. I knew that if he didn't go through that, then there was something unusual. . . . He's a very moody person, and he's allowed to be moody. He's the fighter. I'm not allowed to be moody. I'm not the fighter."

Two weeks before the fight, Tyson sat with a half dozen reporters and called them idiots. "You ruin people's lives. I'm a sucker even to be talking to you guys. I should be ready to rip your heads off, but it's not the right thing to do." He then launched into a wide-ranging variety of topics, including the perceived attacks on his new family from press and public. "All my life," he said, "this bull never bothered me. I take it all with a grain of salt. But my family, my wife and my mother-in-law, they're being cut to pieces. It's new to them. It hits a nerve. . . . My wife went home, and I can be alone. I'm a loner anyway, and I don't think women should be around fighters in the gym. . . . I'll love her to death after it's over." Without mentioning any names, he then said that people in the fight business were bigger crooks than the criminals on the streets where he grew up. "They're not out for my best interests. They tell me they are, but they're not. They say 'I did this for you and that for you,' but that's not true. Whatever they did, they did for themselves. Whatever I get, they get a bigger percentage of it. . . . In my situation, it's very hard to find a real friend. The majority of the people have their hands out. . . . I don't want new relationships. That's how these problems occur. Too many friends—excuse me—too many people who say they're friends. I should have known from my background that people are basically not nice, the majority of them." He said he just wished the fight was today, not two weeks from now. "When I'm in that ring, I don't have no more problems. It's easy to forget problems when people are throwing punches at your head."

As his out-of-the-ring problems mounted and his mood swings became known, people began to believe it might affect his performance in the ring. At one point a 6 to 1 betting favorite, Tyson dropped to 4 to 1 by mid-June. Muhammad Ali was picking Spinks to win, but, like Joe Louis before him, Ali's greatness in the ring did not confer any great analytical abilities when it came to picking winners in fights.

A further snag came in May when Robin Givens persuaded Mike to dump Steve Lott because she did not like him. Only through the intervention of Cayton, who convinced them that things should remain as familiar and stable as possible as Tyson approached the biggest fight of his career, did Givens and her mother relent, and the long-suffering and loyal Lott was reinstated.

Spinks, meanwhile, in a much calmer atmosphere, continued his training at Trump's Castle hotel and casino. But because of fears that Tyson spies were watching the public workouts, every couple of days he would move to a closed session at a nearby gym. "Tyson's not invincible," Spinks told reporters. "He's not the half-man, half-beast you read about in the papers. He's very good but, in the end, he's just a fighter." You couldn't convince Tyson's sparring partners of that, however. On one day, he belted Oliver McCall low, and McCall had to take a rest. He then half-punched, half-wrestled Mike "The Bounty" Hunter to the canvas and fired a left hook to Hunter's head while he was down. McCall said Tyson's punches to his biceps sent a numbness through his arms like the kind that follows an electric shock, after which he couldn't lift his arms in the ring to defend himself against Tyson's devastating shots. Tyson was also merciless with his body shots, punches to the sides, the ribs, that were designed, as Tyson bluntly put it, "to make a man cry like a woman."

Another problem arose in the weeks before the fight. The bout was to be sanctioned by all three governing organizations—the WBC, WBA and IBF—because Tyson was recognized as champion by all of them. All three had come to an agreement that each would take turns administering Tyson's fights under its rules and regulations on a rotating basis. The WBA and WBC had had their respective turns earlier in the year when Tyson fought Holmes and Tubbs; now it was the IBF's turn, which was even more fitting because the IBF was headquartered in New Jersey where the fight was being held. Several years earlier, the WBC, citing questionable medical reasons, shortened its championship fights from the traditional fifteen rounds to twelve rounds. Subsequently, the WBA followed suit. The IBF also decided to go to twelve rounds—effective September 1, 1988. The Tyson-Spinks fight would be fought, the IBF announced, under its rules still in effect, meaning a fifteen-round duration. The WBA and WBC decided to indulge in a power play. Thy insisted that the fight be scheduled for twelve rounds. Bob Lee, president of the IBF, held firm that it would be fifteen rounds, or else the IBF would withdraw title recognition from Tyson. The WBA and WBC, once archenemies, now presented a united front. Many in boxing felt their real purpose was to undermine and hopefully destroy the IBF, which they saw as a threat to their power and authority, since the IBF was American-based. They said if the fight was fifteen rounds, they would strip

Tyson of their titles. Cayton sided with the WBC and WBA and was insistent that the fight be set for twelve rounds.

Tyson continued his gym workouts but took a week off from sparring because of a small cut over his left eye. He took Sunday, June 19, off and spent it with his wife at their home in Bernardsville, New Jersey. He returned to boxing the next day, pounding McCall, Hunter and Melvin Epps in six rounds of work. His fourth sparring partner, Fred Whitaker, was on the sidelines, knocked out of action for three weeks because of the beating Tyson had inflicted on his ribs. Tyson said he didn't give a damn how long the fight was. "We can go twenty or twenty-five rounds for all I care. It's a heavyweight championship fight. It should be a fight to the finish."

In U.S. District Court, Bob Lee sought an injunction on behalf of the IBF enjoining the WBA and WBC from stripping Tyson of their titles if the fight was scheduled for fifteen rounds. Cayton and his attorney, Thomas Puccio, met with Lee to try to persuade him not to withdraw title recognition from Tyson if the fight were to be twelve rounds. Finally, a week before the fight, with everyone refusing to budge from their positions, Larry Hazzard, the Boxing Commissioner of New Jersey, stepped in. On Monday, June 20, stating that the three organizations had created an embarrassing situation, Hazzard declared that the fight would be twelve rounds. Now Lee was faced with a dilemma. He could stick to his guns, insist that it was the IBF's fifteen rounds or nothing and strip Tyson—but that would make the IBF a no-show at the biggest fight of the year, which was being held right in their own New Jersey backyard. Or he could swallow his pride and give in to the WBA, WBC, Hazzard and Cayton. Three days later, he relented. The fight would be twelve rounds, the IBF would not strip Tyson of their title.

Meanwhile, relations between Tyson and Cayton grew increasingly strained as Don King began to flex his muscles, aligned as he was with Givens and her mother against the manager. Anticipating possible trouble, at the beginning of June Cayton had retained a heavyweight attorney, Thomas Puccio, who had run the Abscam bribery trials for the federal government and who had won an acquittal for socialite Klaus von Bulow in his highly publicized trial for attempted murder of his wealthy and comatose wife, Sunny von Bulow. Cayton announced that he had retained Puccio to prepare for possible litigation, that Puccio had reviewed Cayton's contract with Tyson and found it "fully enforceable" for its duration. The contract ran until February 1992. Cayton then declared that he was completely willing to work with Tyson's family on Mike's behalf, to avoid any unpleasant business such as a court case. But Robin Givens accused him on a local New York news program of trying to sabotage her marriage, charging that he had offered someone close to the Tysons $50,000 to help end the marriage. "He said he'd stop at nothing less than our getting a divorce. . . . It's like something out of 'Dynasty,' " she said. But according to Cayton, "Once I knew that Mike was in love with her, and with the Spinks fight coming on, you must know that there was nobody more zealous in keeping Mike happily married than Bill Cayton. . . . I always wanted him to stay married." Cayton says it was Don King who convinced Givens that he was trying to end their marriage. "He was feeding her all these goddamn lies," said Cayton, "and she was believing them. King is a very convincing scoundrel."

Givens grabbed every possible opportunity to speak out against Cayton—accusing him in one TV interview shortly before the Spinks fight of offering someone close to the couple $50,000 if he could facilitate her divorce from Mike. But something else peculiar started to happen. Stories began appearing in the press about the tumult and turmoil going on in the private life of Mike and Robin, and much of it was attributable to Robin and her family. Two weeks before the fight, Robin said she had suffered a miscarriage. Tyson blamed it on Bill Cayton, saying his estranged manager's statements and actions had caused Robin so much worry that she lost the child he had been looking forward to so much.

Barely more than a week before the fight, Robin's sister, Stephanie, a professional tennis player, gave an extraordinary interview to *Newsday*'s Wally Matthews. Speaking from Portugal, where she was playing in a tournament, she told Matthews, "I've stayed completely out of this so far, but it's just gotten to be too much. . . . I've known about Mike from the first day Robin met him. I've felt it's all been a big mistake from the beginning. Michael's supposed to be the good guy and everybody else is supposed to be abusing him. Nobody knows how abusive Michael is." She said that in May, when Tyson was in California with Robin, who was filming a TV movie there, she spent a week with the couple. "The week was a nightmare," she said. "I would call my mom every day to say, 'I can't believe what is going on here.' " She said Tyson was drinking heavily and turned up drunk one day on the movie set. Production had to be suspended after Mike "caused a terrible scene. He started breaking the lights, using foul language, throwing things." She also gave an account of one evening when Mike and Robin "had a fight, and he hit Robin in the head, with a closed fist. He knows how to hit her, and where to hit her, without causing any real damage. We had adjoining bedrooms and I was scared, so I made Robin come into my room and closed both doors. I put the latch on, and the deadbolt [lock]. He just kicked the two doors in. I knew he was strong, but I was amazed. . . . You can be so sweet to him and you'll never know what will set him off. He's the type of person who feels he's Mike Tyson, he can do whatever he wants. He loves to damage things in the house, just for no reason. If he feels like kicking in the TV set, he'll do it. If he feels like punching a hole in the wall, he does it. If he feels like hitting you, he does it. Why? I guess he gets bored. . . . It's just amazing how it's all stayed out of the newspapers. . . . When you're around him, you do live in fear. He's like a bomb, he can just explode. [Robin's] never been alone with him. There's always someone with her, because we're afraid for her. . . . [Robin and Ruth] have tried so hard to make him into a decent human being, and they just can't."

The timing of Stephanie's startling revelations was interesting, because it came shortly after Robin had jetted across the Atlantic to pay her a quick visit. Also, knowing the strong influence Ruth Roper exerted on both her daughters, most observers felt it was unlikely that Stephanie had spoken out independently, without at least the consent, if not the direct instructions, of her mother. Robin, for her part, walked the tightrope, as she had done with her alleged pregnancy, refusing to confirm or deny her sister's charges. She did drop veiled hints, however, telling Wally Matthews "We've had four hard months of marriage. He's under a lot of pressure, and it's made him act in ways I'd never seen before. . . . I can understand Stephanie's position." She then said, "I love Michael dearly. . . . I think we can make a great team. I hope we can have a life together." Privately, however, another responsible New York boxing writer said Robin had confirmed "off the record" that Mike did hit her. Why would she do so, and why would Stephanie speak out so strongly the reporter was asked. "It's obvious," he replied. "They're setting things up for the divorce. These are bad people we're talking about, bad people."

Bill Cayton would not speculate, at least publicly, on the timing of Robin's and Stephanie's speaking out to Wally Matthews. The timing could not have been worse, coming less than two weeks before the fight. He denied Robin's allegations that he wanted to break up the marriage. If Mike was happy, he wanted to see the marriage continue, he insisted, reasoning that a contented and domesticated Mike Tyson would have his mind much more focused on his business in the ring.

Tyson could not understand why the members of his new family should talk about him like this in print, especially now that he was approaching the critical final days before such a major fight. He denied that he hit Robin, but, as Wally Matthews wrote after speaking with him, he "seemed to be seething with a cold anger toward the family that claims to love him. 'You can't say bad things about a person, call them an asshole, and then say that you love them,' Tyson said. 'What they're saying, basically, is that I'm useless. . . . Maybe [Cayton] is breaking down their wills. . . . I can't worry about it. I'm here training for a fight. . . . It's very difficult when someone's telling you one thing, and the other person's swearing to God he had nothing to do with it. My wife and mother-in-law are telling me differently, but what more can I do for them? Maybe I'm not the man for them. . . . I'll get by somehow. I always find a way to get by.' "

Tyson continued, in the days before the fight, to defame Cayton, calling him an "asshole," "ruthless," and "a snake." It was obvious that Tyson, a simple kid, was being pushed and pulled to the breaking point. "They all want something from me. They're all making their living off me. Everybody's got their hands out," he said, echoing his now-familiar lament. He couldn't even turn to his blood relatives, his brother and sister. He and his brother, an ex-serviceman who lived in California, were not close, and his sister, Denise, lived with her husband and two children on the dole, receiving welfare checks twice a month even after her little brother had earned more than $40 million.

King and Cayton spent Monday, June 20, in court in a dispute over the division of Trump's $11 million site fee. King ended up with $2 million, out of which he had to pay promotional expenses and the purses of the fighters on the undercard. King then launched a verbal attack on Cayton, calling him "an inveterate liar, a power zealot, a hypocrite of the first order, an evil man, the incarnation of Satan. The kid gloves are off" said King. He further said that he fully supported Robin and her mother and would help them prove allegations that Cayton was trying to break up the marriage. He then professed fear for Spinks's safety, saying "Tyson's gonna go in and look at Spinks and see Bill Cayton. I just hope he don't get too brutally beaten." Cayton barred King from Tyson's workout six days before the fight, said King's outburst was "one hundred percent bull," and vowed that King "will not, with my approval, be promoting any Mike Tyson fights in the future." Tyson countered: "Bill Cayton is through as far as I'm concerned." But Cayton said, "I will insist that Mike honor the letter and spirit of his contract to its full duration." King allegedly told Givens's mother that Tyson's people were calling Mike a nigger behind his back. Small wonder that the byplay was beginning to overshadow the fight!

After all of this, the final press conference, the final confrontation between the fighters and their camps, was tame by comparison. *Ring* magazine, which still recognized Spinks as champion, used the occasion to present him with a world championship belt, and Spinks responded: "It's a great thrill to be considered a champion." Kevin Rooney jumped in, asking, "Who'd Spinks ever fight? Holmes? We knocked him out in four rounds." Tyson said, "I'm the best fighter in the world. No one can beat me. . . . My objective is to inflict as much pain as possible, to win and win spectacularly. . . . Ever since I was twelve years old, I was groomed to be the heavyweight champion of the world. I've been prepared to handle the pressure, the dealing with the press, everything. I think you guys are basically overbearing sometimes, but none of this bull will affect me in the ring." Spinks said, "I never ran from any man, and I don't intend to run from Mike Tyson." Rooney then grew impatient. "Everybody's being so nice to each other," he said. "I just want to let you know, we're here to kick a little ass." Rooney had taken a beating at the craps tables, dropping some $175,000 over the previous two weeks, but he was still ready for some more action. "Let's get it down," he challenged Butch Lewis. "I got money to bet on Tyson, any amount." Lewis ignored the offer.

Opinion about the likely outcome of the fight was divided. Ex-champs Tony Zale and Rocky Graziano were looking for Spinks to outsmart and outpsych Tyson and pull an upset, joining Ali in his selection of Spinks. Wally Matthews, an astute boxing writer for New York *Newsday*, liked Spinks to TKO Tyson; veteran boxing announcer Don Dunphy, who had been broadcasting fights since Louis-Conn in 1941, also picked Spinks. But Billy Conn, the brash light-heavyweight champion who had come so close to dethroning Louis in that classic confrontation before being KO'd by Joe in the thirteenth round, liked Tyson by knockout. "How soon?" said Conn. "As soon as he hits Spinks." Jake LaMotta, the Raging Bull, was in the Tyson camp, as were former trainer, match-maker and TV commentator Gil Clancy, and Larry Holmes's former trainer, Rich Giachetti. Both liked Tyson by an early knockout. "Spinks will find out he can't run from Tyson, so he'll be forced to stand and fight," said Clancy prophetically. "That should make it an exciting fight but a not a long one."

Angelo Dundee, who had led Ali and Sugar Ray Leonard to world titles, and had been in the corner of ex-champ Pinklon Thomas the night Tyson destroyed him, said, "If Spinks can't hurt Tyson early, forget about it." Ex-heavyweight champ George Foreman also picked Tyson, as did two former champs who had felt the power and determination of Tyson in the ring. "Bonecrusher" Smith chose Tyson by a KO. When asked what Spinks would need to win, he said. "He'd need to take me in the ring with him." And Larry Holmes, KO'd earlier in the year by Tyson, said, "Tyson is very hard to hit and he hits very hard, which makes it a bad combination for Spinks." He picked Tyson to stop Spinks in less than five rounds. Promoter Bob Arum, who had staged some of Tyson's early fights but was now out of favor with Tyson's people because Jim Jacobs believed he had tried to steal Wilfred Benitez from him, hit the nail on the head. He said that when Tyson "nails Spinks for the first time—and, make no mistake about it, he will nail him—the fight will, in essence, be over. There is no way that Spinks can stand up to the overwhelming power of the champ. . . . Tyson will attack Spinks from the start. . . . will cut the ring off on Spinks and land his devastating body shots. If Spinks survives the first-round assault, he will only be postponing the inevitable. Tyson will take him out for good in the second round. . . . Tyson by an early knockout."

On Friday, June 24, Tryson dropped a bomb on his manager. An envelope was delivered by hand to Cayton. It contained a letter which read:

June 24, 1988
By Hand and By
Certified Mail, Return Receipt Requested

Mr. William Cayton
9 East 40th Street
New York, New York 10017

Dear Bill:

Starting now, you are to take no action on my behalf as a boxing manager. Any monies you have received for me as a boxing manager must be promptly forwarded to the office of Michael Winston, my attorney. Any monies you are to receive on my behalf as a boxing manager must be forwarded to my attorney Michael R. Winston.

Also, you are directed to advise all persons and companies that owe me money that you are not authorized to receive any monies due me as my boxing manager.

Sincerely,

Mike Tyson

c.c. Michael Winston
      New York State Boxing Commission
      Sports of the Century, Inc.

RECEIVED

1988

RECEIVED Commission
New York Office

JUN 27 1988

Athletic Commission
New York Office

Tyson's letter to Bill Cayton, delivered to the manager three days before the Spinks fight. Michael Winston eventually fell out of favor with Ruth Roper and was dismissed as Tyson's attorney in favor of higher-profile "celebrity" lawyers.

Tyson had, by virtue of this letter, made the first move to sever his contractual relationship with Bill Cayton. Those who professed to care about him apparently did not mind forcing his hand and taking his mind off the fight just three days before he was due to step into the ring with Spinks. Cayton, in deference to Tyson, had sought to defer any such distractions.

Fighters traditionally weigh in on the day of a fight, because in the divisions below heavyweight they must not exceed the weight limit of that division. However, since a heavyweight weigh-in was essentially superfluous, (there being no limit to weight in that division) and because ABC was going to televise it live during its "Wide World of Sports" program, the weigh-in was held on Saturday, two days before the fight, in the showroom of Trump Plaza, with the fighters, trainers, officials and aides on stage. Bill Cayton was there. So was Robin Givens. And Don King. Givens, either unaware of or unconcerned about a fighter's delicate psyche as a fight approaches, spent the time announcing that Cayton was gone after this fight, contract be damned. The fighters themselves did no talking, except in brief interviews with ABC. Spinks was 212¼ pounds, Tyson 218¼. They departed, each to spend the final forty-eight hours resting, waiting, secluded from the hundreds of reporters and thousands of fans and camp followers who had gathered in this old seaside resort to witness a fight, or, for those without tickets, just to say they were there.

Sunday was quiet, relatively uneventful, the calm before the Monday night storm. George Foreman, the former heavyweight champion, on the comeback trail at the age of thirty-nine after ending a ten-year retirement, fought in Atlantic City and scored an easy TKO over a journeyman named Carlos Hernandez. The promoter of the fight was the now-retired Gerry Cooney. While Foreman was fighting, down the other end of the boardwalk, at Bally's Casino Hotel, Frank Sinatra was giving an open-air concert under the stars. Late in the day, Donald Trump wandered into the Convention Hall that in little more than twenty-four hours would be packed with more than 22,000 people. Now, the hall was empty except for the HBO television crew completing its set-up of technical facilities for the fight coverage.

Trump sat down in the first row in his VIP section, in the seat he had reserved for Sinatra. He didn't like what he saw. The ring was too high. Looking up from the first row, Sinatra's view would be obstructed. Trump called for HBO's producer, Ross Greenburg, and told him he could not risk an unhappy Sinatra walking out during the fight. The ring would have to be lowered a foot. That meant resetting the ring lights, and repositioning all the cameras. But what Trump wanted, Trump got. Greenburg was in no position to argue. His men began dismantling the ring, and in less than an hour, everything was in place again, the ring now a foot lower. (As it turned out—at least as far as Sinatra was concerned—it really didn't matter. Under contract at Bally's, a rival casino, Sinatra decided it wouldn't be good form to be seen sitting with Trump. He did not turn up for the fight.)

The day of the fight began early for Robin Givens and Donald Trump. They were up before dawn to make appearances on ABC's "Good Morning America," from ringside at Convention Hall. Later, Givens would launch a tirade of verbal abuse at the Trump Plaza front desk manager, incensed that she couldn't get her way and have some relatives stay an extra night at the hotel because the rooms were already booked by other guests. "Don't you know who I am?" she demanded. "Yes," the manager said, but he couldn't do anything about extending the rooms. At that, Givens threatened to get her husband, who, she assured him, would take care of this matter. With that threat, she stormed off. Of course, just hours away from his fight, Tyson never appeared at the front desk to argue his wife's case.

In the afternoon, the once-great champion, Roberto Duran, stopped by Tyson's room. Duran had been a boyhood hero of Tyson's, but they had never met. They hugged and began talking. Tyson, intensely interested in boxing history, asked Duran about his ring career, while Duran told Tyson to stay calm, go right to Spinks, who would, he assured him, be nervous. "You'll catch him," Duran said. Duran had once been promoted by Don King, who had made millions out of him. After they parted, Duran linked up with King's archrival, Bob Arum, as his promoter. Now, most of the fortune that he had earned in the ring was gone, somehow frittered away. He did not have a ticket for Tyson's fight. Apparently, none was forthcoming from King, although it is customary that greats of the past are taken care of in this manner. When Tyson found out, he gave Steve Lott $1,500 to buy a ticket for Duran.

Early in the evening, the doors to the Convention Hall opened and the crowd outside on the boardwalk and inside Trump's casino began to fill the hall. Fight fans and those who wanted their money's worth after paying out $500, $1,000, $1,500, or just a mere $100 for the cheapest seat in the rafters, filed in early to watch the preliminary fights and keep their eyes open for the celebrities who would arrive as the main event drew closer.

Bill Cayton, his wife Doris, and Lorraine Jacobs arrived and took their seats at ringside near Donald Trump and his wife and family. At a discreet distance from the Cayton party sat Don King, Robin Givens and Ruth Roper. During one of the preliminaries, Cayton was approached and handed an envelope. He was in for a shock when he opened it. It contained legal papers notifying him that he was being sued by Tyson to break the contract which had been signed just four months earlier and which was for four years' duration. However, Cayton had little time to study the papers. The fight he and Jim Jacobs had worked so long and so hard to make a reality was about to begin.

Tyson bounced from his corner as the echo of the bell faded. He was still burning at the intrusion into his prefight preparations by Butch Lewis, Spinks's promoter. Lewis had entered his dressing room forty-five minutes earlier and created a fuss by complaining about a lump under the tape on one of Tyson's gloves. Steve Lott, in the corner with Tyson that night, recalled, "I have never seen one fighter attack another fighter like Mike attacked Spinks. Vicious punches, incredible body shots. So much for Butch Lewis and his brilliancy."

Tyson threw the first combination, a left jab, a left hook that landed solidly, a right to the body and a right that missed over Spinks's head, all the punches coming in the first ten seconds of the round, in rapid succession, as Spinks covered up. Tyson then missed three punches, but kept the pressure on the challenger. Spinks missed a right and then threw another, which missed high. It was his first offensive, launched more in desperation than in any hopes of doing damage, just to try and keep Tyson off him. Tyson threw another flurry, with a right hand, slightly off the mark, the only punch landing, but the power of Tyson's punches was already apparent, even those that didn't land, and Spinks grabbed and held, forcing the first clinch of the fight, his only respite from Tyson's onslaught. Even in the clinch Spinks found no safe haven. Tyson brought up a left elbow into Spinks's face with vicious force. Cappuccino broke them and warned Tyson, "Hey, Mike, knock it off, man. Knock it off." A left uppercut inside then drove Spinks back. Tyson was constantly coming forward, and Spinks had nowhere to go but backward, retreating on legs not capable at this stage in his career of any longer taking him safely out of danger. There was another clinch, then two rights by Tyson. The first landed hard on Spinks's face and drove him back into the ropes. Every punch that landed was hurting, and that right hand was the beginning of the end. Spinks threw a soft right, almost apologetically, but then covered up completely in a peekaboo defense, still trying to avoid Tyson's blows. Tyson fired off a rapid six-punch combination, with a right to the ribs doing the most damage. It was obvious at this point that Spinks could not fend off Tyson's fury. Still on the ropes, he slid to the adjoining side of the ring, but was again trapped on the ropes—exactly where he didn't want to be with Tyson. He took a thundering left uppercut-hook to the jaw, followed by a tremendous right to his ribs that collapsed him to one knee.

Just one minute had gone by in the fight, and Michael Spinks was down for the first time in his twelve-year professional career. He got up at the count of two, looked to his corner and nodded that he was okay, as Cappuccino tolled the mandatory eight-count and wiped his gloves. He asked him, "Are you OK, Mike?" and Spinks responded the way all fighters do, acknowledging that he was prepared to continue. He came forward to meet Tyson in the center of the ring. Tyson took three steps from the neutral corner where he had been sent by the referee. Spinks, in desperation, threw a final right that missed. At the same moment, Tyson threw a left that also missed. But the momentum of Spinks's missed punch turned his body to the left, and for an instant left his head unguarded. Instinctively, Tyson saw the opening and fired a short, pulverizing right hand that landed flush on Michael Spinks's jaw, finding its way as if guided by some lethal radar between the protection of Spinks's gloves. Perhaps a more perfect, more efficient right hand had not been thrown since the one Rocky Marciano landed on the jaw of Jersey Joe Walcott to win the heavyweight title thirty-six years earlier. Spinks tumbled backward like a felled tree, his head snapping sharply and bouncing off the canvas. His eyes were open, but his body was paralyzed. The medical term is rotational acceleration of the brain, a twisting of the cerebrum as it moves rapidly in the fluid that surrounds it against the inside of the skull. In boxing, it's called a knockout. At the count of four, Spinks tried to turn and rise off his back, but as the count reached ten, he tumbled face-forward into the ropes, intoxicated by the 100-proof power in Tyson's fists.

Tyson turned to the crowd and extended his arms wide, palms up, as if to say, there, you see, the job is done. Kevin Rooney was in the ring now, hugging Tyson, with the beaming Don King also there, attached to Tyson like a leech. Butch Lewis was supporting the wobbly Spinks, and the ring physician tried to steady the groggy fighter. Tyson moved toward him, and Spinks extended his gloved hand to touch Tyson's and acknowledge the victor. Robin Givens climbed into the ring, assisted by Donald Trump. The fight had taken one minute and thirty-one seconds. Tyson told Spinks he had watched him since the Olympics, when Tyson was just ten years old. He told Spinks he had admired him for being a great fighter.

Afterward, in a packed press room, there were the usual postmortems. "He was charging in," Spinks said of Tyson, "and I was trying to catch him in the process. I tried to take a shot at him, and I came up short. That's when he hit me." Eddie Futch would later say that Spinks's failure came when he abandoned his game plan, which had been to jab and move, counterpunch, and make Tyson work, miss punches, and slow down. Futch also said Spinks wasn't scared, no matter what anyone said. But Richie Giachetti, who had been in the corner with Holmes the night Tyson stopped him, said Spinks had the same look on his face that Larry had just before the bell, a look he had never seen on Larry's face in any of his other fights. It was the look of fear.

Tyson, meanwhile, with his wife at his side, stood at the podium and continued his battle with the press. "I wasn't very appreciative of what you guys, the reporters, did to me," he said. "You tried to embarrass me. You tried to embarrass my family. You tried to disgrace us, and as far as I know this might be my last fight." He concluded by offering the opinion that "There is no fighter like me. I can beat any man in the world." Robin took Mike's hand in hers and kissed it, looking out at the press and smiling. In the background, on the podium, stood his estranged manager, Bill Cayton. Tyson ignored him.

For all concerned, the fight was a tremendous financial success. The crowd at Convention Hall paid a live-gate record of $12.3 million. Gross receipts counting theater, foreign, pay-per-view and merchandising would reach an estimated $70 million, making this the largest grossing fight in boxing history, a record previously held by the Leonard-Hagler fight in 1987, which grossed an estimated $60 million. The Trump Plaza casino had a "drop"—the amount of chips purchased by gamblers—of $11.5 million on the day of the fight, which was a record. The four-day weekend drop at the casino came to $30 million. The house profit margin on a drop of $30 million would be about $5 million to perhaps $7 million. Tyson's purse would approach $22 million, of which Kevin Rooney would receive $2.2 million off the top. The manager's share would be some $6.5 million. Michael Spinks, for whom this would be a farewell to boxing, would probably net for himself, after taking care of trainer Eddie Futch, promoter Butch Lewis and Uncle Sam, a nest egg of about $5 million to retire on. Michael Spinks had always been a gentle man. He had said it was painful for him to watch the vultures pick away at his man-child brother, Leon. He had called boxing "a dirty business"; now he could leave it as he had graced it, with dignity.

Tyson talked of retirement. He told Mike Marley of the New York *Post* the day after the fight that it had definitely been his last appearance in a ring. "Don King was laughing, but when he finds out I'm serious, he won't be laughing," he said. "I don't want to deal with this bullshit anymore. . . .

I had fun. Boxing was good to me, but nothing lasts forever. . . . I decided it's time to move on. It's time to call it a day . . . . I don't like reading that my wife is a whore, that my mother-in-law is a sneaky conniver. And then I read that I'm an idiot. I know it goes with the territory, but it's difficult." That night in Atlantic City he had shown the world that he truly was invincible in the ring. But outside the squared circle, his familiar world was crumbling around him.

Chapter 14

The Summer of Discontent

No one's going to be my manager but Bill Cayton. As long as Bill Cayton's around, he's my manager, from the beginning to the end of my career.

—Mike Tyson
May 1988

Happy for him in victory, Tyson's friends were at the same time concerned for him. Over and over, he had vowed he would not end up like Joe Louis, or Muhammad Ali. He would quit with all his money, he said; but things continued to point in a different direction. Tyson indicated he was considering a move to California, where Robin worked and spent most of her time. Those around Mike knew if he established residence in California, he could be hit harder than any opponent had ever hit him if (and it was obvious to all that it was more a question of when rather than if) he and Robin were to divorce. California is a "community property law" state, meaning all property in a divorce is divided 50-50, right down the middle between the two parties involved. Concern for Mike's welfare grew, but no one could point things out to him without seeming to come down against Ruth and Robin.

Cayton, meanwhile, turned his attention to the legal papers he had been served with at ringside, which sought to sever the business relationship between himself and Tyson. He charged that Don King was behind it, stirring things up in an attempt to steal Tyson from him. He labeled King "stupidly greedy," and pointed out that it was he, Cayton, who had been working steadily on Mike's behalf. It was he who had negotiated the compromise with the WBC, WBA and IBF over the duration of the bout—twelve rounds—keeping the IBF from stripping Tyson of the IBF's one-third of the title. Maintaining Tyson as undisputed champion was worth potentially millions of dollars in terms of commercial endorsements. Cayton had, on that front, negotiated lucrative deals not only with Japanese breweries but with Kodak and Pepsi-Cola in the U.S.A. for TV commercials that added considerably to Tyson's income. Another deal had been arranged with Nintendo, the most popular home video game in the country, for a video game called "Mike Tyson's Punch Out," and Tyson had filmed a TV commercial for Nintendo as well.

Cayton pointed out that far from working in Tyson's best interests, King had acted in several ways that might have cost Mike perhaps millions of dollars. Without Cayton's knowledge, prior to the Spinks fight, King had made a deal with a company in California to set up a telephone number which people could call for a fee during the fight and which would provide them with a running account of the bout. This might have kept thousands of people from buying the fight on pay-per-view home TV or from going to theaters to see it on closed circuit, cutting sharply into California revenues. When Cayton got wind of it, he forced King to cancel the deal. And in May, when King had bought his Rolls-Royce gift for Tyson, he had arranged only a $15,000 insurance policy on it, leaving Tyson incredibly vulnerable to a potential lawsuit. If he had had an accident involving any type of injury to another party and been at fault, he could have been sued for millions of dollars once it was learned he was Mike Tyson. This would have come out of his pocket since King's insurance policy would have covered only $15,000. Cayton quickly straightened out the potential mess created by King. (Note: King, after making much public fuss over his Rolls Royce "gift" to Tyson, quietly had informed Cayton that although he'd laid out the funds for the purchase, he did expect Mike to repay him.)

On the day after the Spinks fight, which was also the day after the filing of Tyson's lawsuit against him, Cayton and Lorraine Jacobs, the widow of his former partner, appeared at a news conference to respond to the allegations. Tyson's suit, filed in New York State Supreme Court, charged that Jacobs and Cayton fraudulently induced him to sign new contracts with them in February of 1988, a month before Jacobs died, without his being informed that Jacobs had a terminal illness. Tyson maintained he would never have signed something that would allow Bill Cayton to become his sole manager if he had known Jim Jacobs was fatally ill.

He further charged that he did not read the contracts, nor did Jacobs read them to him or explain the conditions of the contracts to him. The truth of the matter was that Tyson was willing and happy to sign the new contracts at the time, that they were explained to him by an Athletic Commission attorney, and his close friend and confidant Jose Torres was there to look after Mike as well, and, in his capacity as Chairman of the State Athletic Commission, he signed and approved all the new contracts.

At the news conference, held at the offices of Milbank Tweed Hadley & McCloy, the firm in which Cayton's attorney, Thomas Puccio, was a partner, Cayton said, "I'm very disappointed in Mike. I thought Mike had far greater respect for Jim's memory. I'm outraged at this lawsuit." Tyson stated in his legal papers that "Cayton has not been, is not now and will not be [my] boxing manager." To this Cayton responded, "Mike Tyson knew all along that Jimmy and I were truly co-managers. . . . [that] most of the negotiations were conducted by-and-large by me." Tyson's lawsuit said Cayton was not entitled to any portion of the proceeds from the Spinks fight, even though the contract between him and Cayton was in effect and Cayton had handled the negotiations for the entire fight.

Lorraine Jacobs broke down in tears as she expressed her disappointment in Tyson. "It's very difficult," she managed to say. "We love Mike. We've known him since he was thirteen. Both Jim and Bill treated him as they would have treated a son. I just can't believe Mike would do this. It's distressing."

Attorney Puccio was the strongest in his denunciation of Tyson's charges. "Tyson maligns and does dishonor to the memory of his close friend and mentor Jim Jacobs who, with Bill Cayton and Cus D'Amato, guided his career, which has now reached this crowning moment. Jim is no longer with us and cannot defend himself. More than anything else, that is what makes this suit a low blow. . . . Mike Tyson may have been in top form in the ring, but the allegations he made in the lawsuit are not worthy of a champion," said Puccio, who further labeled the charges by Tyson "a sham and totally unsupportable." Although it was obvious that the idea of the lawsuit did not come from Mike Tyson, Puccio was accurate when he said, "It's almost beyond belief that Mike Tyson would put his signature to these charges. . . . Let's put the hat squarely on who it belongs—Mike Tyson. He brought the charges. He's responsible for them."

Don King, meanwhile, who had been inseparable from Ruth and Robin in the days leading up to the Spinks fight, and had labeled Cayton "Satan in disguise" and "the devil incarnate," took an uncharacteristically humble stance. Not wanting to seem too pushy or aggressive in the eyes of Ruth Roper or Robin, he said, "Mike Tyson is my boss. When Mike speaks, I listen." Boxing people wondered how long it would take until that situation was reversed. One day, he said Tyson was "the hottest property in the world," and talked of marketing Tyson around the globe, a Tyson "Ambassadorial tour of fighting in the grand style with a lot of flair and excitement," as Mike when from country to country, taking on national champions. And who better to promote such a tour than the "Only in America" man himself? "It would be extremely difficult for an ordinary promoter to do something with a fighter who has beaten everybody, but I'm an extraordinary promoter. I have imagination. My only hope is that I have the opportunity to earn Mike's trust."

Tyson's next fight was scheduled in two months' time, in London against number-one challenger Frank Bruno, but already there were ominous rumblings that Tyson would not be at Wembley Stadium on September 3. Tyson said he was tired, that he might retire. King said Tyson just needed a rest when he spoke of retirement; if Mike didn't want to fight, "Bruno could be put on hold," no matter that a contract had been signed by Tyson. Of course, King had no interest in seeing Tyson fight Bruno in England because he was not involved in the promotion, which belonged to Jarvis Astaire and Mickey Duff. Privately, Tyson told friends that if he was going to fight Bruno, King was going to be part of the promotion. The battle liens were drawn.

Also entering this three-ring circus was the "boy billionaire," Donald Trump. He suddenly surfaced alongside Ruth and Robin, all smiles, saying he had joined the Tyson family as an adviser to the champion, giving as his altruistic reasons, "[Mike] happens to be one hell of a good guy, that's why I'm here to help him. . . . I'm a friend and adviser." He also said he was motivated by the affection he had developed for Ruth and Robin, who, he said, had been treated "unfairly" by the media and the public. They had been given treatment "they don't deserve." Two days after coming on the scene, Trump's high-powered public relations man, Howard Rubenstein, called a news conference. It was held on July 11 at Trump's Plaza Hotel in Manhattan in the Grand Ballroom. Tyson stepped to the podium and said, "I'm calling the shots. I will manage my own self. Anyone who goes against me can no longer be associated with me," and he made it clear that that included his trainer, Kevin Rooney, who had continued to insist in interviews that "Bill Cayton is an honest man . . . he's careful about his fighter's money." Tyson continued, "I did the sweating inside the ring. . . . without me [Cayton] wouldn't have had a chance of even putting his foot in the door at HBO." (Subsequently, Seth Abraham, HBO's executive in charge of sports, pointed out that Cayton had been negotiating deals and fights with HBO long before Tyson came on the scene.) Tyson announced he had set up a company called Mike Tyson Enterprises, which would include Ruth Roper, attorney Michael Winston and new friend Donald Trump, among others, to advise him on his business and boxing careers.

Attorney Winston said that Jacobs and Cayton had taken advantage of Tyson by not advising him to be represented by an independent attorney when signing contracts with them. "Here was a young man," Winston said, "with no legal experience, dealing with two very shrewd businessmen. That was not fair, it was simply not fair."

Trump had worked closely with Cayton and Jacobs, not only on the Spinks fight, but on the Biggs and Holmes bouts as well, along with other deals not involving Tyson, but now he too said that for Tyson not to have had his own counsel when dealing with the managers was "quite unfair. . . . This isn't a question of taking sides. I'm doing what I think is right." The media was highly suspicious of Trump's motives. the youthful entrepreneur had established a pattern over the years of seeking the spotlight. He was considered a publicity hound, someone who craved public attention as much as he did making money. How much of a "good guy" could he really have felt Tyson was, who had once responded to his greeting and proffered handshake before the start of a news conference by glaring at him and saying "Get the fuck outta here"? Perhaps Trump liked to be at the center of the storm, on TV and in the newspapers at the side of the heavyweight champion. No doubt he also liked the numbers with $$$ signs in front of them that he saw following the Spinks fight, including a live gate of over $12 million and a "drop" at his Trump Plaza casino over the weekend of the fight of some $30 million, of which the casino kept between 14 and 20 percent. It was certainly to his advantage to keep Mike Tyson in the fold and therefore fighting for Trump in Atlantic City.

The usually cynical media was almost universal in its praise for Cayton's abilities as a manager. Mike Katz, writing in the New York *Daily News*, said "[Cayton] turned the books over weeks ago and so far there has not been one instance cited by Winston of dishonesty. No one has accused Cayton of dishonesty before, a remarkable claim in boxing." Ira Borkow, in the *New York Times*, wrote "Cayton, now 70, and in boxing for some 40 years, has before this been known as a tough businessman but an honest one, and never a rip-off artist." Columnist Mike Lupica, in the *Daily News*, said "Robin Givens has worked it out so that Mike Tyson doesn't trust Bill Cayton anymore. . . . Mike Tyson is not being smart. Tyson probably should be worried about his wife, who showed up on their first date with her mother and three publicists. Bill Cayton is an honest boxing manager, something as rare as a day in June when two boxers make $35 million between them. . . . But Robin Givens and Ruth Roper, her mother, have begun to move Cayton out. . . . The wife, and her mother, have become friendly with the shark, Don King. . . . Cayton may have been slow to see what was happening to him, and he may not give Tyson the hugs Jimmy Jacobs did, but Cayton deserves better at age 70 than this. . . . Bill Cayton has a contract. Robin Givens has a bedroom. Somebody stop this fight."

The bottom line was, Cayton's contract was solid and enforceable. Cayton knew it, but wanted to avoid the acrimony that would grow out of a full-scale courtroom battle. Michael Winston knew it, and said he wanted "to see if we can work together to resolve this without litigation." Trump knew it, and was advising the Tyson side to settle the dispute with Cayton. And meanwhile, the British promoters, Jarvis Astaire and Mickey Duff, were growing nervous. They had a contract but no firm commitment from Tyson concerning the September 3 fight at Wembley with Frank Bruno. They were pushing the deadline by which they had to sign an agreement for leasing the stadium. The Wembley people wanted an answer soon, because if they didn't have a heavyweight fight there on that date, Bruce Springsteen and U-2 both wanted it for concerts.

Robin Givens, meanwhile, continued trying to stir up the situation rather than settle it. She said her husband should have stood up to Cayton in a stronger manner, that he should have told him to stop talking to the press about her or "I'm going to punch your face in." She also continued to play what she thought was her teasing game with the truth. In interviews she would say Michael didn't hit her, but he did throw things and had tantrums, that she would never stay in the relationship if she were being abused. Then later, in other statements, she would admit that Tyson was dangerous to the point where her mother hired bodyguards.

Certainly things were not all sweetness and light at the mansion in New Jersey. The Tysons's live-in butler-chauffeur and cook-maid were fired after just three months. They spoke to Mike McAlary of the New York *Daily News* of fights, arguments, a strained relationship and a controlling, interfering mother-in-law. They had been hired by Ruth Roper's assistant and told "You work for Ruth Roper. Anything you see this guy do, you report back to us confidentially. And if you ever cross her, you're finished." The husband-and-wife team of caretakers recalled the first breakfast they cooked for the newlyweds, bacon and eggs. Tyson sat down, said, "I don't like pork," picked up the bacon with his hands and dumped it on Robin's plate. "I thought to myself right then," said the butler, "this is not such a good relationship."

Arguments were constantly overheard, and Mike often slept alone on the couch in his den, the room where he spent most of his time. One night there was an especially loud argument. The next morning, according to the butler, Robin came into the kitchen and asked for an ice pack for her face, which he remembered being "not so good" when he looked at it.

The couple had another disagreement one night when he drove them to the theater in their Rolls Royce to see a play. Afterward, as the butler-chauffeur drove them home, the argument heated up. Robin shouted at Mike "You embarrassed me in front of everybody. I'm sick and tired of you. You're a lowlife. You're a nobody, a no-class nobody." Tyson ordered the chauffeur to "drop this bitch" off at her mother's house and take him home to New Jersey. But Robin insisted the mansion was her house, and that was where she was going. Tyson then jumped out of the car on a deserted Manhattan street corner, and disappeared for four days.

Ruth and Robin invited their friends out to the estate, people Mike didn't much care for and quickly grew bored with, but they didn't like it when he had his buddies out to visit. Finally, the end came for the butler and cook. Mike began to like them, began confiding in them, told him that he loved Robin but she didn't love him. "Ruth Roper gets scared when Mike Tyson starts liking people," said the butler. He and his wife were fired.

Tyson's attorney, Michael Winston, who had charged that Cayton had some of Tyson's money in accounts under his own name, had obtained aa temporary restraining order on June 30 which prevented Cayton or the corporation he had established, Sports of the Century, from receiving any of the proceeds from the Spinks fight. That money would be frozen until the parties involved reached some sort of agreement.

On July 14, Tyson indicated he would indeed fight Frank Bruno in London on September 3, and a meeting was set for the next day between Cayton's attorney, Tom Puccio, and Michael Winston to work out the arrangements. Although Cayton had requested and been granted an extension by the WBC until January for the mandatory defense against Bruno, he, Astaire and Duff were concerned that if the fight didn't take place in September, it would have to be moved from Wembley Stadium, which would seat 40,000 for the bout, to an indoor arena once the autumn weather set in, where perhaps less than 10,000 spectators could be accommodated. This could cost Tyson a million dollars or more in purse money.

Mike, meanwhile, continued to make absurd statements. He said Cayton and Jacobs had actually held him back, that he should have been fighting for the championship a year before he finally did. Considering it was he—not Cayton or Jacobs—who lost twice in the Olympic trials in the summer of 1984 and that in 1985 he had just turned pro and was still fighting largely unknown powder-puffs and that Cayton and Jacobs were bringing him along according to the game plan his own mentor, Cus D'Amato, had laid out, his statement had absolutely no foundation.

Kevin Rooney continued to support Cayton despite the warnings from Tyson to button his lip. He said Bill Cayton had never done anything except help Tyson. He called Cayton a "square shooter," and said all of Tyson's money had been well invested by the two managerial partners. Perhaps the smartest thing he said was that if Tyson and Cayton didn't sit down and work things out themselves, the lawyers involved were the ones who would be making all the money.

Speaking of lawyers, another was added to Tyson's team. With a courtroom battle looming, Ruth and Robin felt they needed a big name to bolster the efforts of Michael Winston, so they retained Peter Parcher to be their trial attorney. Parcher, whose clients included Mick Jagger, Billy Joel, Paul Simon and Bruce Springsteen, said Jacobs and Cayton were derelict not only legally but morally in not seeing to it that Tyson had independent legal representation when he signed contracts with them. "This lawsuit isn't just about money," Parcher claimed. "Since Mike Tyson doesn't get along with Cayton, doesn't he have the right to say "You're fired?" he asked. The attorney, whose clients were from the world of show business, mistakenly compared the practices in the entertainment field with those in boxing. "As a performer becomes a star, on the level of a Tyson, his manager is not entitled to take 33 percent of his earnings. That's not the way it works in the entertainment business." But one-third has always been the standard purse cut due a manager in boxing, where an effective manager performs many functions for a fighter not required of a show-business manager.

On Tuesday, July 19, 1988, all parties gathered in the chambers of Justice David Edwards, Jr., in the State Supreme Court Building on Centre Street in Manhattan. Well, almost all parties. The plaintiff himself—Michael Tyson—did not appear. His appearance was not required by law, since he was represented by counsel, and no doubt could not face the prospect of a direct confrontation with Cayton, especially since it had been the idea of everyone around him except himself. It showed yet another facet of Tyson's increasingly revealed lack of character. This was the heavyweight champion of the world who had just recently announced that he was the boss, that he was running things, that he was taking charge, yet now opted not to turn up in court to face the man at whom he had hurled so many accusations.

During the preliminary hearing, Justice Edwards later announced, some progress was made on two issues: working toward an arrangement that would allow the Bruno fight to take place with all those involved in the dispute participating, even though the larger Tyson-Cayton contractual issue might still remain to be resolved in court at a later date; and disposition of the more than $21 million in Tyson revenues from the Spinks fight, which had been frozen by court injunction.

Thursday, July 21, was spent by the various parties in meetings in the judge's chambers and in private rooms, but it was a day of progress. On hand were Tyson, Robin Givens, Ruth Roper, Bill Cayton, Lorraine Jacobs, Donald Trump, plus attorneys Puccio, Winston, Parcher and various associates. For nearly seven hours they talked and negotiated, and at the end of the day an agreement had been worked out to distribute $16.5 million from the Spinks fight. Justice Edwards vacated the temporary restraining order he had issued on June 29. Mike Tyson was issued a check for $10 million; Cayton and Mrs Jacobs received $5 million; and Kevin Rooney $1.5 million. Several million dollars more in revenue were still to come from the U.S. and around the world. Still unresolved was the matter of whether, when and how matters would proceed toward making the Tyson-Bruno fight for September, less than two months off. Jarvis Astaire was on his way to New York from London at that very moment to meet with everyone involved in a last-ditch effort to try to salvage the September 3 date.

Following the all-day session in court and the resolution

of the Spinks fight money impasse, Thomas Puccio said he had no doubt that Bill Cayton and Mike Tyson would be able to work together in the future. "We're basically down to one issue: money, how much Tyson will get and how much Cayton will get. Bill can advise him on fights, but Mike Tyson will decide where and when he fights," said Puccio.

Michael Winston said, "The two main issues are money and the term of the contract. I think they can build toward a working relationship again if certain issues are resolved." Tyson's attorney was realistic enough, however, to offer the observation that he didn't think the two would ever be buddies who could sit down and share a beer or two. But that night, attending an amateur boxing show at Madison Square Garden, Tyson told Bill Gallo of the New York *Daily News* that he doubted he could get along with Cayton in the future because the manager "took advantage of me." He said Steve Lott was now out as his assistant manager. He said also that he had not reached a decision about Kevin Rooney's future, although he made it clear he was angered because Rooney "went out of his way to go against me." He said he credited only Gus D'Amato for his success, "because he laid down the plans which he handed over to Jacobs. Every step I took was the original idea of Cus, and nobody else." Over the course of the hearings, Tyson continually referred to Cayton as "crude," "despicable" and someone who made him "sick to my stomach." A misinformed Tyson said that Wilfred Benitez, who had been managed by Jacobs and Cayton, was broke and that the other world champion handled by Cayton, lightweight Edwin Rosario, had recently declared bankruptcy. As a matter of fact, the nutty Benitez and his equally irresponsible father were the ones who had themselves raped the Puerto Rican fighter's finances, despite the best efforts of Cayton and Jacobs to try to avert such a situation. When they established a money market fund containing hundreds of thousands of dollars to provide for Benitez's future, the fighter depleted it within 60 days and would accept no financial advice from his managers. As for Rosario, at a Madison Square Garden press conference on July 28 to announce a forthcoming Rosario fight, a smiling Rosario stood next to Bill Cayton at the podium as Cayton,

25 July 1988

Michael Tyson (hereinafter Tyson) c/o Winston &
Bonner, 730 Fifth Avenue, New York and William Cayton
(hereinafter Cayton) 9 East 40th Street, New York
have reached the following agreement in principal to
be later entered into full contract form.

1.   With respect to the New York State Athletic
Commission Boxer-Manager contract signed on February
12, 1988 and now in effect, Cayton will continue
to act as manager under the terms therein
provided until February 11, 1992 except as follows:

   (a)   Cayton will receive 20% and Tyson 80% of the
         net remuneration earned by Tyson from his
         boxing activities.

   (b)   Tyson has the right to have his attorney
         review all fight contracts and to veto any
         fight that he does not want to engage in.

   (c)   Tyson has a right to veto the hiring of a
         trainer and any assistants.

   (d)   Tyson has an absolute right to a full and
         complete accounting of all revenues past, present
         and future by an accountant of his choice.

11. This understanding is subject to the approval of
the New York State Athletic Commission.

12. The fraud claim against Jacob and Cayton is withdrawn.

13. Neither party shall issue any press release or
any other public statements regarding the subject
matter of this Settlement Agreement other than a
joint press release agreed upon by the parties.

Michael Gerald Tyson

William Cayton

Sports of the Century Inc.

by William Cayton, President

7/27/88

*A portion of the agreement reached in July 1988, between
Tyson and Cayton, reducing Cayton's percentage as manager
from the standard 33 percent to 20 percent, at the instigation of
Donald Trump.*

uncharacteristically blunt, labeled Tyson's statement "bullshit," and said "Edwin Rosario is in fine financial condition. He has a six-figure trust fund here in New York."

On Monday, July 25, fresh from a weekend respite, the parties reconvened at Justice Edwards's chambers at the State Supreme Court Building, and behind closed doors the dispute was finally resolved. In a compromise agreement that avoided a protracted court battle, Bill Cayton retained his role as Mike Tyson's manager for the full duration of the contract, which ran to February 11, 1992. But in a major concession by Cayton (which Donald Trump took full credit for imposing on the manager on Tyson's behalf), he agreed to reduce his percentage from 33 percent to 20 percent. As far as the personal services contract between Tyson and Cayton, which covered such out-of-the-ring income as commercials and endorsements, Cayton's percentage was reduced from 33 percent to 16 ⅔ percent on existing deals and 10 percent on any future deals negotiated by Cayton. Tyson retained a right of refusal on any such deals. Cayton won a major point when it was agreed that his company, Big Fights, Inc., would have the exclusive right to license all television foreign rights agreements for Tyson fights and receive a 20 percent commission for doing so, a concession providing tremendous financial potential to Cayton, because the 20 percent commission on foreign rights negotiations was in addition to the 20 percent he would receive from all gross fight revenues. The agreement further stated that Tyson had the right to have his own attorney review all fight contracts, that he could turn down any fight he did not want to take part in (somewhat meaningless in that the WBC, WBA and IBF all had mandatory challengers that Tyson had to face or else risk being stripped of his title, so the only fights he could turn down were the voluntary defenses) and that he was entitled to have his own accountant receive a full accounting of all revenues. Finally, it was agreed that "The fraud claim against Jacob [sic] and Cayton is withdrawn."

The next day, a news conference was called at Trump's Plaza Hotel to announce the terms of the settlement. Along with the parties involved in the litigation, two other pleased parties were on hand—Jarvis Astaire, British promoter of the Bruno fight, and Seth Abraham, whose HBO network would televise it in the United States. They were anxious to sit down and finalize the match as soon as the press conference ended. Cayton said, "I'm pleased this matter is resolved and that Mike and I can work together as we did in the past. We might have gone to court and won, but a court settlement would have led to bitterness. My attorneys decided this was the wisest thing to do and I agreed." He said he hoped Tyson would "enlighten" him as to the specifics of how he had been kept in the dark financially. "The fact is," Cayton said, "before any fight was made, Jim and I would bring Mike into the office and discuss the fight with him. We never made a decision without Mike getting at least the right to know what was going to happen. Of course, he always had the right to refuse. . . . I'm absolutely confident that history will decide he is the greatest heavyweight champion of all time. I'm pleased to be continuing my career with him," Cayton concluded, even though Tyson had refused to stand with him at the podium. Thomas Puccio said Tyson had always had the right to turn down fights or opponents, so adding those points in writing was just "window dressing." When Donald Trump outlined the terms of the settlement, a smirking Robin Givens applauded wildly. Michael Winston said, "I think we accomplished everything we wanted. Mike's calling the shots, controlling his own destiny, and he still respects Bill's ability as a businessman." Lorraine Jacobs said she was pleased it was all over, but when asked if she could forgive Tyson for accusing her late husband of fraud, she said, "I'd really rather not comment on anything."

Then it was Mike Tyson's turn. Stepping to the podium, dressed, for a change, in a tailored suit and tie, he said, "I'm running my show. That contract I was in was like a servant contract. I fought who, when and where they said I should. Cayton did a good job financially, but he didn't inform me of certain things. If I hadn't been married to Robin, my eyes might never have been opened. We had to go through ridicule and scandal. I personally don't get embarrassed myself, but my wife and mother-in-law were embarrassed and might have left me if they weren't so strong." Tyson said he would have liked to have gone to trial because "Deep down inside, I wanted to see my lawyer Peter

Parcher work in court." He said Cayton "is employed by me; I'm not employed by him. . . . The main thing is, if I don't agree to anything, it doesn't have to happen. . . . He's good at what he does, and as long as he abides by all the terms of the agreement, everything will work out. We don't have to get along. . . . As for winning or losing, I'm walking away with a better deal than I had when I started."

Tyson wasn't quite finished, however. As a stunned Jarvis Astaire and Seth Abraham listened, he said, "I think I'm going to pass on the Bruno fight and take six or eight weeks off to relax. I just don't feel like fighting right now. Please, by no means am I scared of Bruno. I just don't want to get on a plane and fly five hours, or three hours, or whatever. I want to stay in the United States." Astaire offered the opinion that Tyson's first decision on his own was a bad one, that it was "commercial suicide." He said perhaps Tyson didn't care about a mere $2 million, but moving the bout from the stadium indoors to Wembley Arena later in the year would cost him at least that, from a projected $8 million to perhaps $5 or $6 million. But Don King, quiet during the court proceedings and conspicuously absent, was spending time with Tyson at the fighter's New Jersey home, and it was a safe bet he wasn't encouraging Tyson to go to England and fight Bruno for his promotional rivals, Astaire and Duff.

Later, when he intensified his attacks on Cayton, King would single out the deal Cayton made for the Bruno fight in London as having been a terrible one for Tyson. It was, in fact, a deal which King would never have dreamt of making on behalf of any fighter, as Cayton carved out angles and advantages for Tyson that King wasn't even aware existed. Cayton's negotiations began with securing $4 million from HBO, which Cayton arranged would remain in the U.S. and therefore would not be subject to British taxes. Next, all foreign TV money outside Britain would be paid to Tyson in the United States—over $2 million—and therefore would also not be subject to British taxes. There was $1.5 million allocated for all expenses, which included (and was quite unusual in this respect) all sanctioning fees, which amounted to some $350,000. Out of the $1.5 million would also come Bruno's sanctioning fees, the promoter's sanctioning fees, the rental for Wembley and advertising costs, plus $100,000 "pocket money" in cash to Tyson for his personal expenses. Bruno was to get a purse of $1.8 million

Cayton had arranged separate deals with Toyota for $500,000 for which the Japanese auto manufacturer would receive advertising and promotional consideration such as having their logo on the ring canvas, the ring posts, and in the stadium, as well as being identified as the fight's "sponsor." Cayton also negotiated a $500,000 deal with the BBC for delayed broadcast rights in Great Britain, plus an additional estimated $500,000 that would accrue from concessions, souvenirs and the like. The gross purse would have come to about $9 million, out of which would come the $1.5 million for expenses and Bruno's purse of $1.8 million, leaving Tyson just about $6 million or slightly under. In addition, Cayton bargained for an extraordinary assortment of "perks" worth perhaps another $400,000. These included sixteen round-trip Concorde tickets, forty additional tickets on regularly scheduled jetliners, suites for Robin and Ruth in one of London's finest hotels, and suites in a beautiful training facility Tyson would use outside London.

Mike Tyson was unmoved and apparently unimpressed. At a meeting that month in the HBO offices attended by Cayton, Tyson and HBO senior executives Michael Fuchs and Seth Abraham, Tyson said point-blank, "I don't want to go to London." Cayton was aware that pulling out of an agreed fight against the mandatory challenger meant risking being stripped of the title by the WBC. And make no mistake, it was Mickey Duff's intention to pressure the WBC to do just that and then move Bruno into an elimination bout for the vacant title as the number one contender, meaning Bruno could win a portion of the title without having to fight Tyson and thereby making an eventual meeting between the two worth much more to Bruno. "Mike," Cayton said, "you've signed a contract, you must honor it." "I don't want to honor it. I don't want to go to London," Tyson reiterated. "You're my manager. Get me out of it. I don't care what it costs." And that was that. Mike Tyson was obviously having ideas put in his head.

As August came, the winds shifted dramatically on two fronts. In the hope that Tyson would relent and fight Bruno in London, as he was contractually obliged to, the fight date was moved back to October 8, when it might still be just possible to squeeze it in outdoors at Wembley. During the second week of August, Jarvis Astaire announced in London the fight would take place, and on Monday, August 15, at a Wembley news conference, Bruno said, "People are making Tyson sound like a monster, but no man is unbeatable, and I am a stone [14 pounds] heavier than him. This fight is all about power. . . . I have been watching videos of Tyson, and I have spotted quite a few weaknesses. . . . He's going to get murdered, not me. . . . He doesn't scare me." Wembley was scaled for a live gate of $7.65 million with a sellout, which the promoters said they expected. That would make it the biggest financial windfall in British sporting history. John Morris, secretary of the British Boxing Board of Control, expressed his faith in Bruno's forthcoming effort. "In no way will Frank Bruno be a lamb led to the slaughter," he said. "We could have the biggest boxing upset of all time here." Terry Lawless, Bruno's manager, said Frank's aim was more than just going in to grab the $1.8 million purse. "Frank has desperately wanted to fight Tyson since they first met. I have never known anyone so desperate to fight someone. It's a pride fight for Frank," said Lawless.

On that same Monday, August 15, some 3,500 miles away, in Cleveland, Ohio, Tyson was hedging. "We really haven't decided if we're fighting him or not," the champion told the press who had gathered for a Don King-arranged ceremony in which Tyson was being presented with the ceremonial key to the city. Tyson was staying with King at the promoter's home outside the city. As a matter of fact, the two had of late been virtually inseparable, and the suspicion was that King was up to no good, with the malleable young champion in his grasp. But in an effort to subvert the Bruno fight, Don King was overplaying his hand and was in the process of making a major blunder.

The previous week, King had been with Tyson in Los Angeles. Jose Ribalta and his manager, Luis DeCubas, were summoned from their homes in Miami and the four met to negotiate a fight. King told Ribalta and DeCubas that Tyson would fight the Cuban-born heavyweight in October, not

Frank Bruno, and had them sign an agreement to that effect which offered a purse of $700,000 to Ribalta. When Cayton, Astaire, and Duff, got wind of it, along with Ruth, Robin and attorney Winston, the shit hit the fan. Tyson had listened to Don King singing him the "You're the Boss, You're Calling the Shots" song and had acted, as usual, impulsively, jumping right in to dance to the tune without being properly informed. A month earlier, Tyson had complained in his legal papers that he had never been represented by his own attorney when dealing with Jacobs and Cayton. Now that he had an attorney, he didn't consult him. But it did not take Winston, Ruth Roper and Robin Givens very long to come to the conclusion that King had been working behind their backs to deal independently and directly with Tyson and had put Tyson in tremendous legal jeopardy. Just three weeks earlier, a legal war had been averted when a new agreement was reached with Bill Cayton. That agreement was that Cayton remained the manager, and one of the key points in the contract with Cayton stipulated that Tyson could not engage in any fights except those specifically approved by his manager, despite all the rhetoric that Tyson was "the boss." They also knew King was smart enough and experienced enough to realize exactly what he was doing.

King then announced he had Tyson's signature on a contract to promote his next fight. "I have a written contract," he declared, looking like the cat who had just eaten the canary. "Rest assured, I've got paper. I don't do nothing just oral." He said he had done what he had done with no other intention except "love," insisting it was not a desperate act of disruption on his part. Thomas Puccio advised Bill Cayton to sue King for tortuous interference with his contract with Tyson. "The contract King purports to have isn't worth the paper it's written on," declared Cayton. Astaire and Duff saw King's move as a direct attempt to sabotage the fight at Wembley, and were also contemplating legal action. So, suddenly, in one greedy move, Don King had alienated the two women he had spent months smooth-talking in an effort to win their confidence, had put Tyson in potential legal hot water, and was facing a possible lawsuit from the champion's manager, as well as another from the

British promoters. But one week later, a single punch thrown not in the ring but in the middle of the night on a steamy Harlem street would turn everything topsy-turvy, the first in a series of events that would generate more newspaper copy, magazine stories and TV reports than any of Tyson's thirty-five fights, as his life began more and more to resemble, at one and the same time, a television soap opera, a slapstick comedy and a Greek tragedy.

Chapter 15

Those Lazy, Hazy, Crazy
Days of Summer

*If anger is not restrained, it is frequently more hurtful to
us than the injury that provokes it.*

—Seneca

On Tuesday, August 23, 1988, Tyson was due in Catskill,
where Kevin Rooney expected him to put in his first day of
training for the Bruno fight. Instead, at 4:00 A.M. on August
23, Tyson and two friends pulled up in his Rolls Royce to 43
East 125th Street, the heart of Harlem, just off the corner of
Madison Avenue. Tyson's two companions were Walter
Berry, the former St. John's University basketball star then
playing with San Antonio in the National Basketball Association, and Berry's cousin, Tom Smalls. At that address was
a clothing store called Dapper Dan's, frequented by customers ranging from fancy Harlem dandies and rap music stars
to pimps and drug dealers. (Also at that address, according
to police, was an unlicensed after-hours club in the base-
ment.) Owing to the nocturnal nature of much of its clien-
tele, Dapper Dan's was open when Tyson arrived to pick up
a custom-made $800 white leather jacket.

Mitch Green lived on 160th Street in the Jamaica section
of the borough of Queens, but he considered Harlem his
turf and it just so happened that he was hanging around
with some friends nearby. Word quickly filtered to him that
Tyson had just arrived at Dapper Dan's, and he made an
instant decision to go and confront the heavyweight champion. A former street gang leader who had spent time in a
juvenile detention center, Green had turned to boxing and
after a solid amateur career, became a professional in 1980,
when he was twenty-four years old. Standing 6'5" and possessing considerable talent, he had the potential to go far.
After racking up a string of wins under the management of
Shelly Finkel and Lou Duva, NBC Television included him

in a group they called "Tomorrow's Champions" in a televised boxing series of the same name. Green lost a twelve-round decision to former champion Trevor Berbick, his only loss until he dropped the ten-round decision to Tyson in May of 1986, by which time he had switched management to the Don and Carl King team. Despite lots of big talk, Green, who still faced a bright future as a fighter, never fought again. He developed a pattern of erratic behavior that made him too unstable to fight. His driver's license had been suspended or revoked a remarkable fifty-four times, and charges against him from 1983 to 1988 included driving without insurance and driving under the influence of drugs, plus five accidents involving personal injuries to others. After one arrest, a urine test performed on him came back positive for angel dust, and his behavior at Gleason's Gym on the one or two days he turned up there in 1988 to make an attempt at training led those present to conclude he was functioning under the influence of some foreign substance in his body. He was also arrested for robbery when he commandeered a gasoline station, chased the attendant away and began pumping the gasoline himself for customers and pocketing the cash. He provoked a highly publicized confrontation with Don King at a 1986 news conference when he arrived uninvited and threatened King's life, and he had previously invaded a Larry Holmes news conference, challenging the then champion to a fight and pointing his finger directly into Holmes's face until one of Larry's bodyguards bit it! This, then, was the Mitch Green who decided to drop in on Mike Tyson at Dapper Dan's.

According to various accounts, Green went inside the clothing store and began egging Tyson on. "I was telling him," Green himself said, " 'You know I didn't really fight you. You really didn't beat me, 'cause Don King done took my money.' " He then began yelling, "Don King robbed me," to which Tyson allegedly responded, "Don King robbed me, too. He robs everybody." "You're with Don King," Green said to Tyson. "You both owe me money." Tyson said he left the store and headed for his car to end the showdown with Green, but Green followed him out to the street and grabbed him, ripping his shirt. "It happened so fast," Tyson later said. "I was very upset that he ripped my shirt, and I was upset that he came back again. I was getting paranoid because he was close to me, so I defended myself. I had no choice but to defend myself. I wasn't planning to punch him. I was fighting because I was scared. I hadn't had a street fight in seven years, I was getting scared."

Tyson apparently told Green that he was talking bullshit. "You're going to tell me I didn't beat you?" Tyson asked. "I won that fight. I beat you." According to Green, Tyson said, "We can do it again now." Green said he saw Tyson adjusting the gold rings on his hand as if he were getting ready to punch. Now out on the sidewalk, Green said Tyson "sucker-punched me and ran, and his boys held me, like they were breaking up a fight, while I was trying to get to him. They hit me cheap shots, too. . . . Mike Tyson, heavyweight champion of the world, a cheap shot like that." Tyson and witnesses, however, say it was Green who threw the first punch, striking the champion in the chest. In an instant, Tyson fired one right hand, gold rings and all, right between Green's eyes, inflicting a wound that required five stitches to close. In the ensuing scuffle, Green broke the sideview mirror off Tyson's Rolls Royce. Both men then went off to the hospital, Green to North General to be stitched up, and Tyson to Manhattan's Mount Sinai to have his hand looked at. He arrived at the emergency room at 5:30 A.M. complaining of a bruised hand and was treated and released forty-five minutes later. Green proceeded from the hospital to the 25th New York City Police Department precinct house to file assault charges against Tyson, which Tyson later termed "ludicrous . . . I'm a victim, and then he presses charges on me." Tyson said he did not plan to file countercharges.

Later in the day, the hand still bothering him, Tyson went to an orthopedic hand specialist, and X-rays revealed his one-punch fight with Mitch Green had cost him dearly. He had suffered a hairline fracture of the third metacarpal bone, the bone on the back of the hand running from the middle knuckle back toward the wrist. His hand was set in a protective cast for three weeks. Now the October 8 date in London, which was still being worked on, was in danger of cancelation before it was even set.

In the days following the incident, the TV newscasts and newspapers had a field day questioning Tyson's motives and judgment in being out and about at four o'clock in the morning, especially on the day he was to begin training, and reporting Mitch Green as he ranted and raved at a news conference he called on TV talk shows. "He was acting like a sissy . . . he's scared of me," said Green. "He's a homo, ho–mo. He may go both ways, but he's a homo. . . . He's a half-retarded, henpecked little sissy . . . Where's Michelle. I want Michelle. . . ." What Green was trying to do was parlay the highly publicized incident into a million-dollar rematch with Tyson, and for several weeks thereafter he actually succeeded in creating enough interest to make a future showdown—in the ring—a distinct possibility. Green challenged Tyson, and Bill Cayton liked the idea of a "grudge match," saying Tyson-Green was "absolutely a very attractive fight now." The hype was on, even as the British promoters of Tyson-Bruno secured an October 22 back-up date at Wembley, anticipating that the injury to Tyson's hand might push their bout back two more weeks.

There was just one obstacle to a Tyson-Green fight, a little matter of rules. No sanctioning group would permit a fight for the title unless the challenger (that is, Mitch Green) was ranked in the top ten, and because of his more than two years of complete ring idleness, he was unranked. In order to become ranked, he would have to defeat someone in the top ten first. Such disparate figures as Seth Abraham of HBO, Green's former manager, Shelly Finkel, and his former promoter and current arch-enemy, Don King, made a concerted effort to get him a fight, but Green really wasn't interested. He kept insisting he didn't need to fight anyone first, just Tyson. Even his current managers acknowledged their man didn't really want to fight. He turned down several fights his managers had been trying to make since his 1986 loss to Tyson, one for $40,000 and another for $25,000, plus an easy one for $7,500, saying he wouldn't take them because it was beneath his dignity to fight for such low purses.

Finally, in exchange for dropping his charges against Tyson, which he did two days after filing them, Bill Cayton gave Green a letter of agreement saying he could have a fight with Tyson, *if* he got himself in shape and back in the rankings. "How do you like that? I'm a hot item right now," said Green, with an inflated opinion of his own worth. Tyson issued a statement which said, in part, "I can beat this guy anytime, anywhere, anyplace. I will teach him a lesson in the ring that he should have learned already." Calling Green's attack on him a "cheap publicity stunt," he called on Green to "be a man for once . . . get into shape, get his act together with some good tough prelim fights so that he's ranked again [and] I'll definitely teach him a lesson in the ring that he'll never forget."

Despite all the publicity and interest generated by this apparently chance encounter of two heavyweight ships passing (and colliding) in the night, Mitch Green made no effort to follow through on any of the things being done on his behalf to help him get in shape, and before long all talk of a Tyson-Green bout was dropped and forgotten. The next time Mitch Green was heard of was four weeks later, when he was arrested on a Harlem street for disorderly conduct after stopping his car and causing a traffic jam while he raved and cursed about Mike Tyson. Officers from the Emergency Services unit had to use electric stun guns to subdue the crazed fighter. Two days later, he was arrested once again, this time for third-degree assault after his girlfriend called police and said the boxer, who was the father of her child, had beaten her.

One footnote: The inscription meticulously sewn onto the back of the white leather jacket that Tyson had stopped by Dapper Dan's to collect, read in large letters, "Don't Believe the Hype."

On September 1, earlier than expected, the cast was removed from Tyson's right hand, and he was given the go-ahead to resume serious training in Catskill for the Bruno fight. He would return to Catskill for a week, before accompanying his wife to the Soviet Union where she was scheduled to tape two special episodes of her TV sitcom. While in Moscow, Kevin Rooney was to join him, and Tyson would train there for a week, come back to the United States for several days, then move his training base to London on September 25. He left his doctor's office in midtown Manhattan with a protective, removable plastic support on his hand, and although he could resume training, he would not use the right hand until it was no longer sore.

On September 2, he worked out in the gym, then stayed out late at the Albany-area nightclub he frequents, Septembers, in the town of Colonie. The next morning, he arrived at the gym alone at 10:00 A.M. in his BMW, removed his hand brace and went through a light workout with the bags and in the ring, although there was no sparring. He was supervised by Rooney. He showed a visitor his hand, which was clearly still swollen across the back, where the break had occurred. After the workout, he returned to the house with John Etheridge, a reporter on the London *Sun* newspaper, and Etheridge's photographer, in tow. The weather was beautiful, and after climbing to his pigeon loft and letting his birds out to fly, he sat down on the porch and gave Etheridge a relaxed interview. He talked about how he was finding himself as a person, how he was no longer into jewelry, into buying cars, how he was discovering that money was not really important. He reminisced about the days when he had no money and was happy to buy used leather jackets at rummage sales for $30 around the Catskill area; about how he would beg his friends to buy him a Whopper at Burger King; and how they tried to talk their way into the local movie theater at two-for-one prices. He seemed nostalgic about the old days, perhaps implying life was simpler before fame, success and money complicated it.

Shortly after noon he ended the interview. He wanted to shower, change and drive to Atlantic City, a good three and a half to four hours from Catskill, to see Buddy McGirt defend his junior welterweight title against Meldrick Taylor. But after the newspapermen departed, he felt groggy and could hardly keep his eyes open, tired from his late night at Septembers. Jay Bright strongly advised him not to attempt the long drive to Atlantic City and back in his fatigued condition, and Tyson saw the wisdom of this. He rested, watched on TV as McGirt lost his title to Taylor, and then drove the 40 miles to Colonie where he once again spent the night at Septembers.

On Sunday morning, September 4, the entire United States eastern seaboard, from Florida to New England, was blanketed in bad weather. Torrential rains had fallen all night in New York, and it was still pouring in the morning when Mike woke up, watched a movie on his VCR, and then sat in the living room reading a magazine. Around eleven o'clock he told Camille Ewald he had nothing to read and he was going to drive the two miles into town to buy some magazines. She told him to be careful because of the terrible weather. Mike then went outside and got behind the wheel of the $71,000 BMW 750iL, a 12-cylinder powerhouse he had purchased as a gift for Robin.

Many of Tyson's friends will joke that Mike Tyson behind the wheel of a car is more dangerous than Mike Tyson in the ring. Teddy Atlas recalls Mike's mounting the sidewalk and hitting a mailbox while trying to drive the first used car Cus D'Amato bought for the teenage fighter. Jay Bright laughingly said he hides behind trees when Mike gets in the car to drive. D'Amato once told his young fighter, after taking a drive with him, "Mike, I'll never have to use a laxative again." Tyson had no luck with cars, even when he wasn't driving. Before he and Robin were married, following an argument, she got into his Mercedes 560SL and slammed it into the rear of his Rolls-Royce, damaging both vehicles. On this rainy morning in Catskill, the BMW was parked on the grass. Tyson turned on the ignition, hit the gas pedal and the wheels began spinning in the wet grass and mud. Camille came out on the porch to try to tell him there was a telephone call for him. At that moment, the wheels suddenly grabbed and the car shot forward out of control. It lurched about 30 feet, and the right front bumper slammed into a chestnut tree at the edge of the property. It bounced off the tree, sustaining heavy damage to the front end, then came to a stop in some shrubs a short distance away. When Camille got to the car, Tyson appeared to be unconscious. His head was slumped back, his eyes closed. She slapped him a few times, and when he came to, asking her, "Camille, what happened?" "You hit a tree," she told him, and then he drifted off into unconsciousness again. Jay Bright phoned for an ambulance, which came from Catskill in about ten minutes. Tyson, according to one of the attendants, was still unconscious, although his pulse, breathing and blood pressure were normal. They rushed him to Catskill Hospital, but a short time later it was decided to move him to the larger Columbia-Greene Medical Center about fifteen minutes away in Hudson, New York, where a CAT scan could be performed.

Meanwhile, Ruth Roper and Robin Givens were notified in New York City about the accident and immediately began the two-hour drive to Catskill. Tyson had wanted Robin to spend a few days with him there while he trained and before they both left for the Soviet Union, but she had opted to stay in the city to attend the U.S. Open Tennis Championships which were under way. Before starting out for Catskill, Roper had told Camille they would want to transfer Mike to Columbia-Presbyterian Medical Center in Manhattan, where they felt he would receive better diagnostic treatment.

When Camille went to see Mike at the hospital in Hudson, around one o'clock in the afternoon, the fighter was fully conscious and in good spirits, though rather embarrassed by the mishap and the fuss. Camille told him that Ruth and Robin wanted him transferred to New York City, but Mike said he wasn't going anywhere until he had something to eat. He was starving, and food was his major concern at that moment. Jay Bright went to a Chinese restaurant and brought him a large quantity of fried rice and beef with broccoli, which the champion ravenously consumed. Mike joked with Camille about what a "nice Labor Day weekend" it had turned out to be, with him in the hospital, and the two laughed about it.

His spirits brightened further when Robin arrived later in the afternoon, along with her mother and their public relations representative. By then, Tyson had undergone a CAT brain scan, an EEG and an EKG, and Bill Cayton had been informed by Columbia-Greene doctors that Mike was "absolutely okay." Shortly after 7:00 P.M. with local newspaper and TV cameramen waiting outside, Mike was brought out, strapped to a stretcher, looking bewildered and embarrassed, and placed in an ambulance for the trip to Manhattan. In response to a question, he nodded and quietly acknowledged that he was feeling fine. Robin got in the back of the ambulance with him, and as photographers jockeyed for position to take pictures through the ambulance window, she blocked their view with her hand until a towel was placed across the window to curtain off the view. Earlier in the afternoon, there had been an unpleasant shouting match between Robin and trainer Kevin Rooney, when he arrived at the hospital to visit Tyson. Robin had tried to prevent him from getting into Mike's room, but he had brushed past her and gone in to see his young charge.

Shortly after 9:00 P.M., Tyson's ambulance arrived at Columbia-Presbyterian Medical Center in Manhattan, where reporters, photographers and TV cameras were waiting. As Tyson's stretcher was taken out of the ambulance, Givens became involved in another scene, shouting at the newspeople to "leave him alone, nothing's the matter, give the guy a break." No one was bothering Mike, just taking his picture, but Givens suddenly jumped right over her husband's stretcher, which was momentarily on the ground, and lunged at a TV cameraman, pushing him until he admonished her to "Take it easy, lady." Thus she became the focal point of the next day's TV newscasts and newspaper photos.

In the hospital, Tyson was once again subjected to a battery of even more sophisticated tests. Late that night, the Assistant Professor of Neurology at the hospital, Dr. Carolyn Britton, told the media that Mike had "suffered minor trauma to the head and chest wall" as the result of banging into the steering wheel when he hit the tree. She said he would remain in the hospital to undergo further observation and diagnostic testing, but his condition was "quite stable" and he was "neurologically normal."

The next day, Mike was isolated in a private room on the ninth floor, with security guards posted to protect his privacy. The two women compiled a list of approved visitors to Mike's room. Bill Cayton and Kevin Rooney were not on it. They had made it clear many times that the people who had been with Mike all along, from the beginning, were not part of their group. Even Cus D'Amato, who, despite some errors in judgment had done more for Mike Tyson than anyone else, was no longer in favor with the two women. Robin had said in the past she was "tired of constantly hearing about an old dead man I never knew," and said she didn't want her life infringed upon by the "ghost" of Cus D'Amato. The past meant nothing to these women. They were calling the shots now. Bill Cayton tried as gracefully as possible to excuse the fact that he was turned away when he tried to visit Mike, but Rooney was enraged. So were others, including Broadway and film star Danny Aiello and photographer Brian Hamill, who were also unceremoniously rejected when they arrived at the hospital. All had known Tyson from the early days and were friends in the true sense with no ulterior motives. Aiello and Hamill were personally turned away by Robin, who gave them a curt "no," without explanation or even cursory thanks for dropping by.

The list of those who could enter the inner sanctum and visit Mike was a joke. It included, besides Roper and Givens, Roper's assistant and henchwoman, Olga Rosario, Peter Parcher and Steven Hayes, the two attorneys retained by Roper to represent Tyson, Donald Trump and his wife, Ivana, and Howard Rubenstein, Trump's public relations man, who had, not accidentally, been retained by Roper and Givens to represent them as well as Mike. "Mrs. Trump!" exclaimed Danny Aiello. "We've known Mike since he was a kid. Trump knows him for half an hour," he told Pete Hamill.

Roper spoke touchingly of her daughter's loyalty. "Robin is hanging in there with her man, as usual," she said. "When he gets bruised, she hurts." Don King, on the outside looking in, offered his opinion that something was evidently wrong with Mike, he was confused, and those around him, suggested the benevolent promoter, shouldn't be so concerned about Mike fighting and making money. Instead they should be interested in his welfare as a human being, said the noted humanitarian King. Sugar Ray Leonard put forth the opinion that "there is something bothering Mike, probably something that stems back to when he was a kid. Larry Holmes said Tyson needed some guidance and good advice, and sent Mike a telegram offering to help if Mike wanted to talk to him. Muhammad Ali said he had never gotten in trouble while champion, but said Mike was "still young and he's got a few little faults and habits, which we all have, that have got to be corrected. He's in a position now where the world is watching him, and I think after a few mistakes he'll realize that . . . . If he wasn't famous and he wasn't where he was, he wouldn't make the news. But he's popular."

On Tuesday, Tyson underwent further testing. It was determined he could be released within a day or two, but Dr. Britton then said the words that Jarvis Astaire and Mickey Duff didn't want to hear. She said Mike had been unconscious for about twenty minutes following the accident, and he had suffered some temporary amnesia. His doctors recommended that he should not train for thirty to sixty days, making an October date at Wembley an impossibility. In London, Jarvis Astaire acknowledged that both October 8 and the back-up date of October 22 were now out of the question. He said there was no choice but to implement the contingency plan of moving the fight indoors to a much smaller venue, the Wembley Arena, and a tentative date of December 16 was set. Astaire made it clear there would be no stepping aside by Bruno to allow Tyson to fight an interim challenger. "Bruno is the nominated next challenger," he said. "We have a contract for Tyson to fight him, and that is what will happen. . . . If anything, this should give Frank encouragement. The invincibility of Tyson has taken a bit of a blow. Once he gets over his initial disappointment, Frank is going to fancy his chances even more. Psychologically, what's happened must worry the champion."

Back at the hospital, Tyson was getting petulant and restless. The security guards assigned to him described him as a "big baby," complaining all the time and watching television constantly, throwing the white hospital gowns at nurses and attendants and telling them he only wore black.

The front page headlines all week had riveted people to the Tyson story: "Iron Mike KO'd in Crash," "Car Skid KO's Tyson," "Iron Mike Faces Brain Scan," "Tyson's Bout [vs. Bruno] KO'd," "Alone at the Top, Tortured Tyson Has Nowhere to Turn," "Tyson-Bruno Off, Doctor Says Champ Needs Time to Recover." But the New York *Daily News* headline on the morning of Wednesday, September 7, set off more reaction, controversy, claims and counterclaims than any Tyson had previously had in the three years since he first hit the news: "EXCLUSIVE: TYSON TRIED TO KILL SELF," said the paper's front page in two-inch bold black letters. The subheading said, "Friends Reveal Suicide Threat." The story, written by columnist Mike McAlary, was, to say the least, sensational. It claimed that on Sunday morning, Tyson, whose mind "was racing and tortured," called Givens in Manhattan and told her, "I'm going to go out and kill myself. . . . I'm going to crash my car." The story says Tyson then went to the BMW and hit the gas pedal without putting on his seat belt, and "aimed the car into a tree." McAlary presented an entire dossier of allegations, among them that the previous Thursday Tyson "had threatened to kill Givens," and that the next day, "according to . . . friends," two shotguns were delivered to Tyson. "I'll kill you and then me," McAlary reported Tyson as saying to Robin.

According to McAlary, when Givens arrived at the hospital upstate on Sunday afternoon, Tyson said to her, "I told you I'd do it . . . and as soon as I get out of here, I'll do it again." McAlary said for several weeks Roper and Givens had tried unsuccessfully to get Mike to see a New York psychiatrist, Dr. Henry McCurtis, who was the Director of Psychiatry at Harlem Hospital and who specialized in the treatment of athletes suffering from stress. While in the hospital, Tyson had at last spoken with Dr. McCurtis. Although the psychiatrist would not discuss Tyson with him, McAlary's "sources" told him that Dr. McCurtis believed "Mike Tyson should be committed for psychiatric evaluation." The reporter went on to reveal, "Only a small circle of people know what is said to be Tyson's problem, that he has a chemical imbalance that prods him to violent behavior. . . . As a child, the champ reportedly took medication for this afflication. But then he became a boxer and quit the medication. His old trainer, Cus D'Amato, believed that he could control Tyson by keeping him in the ring. But . . . evidently there is no controlling his demons. . . . The people with knowledge of Tyson's problems include Donald Trump and public relations man Howard Rubenstein. Tyson's lawyers—Peter Parcher and Steven Hayes—also understand the situation. . . . They are more interested in the fighter's future than his next fight." McAlary included Givens and Roper among those truly concerned for Tyson's well-being, painting Cayton and Rooney as money-grubbing and interested only in milking every last dollar from Tyson: "The nonfight people were trying to help the heavyweight champion of the world save his life. The second set—the fight people, Cayton and Rooney—were trying to save a meal ticket."

The writer further portrayed Givens as the long-suffering

wife, saying she was "distraught" when she entered Mike's hospital room, while depicting Tyson as a monster. "The Tyson marriage that you see on television—the smiling pictures you see on gossip pages—is a lie. Mike Tyson, his friends and relatives say, is a wife-beater. They say he has learned to hit his wife with the bottom of his hand, boasting that this is a blow that when delivered correctly leaves no mark.

"The champion is also said to be big on choking," McAlary wrote. "He grabs Givens by the neck, friends say, and shakes her. . . . Mostly, Tyson curses his young wife. He does this in public. He also takes phone calls from girl-friends in front of his wife." McAlary then states that two months earlier Tyson and Givens had vacationed at Donald Trump's hotel on Paradise Island in the Bahamas. While there, Tyson got into a fight with both his wife and her friend, Lori McNeil, one of the premier professional women's tennis players, who was also at the hotel. "Tyson is reported to have smacked both women," said the sensational *Daily News* story. "According to friends of the couple," wrote McAlary, "Givens suffered a black eye and swollen jaw. She spent most of her vacation waiting for the bruises to clear."

Those who bought the *Daily News* that morning certainly got their money's worth. Tyson could not believe it when he saw the paper. He called Camille in Catskill and rhetorically asked her, "Who the hell said I was committing suicide?" Reaction was swift. Respected columnist and author Pete Hamill wrote: "I have only one response to this story. Bull." Pat Putnam, of *Sports Illustrated* magazine, wrote, "The story made for juicy reading, but there was a problem: It was a plant, and an artless, bubble-headed one at that." One by one, those who really knew Tyson reacted. Bobby Stewart said, "I dispensed the medication [at the Tryon school], probably most of them [the boys] were on medication at the time, something to slow them down. Mike was not on anything." Teddy Atlas said Mike was not on any medication while at Catskill, something he certainly would have known about as the fighter's trainer, friend and housemate. Kevin Rooney also confirmed this and called the story "bullshit." Bill Cayton termed the *Daily News* story "obviously a plant . . . outrageous . . . a pack of falsehoods and untruths . . . despicable lies." All those who knew Tyson treated the allegations of attempted suicide as a joke, pointing out that a person doesn't run a car thirty feet across a wet lawn into a tree if he's trying to kill himself. As for McAlary's charge that Tyson wasn't wearing his seatbelt, it wasn't necessary—the BMW, as Mike well knew, was equipped with an inflatable bag safety feature in the front seat. The collision into the tree wasn't even of sufficient force to release the air bag!

Donald Trump was unavailable for comment. Award-winning sports columnist Jerry Izenberg wrote in the New York *Post* that the McAlary piece was "a calculatedly leaked story—apparently from one of the attorneys his wife's family chose for [Tyson] and he described the entire situation as "an emotional tug of war over [Tyson] in which the participants are engaged in a deadly game of media roulette with a bullet in every chamber. . . . With no place to hide, no place to think things out and no place for Mike Tyson to catch his breath . . . unless the heavyweight champion gets the one-on-one help he so desperately needs with absolutely nobody else involved, it is a story with a frighteningly predictable ending."

Tyson's sister went to visit him at the hospital the day the story appeared. She said Mike laughed about the suicide report and told her, "I wouldn't even know how to do it." In a telephone interview with sports reporter Carl White, Tyson said the story was "ridiculous. . . . . They're trying to make a freak show out of my life, to say I would try to kill myself. Nobody has more, better reasons to live than I do. . . . No one loves living more than I do . . . . I have way too much butt to kick in the ring to try to kill myself out of the ring . . . why does my wife have to be a bad person? We're both basically good people. We're high-strung but we're basically good people." Tyson added, "I love my wife. I don't beat on my wife. I'm never going to leave my wife. My wife's never going to leave me."

Chapter 16

To Russia . . . With Love?

The unfortunate thing about public misfortunes is that
everyone regards himself as qualified to talk about them.
—E.M. Cioran

On Wednesday evening, unannounced and undetected, Tyson was released and slipped quietly out of the hospital into a waiting limousine with his wife and mother-in-law. All week it had been said he would go to Catskill to get some rest under the care of Camille Ewald, but instead Ruth and Robin took him to the New Jersey mansion. A final barrage of ultrasound tests, electrocardiograms, radioisotope scans and blood tests showed that there had been no damage done to his heart despite the bruising to his chest from the impact with the BMW's steering wheel.

Tyson's true friends believed that most of what was going on, from the "revelation" by Robin's sister that Mike beat his wife to the story of his suicide attempt, his emotional instability and, again, his violent behavior toward Robin, was nothing less than a carefully orchestrated plot to establish grounds for a divorce that would allow Givens to walk away with a big settlement of cash and property.

Lori McNeil, Robin's tennis player friend, issued a statement concerning McAlary's allegations that Tyson hit her and Robin during their vacation in the Bahamas: "The player they made reference to is not me, nor do I know who they are referring to. I have never been to Paradise Island."

But accounts of a wild scene in the Bahamas did emerge independently from hotel employees. Apparently Givens left their $2,000-a-night suite to go out for the day, and Mike heard that her old flame, Eddie Murphy, was also vacationing somewhere on the island. According to those at the hotel, he confronted her in the lobby when she returned late in the afternoon, accusing her of sneaking off to visit Murphy. Givens denied she even knew where Murphy was staying. That night, a sulking Tyson drank heavily at the hotel bar while Givens sat with him. From his early days in boxing when he wouldn't touch alcohol, Tyson had become a heavy drinker. Shortly before 11:00 P.M. hotel security said a woman staying with the Tysons reported a disturbance in their suite.

When two security guards arrived and entered, they said they saw Tyson hitting Givens, while she screamed for him to stop. Seeing the security guards, Tyson became more enraged, punching one of them and chasing them into the hallway as they begged him to cool down. They were not anxious for a confrontation with the formidable Tyson. Givens told the guards they were useless. "You think they'e going to protect you against me?" Mike asked her, and then started to strip off his shirt as if he was getting ready for more action. The guards retreated, and while Tyson's temper was momentarily defused, Givens reportedly packed a bag and left for the night. The next day, however, after Tyson calmed down, the two were back together. Tyson was billed for nearly $400 in damages, which included a door kicked off its hinges and splintered during the previous night's outburst.

It was painfully obvious there were serious problems in the Tyson-Givens marriage, a union of two people who were quite ill-suited for one another. Too many friends of both talked about constant fighting and arguing. Even before they married, there was the incident in Steve Lott's apartment, just one of many. Tyson told Colin Hart of the London *Sun* that he and Givens, then just his fiancée, fought all the time. "She knows she can't hurt me if she kicks me in the head," he said, "so she tries to kick me in the groin."

On Thursday, September 8, against his doctors orders and quite unexpectedly, Tyson showed up at Kennedy Airport with Robin. The Tysons went immediately to a VIP lounge, away from reporters, photographers and a crowd of about 200 people waiting to catch a glimpse of the couple. They were then taken through a security entrance and escorted onto the first-class section of the Scandinavian Airlines plane bound for Moscow via Copenhagen. Givens said Tyson had decided to accompany her to get away from all the commotion. She denied the suicide report was accurate, saying her husband had too much to live for—including her—to want to kill himself (although Mike McAlary had reported in his story, which was completely pro-Givens and Roper, that the young actress had been calling people from her car phone all the way to Catskill the previous Sunday, telling them "Michael just tried to kill himself").

On Friday, September 9, Tyson and Givens arrived at Sheremetyevo Airport in Moscow, still denying the suicide reports. (In New York that same Friday, sportswriters on two separate newspapers speculated that Tyson's massive muscle buildup over the previous three or four years, his mood swings from euphoria to depression, his violent temper tantrums could be attributed to steroid use, since all of these symptoms can be side effects of the muscle-building artificial hormone.)

In Moscow, Mike spent the first few days visiting Soviet amateur boxers, sightseeing at Lenin's Tomb, becoming annoyed that the Soviets knew the visiting soccer star Pele very well but had little idea who he was, greeting his mother-in-law, who joined the couple a few days after their arrival, and pining to get back to the States and back into the ring. He told reporter Barry Levine he was ready to go back to New York just three days after he got to Moscow, a trip it was believed Givens forced him to make against his doctors' orders because she didn't trust him alone while she was away for two weeks. Mike was unhappy that his mother-in-law had joined them in Moscow, unhappy with what he described as their cockroach-infested room in the famous Rossiya Hotel and unhappy with the quality of Soviet food.

On their final night in Moscow, he finally blew. He became completely irrational. He climbed out along a railing in the hotel and hung from it for ten minutes. He also terrorized Robin, Ruth and Phyllis Polaner, whom Roper had recently hired to work as an assistant to Robin and Mike. Tyson reportedly stabbed at Polaner with a fork and kicked at her. He then chased the three women, in their nightgowns, out of their suite. They ran to the lobby for safety, but Mike followed them. They tried to calm him as hotel security guards watched, but then Tyson confronted the guards, asking them what they were looking at and making threats. Roper was so concerned for their safety that she hired several former New York City detectives to provide private security at the Tyson mansion in New Jersey when they returned home. She was finally convinced that she and her daughter had to get away from Tyson before he did something drastic to them in one of his rages.

While Tyson was in the Soviet Union, the various parties concerned with his boxing future were meeting in New York, trying to resolve their differences. Tyson's continuing troubles outside the ring had cost him several major endorsements, including Pepsi-Cola, which did not renew the deal it had with Tyson for TV commercials leading up to and following the Spinks fight. Several meetings were arranged between Cayton and Howard Rubenstein (the P.R. man retained by Ruth Roper to represent Tyson) and between Cayton and the Parcher and Hayes legal team (also retained by Roper), in an effort to bury the hatchet and work in the common interest of advancing Tyson's career. Cayton said he was willing to be reconciled even with Donald Trump, who had forced him to accept a reduction in his managerial cut from 33 percent to 20 percent.

Dan Klores, the Rubenstein P.R. man who was with Tyson constantly in the hospital, privy to all the Tyson-Roper-Givens conversations and therefore a prime suspect in Cayton's eyes in the plant of the suicide story, called the manager to say he was innocent. So did attorney Parcher. Trump said he was being falsely accused of being the story's source by Cayton because "I killed [Cayton] on the contract" renegotiation. Ever the diplomat and concerned as always to act in Tyson's best interests, Cayton simply said, "We're ready to work for Mike Tyson instead of against each other."

On Tuesday night, September 20, Mike and Robin returned from Moscow. When Tyson spotted the security guards hired by Ruth at his home, he was not pleased. He told Robin to get rid of them. Then he and his friend Rory Holloway, drove off in the middle of the night shouting at the security men to "fuck off." Shortly after 3:00 A.M. he arrived at Camille Ewald's home in Catskill, but left there a little after 8:00 A.M. and drove back to his New Jersey home. He then went out for a midday jog. While running, he spotted a WNBC-TV news crew taping him on the quiet street outside his house. He responded to their presence by throwing his Walkman radio at them, then running over and grabbing the camera. The taped incident, of course, made the TV newscasts around the country, but neither Tyson nor the television station had any further comment regarding it.

The next day was an emotionally draining one for the champion. He sat down for a marathon therapy session with Dr. Henry McCurtis, the psychiatrist Roper and Givens had been encouraging him to consult. Also present were the two women. Afterward, Tyson and Givens spoke with Mark DiIonno of the New York *Post*, and Tyson said he was a manic depressive. "I was born with this disease. I can't help it. . . . this is the way I was all my life," he said. He talked of going through three- and four-day periods without sleeping, of being extremely depressed and "very, very high-strung." Givens was quick to apportion blame, saying, "He's been [like this] for many years and they've been ignoring it." Givens vowed to stand by her man, saying she and Mike were in tears during the session with Dr. McCurtis, whom two weeks earlier Tyson had ordered out of his hospital room, threatening to kill him. Now Mike said he would make the effort to work with Dr. McCurtis to understand his illness. "How can you turn your back on someone who is making a commitment to try?" asked Givens.

Dr. Gene Brody, who had been Tyson's personal physician until Givens and Roper came on the scene and who had also been Jim Jacobs's doctor, discounted the manic-depressive story. He said that most doctors could tell when a person was a manic-depressive and that Mike had seemed perfectly normal to him.

On Friday night, September 30, much of the country sat transfixed as Mike Tyson, Robin Givens and Ruth Roper allowed the ABC News program "20/20" to come into their New Jersey mansion and put the young couple's personal life under the microscope of the television camera's lens. The interviewer was Barbara Walters, who had carved out a reputation for being able to secure hard-to-get interviews and make people reveal things about themselves they would not tell other interviewers. In this instance, Walters's skills at eliciting information were hardly necessary. Givens was ready and willing to air the dirty laundry for everyone to see. Walters, good friends with Donald Trump and thus able to get access to the Tyson family, was willing to provide Givens with the forum to discuss the family's personal problems.

Speaking with Walters individually, Ruth Roper said she had become a "surrogate mother" to Mike, that she loved him like a son, that she wasn't trying to control him or his money, but that "people who earn a living through Michael" found her close relationship with him intimidating. Walters then asked, "Like Bill Cayton?" to which Roper replied, "Yeah, like Bill Cayton, to be very direct." Don King's involvement as an instigator in the whole Tyson mess was never explored by Walters. In a separate interview taped with Cayton at his office and inserted in the program, Walters asked him whether he was concerned that if Tyson had to take psychiatric medication to control his emotions he might not be able to box. "If Mike Tyson needs medication," replied the manager, "I want him to take medication. Whether he boxes or not is of no great interest to me." "You make money from him," shot back Walters. "I have money," the millionaire Cayton pointed out to her. "I don't need Mike's money."

Walters did a one-to-one interview with Tyson, during which he told her, "I'm not a psychopath or a maniac or anything. . . . I've seen some doctors and I have a very slight illness that I had all my life, just being extremely hyper. . . . I'm a moody person by nature. . . . At times I raise hell, yeah, and I like to raise hell because that's basically my nature, coming from my background." Tyson denied the reports that he hit Robin. "My wife and I have arguments," he said. "I grab my wife and hold my wife, I shake my wife up, but I never struck my wife."

The interview with Tyson, which was taped several days before broadcast, had concluded when Givens, who did not participate, approached Barbara Walters and said to her, 'You're not getting the story straight." She volunteered to tell the truth, and so the camera rolled again, and with Mike at her side, without speaking up once to contradict her, Givens said of their marriage, "It's been torture. It's been pure hell. It's been worse than anything I could possibly imagine . . . every day has been some kind of battle, some kind of fight, with managers, with members of the family. . . . The fights with [Mike] make me wonder why I'm going through the other fights, the other battles. . . . He's got a side to him that's scary. Michael is intimidating, to say the least. . . . He gets out of control, throwing, screaming, he shakes, he pushes, he swings . . . and just recently I've become afraid, very very much afraid. . . . Michael is a manic-depressive. He is. That's just a fact. . . . The type of disease Michael has . . . it's something he's had for a very long time. It went untreated, therefore it got worse." Givens insisted, though, that she loved him, that he wasn't a bad guy, he had a sense of humor, he was smart and gentle.

Walters asked Givens about the lack of a prenuptial agreement. "Why should there be?" replied the actress. "There's a certain sense of idealism that comes with being young that I wouldn't trade for anything in the world. We got married to be together forever, not to play for divorce." At this point, Mike jumped in and said, "I do have many millions. My wife would just have to ask for it and she has everything I have. If she wants it right now, she could leave right now, take everything I have. Just leave . . . she has the power to do that. She's still here, she tolerates my shit, and I love my wife." Mike said he was aware his illness had to be "taken care of," but he said he was not taking the Lithium his doctor had prescribed because "I'm handling myself very well." Givens concluded her remarks by giving credit to her always-present mother. "I don't know what Mike Tyson would be without my mother, what we would be. She's been the glue that's kept us together . . . and I do come with a package, that's how I am. My mom, my sister." Robin expressed her concern that if she and her mother left Mike he would be alone: "He would have gotten so bad that I think maybe one day he would have been more deliberate [than the car accident of two weeks earlier] and killed himself, or hurt somebody else."

Privately, Tyson had told Camille Ewald while staying in Catskill the previous weekend he was not taking the Lithium because he didn't like what the pills did to him, how they made him feel sluggish and dopey. "I like the way I am, the way I used to feel," he told her, and ignored persisting calls from his doctor reminding him to take the mind-controlling drug. Dr. Gene Brody, Mike's physician, had said repeated blood tests he'd given Mike had never revealed any "chemical imbalances" in Tyson's system.

Both Tyson's friends and impartial observers were shocked

in the wake of the televised interview. Bill Cayton said he did not believe Mike was a manic-depressive but was turned down by Ruth Roper when he asked if Mike could be seen by an independent doctor—alone. "I feel it's imperative that Mike have at least one other psychiatrist examine him," said Cayton. "What are they [Ruth and Robin] afraid of? That they'll be contradicted?" Tyson's friends said there was a concentrated effort on the part of the two women to cut Mike off from all those previously close to him. They said the women constantly changed the phone number at the house so no one could reach him. Camille Ewald said Mike was "an emotional captive" who had confided to her the previous weekend at her house that he was very unhappy with his marriage. Jose Torres said Mike was not a manic-depressive, but a confused young man who had been manipulated and brainwashed. "Ruth Roper is a dangerous woman," he said. "She has complete control over Tyson." Other friends termed the entire affair a "diabolical plot" against Mike and were shocked that he could sit quietly stroking his wife's neck while she aired all their private business, true or untrue, on national TV. They said Mike appeared to have been drugged, perhaps with a dose of Lithium, before the interview. They felt he had been humiliated by his wife and mother-in-law for their own self-serving ends.

Slowly, as the feedback filtered to him over the weekend and it dawned on him just what had taken place, Tyson grew enraged. He knew he had taken a prescribed combination of Thorazine and Lithium before Barbara Walters and her TV crew arrived at the house. On Sunday morning, Tyson's rage erupted. In an argument with Robin he picked up a sugar bowl and threw it across the room, smashing it. He then allegedly threw some chairs through the windows, while Givens ran to the phone to call Dr. McCurtis. While Mike continued his rampage, she and Ruth escaped from the house and drove to a nearby gas station, where they called their friend, Shelly Finkel, who had been at the house with Mike and the women the previous day, to celebrate Roper's birthday. They then telephoned the Bernardsville police, asking them to come to the house. When the police arrived, Givens and Roper returned. Dr. McCurtis phoned back and told the women to leave the house as soon as possible, advising them to arrange for emergency psychiatric evaluation for Mike. He also spoke to the police at the house and told them he was worried about the safety of Givens and Roper.

Tyson was calm when the police arrived, but became agitated again when Givens brought them into the house to show them the damage. He began to yell that he owned the house and everything in it, that it was none of anybody's business if he wanted to break his own things. Givens and Roper packed their bags, preparing to leave for Roper's apartment in Manhattan. When they left the house, Tyson came outside and began to confront them once again, and another shouting match developed. Tyson then turned his attention to the police, telling them in the language of the streets that he did not want them on his property. "Fuck you all," he shouted. "Fuck you cops, you scum. Get the fuck off the property, and fuck off." With that, he got into his Mercedes and drove off.

Givens did not file a formal complaint, so no arrest was made, but she did go into the Bernardsville police station and give a detailed seven-page statement about what had transpired, thus establishing an "on-the-record" account of the incident.

Meanwhile, Tyson arrived in Manhattan, trying to meet up with his fellow boxer and friend Mark Breland, who was managed by Finkel. He missed their rendezvous. Mike had telephoned his sister, Denise, and made her promise him that he would be buried next to their mother. She became concerned and called Bernardsville police, asking them to return to the house and break in if they got no answer. When they got to the house, however, Tyson's friend, Rory Holloway, answered the door and said that Mike had left. Tyson's bother, Rodney, speaking from Los Angeles, also expressed concern to Mike Katz of the *Daily News* about Mike, describing Ruth and Robin as "manipulative."

On Monday morning, Givens flew to Hollywood to resume taping her TV show. That same morning, October 3, something very unexpected happened. Mike Tyson paid a visit to his estranged manager, Bill Cayton, and his estranged friend, Steve Lott. He ran up the stairs to Cayton's private office and embraced his manager, the first thaw in their relationship since the death of Jim Jacobs nearly seven months earlier. He hugged Steve Lott as well, and they all sat down to talk. Mike was warm and outgoing. He told Cayton he was anxious to get back into the ring and fight. He didn't mention the previous day's incident at his home. Cayton said he would go ahead with plans to have Mike meet Frank Bruno in London on December 17. First, however, he wanted Mike to undergo complete neurological and psychiatric evaluations, just to be sure.

The next day Tyson was examined by Dr. Abraham Halpern, Clinical Professor of Psychiatry at New York Medical Medical College, who gave him a clean bill of mental health. "I saw Mr. Tyson and, from a clinical standpoint, he showed no signs of a major mental disorder. Certainly there's no sign of a manic-depressive condition or psychosis," Halpern said, adding that he had spoken with Dr. McCurtis and that McCurtis had said he had never diagnosed Mike as being manic-depressive. "Dr. McCurtis spoke of a mood-regulatory disturbance," reported Dr. Halpern, "and that's a far cry from a major mental illness such as manic-depression." He said Dr. McCurtis had examined Mike once, but got most of the information about his behavior from Ruth and Robin. Mike had been put on the Lithium by Dr. McCurtis on "a trial basis" to "stabilize" his moods, a treatment Dr. Halpern termed "not unreasonable," although not necessary. "He needs to be goal-oriented again," Dr. Halpern said. "He wants to box, and the training would be most therapeutic right now." He did suggest Mike should see a psychotherapist, "somebody to talk to that he trusts to relieve his pressures," and added that Mike "misses his wife terribly and he loves her." If, indeed, Dr. McCurtis had never diagnosed Mike as manic-depressive, then it was Givens and Roper who decided to use that term to describe Mike's condition. When the neurological experts confirmed Mike was showing no signs of injury from the car accident, Bill Cayton said "All systems are go" for the Bruno fight in December. Tyson flew to Detroit for the weekend to see Mark Breland fight. Then he would head for Catskill to begin training.

By now, although Mike was still obsessively attached to Robin, the people closest to him could hold their peace no longer. Jay Bright said the people "who know Michael and who genuinely care about him are disgusted by what they saw on that show. To see his wife emasculate him on national TV like that was offensive and vile." Camille Ewald said, "If that was my wife sitting next to me saying those things I would have choked her." And Ewald now had much more to say. Roper and Givens were angry with her because, like Cayton, she had wanted Mike to be examined by other doctors besides Dr. McCurtis. She now revealed that when Mike began earning large purses, Jim Jacobs had arranged for Camille to be paid house expenses by Mike, such as phone, electricity, repairs, taxes, an amount coming to thousands of dollars a year, nothing to Tyson, nor did Mike have any objections about taking care of the woman who had cared for him (and silently put up with, as he termed it, "my shit"). When Roper came on the scene, everything was paid through the company she formed, Mike Tyson Enterprises. Roper and Givens told Ewald they thought it was only fitting, since she was an old woman and Mike was paying the bills, that she should leave the house in Catskill to Mike in her will. To tighten the vise on Ewald, they stopped sending her expense checks. At one point, Kevin Rooney had to bail her out when her telephone was about to be disconnected for nonpayment by the phone company. "I don't think we should pay the bills," Roper told Ewald over the phone in September, "unless Mike will be inheriting the property." Ewald became angered with Roper when the mother-in-law asked why Mike was paying for the house upkeep and not Cus's other fighters, Jose Torres and Floyd Patterson. Eward told her it was because Torres and Patterson never lived in that house. When he learned what was happening, Bill Cayton took over payment of the house bills.

Ewald also said Roper had refused to pay thousands of dollars in outstanding bills to the private limousine company that chauffeured Tyson, because the company refused to report back to her every place they drove Mike, every stop he made, who he went to see.

With Tyson willing and anxious to fight, Bill Cayton outlined a plan for him that in the space of twelve months would earn him $50 million gross. It would start in December with the scaled-down (due to the move indoors) purse of $6 million against Bruno in London; then in Rio, during Carnival in February, $9 million for an easy defense against Brazil's Adilson Rodriguez; in April, $5 or $6 million for a mandatory defense in the United States against number one IBF challenger Carl Williams; followed by a bout for perhaps $10 million in Milan's soccer stadium against Italian challenger Francesco Damiani in June; then would come The Big One, the next "super fight," late in the year, a closed-circuit and pay-per-view $20 million payday for Tyson against undefeated world cruiserweight champion Evander Holyfield. Tyson would finish the year in Japan, which desperately wanted him for another performance, against forty-one-year-old former heavyweight champion George Foreman. The only thing Bill Cayton had not taken into consideration, the one thing that would rend all these plans asunder, was the sudden reentry into Mike Tyson's life of Don King.

Chapter 17

Divorce . . . and Don King

The devil can cite Scripture for his purpose.

—Shakespeare

Don King had been waiting patiently, quietly, biding his time. Better than anyone, he knew how to exploit a weakness, and when he saw the opening left by the rift between Mike and the Roper-Givens team, it was the opportunity he had been waiting for. He moved quickly to fill the void and renew his relationship with Tyson. With Ruth and Robin in Hollywood, King quickly reestablished contact with Tyson, offering to help him protect his assets, most of which had been transferred into Mike Tyson Enterprises, which was Tyson's company, and of which he was president, but which Ruth Roper actually controlled. King and Tyson went to the offices of Tyson Enterprises to check on Mike's financial records, but found the office locked. The key was with Ruth Roper—in California.

King proceeded to take Tyson from financial institution to financial institution, changing his accounts. Since his marriage and the formation of Tyson Enterprises, all Tyson's accounts had become joint, meaning Robin had complete access to them as well as Mike. King quickly saw to it that this was changed. Mike transferred all his assets into new accounts with only his name on them, making it impossible for Robin to use any of his funds. Only Tyson now had the authority to write checks, and, with King's help, he canceled all his joint credit cards.

In Los Angeles, meanwhile, Robin Givens retained the noted celebrity divorce lawyer, Marvin Mitchelson, almost as soon as her plane touched down. And on Friday, October 7, 1988, in Los Angeles County Superior Court, she filed divorce papers against Mike. The grounds were cited as "irreconcilable differences." In part, her divorce papers read, "My husband has been violent and physically abusive and prone to unprovoked rages of violence and destruction."

She specifically mentioned the hotel incident in Moscow, saying Mike began to "lose control over his emotions . . . [and] started throwing champagne bottles around our room. At the peak of his manic state, Michael went down to the bar and started drinking vodka, glass after glass, like it was water. He then returned to our room, grabbed a handful of Lithium and locked himself in the bathroom, saying he was going to kill himself." After recounting his alleged chasing her, her mother and their assistant to the lobby, his threats to a Soviet security man, and his hanging from a balcony for ten minutes, threatening to kill himself, she went on to claim, "On the plane [returning from Moscow] Michael swore at me, called me a 'whore' and a 'slut,' and said he was going to kill me, that he had guns at home. He told me, 'The world will forgive me because I have succeeded in making everyone think you are the bad one.' " She also recounted the previous weekend's outburst in New Jersey, saying Mike had awakened her when he was drunk by jumping on her bed and punching her in the body and head. "He started throwing dishes and liquor bottles at me and hit me with one dish that shattered all over me."

In New York, Raoul Felder, one of the most successful and high-powered divorce attorneys in the United States, was sought out by the press for his opinion on what promised to be the most publicized divorce in recent years. Felder came down firmly on Mike Tyson's side. "The woman's married eight months," he said, "and this poor guy got his money by getting beaten up and she's going to seek half of it, and she expresses her love rather peculiarly by suing him for divorce," Felder termed Givens's action "a very obvious and, I must say, a rather shabby ploy." Knowing that Mitchelson had filed the divorce action in Los Angeles because California had a 50-50 community property divorce law, where Givens stood to collect half of Tyson's estimated $40 million in assets, Felder suggested that Tyson seek to have the divorce action moved to New Jersey or New York, where his assets would not be in nearly as much jeopardy.

After covering his assets in New York, Tyson had flown off with Don King to isolate himself at the promoter's home outside Cleveland. Before departing, he, King, Bill Cayton and other Tyson advisers, met at HBO's offices. King and Cayton made peace, uniting to protect Mike and work in the common interest against Roper and Givens. They considered a counterattack: filing to have the marriage annuled on the grounds that Givens had tricked Tyson into marrying her. According to Cayton and others, on January 15, 1988, about three weeks before the marriage, Ruth Roper had called Jim Jacobs and told him Robin was three and a half months pregnant. Jacobs felt Tyson should marry Robin—for a very practical reason: Tyson's endorsement contracts contained moral clauses, and he and Cayton felt Mike's lucrative outside-the-ring income might be jeopardized by an out-of-wedlock pregnancy, especially if things got nasty. Still, the elopement on February 7, sans prenuptial agreement, had taken the managers by surprise. Events that followed Roper's phone call to Jacobs led those around Tyson to believe the fighter had been deceived. Givens never appeared to be pregnant, and she herself gave conflicting stories, although she certainly led Mike to believe she was. Mike had even mentioned that Robin was pregnant while they were in Japan in March. Further information surfaced when Givens's gynecologist, Dr. Sheldon Cherry, confirmed that she did indeed have a "spontaneous miscarriage" on June 3, three weeks before the Spinks fight. However, Dr. Cherry said the actress was about six or seven weeks pregnant at the time, which meant she had conceived well into April. So, barring an earlier pregnancy, which she never claimed, Robin could not have been three and a half months pregnant in January.

Don King had retained Howard Weitzman to handle Tyson's divorce litigation. Before leaving New York for Los Angeles on Monday, October 3, following the rampage at their New Jersey home, Givens had written a check against an account of Mike Tyson Enterprises, Inc. By the time the check reached the Chase Manhattan Bank for collection later in the week, Tyson's accounts had been transferred and it bounced. Givens was furious privately, but denied writing the check. Unfortunately for her, it turned up in the hands of Tyson's attorney. It was written for $581,812, payable to Robin Givens Productions, and noted in her handwriting "Reimbursement on expenses."

On Sunday, October 9, while Don King took Tyson to services at Cleveland's Holy Trinity Baptist Church—certainly a new environment for the champion, who was presented with a Bible and told by Pastor Henry Payden, "Mike, you have a way of knocking men down, but Jesus has a way of picking people up"—Ruth Roper and Robin Givens were busy in Los Angeles. Four days after retaining him, the women dropped Marvin Mitchelson as Robin's lawyer. Over the years, Mitchelson had become one of the highest of high-profile divorce attorneys, representing Joan Collins, Bianca Jagger and Soraya Kashoggi. He had fallen on hard times in recent years, beset by numerous legal problems himself involving a variety of serious charges. Roper and Givens had second thoughts about having retained Mitchelson. They hired none other than Raoul Felder to represent Robin, the same Raoul Felder who just days earlier had publicly sided with Tyson and called Givens's divorce action a "shabby ploy." Now that he had reviewed the case more thoroughly, Felder told the press that Robin "was beaten, abused and so forth, and apparently it's undenied [by Tyson]." There was no doubt that Felder knew his business, however. *Forbes* magazine said of him: "Raoul Felder is the divorce lawyer of choice for many of the power set. He's represented dozens of the rich and famous during the thirty years he's been practicing. Felder's divorce practice is now the nation's largest, grossing him some $15 million per annum."

Felder announced that Robin loved Mike, that he hoped to negotiate a settlement to avoid a dirty public trial, that he would meet with Howard Weitzman, Tyson's lawyer, "to try to resolve this quickly, equitably and civilly," that Robin said she would settle it quickly "if Michael apologizes to me," and Felder maintained that Robin had never said she was pregnant prior to the couple's marriage. "The pregnancy came after the marriage," he said. Neal Hirsch, a West Coast associate of Felder's, would have direct responsibility for handling the case for Givens.

Tennis star Lori McNeil then resurfaced to lend documentary support to her friend Robin. Having denied Mike McAlary's story in the New York *Daily News* about Tyson's rampage in the Bahamas in July 1988, she now told McAlary she had lied in doing so because she was "very afraid of the whole situation." Now, she said, she was really telling the truth: "I'm still afraid, but I think that it's something that should be told. It's something I've seen and it's the truth. People don't really know the other side of Mike Tyson."

McNeil now described the "real" version of what had happened that night in the Bahamas. The threesome had had dinner, she said, and they were all drinking, especially Tyson. "He drinks a lot anyway," she said. Back in their suite, Robin complained Mike had been flirting with another woman at the bar. A few minutes later, with Givens and McNeil apparently in a room separate from Mike, "He kicked in the door, and then he came into my room after Robin. He dragged her back to his room," said McNeil. "I went in there and he was hitting Robin and dragging her and saying he was going to kill her. He was choking her . . . She was screaming. So I called security. . . . Security came in and he was hitting Robin and choking her. And they chased him out into the hall. He made a big scene in the hall with security. He was totally out of control. . . . He hit me in the mouth . . . and busted my lip. I was trying to stop him from hitting Robin. . . . He was swinging with his fist. I saw him kick her." McAlary also reported Givens as saying, "The time in the Bahamas was the first time Michael ever hit me in the face. . . . He was choking me and I went into the bathroom to vomit. I was leaning over the toilet, and Michael kicked me in my rear end."

One week after Givens had filed for divorce in Los Angeles, Mike Tyson came back punching with a countersuit. In a ten-page document filed in New Jersey State Superior Court on October 14, 1988, the world heavyweight champion charged in his own divorce petition extreme cruelty on the part of Robin Givens, alleging his wife of eight months had "tricked" him into marriage with a false claim of pregnancy and that he was "the hapless victim of intentional fraud." His papers further charged that when she married him, Givens was "motivated solely by personal aggrandizement and a need to enhance her level of public recognition and personal wealth. . . . Having been tricked into marriage by the defendant, the plaintiff found himself constantly manipulated by her and her family to the point of personal distraction regarding his own welfare and career. . . . [She then began] a campaign to publicly humiliate him, strip him of his manhood and his dignity and to destroy his credibility as a public figure," after which she left him "with as much notoriety as possible and [sought] whatever personal gain might be available to her both in terms of media notoriety and asset acquisition."

On the night that Tyson filed his countersuit, Givens had a second appearance on "20/20" with Barbara Walters. A tear trickled down her cheek as she maintained, "Nobody can love Michael more than I love Michael. . . . I didn't get married to get divorced. I'm twenty-three. I'm idealistic." She said she had filed for divorce in California simply because that was where she lived, not because she stood to get half of Tyson's fortune under California's divorce laws. "If I offended his fans, I apologize. If I offended him, I apologize."

Tyson, needless to say, would have no part of a second appearance on the program. Instead, at the home of Don King, he gave an interview to the Chicago *Sun-Times* charging that Roper and Givens "don't like black people. . . . They use them, but they don't like or respect black people. They want to be white so bad. The way they talk about black people, you'd think you were living with the Ku Klux Klan. . . . They thought they were royalty. She and her mother want so much to be white, it's a shame. And they were trying to take me away from the people I grew up with and throw me into their kind of high-class world. . . . The issue really is not money. I don't blame anybody for trying to get money. It's just the idea that they played the scheme on me. It was like a sting game. They drew me in. They worked on my emotions because I was in love. . . . She just tried to ruin me and destroy me. Not only did she want to take my money, but she wanted to ruin me, embarrass me, take away my manhood and humiliate me on television so that no woman would ever want me again. And that was evil." Tyson concluded by saying, "She had her chance and she blew it. She blew the opportunity of a lifetime. Nobody is going to ever want her. She just missed out on the train."

Things took yet another unexpected turn a few days later when Raoul Felder read a statement to the press from Robin saying she would grant Tyson a divorce and that "I will not seek or accept any money for myself. . . . I never wanted anything but what was best for Michael. I never wanted anything for myself and I never sought anything for myself." The statement went on to say, "I never married Michael for his money. . . . I represented a threat to many other people and that threat was engendered by my love for

Michael. I have never said one bad word about Michael or done anything to hurt him personally." The woman who had chosen to go on national television and talk about her marriage now said, "We were not permitted the dignity of dealing with our private problems," and concluded "I wish him well."

"I interpret this to mean they give up all claim to money and property that belongs to Mike and we have achieved a knockout here," said Tyson's attorney, Howard Weitzman, who speculated that Givens may have been concerned about her deteriorating public image and her fear over what might have been divulged had the divorce case gone to trial. He said that the day before Robin issued her public statement that she did not want any money from Mike, Raoul Felder had called him and asked for an $8 million settlement. After consulting with Robin, he had then lowered the demand to $2 million, the money Robin said she had in her possession, but she had refused Weitzman's demand that her accounts be subject to an audit.

On November 7, Tyson said in the New York *Post* that Givens was trying to "steal" his money: "It turns out she was lying when she said she didn't want anything from me." He said she wanted to keep the New Jersey mansion, now worth about $8 million with its furnishings and improvements, plus more than $1 million in jewelry. She also wanted him to forget about having his lawyers check into the disappearance of $5 million which occurred, according to Tyson, during her shifting from one bank account to another. "The nature of those two women," Tyson told the *Post*, "is to be mean and vindictive. She [Robin] said she wants nothing but she refused to sign a release. . . . Those two are the slime of the slime. And anyone associated with them is slime. . . . She stole from me, and she said I beat her up. If it was such a living hell, how come she wants to get back together?" He said Givens had been sending signals she was interested in a reconciliation. "They tried to turn me into an imbecile. They got enough already from me. Everybody could see it, everybody but Mike."

On Saturday, November 5, Mike Tyson was in Las Vegas to attend the Sugar Ray Leonard–Donny Lalonde fight. Also in Las Vegas was Robin Givens. At a meeting that day in the Alexis Park Hotel, the battling couple sat down face to face for the first time since Givens and Roper had bolted from the New Jersey mansion six weeks earlier. Tyson and his attorney, Howard Weitzman, were in the room, along with Don King, when Givens arrived with her attorney, Neal Hirsch. She walked straight to Mike, embraced him, and tilted her face up to kiss him, but he pulled away and only let her kiss him on the cheek. She sat next to Mike and kept easing her chair closer and closer to his. She even tried to stroke his leg, which he wouldn't let her do. Then, taking his chin in her hand, she turned his face toward hers and said, "Mike, isn't it true you still love me? Isn't that why you call me all the time? Let's go into another room alone and talk. I need to talk with you alone." Tyson refused to take the bait. "You're a conniving bitch. I don't trust you," he told her. "It's over between us. I want you out of my life. You were my dream once, now you're my nightmare." The meeting ended at that point, as Givens stormed out, saying, "You haven't heard the last of Robin Givens."

Eleven days later she struck back with a vengeance when her attorney, Raoul Felder, filed a libel suit against Tyson in Manhattan Federal Court for $125 million. The suit asked for $25 million for damages and injury to Robin's "good name, professional reputation and social standing," plus $100 million in punitive and compensatory damages. It accused her estranged husband of holding her up to "public contempt, ridicule, embarrassment, disgrace and prejudice" by libeling her with his statements in the November 7 New York *Post* article, and described the allegations that she was trying to steal his money as "false, defamatory, malicious and libelous."

Howard Weitzman called the lawsuit "outrageous and ludicrous," saying, "This young lady once again is attempting to shift blame for her conduct to someone else and blame them for any problems she perceives she's having. . . . What you have once again is Robin Givens bickering in public with her estranged husband and attempting to generate publicity for herself." Besides, added Weitzman, "Truth is the best defense against libel."

At least Robin and Mike were reunited in one sense. They were named as co-defendants in a lawsuit filed by Jack/Paul Waltzer, Inc., a Manhattan furrier, for nonpayment of a $91,000 bill. It seems that the furrier had sold

Mike and Robin a Russian golden sable coat that was to be a birthday present for Ruth Roper on October 1. The couple gave it to Ruth on her birthday, but unfortunately the next morning came the big blow-up, followed by the women's departure for Los Angeles and the filing of divorce papers. When the bill subsequently arrived, Mike understandably refused to pay it and said he wanted his mother-in-law to return the coat, which she refused to do.

Robin and Mike kept talking to the press. In a *People* magazine story, Robin said, "If I had to do it all over again, I'd let him do whatever he wanted to do. . . . I would not say a word if Michael stayed out for three or four nights, which is what he did." She also said about herself, "I'm one of the nicest, most fair people I know. . . . I think [Mike] is probably going to turn out to be the all-American tragedy," she predicted. At a Chicago news conference on December 13 (where he was dressed in a full-length white mink coat, with jeweled gold bracelets on both wrists), Mike fired back: "In Hollywood you make money by being either the best person or the worst person. She's making the most money on being the bitch of Hollywood." He denied her allegation in *People* magazine that he had admitted his weight was up to 255 pounds. He said he weighed 240 and would be back in training in a few days for his fight with Frank Bruno. He again claimed Robin had stolen "millions of dollars" from him.

Yet, incredibly, Tyson was still irresistibly drawn to Robin. On Sunday, December 4, Robin was in New York City, staying at her mother's apartment. She phoned Mike, who had apparently been phoning her constantly since their breakup, and told him, sobbing, that everyone hated her and she was going to lose her role on her TV sitcom. Mike took the bait and came running. He picked her up in front of her mother's building, and the two went for a drive. She tried to get him to abandon his personal and business relationship with Don King. A bit of sexual teasing went on in Tyson's Rolls-Royce as well; then she told Mike she had to go to the airport to catch a flight back to Los Angeles, jumped in a cab, and was gone. Tyson later said he was a "sucker" for meeting her and thinking they could get back together, but three weeks later he was in California and the estranged couple were together again, on a movie date. Don

King, at home with his family for the Christmas holiday, was not pleased when he learned of the Tyson-Givens rendezvous. In the meantime, attorney Weitzman discovered another check—this one for $2 million—signed by Robin Givens four months earlier and transferred into the account of Robin Givens Productions. The word "gift" was written on the check.

During all of this marital intrigue and turmoil, Mike Tyson and Don King were inseparable. Tyson spent a great deal of time sequestered at King's home outside Cleveland, where virtually no one, including Bill Cayton, could reach him. Cayton adopted a conciliatory attitude toward King, saying publicly that the promoter had worked in Mike's best interests by helping him transfer his assets into accounts safe from Robin Givens and Ruth Roper. But ominous rumors began to filter from Ohio to New York in October: King was trying to subvert the December 17 date for Tyson to meet Bruno in London by working to move the fight to Las Vegas; King was trying to influence Tyson to fire his trainer, Kevin Rooney; Tyson was seriously considering buying a home in Cleveland to be close to King.

Many people were at a loss to explain Tyson's attraction to King, which they likened to that of a moth to a flame, but Kevin Rooney told columnist Denis Hamill in *Newsday*, "It's because of [King's] black ghetto, jive jailhouse background. It's the black thing. King is literally putting the con on him with his flash and black talk. See, Mike was in reform schools but King went to the big house for murder. And the only reason Mike never went to the big house is because of Cus D'Amato. But growing up, Mike looked up to hoods. Now he's looking up to an ex-hood with a legal license. If he falls into that trap it will be sad. See, King is trying to make him cut all his ties to Cus the same way Ruth and Robin did. . . . I work in a jail [coaching boxing] so I know what's going through Mike's head right now. He wants to be with one of his own, a ghetto ex-con."

Meanwhile, word reached Cayton that Tyson had reinjured his broken hand. The original break was not a serious one, but Tyson, ignoring doctor's orders, did not allow it to heal properly. He failed to wear his removable brace regularly after the cast was removed late in August, which kept the injury aggravated, and he was not wearing it the morning of his car accident. A cast was put back on the hand while Mike was confined in hospital, and when he departed for Moscow with Robin, the cast was in place. But photos taken of him in Red Square just a couple of days later showed no cast on his hand. Mike apparently had removed it himself. Now, a month later, amid reports he might have been fooling around in King's gym, possibly punching a heavy bag, the hand had swelled again and there were fears it might have been refractured. However, Dr. Richard Rhodes, who examined the fighter in Cleveland, said it was not a break; the hand had become swollen because it had never properly healed.

Tyson, no doubt encouraged by Don King, was now insisting that the Bruno fight be moved to the United States, just as he had originally told Cayton in the summer, even as public talk of the fight being held in Wembley continued. The December 17 date was also looking unlikely, since the Vegas casinos considered the week before Christmas "dead" time, when their business dropped off too much to warrant the expense of investing millions of dollars to bring the fight to Las Vegas. In mid-October Jarvis Astaire, Mickey Duff, Bill Cayton and HBO executives huddled in New York for two days to try to work things out, while Tyson remained in Cleveland. Frank Bruno said he wanted the fight in Britain, where Tyson had agreed to fight him. It wasn't a question of money, said the challenger. "I want to win the title in front of my own fans." King had no involvement in the London fight, which is why many suspected he was working hard behind-the-scenes, with Tyson's cooperation, to shoot it down. In Las Vegas, his power base, he might somehow worm his way into the promotion. But King continued to maintain he was working to put Team Tyson back on track, including Bill Cayton-manager, Kevin Rooney-trainer, and, of course, Don King-promoter.

Tyson now insisted he could not travel to England to fight because his divorce litigation and negotiations made it necessary for him to remain close to home. Astaire and Duff had Bruno fly to New York to argue his case in public. At a news conference, Bruno said he'd had just about enough with the constant delays and uncertainty. "The promoters don't know what's going on, Tyson's manager doesn't know what's going on, I'm the number one contender and I don't know what's going on," he complained. "The only one who knows what's going on is Tyson, and he's nowhere to be found. First it was his legal fight with his manager, then he broke his hand, then he smashed up the car, now he's getting divorced. Every day you pick up the paper, there's something new. Frankly, I'm getting ticked off about it. His problems are not my problems, but I'm being affected by them. I would like to win the title in front of my countrymen. I owe my countrymen a lot."

However, after continued meetings with Cayton, convinced it was Tyson's intention to bypass a trip to London, contract or no contract, Astaire and Duff relented and agreed to move the fight to the United States. As a result of the concession, Tyson would take a reduced purse, and Bruno and company would have theirs doubled, from $1.8 million to some $3.6 million. Meanwhile, Tyson, who had said he couldn't leave the United States because of his pending divorce, turned up with Don King in Venezuela, where they attended the annual convention of the WBA.

Tyson's father, Jimmy Kirkpatrick, who had abandoned his family twenty years earlier and who hadn't seen Mike since the funeral of the champion's mother six years earlier, now turned up again. The sixty-four-year-old disabled veteran was living on a small government pension in a public housing project in Brooklyn. In a television interview he said he was now a born-again Christian, a very changed man from the one who had abandoned his family, and he would like the opportunity to sit down with Mike and talk to his famous son. Even though he had no contact with Mike, he said it made him very proud when he walked down the street in his poor neighborhood and heard people say, "That's Mike Tyson's father." Tyson learned of these public overtures, but he was not yet ready for a reconciliation. Perhaps he did not yet have it in his heart to forgive him, or perhaps he was suspicious of his father's motives. Back in the Catskill days, Bobby Stewart had once asked him, "If you ever make any money, which you probably won't, what if your dad surfaced and you had something?" Tyson had replied, "I'd have nothing to do with the scumbag." Stewart said, "Your mother died probably in part as the result of him leaving her, so just remember that." And maybe Mike did.

*   *   *

Any delusion on Bill Cayton's part that he could somehow work cooperatively with Don King ended on October 21, when, without consulting anyone, Tyson signed a four-year contract granting King sole and exclusive rights to promote his fights. The nine-page document makes for fascinating reading, because the contract, signed willingly and voluntarily by the heavyweight champion, is almost totally in Don King's favor. Legal experts termed it "a promoter's contract, not a fighter's contract." It was almost as if Tyson signed it to spite Bill Cayton. The day before it was actually signed, King telephoned Cayton and told him he had a four-year exclusive promotional deal with Tyson. "Mike has given me power of attorney," said King, "and I'm taking over everything." The call was made from the Chicago offices of King's attorney, Charles Lomax, and Tyson was also on the line. Cayton told them he found it all totally unacceptable, but Tyson jumped in and said, "Yes, I've given him power of attorney," with Lomax clarifying for Cayton that it was a limited power of attorney. Jacobs and Cayton had never had that power; Mike signed exclusively in matters concerning his own money. Tyson then got back on the line and and began cursing Cayton in vulgar gutter language, at which point Cayton told him, "I will not accept that language from you." Tyson replied, "You're threatening me." Several days earlier, at the WBA convention in Venezuela, Tyson had used similar abusive language about Cayton, referring to him as "that white motherfucker who stole my money."

The day after the phone conversation, Tyson signed the agreement. It said, "Whereas, Tyson wishes to grant to DKP [Don King Productions] the sole and exclusive right to secure, arrange and promote all professional boxing bouts requiring Tyson's services. . . . for a term of four years commencing on the date hereof [October 21, 1988] . . . DKP shall promote not less than three bouts requiring Tyson's services during each year of the term hereof. Such bouts shall be on dates and at sites to be designated by DKP and shall be against opponents to be designated by DKP with Tyson's consent, such consent not to be unreasonably withheld."

The financial arrangements were thus: King would pay

Tyson $1 million for each fight, plus $200,000 for training expenses. In addition, Tyson would get two-thirds of the net receipts, 80 percent in the case of closed-circuit and pay-per-view bouts. King defined net receipts as total gross receipts from all sources "less DKP's out-of-pocket expenses, including without limitation all applicable taxes and the amount paid to Tyson" (i.e., the $1,200,000 guarantee per fight).

The contract further provided that if "any court in any jurisdiction" declares the exclusivity of the contract to be illegal, King would still have the right to promote three Tyson fights a year on a nonexclusive basis. It stated that "Tyson represents and warrants to DKP that he is free to enter into this Agreement . . . and agrees to indemnify and hold DKP harmless against any and all liability, cost or expense, including reasonable attorneys' fees, that DKP may incur as a result of any breach or inaccuracy of any of the foregoing representations and warranties." It also gave King the right to have Tyson examined by a doctor of the promoter's choosing in case the fighter claimed he could not perform due to injury, and that if Tyson retired during the term of the agreement, it would be suspended and then would remain in effect if Tyson came out of retirement at any point in the future to fight again.

Promoter and attorney Dan Duva said it was ludicrous that Tyson should sign a contract like that, especially since he and King had no legal right to enter into a contract with each other without Bill Cayton's consent, according to the contract between Cayton and Tyson. Duva termed it a "blatant breach of contract by Mike Tyson and a blatant interference with a contract by Don King." Duva further said it was foolhardy of Tyson, the most valuable athlete in the world, to sign an exclusive contract with anyone. He could make the most money by putting his services up for bidding on the free market among promoters on a fight-by-fight basis. If Cayton and Tyson were interested in an exclusive contract, however, with King or any other promoter, Duva estimated it would be worth a $5 million up-front signing bonus to Tyson, plus a guaranteed $100 million over the four-year term! King paid Tyson no bonus, guaranteed him a mere $12 million for the four years, an amount Tyson could earn in one fight, and King, doubtless realizing that

PROMOTION AGREEMENT between MICHAEL TYSON
("Tyson"), 110 Ravine Lake Road, Bernardsville, New Jersey
09724, and DON KING PRODUCTIONS, INC. ("DKP"), a New York
corporation with offices at 32 East 69th Street, New York,
New York 10021.

WHEREAS, Tyson wishes to grant to DKP the sole and
exclusive right to secure, arrange and promote all professional boxing bouts ("Bouts") requiring Tyson's services as a
professional boxer and DKP wishes to secure, arrange and
promote such Bouts.

1.   Tyson hereby grants to DKP the sole and exclusive right to secure, arrange and promote all Bouts requiring
Tyson's services as a professional boxer during the term
hereof, and DKP undertakes to secure, arrange and promote
such Bouts, all upon and subject to the terms and conditions
hereinafter set forth.

2.   This Agreement shall be for a term of four (4)
years commencing on the date hereof.

Dated: Chicago, Illinois
          October 21, 1988

MICHAEL TYSON

By: _____
     Michael Tyson

By: _____
     William D. Cayton, Manager

DON KING PRODUCTIONS, INC.

By: _____
     Don King, President

A portion of the four-year exclusive promotional agreement signed between Don King and Mike Tyson. Cayton had refused to sign, causing Tyson to file suit to break his contract with the manager. Cayton, in turn, has instituted a lawsuit against King for interfering with his contract with Tyson.

the contract would be answered by a lawsuit from Cayton, put in a provision for his own protection making Tyson liable for all legal fees arising from any litigation!

Lee Pollock, a noted attorney from White Plains, New York, who was familiar with contracts, agreed with Duva. What bothered him most was the failure of the contract to make any provisions for an independent accounting of expenses. He said, a "very troublesome aspect of the agreement is its failure to define the term net receipts, from which Mike's 66 2/3 percent would be derived. To prevent Mike's share of the receipts from being siphoned off, it is essential to specify the out-of-pocket expenses which may be deducted from the gross receipts before application of Mike's 66 2/3 percent. . . . Since information concerning the expenses is in Don King Production's control, I would urge that there be a specifically imposed obligation to account for all expenses prior to DKP's receiving its share, and that there be an obligation to place all receipts in a trust or escrow arrangement until there has been a satisfactory accounting." None of those protective clauses appeared in the agreement Tyson signed.

The contract, on its final page, did recognize that Tyson had a manager's contract with William Cayton "whereby Cayton's approval of any bout is required." The contract was forwarded to Cayton for his signature. Naturally, he refused to sign it, and without his signature it was not valid. Instead, Cayton and his long-time attorney, Irving Gruber, went straight to the New York State Athletic Commission and sat down with the new chairman Randy Gordon (who had replaced Jose Torres) to discuss the situation. Cayton made it clear he was optimistic he could have a settlement without litigation and work out a deal with King in the best interests of Tyson. "But obviously," said Cayton, "an exclusive four-year promotional contract is not in the best interests of Mike Tyson." He felt he held a trump card, in that his boxer-manager contract with Tyson contained a provision for "specific performance," which Cayton said left the decision on who Mike fights, where he fights, when he fights and for how much money in the manager's hands, although Tyson did retain the power of veto. The bottom line was, however, that if Cayton did not approve a fight, contractually Tyson could not fight. And Cayton made it clear that unless King and Tyson reached some agreement with him, he would file a complaint with the Athletic Commission that could lead to King's losing his promoter's license. What Cayton did was exactly the right thing, according to attorney Lee Pollock. "Bill Cayton's refusal to sign the agreement," he said, "is not only justified, but necessary for Cayton to fulfill his obligations [to work in his fighter's best interests] as Mike's manager."

Tyson and King were angry that Cayton would not concede defeat and sign. Tyson termed it a "low blow" and said Cayton was "against us." King said he and Tyson were inseparable and nothing or no one was going to break them up. Late in October of 1988, King and Tyson headed for Las Vegas, where King was promoting the lightweight title fight between Julio Caesar Chavez and Jose Luis Ramirez, which HBO was televising. Two days before the fight, it was announced that Tyson would become a promotional partner of King's, and his first venture as a co-promoter was the Chavez-Ramirez fight. "Me and Don King have made a deal," said the naive Tyson. "He'll be working as my associate and partner," said King. "We love each other, so we're partners. He's working with me in every fight."

On the day of the fight, Bill Cayton and Lorraine Jacobs met King and Tyson to try to reach a compromise. The parties were actually close to reaching an agreement for King to promote Tyson on a fight-by-fight basis, when Tyson reversed himself and insisted King be given the four-year exclusive. The meeting broke up, and everyone proceeded to the arena at the Las Vegas Hilton to watch Chavez defeat Ramirez. Kevin Rooney was at ringside, acting as a commentator for HBO. When he spotted "promoter" Tyson in the ring before the main event began, he shouted up to him, "You look fat. When are you getting back in the gym?" Tyson looked down at his trainer from the ring and said, "Fuck you." And so, the impasse remained. Cayton had a valid contract, but an unwilling fighter whom he couldn't force to fight against his will. King had an invalid contract, but, as he was boasting, "I can deliver the fighter. Cayton can't." Tyson, who had claimed that one-third was too much to pay Cayton and had renegotiated his manager's share down to 20 percent the previous summer, now found one-third an acceptable amount to pay Don King, according to the contract he had just signed with the promoter. King further protected himself in the limited power-of-attorney agreement he had with Tyson, which said King was liable only for "willful default, and not errors of judgment." That meant if King made a mistake of some sort while acting on Tyson's behalf, Tyson would have to prove that King had done it intentionally and fraudulently in order to recoup damages in court.

Bill Cayton received an unexpected phone call that week. It was from Robin Givens. She called to apologize to the manager, saying how sorry she was for all the things she had said about him which she now knew were untrue and which she said had been fed to her by Don King. "I think she was sorry," Cayton said, "because she knows that I was always on her side, because I was in favor of the marriage."

Another voice now surfaced: that of Donald Trump, Tyson's erstwhile adviser. Trump wanted to collect an overdue bill. It seems that when he stepped in to "advise" Tyson in his dispute with Bill Cayton before and after the Spinks fight, he had what he termed "a verbal agreement made in front of witnesses" with Tyson to receive a fee for his services. The fee was $2 million for helping Mike renegotiate his contract with Cayton. "When Cayton saw me come down the pike with my killer lawyers, he did a total el foldo," boasted Trump. "I proceeded to beat the hell out of his manager to get the ridiculous fees reduced. Now that it's all settled, it's time for Mike to pay. Mike would still be in that contract mess if it wasn't for me." Now, he wrote to Mike: "As per our conversation, I know that you now feel it is time to live up to your promise of making a $2 million contribution to various charities as selected by me. . . . Over the course of your career, I have probably saved you substantially in excess of $50 million, and therefore the $2 million contribution, all of which will go to worthy charities, is very reasonable. . . . It is great getting your phone calls and I am always here to give you advice."

At the end of October, King and Tyson jetted off once again, this time to Mexico City to attend the WBC's annual convention, where Tyson was presented with a solid gold and jeweled championship belt by Jose Sulaiman and where he joined arm-in-arm with King and Sulaiman after Sulaiman was reelected WBC president.

As mid-November came, the impasse remained between Cayton and King. Tyson said he didn't want to fight Bruno on January 14, the new date which had been set, because he wanted to take it easy and not train during the holiday season. Cayton continued to threaten lawsuit if things could not be resolved out-of-court with King and Tyson. He was determined to stand his ground, although he hoped for some agreement that would allow the Bruno fight to be staged, even while the larger issues remained unresolved, so that Tyson, who was getting fat and out of shape from inactivity, could get back into training. He said he would not sign the exclusive promotional contract despite an offer from Howard Weitzman that Cayton's attorney should draft a letter, which Tyson would sign, absolving the manager from any responsibility should Tyson come to the realization that the promotional contract was indeed a bad deal for him.

King, attached to Tyson like a Siamese twin, continued to keep Mike on the move. They distributed Thanksgiving turkeys to poor families in Tyson's old neighborhood and in Harlem. Then it was on to Chicago, where they gave out more turkeys, visited the Reverend Jesse Jackson at his Operation Push headquarters, attended a memorial service for the late Mayor Harold Washington, went to a fund-raiser for a black priest who was a friend of theirs (he had actually performed the Tyson-Givens nuptials) and whose church had burned down. Then they went to Hyannis, Massachusetts, where they taped a segment for a Special Olympics TV show with the Kennedy family at their compound on Cape Cod. Tyson's attorney told Jarvis Astaire that Tyson would be reporting to Catskill by the end of November to begin training with Kevin Rooney, and it looked for a while as though the January 14 date would be met. But no breakthrough came in the contract dispute, and on November 22, the date was canceled, as Cayton held firm. "I wouldn't let a stranger sign that contract," he said. "If Don King gets control of Mike Tyson, he controls boxing. I'm not going to let that happen." Howard Weitzman blamed Cayton for the latest postponement, writing to Jarvis Astaire that Cayton "is determined to prevent Mike from fighting except upon the unreasonable terms which he has attempted to dictate to Mike." Responded Cayton, "Don King hates me because I'm the one guy keeping him from taking over Mike Tyson and boxing. Tyson hates me because I wouldn't let him commit economic suicide."

The next day, November 23, 1988, Tyson filed a lawsuit in Manhattan federal court, seeking once again to break his contract with Cayton. Weitzman maintained this action was strictly Mike's doing, that King and his attorney, Charles Lomax, wanted to try to settle the dispute with Cayton. Four days later, with Jesse Jackson and Don King in attendance, Mike Tyson was baptized at the Holy Trinity Baptist Church in Cleveland. Clad in a white robe, Tyson was immersed in a baptismal pool in the church as 700 parishioners watched, then he sang and clapped his hands along with everyone else to the sounds of gospel music. "I felt so clean, so pure and reborn," said the champion, "and I think it is going to change my life. . . . Baptism is an unbelievable experience."

On November 30, Kevin Rooney telephoned Camille Ewald from the gym in Catskill. He was very surprised when a familiar but unexpected voice answered the phone. It was Mike. Rooney had heard rumors that Tyson was planning to get back to the gym, but he had no idea the heavyweight champion was two miles away at Camille's. Tyson said he would be in the next day, and indeed, on December 1, Tyson walked into the little gym above the police station for the first time in three months. Rooney put him through a moderate workout of floor and bag exercises, but all was not well. Tyson became annoyed at Rooney's loose lips. The trainer had recently appeared on the Madison Square Garden Network with sportscaster Dave Sims and voiced some personal opinions that in hindsight were perhaps better left unsaid. Rooney had made the comment that he thought it would be good for Mike to date Robin again, since he knew the two had had a Manhattan rendezvous a few days earlier. He also said he thought Tyson's baptism had been "orchestrated," by King and Jesse Jackson. Mike felt Kevin was interfering in his personal business, and he responded by doing what it had been rumored for weeks he intended to do. He fired Rooney, who had been his friend for eight years and his trainer for six. Unable to do it to his face, or over the phone, Tyson announced it in the newspaper, saying Rooney had "fired himself" by not heeding his warnings not to discuss his (Tyson's) personal affairs publicly. Rooney countered by saying that he was still Tyson's trainer until Mike told him otherwise "to my face, like a man." Rooney further said King was behind it. Like Cayton, he felt King was poisoning Tyson's mind. (All things considered, it was not a good holiday season for Rooney. In the midst of a divorce himself, he was sentenced to three years' probation for assaulting the boyfriend of his estranged wife a year earlier. The sentence came just two weeks before Tyson let him go.) Tyson continued to confirm that his decision on Rooney was final, and that if need be he would train himself until he secured a replacement.

On December 15, at a Los Angeles news conference with all parties present, the long-awaited and five-times-in-five-months postponed fight between Mike Tyson and Frank Bruno was officially announced. It would be promoted by the Las Vegas Hilton, which would pay a $7 million site fee to stage the fight which by now had built strong worldwide interest due to Tyson's out-of-the-ring tragi-comic life. "I'm happy to be back," said Tyson, the heavyweight champion. "I've been channeling all my energy and vision into this fight," said the challenger Bruno. "I've got the power to do what needs to be done." The fight would take place on February 25, 1989, the twenty-fifth anniversary, coincidentally, of Muhammad Ali's victory over Sonny Liston, which had given him the Heavyweight Championship. Although King was not the promoter of the Tyson-Bruno fight itself, he was the promoter of the undercard, which he loaded up with fighters controlled by Don King Productions. In order to have the fight go forward, Bill Cayton had compromised a great deal. Because certain safeguards he had always insisted on to protect Tyson were not in this fight contract, Cayton did not sign it. Cayton would be allowed to attend all press conferences and the weigh-in, but he really had no say over what Tyson did. It had clearly become King's ballgame. Howard Weitzman was quick to point out that although Cayton had this level of participation and although he would be listed as Tyson's manager, it did not mean that

Tyson recognized Cayton as his manager, and the lawsuit the champion had filed to try to break his managerial ties with Cayton still stood. (As regards Donald Trump's claim for $2 million for services rendered, Weitzman said, "Mike Tyson doesn't owe Donald Trump anything.")

Tyson set up his training camp in Las Vegas, ensconced in promoter Don King's Vegas home, with a guard dog, Terminator, stationed nearby to keep unwanted guests away. The year came to an end with his former attorney, Michael Winston—dismissed by Ruth Roper several months earlier, then retained by King to handle Tyson's affairs, only to be dismissed again in favor of Howard Weitzman—refusing to hand over files in his possession pertaining to Tyson until the champ paid $17,000 in legal fees he said was still owed to him.

Chapter 18

The Bruno Fight . . . At Last

*I have known the time when a pugilistic encounter
between two noted champions was almost considered in
the light of a national affair; when tens of thousands of
individuals, high and low, meditated and brooded upon it,
the first thing in the morning and the last at night, until
the great event was decided. . . . In the days of pugilism
it was no vain boast to say, that one Englishman was a
match for two of t'other race; at present it would be a vain
boast to say so, for these are not the days of pugilism.*

—Lavengro
George Borrow

There was much speculation as to who would get the plum
assignment to replace Kevin Rooney as Mike Tyson's trainer.
Angelo Dundee, an excellent in-the-ring motivator, and Joey
Fariello, a disciple of Cus D'Amato who handled Mark
Breland, were talked about, but they were white, and it was
widely believed that King was persuading Tyson to replace
his all-white corner of Rooney, Lott and Baranski with
black cornermen. Among the black trainers whose names
were mentioned were such men as George Benton and the
master, Eddie Futch, who had handled Joe Frazier, Larry
Holmes and Spinks. Futch had once been secretly approached
by Jim Jacobs early in Tyson's career, not necessarily about
replacing Rooney, since a promise had been made to
D'Amato that Rooney would always be with Tyson, but
certainly about joining with Rooney. When word of the
approach leaked out, Jacobs vehemently denied ever talking
to the great trainer, but Futch and Tyson both eventually
confirmed that such a meeting had indeed taken place. One
drawback to anyone on a level with Futch was money. King
and Tyson were certainly not going to pay a new trainer
anything approaching the 10 percent Rooney received as the
standard trainer's fee.

Eventually, early in January, Tyson settled on an unknown young black man named Aaron Snowell from Pennsylvania. Snowell had never fought. Although he claimed he had trained Tim Witherspoon, he had actually just hung around the gym and helped out, according to Witherspoon himself, whose trainer had been "Slim" Jim Robinson. Boxing people regarded Snowell as nothing more than a "gym rat," someone who hangs around at fight gyms. But Snowell had three key qualifications: He was black, he would work cheap for the opportunity, and when Witherspoon had split with King, Snowell had remained loyal to the promoter. When Tyson began sparring at Johnny Tocco's Ringside Gym in Las Vegas early in January of 1989, Snowell was in place, supervising the workouts. Joining him in handling Tyson's training was the champ's buddy from Albany, Rory Holloway, who had assumed the position of assistant manager formerly held by Steve Lott, although he was in no way as competent to deal with camp duties and coordination as Lott had been. Holloway was simply a young guy who was in the right place at the right time, having met Tyson when the teenage future champion was competing as an amateur in the New York Empire State Games in which Holloway was playing basketball. The two became friends. One Tyson insider who knew Holloway quite well described him as "a puppy, completely dependent on Mike." Newsday reporter Tim Layden described Holloway as "a very odd guy who fell into a situation and has taken advantage of it. He's completely infatuated and misguided as to his own worth on the face of the earth." And so, the corner for the champion was being put in place.

"It's ridiculous for me to pay someone like Kevin Rooney 10 percent of my purse when there's no loyalty on his part," said Tyson, with Don King at his side, during a small press gathering at the Hilton on January 7. Tyson said the turmoil that had surrounded him was because "When I have these long layoffs I get in trouble. The way I am is the way I am: high-spirited, energetic and wild. I'm going to live the way I want to live anyway. I have to live my life. Once I start to change, that's the first sign of failure." He added that "My friend Frank Bruno is in real trouble." Tyson said he was down to 230 pounds from a reported high of 255 and that he would be "perfectly comfortable" going into the fight without any trainer in his corner if need be. King just beamed and reiterated his oft-repeated "Tyson is the boss. When Mike speaks, I listen," nonsense, while continuing to control Tyson and not let him out of his sight.

Tyson and King were due to give depositions to Thomas Puccio in the champion's lawsuit to break his contract with Cayton. The deposition, a pretrial questioning procedure conducted under oath but outside the courtroom, was to be held in Las Vegas according to a ruling by a federal judge in New York, so as not to disrupt Tyson's training. Tyson's questioning by Puccio took place on Monday, January 9, and Tuesday, the 10th. King watched the procedure on a closed-circuit TV monitor in another room, while in a separate room Cayton, his wife, Doris, and Lorraine Jacobs, also view the proceedings on a television monitor. They heard Tyson revile the man who had helped guide his career to its present peak, saying, "I want to terminate him. I don't like him. I don't want him around. He gets me sick to my stomach. I just want Don King as my promoter. No one's going to dictate my life when I generate the capital." He called Cayton "crude and diabolical and a funny old man," and one could hear the words of Don King every time Tyson opened his mouth. Every time there was a recess, King dashed in to consult with Tyson.

"Regardless of the price, my intention is to terminate him," said Tyson of his manager when the questioning resumed. "He's a horrible, wretched guy, a liar, a hypocrite, not a very nice man." However, he offered little in the way of substance in his testimony, admitting he knew very little about his finances and business, despite accusing Cayton of stealing from him. "I didn't know nothing. Basically, I was a space cadet," he said.

Attorney Puccio asked Tyson about a $10 million check he had received following the disbursement of funds from the Spinks fight. Tyson said he did not know where the money was or if it had been deposited. "I handed you the check in court," said Puccio. "What did you do with it?" Tyson said he had put it in the bank. No, he had given it to his accountant. That is, he had given it to his lawyer to give to his accountant. "Do you know where the money is deposited?" asked Puccio. Tyson replied, "No." "You don't know where this $10 million went?" he was again asked. "No," came the answer. Tyson also said he had no idea how much money he had before the Spinks fight, and denied he had ever been shown any post fight financial statements by his managers. At another point, Tyson told Puccio, "I'm the boss." Puccio asked him, "Where does it say in the contract you're the boss?" Replied Tyson, "Let Bill Cayton fight."

During the questioning, Puccio got Tyson to admit under oath that he had signed several agreements with Don King without the knowledge or consent of Cayton, which was a violation of Cayton's contract with the fighter, and when Puccio asked whether Tyson was a silent partner in putting together the undercard of the Bruno fight, attorney Weitzman told Tyson not to answer. Tyson complained that the questioning was "pissing me off" and "stressing me out." Unbelievably, during the deposition he made vulgar sexual gestures to Joann Crispi, an attractive attorney who was an associate of Puccio. Then, after defending King as the person "who helped me to blossom into a man" and calling Cayton a man "with a slavemaster mentality," he had the audacity during a recess to walk right up to Ms. Crispi and tell her, "I want to fuck you."

Puccio was extremely pleased following the two days of depositions. He felt Tyson had demonstrated he had no substantial case against Cayton and that he was unable to substantiate claims Cayton had misappropriated his money. He described the information he had obtained on the secret contracts signed between King and Tyson as "devastating."

The day following the depositions, Tyson, no doubt still feeling "stressed out," broke training and disappeared from Las Vegas without bothering to inform either King or his "trainers" that he was leaving. Several hours later, he stepped off a plane in Vancouver, Canada, where Robin Givens was on location filming an ABC-TV movie, "The Penthouse." It seems Tyson had phoned her to say he missed her, and she suggested he fly up. He caught the next plane out of Vegas, not even taking a change of clothes or a toothbrush. When he arrived at the hotel, he found reporters, photographers and TV cameras waiting for him. Since the trip was completely spontaneous, someone must have tipped them that he was arriving. Someone in Vancouver. Someone who knew he was coming. That narrowed the choices considerably.

As Tyson stalked the Hotel Vancouver lobby, trying to find out where Robin was, the cameras were on him and he blew a fuse. He grabbed a $1,200 Nikon F3 camera out of the hands of a photographer for the Vancouver *Sun*, and hurled it against a wall. Mike Timbrell, a cameraman for Canada's BC-TV, was taping the incident when Tyson lunged at his $70,000 TV camera and tore the viewfinder off it, smashing it to the ground. He then tried to grab the camera, but Timbrell broke free from Tyson and escaped onto the street through the hotel's revolving door. The cameraman suffered minor injuries to his hand in the scuffle with the heavyweight champion, but said he did not plan to file assault charges. The Vancouver *Sun* said it would bill Tyson for damages to the Nikon.

Once upstairs, Tyson found a gift Robin had left for him in her suite and a note telling him to come on up to where the filming was taking place. He dashed up, and Robin greeted him warmly, introducing him to the cast and crew. He watched her work for about two hours, until 8 P.M. and when the filming was finished for the day, she walked over to Mike and gave him a big kiss. Hand in hand, they returned to her suite, and did not leave it until the next morning. They ordered dinner from room service, including two dozen raw oysters, and put the "Do Not Disturb" sign on the door.

In Las Vegas, King was furious when he learned where Mike was. The one person he wanted to keep Tyson away from, even more than Cayton, was Givens—and her bed. If Mike became reconciled with her, King knew he risked being dumped once again. However, at midday Thursday, Tyson boarded a plane at Vancouver airport and arrived back in Las Vegas late in the afternoon, his whirlwind twenty-four-hour excursion to Canada over. Givens told reporters that she and Mike were continuing to see each other as often as they could, even as their divorce proceedings went ahead. "We're doing better than we ever have before, just being friends. Right now, we're happily estranged," she said. She revealed there were many show business offers coming in to her now, and acknowledged "Certainly all that's happened has raised my recognition factor."

On Friday, January 13, with the Bruno fight six weeks off, Tyson returned to Tocco's Gym and boxed nine rounds, pounding his three sparring partners hard. The sessions were closed to the press, and Tyson's security guards got into several scuffles and shouting matches outside the gym with newsmen.

On Wednesday, January 18, it was Don King's turn to give depositions in the Tyson-Cayton lawsuit, which were conducted in New York City at the offices of Puccio's law firm. Puccio questioned King about his son's involvement in his business, suggesting that King had acted as both a promoter and manager, a violation of boxing commission rules. King's attorney, Bob Hirth, an associate of Charles Lomax, responded that Bill Cayton was the only person he knew who acted as both a manager and promoter. Puccio also questioned King about the involvement of Rory Holloway and John Horne with Tyson. Both were constantly at the fighter's side, and Horne was reputed to be "King's man," there to keep tabs on the champion and report back to King. In response to Puccio's questions, King denied that he or his company had paid either man any money. Puccio sought to establish that Holloway and Horne might also have interfered with Cayton's contract with Tyson. King testified that he had gone from New York to California in April of 1988 in response to a phone call from Tyson, who had asked him for help in dealing with Cayton. King said Tyson told him Cayton "was no good, that he hated him, that he wasn't going to fight for him, that he was the worst man he ever met. . . . [Mike] said, 'I want to know the business side of boxing. I'm tired of [Cayton] messing with my life.' " When asked what his relationship was with the champion, King said, "He's a friend of mine," and added, "The fact is Mike Tyson always called me. I've never called Mr. Tyson." King said that far from interfering with Tyson and his managers, he had even encouraged Mike to remain loyal to them when Mike wanted to leave Cayton and Jacobs. "[Mike's] brother came to me earlier, I think before the Berbick fight, and asked me what I would do for him [Tyson]. I ran right to Jim and Bill, just like I always did." (This may well have been true—when Jacobs was alive. It was only after Jacobs's death that King began his seduction of the heavyweight champion.) King also testified concerning what Puccio termed the two "illegal" contracts he had signed with Tyson. At one point the promoter said he actually took fewer years in the four-year exclusive promotional deal signed on October 21 than Tyson wanted to give him. "Mike said he wanted me to be his promoter for life, but I said let's just make it for four years," said King, who acknowledged that he had never informed Cayton about the deal. When Puccio pressed him and asked if it was not customary for the promoter to deal with the manager and not directly with the fighter, King replied, "You can't ask a normal question when dealing with an abnormal situation."

Bill Cayton was in the room, along with Lorraine Jacobs, during the questioning of King, but that didn't stop the promoter from defaming the manager while under oath. "You are representing Satan," he told Puccio, and went on to label Cayton "a hypocrite, an inveterate liar, a tyrant, a power zealot. . . . When I said he was Satan in disguise, the disguise is gone, he's just Satan. . . . The man is an egotistical maniac. No one likes Bill Cayton. He's never been liked by anybody. No sooner did Jim Jacobs die, the man went completely berserk." King termed Cayton's contract with Tyson "an ownership. This is a slave contract, an unbridled contract over this human being."

King said Tyson had also called him in May of 1988 and asked him to come to Albany, where the fighter negotiated a contract (never put into effect) with King to promote his first fight following the Spinks bout, even though Tyson knew full well that he had a signed contract with Astaire and Duff to fight Bruno in London. Then King said, "You have to understand one thing. I am the best promoter in the world. My record substantiates that . . . despite a few allegations by dissidents. My record is irrefutable." When Puccio told him "You're not here to make speeches," King replied, "You subpoenaed me, now you've got to deal with me."

When the formal portion of the deposition was over, King launched another tirade, aimed directly at Cayton sitting just a few feet away. "You are a lying hypocrite," he screamed. "Jimmy Jacobs was the most loved man in boxing. You are the most hated." Cayton called King a liar, and King responded by calling him a "despicable liar." Then, in the presence of Lorraine Jacobs, King became vulgar. "You're a liar, Bill Cayton, you're a lying motherfucker. You desecrate Jim's memory." "You're a lowlife," Cayton retorted to the ex-con promoter, who replied, "I certainly am, when I look at a despicable motherfucker like you. . . . You never were loyal to Jim." King stomped out of the room. Puccio wasn't flustered, saying, "It's all part of his act, which you have to listen to if you want to hear him . . . [it's] the price you have to pay in order to get him to testify." Lorraine Jacobs was upset for Cayton, but the manager just called King "one hundred percent bluff and bluster."

While all this was going on, Frank Bruno was quietly training in the Arizona desert, having arrived in the United States on January 5. The fight had caught the imagination of the British public, with whom Bruno was extremely popular and was the biggest sporting event involving Great Britain since the winning of the World Cup soccer championship in 1966. The fight would be televised in as many as forty closed-circuit locations throughout England and Ireland, even though it would begin there at three o'clock in the morning on Sunday, February 26, local time. Those with satellite dishes would see the fight live at home on Sky Television, and the BBC would replay it on tape on Sunday afternoon. Jonathan Martin, the BBC's Director of Spots, said a "massive audience" was anticipated. The intense interest was a tribute to the twenty-seven-year-old Briton, who would make the thirteenth attempt in this century by an Englishman to win the Heavyweight Championship of the World, the previous twelve having been unsuccessful, and despite their affection for him, even his countrymen knew Bruno was a long shot to fare any better.

Franklyn Roy Bruno was the youngest of five children of Jamaican immigrants to England. His father was a baker, and Bruno's neighbors in Barmouth Road, Wandsworth, where he grew up, remember young Frank as a quiet, polite, and well-mannered boy. However, at the age of eleven, the big lad hit a schoolteacher during an argument, and was packed off to reform school. Unlike Tyson, it was the only trouble Bruno ever was in. Even in reform school he was known as a gentle boy who worked on the weekends at a home for the elderly, often taking wheelchair-bound residents out for walks. When he returned to Wandsworth at the age of sixteen, he was over 6 feet tall and weighed more than 200 pounds. He began working out in amateur boxing gyms, and at the age of eighteen he became the youngest British amateur heavyweight champion in history. It was around this time that he met Laura Mooney, a white girl who had grown up in the London borough of Hammersmith and who worked at a children's nursery. the couple began living together, a relationship that continues to this day and which has produced two beautiful young daughters.

Bruno turned pro in 1982 and won his first twenty-one fights by knockout, against generally mediocre opposition, his biggest wins coming against veteran Americans Scott Ledoux, Barry Funches and Jumbo Cummings. On May 13, 1984, at Wembley, he was matched against future champion James "Bonecrusher" Smith and was leading in the fight when he was KO'd by Smith in the tenth round. After rebuilding with wins over Phil Brown, Anders Eklund, Lucien Rodriguez and over-the-hill former champion Gerrie Coetzee, he was matched for the Heavyweight Championship against Tim Witherspoon at Wembley. Again, he was leading on the scorecards going into the eleventh round, but was KO'd by Witherspoon, coming so close, but failing in the end to win the WBA title. Four victories in 1987, all by KO, against trailhorses Chuck Gardner and Reggie Gross and faded names such as James "Quick" Tillis, who was no longer quick, and Joe Bugner, whose glory was more than a decade behind him, somehow catapulted Bruno back into the number one challenger's position. The combination of his not wanting to risk that top ranking, which meant another title opportunity, and the five months of delays due to Tyson's star-crossed life, meant that Bruno would step into the ring against Tyson on February 25 after sixteen months of inactivity.

Tyson's inexperienced handlers continued to wield a heavy hand. Rory Holloway warned reporters who were allowed into the gym one day that "Anyone asking questions about Mike's personal life will be escorted out of here." Tyson told the newsmen he was considering bringing Kevin Rooney back into the fold, but not for the Bruno fight. He did make another addition to his corner: Jay Bright, his long-time housemate in Catskill, was brought in to assist with his training and work his corner. Bright knew the D'Amato philosophy from living in the house with Cus and Camille for ten years, but he was even less experienced than Aaron Snowell. Bright had never fought (although he liked to say he'd had a few amateur fights) and had never worked with a fighter before. But he was familiar with Mike, which would give the champion a certain element of comfort, and as Steve Lott said, Mike would do whatever he wanted to anyway once the fight started. Bright said he was just happy to be able to help out Mike and that he wasn't concerned what the champion, whom he looked upon as a "brother," paid him.

Both the British and American press were upset at being unable to reach Tyson. Only one journalist from a New York tabloid had unrestricted access to both King and Tyson, but he was known as "King's designated writer." Anyone who wrote impartially—journalists like Mike Katz, Phil Berger, Wally Matthews—were kept as far away from Tyson as possible. Several moonlighting Cleveland police officers served as bodyguards, keeping the press at arm's length. The new Tyson entourage, sporting purple and gold jackets supplied by King that said on the backs "It's a Family Affair—Team Tyson," had little knowledge of, or regard for, a journalist's right to ask questions in an unrestricted format. King had claimed he cut Randy "Tex" Cobb's purse in the Holmes fight because Cobb did not come to Houston early enough to help promote the fight, yet he was apparently not interested in letting Tyson help promote the Bruno fight by talking to reporters, even though many seats remained, and would remain, unsold at the Hilton. Without access to Tyson, some newspapermen had to rely on their own imaginations to come up with story angles. Britain's *The News of the World* carried a story that Tyson and King were approached by two characters who offered an incredible $80 million if Tyson would throw the fight to Bruno. The source of this story was not revealed, but the paper reported that Tyson furiously ordered the "bums" out of his sight "before I kill them." The British press also made quite a fuss about Bruno employing a hypnotherapist, Dr. David Silverman of Las Vegas, to help put him at ease and build his confidence. "When I wake up [from the hypnotic trances]," said Bruno, "I feel as if I could fight King Kong, let alone Mike Tyson."

The champion, as usual, had his hypnotist, John Halpin

of New York, in camp with him. Along with watching movies and listening to rap music, Tyson spent some of his relaxation time racing around the desert in his new white four-wheel drive, $170,000 Lamborghini LM002 off-road vehicle, for which he paid cash and which he had no trouble getting up to 120 mph on his joyrides, since it had a 450 horsepower engine.

Several months earlier, a drunk and loud Tyson had made a fuss at the Las Vegas Hilton gambling tables, shooting dice, cursing, and "causing a whole lot of commotion," according to one witness. He had been asked to leave by hotel security. But now, in training, Tyson kept more to himself, out of the public eye, and, according to Hilton Hotel security personnel, the champion was this time staying out of trouble.

Bruno shifted his training camp to Las Vegas from Arizona and went about his business in his usual no-nonsense, dignified manner. Colin Hart of the London *Sun* newspaper, said Bruno was "easily the most popular sportsman in Britain," a phenomenon he found somewhat curious since "he hasn't won anything." BBC boxing commentator Harry Carpenter said the British were a people who preferred "a good loser to a flashy winner." Another reason for his popularity might well have been that the British people (and many Americans as well who were rooting for Bruno) felt that he conducted himself with the demeanor of a champion, while Tyson had demonstrated time and again that his personal conduct left much to be desired.

The usually placid Bruno did become annoyed at the poor treatment he said he and his party were receiving at the Hilton, saying the hotel was "treating me like a dog. . . . This is the worst [hotel] I have been in for looking after a fighter." He complained he even had to purchase a Tyson-Bruno souvenir T-shirt, since the Hilton wouldn't give him one. However, from his purse as well as from his share of closed-circuit TV revenues in Great Britain, Bruno stood to net $2 million for himself, to add to his personal worth that was already estimated at $5 million, so he was willing to put up with the Hilton's behavior toward him.

While keeping Tyson away from the boxing journalists, King engineered a series of appearances on TV talk shows, where Tyson would not be pressed very hard on controversial issues such as his relationship with King. On most of these shows, King appeared as a guest alongside Tyson. On the "Phil Donahue Show" Tyson said he still loved Robin, "but it's an unhealthy situation. I can't live with her. . . . We both made a mistake. We were young and got married." Of his mother-in-law, whom just a few months earlier he had defended, saying that he loved her and considered her part of his family, he simply said, "I have no relationship with the woman." On a satellite interview with David Frost in London for "TV-am," he said he was not interested in a reconciliation with Givens, and that his new-found Christianity gave him comfort in times of trouble. In several interviews on ESPN, the cable sports TV network, Tyson said he didn't think he'd end up broke when his career was over, but acknowledged that "smarter businessmen than me has [sic] been tricked out of all their money." About his preparations for the fight, he said he would be completely ready, because he was aware that if you go into a fight only halfway prepared, "you're going to be pickin' your butt off the canvas." He said he was ready to get back into action. "I just want to fight. I'm very hostile at this particular moment in my life." The low point came on the "Arsenio Hall Show," a late night variety program. Hall, a black comedian, seemed both incapable and unwilling to ask King and Tyson any hard questions, and Tyson used the appearance to slander Bill Cayton shamelessly once again, saying, "When I was with the opposite people, when I was with Bill Cayton . . . people that was [sic] actually stealing my money and had the complexion for the protection," injecting race as an issue, which in fact it never had been in all his years with D'Amato, Jacobs, Cayton, Ewald, Atlas and Rooney. But when Hall gave him the opportunity to tell how Cayton had stolen from him, Tyson could offer no specifics beyond saying, "It's very simple, then again it's very complex, because I had no experience." Tyson gave King credit because "he showed me God." "Now I'm with Don," he said, "and we're two black people, and we're generatin' power."

King, for his part, termed his association with Tyson "a wonderful relationship . . . demonstrating to America, to friend and foe alike, that two people of color can come together and do just as any other people would do. . . . We understand who we are and love ourselves." He praised

Tyson as a champion who in the future would show he was the greatest of all time, saying "I'm like John the Baptist, a voice crying in the wilderness, talking about one that's coming greater than I," and, gesturing toward Tyson, concluded his speech: "This is a bad nigger, babe."

While in Los Angeles with King early in February taping several TV appearances, Mike unexpectedly turned up at Robin's house carrying six dozen red roses. He spent the night with her, and the next day the couple were out strolling and embracing on fashionable Rodeo Drive in Beverly Hills. Several days later, Robin signed, at last, the divorce decree, and King wasted no time getting Mike legally apart from Givens, once and for all. Although Tyson had won the right several weeks earlier to have his deposition with Cayton's attorney Tom Puccio conducted in Las Vegas so as not to interrupt his training routine, now, with the fight just eleven days away, King hustled Tyson onto the promoter's private jet and flew with him to the Dominican Republic, a five-hour flight, where a divorce could be obtained in twenty-four hours. All that was required was an overnight stay. On February 14, a mutual divorce was granted to Mike Tyson and Robin Givens, after which the promoter and his charge returned to Las Vegas, with King chanting "Free at last, free at last," as they were met by reporters at the airport.

The specific terms of the divorce, by mutual agreement, were not announced. Raoul Felder said his client, Givens, "will keep what was hers, including all of her jewelry, and he will keep what is his." But, of course, it wasn't quite that simple. Felder acknowledged there would be an audit at a later date, that would set "a floor to what she receives," Robin was going to do quite well. She would not get the New Jersey mansion, but she would keep the couple's luxury cars and the house in the Hollywood Hills that was in her name but which Tyson had purchased and furnished at a cost of more than $1,250,000. This, along with the jewelry Mike had lavished on her, plus several hundred thousand dollars' worth of clothing, meant that Robin would come out of the marriage with millions of dollars in assets. And still unanswered was the question raised by Tyson of what had happened to millions of dollars in cash he said was transferred from Mike Tyson Enterprises accounts to accounts controlled by Robin Givens Productions. One thing she had to give up was his name: A stipulation of the divorce said she could no longer use the name Tyson,

Back in New York things were also happening. Kevin Rooney's attorney arrived in the U.S. District Court in Albany, New York and slapped Mike Tyson with a $10 million lawsuit on Rooney's behalf, claiming breach of contract. It was based on what he said was an oral agreement that he had to be Mike's trainer for life, with a set fee of 10 percent. Coming when it did, the lawsuit was impetuous and ill-advised. Tyson had been saying "Kevin is my man," and making it clear he intended to reconcile himself with his trainer following the Bruno fight, which he was making Kevin sit out as a sort of punishment. Now he was furious. He said Kevin "just did something unprofessional" by speaking out on matters involving Mike's personal life, but now, by suing the champion, Rooney had gone "out of his way to make it personal. Now he'll never be involved with me again, never." Rooney fired back that Tyson had never even called to discuss the matter with him, that he only read about it in the newspapers. "What was I supposed to do, sit around like a jerk?" asked Rooney. "Fuck him. He's a jerk," said the dismissed trainer.

With the fight now just a few days off, grizzled old gymkeeper Johnny Tocco said Tyson seemed ready. "I've seen him train for five fights now. I've never seen him let up on any sparring partners. He's an animal. He's got seven sparring partners now and he needs them because he keeps hurting them. He gets them hurt, and he wants to finish them off whether it's gym work or a fight." Tocco said Snowell and Bright seemed to be a bit disorganized. "They both are yelling instructions to him, which isn't too good, but I don't think he listens to anyone in there, anyway. All he needs is someone to tie the gloves on, and anything in front of him he goes after. Anything in front of him, once that bell rings, you're gone." Michael Spinks, who was in Las Vegas, said, "Boxing is the best job in the world to let off steam, and people are in trouble when Tyson wants to let off steam."

At the final prefight news conference, Tyson said he liked "the single life," that he was "very happy at this particular moment in my life and Don King put a big hand in it." "Thank you, champ," answered King. About his topsy-turvy year, Tyson said, "I'm a human being, I'm bound to slip on a banana peel," but he said people shouldn't feel sorry for him. "That insults me," said Tyson. "I ask for no sympathy. I despise sympathy. I hear people say, 'Poor Mike Tyson.' There is nothing poor about me."

"I don't think people respect him," said Bruno of the champion. "He's done too many crazy things. He's young and he's got to do some serious, serious learning to bring him off his pedestal. I'm the one to do it." Responded Tyson: "He's a good fighter, believe it or not. He didn't get to be number one by laying on his butt. When you look at him, he's very threatening-looking, but I give him no chance. I'm basically not a hostile person, but I'd say he's in some trouble." With King and his new triumvirate of camp coordinator John Horne, plus cornermen Snowell and Bright, surrounding him, Tyson said, "I'm glad to be back in the ring, because this is where I dominate."

When King began to insult absent manager, Bill Cayton, Jarvis Astaire walked off the dais. Cayton was resting in New York, on doctor's orders, following several days of hospitalization. He had just returned from testifying as a defendant in London in a lawsuit precipitated by King, who, according to Cayton, had made an unauthorized deal for ITV to televise the fight in Britain. The suit was decided against ITV by the High Court and in favor of Sky TV, and the court also issued a financial judgment against ITV for $700,000, but following his successful testimony, Cayton returned to New York suffering from exhaustion. At the Las Vegas news conference, King accused Cayton of entering the hospital to avoid giving a deposition in the Tyson lawsuit.

In New York, both prior to and following his trip to London, Cayton had been working quietly behind the scenes to see if some compromise could be worked out with King to avoid disruptive litigation. In the waning days of January 1989, Cayton spoke by phone with James Binns of Pennsylvania, an attorney who was the WBA's legal adviser and a major power broker in that organization. Binns was an ally of King, but he had also helped Cayton and Jacobs on various matters and Cayton felt he was an honorable man who could be trusted. In that phone conversation, Cayton advised Binns confidentially that he and his attorneys were on the verge of filing a formal complaint against King with the New York State Athletic Commission for interfering with Tyson. Binns said, "Bill, I hate to see it come to that because if it does, the chances of a settlement are remote." Binns explained that once the commission took over jurisdiction of the matter, a private deal between the parties involved would then be out of their hands. Cayton responded, "I have no choice in the matter. You know what's been said, you know what Don's done." Binns interjected. "Let me talk to Don," he suggested. "Maybe there's a way of settling this." Cayton said he'd prefer that Binns not intercede with King, reminding the attorney that he had been close to a settlement several times, including at the recent meeting in Las Vegas prior to the Chavez-Ramirez fight, but each time things had collapsed. Cayton had offered a settlement based on King working with them on a fight-by-fight basis, or a group of fights (Cayton had offered King the opportunity to promote the final four fights of the seven fight HBO contract with Tyson) but King and Tyson were insisting on the four-year exclusive contract. Binns asked Cayton if he could talk with Tom Puccio, Cayton's lawyer, and Cayton reluctantly agreed. Puccio agreed with Binns and convinced Cayton to give Binns a shot at dealing with King. "If he can do it," said Puccio, "why not let him?" Before long, Binns notified Cayton that he had spoken with the promoter, and King was ready to sit down and try to hammer out some arrangement. Cayton consequently agreed to hold off on the filing of his formal complaint against King. It was agreed King would come to New York to meet sometime during the first half of February, before Cayton's trip to testify in London, but that meeting was never arranged, although the attorneys for both sides did begin talks. During Cayton's absence, however, things fell apart; as he was to learn once again, accommodation was not in King's vocabulary. Even King's ally, James Binns, apparently threw in the towel in exasperation. During the week preceding the Bruno fight, Binns said, "Bill Cayton has been very reasonable. He made King a very good offer." Larry Holmes, from afar, still issued warnings to Tyson about King. "You don't get off the horse that brought you over the bridge to get on another horse," said the ex-champion. "Especially not that horse. I know that horse too well."

The weigh-in was held on Friday, February 24, the day before the fight, on the stage of the Hilton's Showroom Theater. Several thousand British fans were in Las Vegas for the fight, among them former European and Commonwealth heavyweight champion Henry Cooper, still much beloved by his countrymen for his two game but unsuccessful efforts against Muhammad Ali a generation earlier. Most of the Brits sported T-shirts with a picture of Bruno superimposed over the Union Jack, and a rowdy group was among the hundreds of people who jammed in to watch the weigh-in. When Bruno entered, wearing an aqua-blue sweatsuit and a red baseball cap, his fans began chanting "Bru–no, Bru–no, Bru–no." Tyson indicated Bruno should step on the scale first, which he did. His weight was announced at "228 pounds—16 stone, 4 pounds." Tyson came in at a trim "218 pounds—15 stone, 8 pounds." When he stepped down, he tried to engage Bruno in a stare-down match, but Bruno was having none of it. He avoided Tyson's eyes, looking down, at which point the champion pulled his red-and-black bikini underwear shorts down to give Bruno a look at the "family jewels." It was a primitive, rude gesture on Tyson's part, but George Francis, Bruno's trainer, said it did not bother his man, although it did prompt a headline in the next day's *Mirror* in London that said, "Tyson Flashes a Warning." There was little betting on the outcome of the fight, since the Las Vegas line had Bruno a solid 7½ to 1 underdog. Most of the betting centered on whether Bruno would last more than one round, or more than four rounds, or whatever. Back in Catskill, Kevin Rooney said he would be rooting for Tyson, who he thought would stop Bruno, although he did say the fight could be tougher and go on longer than many expected. He himself would be spending Saturday night coaching several amateur fighters he was training in an amateur tournament in Schenectady, New York.

On Saturday, February 25, 1989, Frank Bruno was the first to enter the Hilton's indoor arena, wearing a bright red robe trimmed in shiny gold lamé. Moments later came Tyson, who tossed a terrycloth towel off his shoulders halfway down the aisle to enter the ring traditionally barechested. During the instructions at center ring from referee Richard Steele, it was Bruno who stared directly at Tyson and the champion who averted his glance.

At the opening bell, both men advanced strongly toward each other, and after barely seven or eight seconds, the crowd, hardly settled in, was stunned when Tyson hurt the towering Brit with a right hand. Bruno's knees wobbled, and he stumbled backward. Another right caught him, mostly with forearm, but the force of the inaccurate punch, with Bruno already hurt, sent him to the canvas after just eleven seconds had expired in the round, and many thought they might be witnessing the fastest heavyweight title fight in history. Tyson, who often used dirty tactics in his fights, fouled Bruno by punching the challenger after he was clearly down, but referee Richard Steele chose not to penalize, or even warn the champion. Bruno rose to his feet immediately, and Tyson later recalled telling himself when he saw Bruno get up, "Oh, man, this guy means business." Bruno then held Tyson behind the head with his left arm and clubbed the champion repeatedly with rights to the head. Tyson, in turn, replied with his own dirty tactics, banging Bruno in the face with his elbow. Bruno was bleeding from the nose. Bruno then spun Tyson into the ropes, and with the champion's back to him, whacked Tyson with several rabbit punches. Steele stepped in and called a halt to the action, waved Tyson to a neutral corner, and informed the judges at ringside he was deducting a point from Bruno's score for the challenger's tactics. Moments later the crowd was electrified when Bruno connected with a right hand which clearly hurt Tyson. Bruno followed with a solid left, and Tyson's legs turned wobbly for an instant, the champion losing his footing but not going down. It was, however, the worst Tyson had ever been hurt in any of his thirty-six fights, and Bruno was coming back very impressively and strongly. With thirty-five seconds to go in a thrilling first round, Bruno again hurt the champion with a hard left hand, and Tyson responded by clubbing Bruno with another illegal elbow to the head. The bell ended the round, and the crowd responded with cheers, having witnessed much more than they had expected at the start of the evening. In the corner, Lawless told Bruno, "You hurt him."

In round two, Bruno continued to hold Tyson behind the head with his left hand, despite warnings from referee Steele. He landed two solid lefts to Tyson's body, bringing chants of "Bru–no, Bru–no," from the 2,000 British fans among the 9,000 in attendance. Bruno followed with a good left hook–left uppercut combination, but a sharp right hand to the jaw by Tyson hurt him. Tyson then subjected his opponent to a flurry of punches as the round came to an end. In the corner, Jay Bright encouraged Tyson to "throw those punches with bad intentions, man," while in Bruno's corner, Lawless urged his man, "Frank, get yourself together now . . . you took his best shots."

In the third round, Tyson attacked Bruno's body, while Bruno started by continuing to land his left effectively. Bruno forced a clinch, and Tyson dug a brutal right hand to Bruno's ribs. Tyson then lunged and missed several punches, but landed a good right to Bruno's head in the final minute. The Londoner responded with a solid right to Tyson's head and dug several lefts to Tyson's body just before the bell. Tyson then shot a left to Bruno's face clearly after the bell ending the round, another one of his customary dirty tactics. It brought boos from the crowd, but no penalty from referee Steele. Aaron Snowell admonished his man during the rest period to use "body shots, a lot of those 'sevens,' stay inside."

Tyson opened round four with a big right to Bruno's head, while the challenger pawed with an ineffective, slow jab. The two men exchanged solid lefts, and Tyson nailed Bruno with a good right to the body. Tyson's body shots were beginning to take their toll, knocking some of the starch out of Bruno and slowing him down. Inside the one-minute mark, Bruno was stunned by a right to the head, followed quickly by two lefts and then two sharp left jabs. Tyson ended the round strongly, with a left uppercut and another left elbow.

Round five was the challenger's last stand. During the first minute there were several mauling clinches, with Bruno clutching behind Tyson's head once again, prompting Steele to shout, "Last warning—you're holding, Frank." Just past the halfway mark, Tyson hurt Bruno badly with a left hook, followed by a right uppercut. Bruno was forced to clinch to try to clear his head. Tyson then came out of the clinch with a pulverizing right hand, the first in a ten-punch combination that came from all angles, punctuated by several damaging left uppercuts. With twenty seconds to go in the round, Tyson backed Bruno to the ropes and fired a damaging right hand to Frank's ribs, two right uppercuts, and a left hook to the head. Bruno was nearly helpless. Seeing this, Terry Lawless jumped onto the ring apron to try to stop the fight. Ringside officials tried to stop him, but Richard Steele had also seen enough. He jumped between the fighters as Tyson got one final right-hand punch off, landing it on Bruno's bloodied face. It was all over as Lawless made it into the ring, the stoppage coming at 2:55 of the fifth round. Tyson quickly moved back toward Bruno to embrace his beaten challenger. Once again, as he had demonstrated against Spinks, adversity outside the ring—this time a broken hand, mood-altering drugs, a car crash, and a divorce—did not affect his performance inside the squared circle, which was his domain. True, he did show signs of rust, but he also showed he was, far and away, the best heavyweight in the world. Speaking of Bruno and the rest of his opponents after the fight, Tyson said, arrogantly but accurately, "How dare they challenge me with their primitive skills. They're as good as dead."

"He beat me fair and square," acknowledged Bruno. "I have no excuses."

Bruno's performance was praised in the American press, which labeled him "the gallant Briton" with "a stout heart" who "fought with valor." When he returned to England three days later, he was met by a crush of fans and reporters at Heathrow Airport. Bruno managed to say he was sorry he hadn't brought the title home and hoped to meet Tyson again in the ring, in London, when "I reckon I would stop him next time. . . . I proved he's only human, he can be hurt." After that, fans and reporters broke through police security barriers and the scene turned to chaos. It was as if Bruno had brought home the belt. Scuffles erupted, cameras were knocked over as well as people, and Bruno, along with his girlfriend, were quickly escorted by police to a waiting car. Clearly, Bruno had done Great Britain proud. "If he had not been up against such a great fighter," said

John Morris, secretary of the British Boxing Board of Control, "we might now have our first heavyweight world champion this century. He showed all the knockers who said he had no right in the ring with Tyson that they were utterly wrong. . . . He hit Tyson harder than anybody ever has, and I am proud of him"—an opinion that was generally reflected throughout the country.

Back in the United States, King and Tyson appeared on the "Arsenio Hall Show" again, where they apparently had a free platform. King said he was proud because "We made history. This was the first time Mike had blacks in his corner." King, ever injecting race, although constantly denying he was a racist, seemingly had no concern for the competency of the corner, just that three black men—Snowell, Holloway and Horne—were in it, along with Jay Bright, who was white. Others had more concern. Jerry Izenberg wrote in the New York *Post*, "As the fight wore on . . . Tyson's corner looked and operated as if it had just stepped out of the Inter-City Golden Gloves semifinals. . . . Collectively, they provided no answers. . . . Beyond lifting the stool into and out of the ring, they contributed little. . . . On another night, with another opponent, it could have been a disaster." And Michael Katz, in the New York *Daily News*, wrote that Tyson was "filled with arrogance, pumped up with poison. He does not need a trainer, he said after a performance that could have embarrassed a Golden Gloves novice. . . . Mike Tyson should get down on his knees and beg Kevin Rooney to take him back."

With the fight behind them, Cayton and his attorneys, Puccio and Gruber, no longer had a need to keep the lid on, and Cayton was finished with trying to work out an accommodation with the stubborn King. Barely thirty-six hours after the fight, at the opening of business on Monday morning, Cayton filed his official complaint against King with the New York State Athletic Commission. The twenty-four-page document charged the promoter with "deliberate disregard of the Tyson-Cayton boxer-manager contracts, commission rules and established boxing practices." The Cayton complaint asked that the Athletic Commission fine Don King and his company and revoke King's promotional license if it was determined he had violated Cayton's contract and commission regulations. Letters were also sent to both

Tyson and King by Puccio warning them that if they attempted to arrange any fight without the participation and approval of Cayton they would be in violation of Tyson's contract with his manager. Puccio said anyone interested in arranging a Tyson fight would be informed they must deal only through Bill Cayton. "We allege that Don King has in effect attempted to steal Mike Tyson," said Puccio, who also said Tyson might have misappropriated between $800,000 and $1 million which the Hilton paid to him directly (a rules violation by the Las Vegas hotel) in order to reduce the amount due to be paid to Cayton. The manager said, "I truly believe that if Mike could get out from under the influence of Don King, he would come back to me. Really, he loved me when he was younger." On the wall of Cayton's office, in fact, was a photo Tyson had inscribed "To my dear friend and the man I love greatly, From your boy, Mike." Cayton said the problem was, "I haven't been able to get to him. They have an iron curtain around him that I can't break through . . . [but] I will not ignore my responsibilities by surrendering to the extortionist demands of Don King. As long as I am Mike Tyson's manager, I will not allow him to be added to the scores of boxers over the years who claim to have been raped and pillaged by Don King. . . . I will do everything in my power to keep him from committing economic suicide with Don King."

One week later, on March 7, Cayton and Puccio dropped their other bomb, and it was a big one. They filed a giant lawsuit against King in the U.S. District Court in New York, alleging no fewer than thirty-eight charges of federal antitrust violations, racketeering, defamation, extortion, mail and wire fraud, and interference with contractual relations. The lawsuit charged that through a "pattern of racketeering" King had monopolized heavyweight championship boxing and that a desire to continue this control of the heavyweight division was King's motivation for undermining Cayton's contract with Tyson. The suit alleged: "King maintains this monopoly by, among other things, signing champions to long-term, exclusive promotional contracts. Potential contenders are in turn told that to fight King fighters in championship fights, they must sign with King themselves. . . . King generally waits until a manager, or promoter, has developed a fighter to the point where he is of commercial appeal. . . . King falsely convinces the fighter to trust him . . . that he can make more money for the fighter and that, unlike the current advisers he acts out of love and racial unity. . . . Should the fighter subsequently tire of withering purses and diminishing bank accounts and seek to break free, King threatens to have the fighter disciplined or barred from competition by sanctioning bodies. . . . When King realized that Tyson would be able to dominate the heavyweight division, it became imperative to sign Tyson to a long-term deal. . . . Should King succeed in forcing Cayton to ratify an exclusive promotional contract with King . . . King will eliminate competition among promoters in the relevant market." Cayton asked for an injunction to prevent King from negotiating deals or signing contracts with, or for, Tyson.

Late in March, Howard Weitzman questioned Bill Cayton for four hours in a deposition related to Tyson's lawsuit to break his contract with his manager. Weitzman pursued a line of questioning aimed at trying to establish that Cayton had violated Athletic Commission rules, which allow only one manager for a fighter. Weitzman questioned how Cayton could have been Tyson's co-manager while Jacobs was alive. However, there was no violation of rules. It is common for fighters to have a manager and a co-manager in New York State. As a matter of fact, when Carl King moved in on "Bonecrusher" Smith in 1986, he became co-manager with Smith's true manager, Alan Kornberg. Co-manager is simply a common usage term, the second party involved with a fighter actually being an assignee for a specific percentage, designated by the manager.

Still grasping at straws, Weitzman "revealed" he had determined in the course of the deposition that Cayton did not have a valid manager's license when he signed his new contract with Tyson in July of 1988, making the contract voidable. However, this revelation (a "big bombshell," according to Don King), had a very short life. Four days later, Athletic Commission Chairman Randy Gordon said Bill Cayton did indeed have a valid manager's license all along. Tyson's attorney then charged Cayton with double-dipping into Tyson's foreign-rights earnings, since Cayton's company which marketed Tyson's fights overseas received a 20 percent commission, this in addition to the 20 percent managerial fee Cayton received. The only problem here was that the 20 percent marketing commission was clearly defined in the July 1988 contract which Tyson had signed and which had been reviewed and approved by the champion's attorney.

During the first week of April, King struck back by filing a frivolous countercomplaint against Cayton with the Athletic Commission. King charged that Cayton had "financially abused" Tyson "through fraud, the use of unlicensed sham corporations and blatant conflicts of interest." It seemed to be the ultimate example of the pot calling the kettle black.

Chapter 19

Rich and Famous

When you begin with so much pomp and show,
Why is the end so little and so low?

—Roscommon

When Mike Tyson's whirlwind year of turmoil began at the start of 1988, he was on his way to becoming the richest athlete in the world, not only from his purses but also from his commercial endorsements, remarkable in themselves since large companies with products to market generally don't choose to be associated with boxing. Yet, by the time Tyson fought Michael Spinks, Cayton had negotiated some noteworthy endorsement contracts for his fighter. The smallest earned him a mere $50 thousand, but it was made early in his career in large part as a public service and an image enhancer. (It was with the Greene County Chamber of Commerce in Catskill, New York, and allowed them to use Tyson's image in their promotion of his adopted home county as a holiday resort.) Another early endorsement deal was made with Summit Bank of Virginia for $125,000. Tyson was paid $250,000 for his first national TV commercial, a camera advertisement for Eastman Kodak, which used still-photo images of Tyson and his late mentor, Cus D'Amato, with Mike's voice-over. A deal was also made for two years at $750,000 per year with the Nintendo video game manufacturer, which marketed the "Mike Tyson Punchout" game cassette and used Mike in a TV commercial. (The Nintendo endorsement proved to be a windfall. Tyson received a royalty of $2 on each $40 game sold, and from 1987 to mid-1988 this alone netted him an additional $4 million.)

Tying in with the Tubbs fight in Tokyo, Cayton had made deals with Suntory Beer for $700,000 and Toyota cars for $800,000. In addition, waiting in the wings, Cayton had future endorsement contracts lined up with RJR/Nabisco, the 3M Corporation for one of its adhesive products, and a major battery manufacturer.

Then came the blockbuster. Cayton tied Tyson in with Pepsi-Cola and a major national advertising campaign built around the Spinks fight. It was a high-profile, prestigious association for Tyson, putting him in a league with Michael Jackson, who had also been used in a major Pepsi advertising-endorsement campaign. Several commercials were filmed and run in the months leading up to the fight and in the weeks following it. For the right to use Tyson as a spokesman, Pepsi paid $1 million. (In addition, although Pepsi will not acknowledge it, it is believed there was later talk of an extension of the company's arrangement with Tyson for an incredible fee of $8 to $10 million.)

Furthermore, Cayton was said to be working on a movie deal for a film tentatively titled *Cus and the Kid*, which would further perpetuate the D'Amato-Tyson myth. Toyota was also said to be interested in extending its relationship with Tyson for millions of dollars more.

But by September of 1988, things began to crumble. His volatile marriage, his lawsuits with Cayton, his street fight with Mitch Green, his car accident amid unsubstantiated rumors of attempted suicide, and, as *Sports Inc.* magazine columnist Thomas Hauser wrote, "whispers that Tyson's sexual conduct is beyond the pale of acceptability," all combined to make the corporations Tyson was involved with take a hard second look. In rapid succession, Pepsi announced its advertising campaign involving Tyson had ended and was not being renewed. Both the battery manufacturer and the 3M Corporation abandoned plans to become commercially involved with Tyson. Japan followed suit, with Suntory Beer and Toyota allowing their deals with Tyson to expire. It was no coincidence that all Tyson's endorsements were disappearing. Marty Blackman, an advertising consultant who specializes in athlete endorsements, said, "The basic problem is that companies didn't research Mike Tyson as well as they should have. Had they spoken to people in boxing, they would have been a little more cautious. Mike Tyson has shown a pattern of unpredictable behavior and now, with this guy, everybody's wondering, 'What's next?' We are advising clients to proceed with caution."

Certainly, Cayton and Jacobs, when orchestrating their

careful plans for the marketing of Tyson, had always been aware of the "image" where advertising is concerned. Thus they had taken great care to guard and enhance his public image as best they could, involving him in voluntary public service projects such as anti-drug campaigns; an anti-illiteracy, stay-in-school campaign (conceived by PR man Howard Rubenstein), and homes for the mentally retarded. But, after receiving some good publicity, including a major feature on the HBO network about his involvement in the homes-for-the-retarded project, Tyson had withdrawn from such public-spirited activities.

At the age of twenty-three, Mike Tyson's gross earnings have been staggering. In the four years since he turned professional, he earned an incredible amount of money. Through his fight with Tyrell Biggs in the fall of 1987, Jim Jacobs said Tyson's earnings were $15 million. HBO subsequently negotiated a seven-fight deal that would pay Tyson $26.5 million. Over and above his HBO fee, he earned another $5 to $6 million fighting Tony Tubbs in Japan and more than $20 million when he fought Spinks. He made $3 million or so, plus his HBO fee, for the Bruno fight, and his commercial endorsements plus Nintendo royalties brought him another $7 million. This means that in four years, Mike Tyson had gross earnings of approximately $76 million. After paying his trainer and manager their percentages, plus his taxes, he has netted some $35 to $40 million for himself. This has allowed him the freedom to buy Don King and his new Team Tyson members gold and diamond Rolex watches, plus a $150,000 Piaget wristwatch for himself. It enabled him to go into a Las Vegas dealership the week of the Bruno fight and purchase a white Mercedes convertible, then several days after the fight, to impulsively walk into another dealership on Ventura Boulevard in Woodland Hills, California, telephone Don King to wire him $205,000 and drive out three hours later with a 400-horsepower black Ferrari Testarossa. He also owned the luxury four-wheel drive vehicle he used in Las Vegas, a $120,000 Rolls Royce Silver Spur, a white $165,000 Rolls Corniche, a Bentley, a Jaguar, a BMW, a Porsche, a Lamborghini and an Aston-Martin Lagonda.

While they were controlling his financial affairs, Cayton

and Jacobs put his money in ultraconservative investments including, as of 1987, $1,213,000 in a Merrill Lynch Cash Management Account and $1,466,000 in tax-exempt securities, plus a single-premium life insurance policy which will begin paying him $250,000 a year, tax-free, for the rest of his life beginning on his twenty-seventh birthday in 1993. *Forbes*, the business and finance magazine, listed Tyson in 1988 as the youngest of their top-forty money earners, crediting him with $55 million to that point.

It is rare to gain access to a public figure's private financial records, but when Tyson became involved in his dispute with Bill Cayton, he was required to provide the court with his financial statements for 1987. They give a revealing, and somewhat puzzling, glimpse of how Tyson spent his money for that year (which was *before* he earned $10 million in the Tubbs bout, $20 million for his match against Spinks and $7 to $8 million for the Bruno fight). In 1987, Tyson listed $228,627 as expenses for "Apartment Equipment and Furniture." His New York City apartment rent was $18,150. His combined telephone bills for his New York City apartment, his Albany residence and his phone at the Catskill house came to $6,612. He listed $20,000 under "House Repair, Catskill," plus $15,370 in payments to Camille Ewald. Robin Givens, then his girlfriend, was down for $7,560; but under the separate heading of "Jewelry" Tyson listed expenditures of $219,819. For "Clothes," the champion spent $178,314. He paid out $19,055 in fees to his accountants and listed $13,241 in legal fees. He put down $19,315 under the heading of "Travel Expenses," but separately listed $22,222 for "Airfare." He spent $35,480 for hotels in 1987 and $157 for records and tapes. Curiously, under the heading of "Food," he put down just $55 for all of 1987! (No explanation is offered on the statement.) He spent $864 for a pet Sharpei dog and paid out $8,226 in "Contributions."

According to the financial statement, compiled by the accounting firm of Kaufman Greenhut Lebowitz and Foreman, Tyson had several expenditures of particular interest. He indicated he spent $71,708 on limousine and car rentals, even though he owned a fleet consisting of some of the most expensive cars in the world. And he put down as the largest single expense, "Cash Drawings" totaling $332,545, which averages out to $6,400 a week. With other items added in, his total expenditures for 1987 were listed as $1,430,412. This was against taxable earnings for the year of $7,056,082, out of which he paid $2,262,536 in federal, state and local taxes. His total net worth as of December 31, 1987, was listed at $5,187,097. One final expenditure of $105,000 was itemized as being for "Settlement of Lawsuit." It was the money paid to keep the case involving the Los Angeles parking lot attendants out of the courts.

The personal lives of celebrities always seem to generate a fascinated interest on the part of the public, and Mike Tyson has certainly been no exception to the rule. There has been speculation for some years both within and outside boxing circles that he might be homosexual, but absolutely no evidence has been offered to substantiate the obviously sensational stories that have appeared from time to time in the press. The subject was broached directly during an interview with Steve Dunleavy on July 30, 1988, on America's Fox Television Network. "I got a call at my office about two months ago," said Dunleavy as he talked to the champion in his Catskill home. "A very, very well-known lawyer, who has a client who will even say Mike Tyson is a homosexual." "Yeah?" responded Tyson. "Do you think someone's behind this?" asked Dunleavy. "What can I say?" asked Tyson. "You know what I'm getting at," said Dunleavy. "I mean, is there a person?" Tyson, not taking the opportunity to vehemently deny the innuendo in the question, replied, "Well, eventually there is. I believe who they are [sic] but what can I say? You hear the same stories. 'He has so many women.' 'He's a homosexual.' The two don't intertwine, you know what I mean? 'His family is crazy.' 'He has a wild life.' By nature I'm wild, regardless of my mentality, that's the way I am."

Dunleavy did not pursue the line of questioning any further in his on-air interview, but speculated afterward, "Those rumors have been going around for years and years. I mean, if it goes to two, three, four years you have to ask if it's more than just a rumor. . . . I will give you what I think is the truth, as opposed to what I know is the truth. The very fact that he had been in the slammer, there had been some allegations that he had to go along with the scene. . . . He had some time in bad places. Spofford (Youth Detention

Center) is about as bad as you'll get. Obviously, that triggered the rumors, whether they be scurrilous or legitimate." Dunleavy's overall impression of Tyson was that he "found him deliciously innocent on one hand, totally lethal on the other, and a lot smarter than either of the former would suggest."

Joe Bruno, a long-time and well-connected writer on the boxing scene in New York, has also been aware over the years of the talk about Tyson. He bluntly says, "I have no proof . . . but I know when you're in jail you do strange things, and he's not out and out denied anything. . . . I believe it. I believe he sucked a prick once in a while." Bruno said a Mafia figure he is acquainted with in New York's Little Italy section came to him and said "he knows for a fact that Tyson's a stone fag, a stone fag means an out and out fag. Usually these [Mafia] guys don't make up things, they usually find out things like this, it's usually from reliable sources that you can't name." One of New York's most respected boxing writers said a journalist colleague of his who is a homosexual came to him one day with some information he thought the boxing writer would find interesting. "I met some interesting people the other night at [a] gay club . . . three guys, one was a big black guy introduced as 'Mike.' He was a fighter." The boxing writer, knowing his colleague knew nothing about boxing, said, "You don't mean Mike Tyson?" He said yes, that's who it was and proceeded to describe him. He said the two men who accompanied Tyson that night were white.

But the bottom line is, with all the innuendo in print, on TV, in casual ringside conversation, there is absolutely no proof that Mike Tyson is homosexual or bisexual. Ted Atlas, who lived with and roomed with Tyson for more than two years, said there was absolutely no hint of any homosexual behavior or tendencies in the time he knew Tyson and so puts no credence in the rumors.

In fact, there was at least one incident involving homosexual activity at the house in Catskill, but it did not involve Tyson. One of the other young men who lived there, who was older—in his twenties—had a young boy move into his room with him for about a year. There was little doubt among the rest of those in residence what the nature of the relationship was. D'Amato was furious at the older boy and would not speak to him, but for some reason he did not move forcefully to bring an end to the situation.

Although there is no proof of homosexuality, Tyson certainly has exhibited odd behavior on more than one occasion. On the night he fought Reggie Gross at Madison Square Garden, Tyson was in the dressing room area following his brief bout, walking in the hallway with his arm around the neck of a reporter he was talking to. Tyson often does this and there is nothing implied beyond the message that it means Mike likes you. However, on this night, when another reporter he was familiar with passed them in the hallway, Tyson looked at him and said, "You're probably jealous because I'm with another man." The reporter's reaction: "It struck me as strange . . . a weird fucking thing. I mean, why did he say that?"

Another time, a well-known boxing writer who wears his hair rather long was sitting on a couch next to Tyson conducting an interview. As the reporter later recounted, "Tyson was leaning more and more on my shoulder, like he used to do with Jimmy [Jacobs], he was sort of distracted, and in an offhanded way he started stroking my hair like I was a girl. I looked at him and said, 'Mike, what the fuck are you doing?' And he sort of snapped out of it and took his hand away."

The overwhelming evidence, however, points to Mike being, as his manager Bill Cayton bluntly terms it, "the ultimate heterosexual . . . who can screw women endlessly."

Often, it seems, Tyson exhibits a rage against women, perhaps dating back to his days in Catskill and before when they rejected him and made fun of him. Jose Torres, a former Tyson intimate, said the champion "has this problem with women. He told me he likes to hurt them when he makes love to them, likes to pound them, likes to hear them scream with pain, to see them bleed. I told him, 'Mike that's not the idea.' " Two reporters who covered Tyson at the Albany *Times-Union* from his early days in Catskill, Tim Layden and Joe Mahoney, say Tyson has always had women problems. "Mike's biggest problem far and away is women," said Layden, who predicts, along with many others, "that's the problem that's going to wind up nailing him some day." Mahoney, the newspaper's police beat reporter, agrees that women are Tyson's "Achilles' heel."

A friend of Jim Jacobs recalls leaving Jacobs's office one day in December of 1985 and strolling uptown with Tyson. He recalls vividly every time Tyson passed an attractive woman, he would walk up close to her and make remarks under his breath that they heard and were obviously not pleased.

While living in Catskill, Tyson would often frequent, as he still does, a club called Septembers, which local police describe as a "meat market," where someone can be fairly certain of meeting a companion for a "one-nighter," in other words, a typical singles and young-couples hangout. Local authorities also say that probably half the total cocaine arrests in the town of Colonie take place in Septembers parking lot, including that of a prominent local college basketball star in 1988. On numerous occasions during the years when he was under the guardianship of D'Amato, Tyson would pick up a young woman at Septembers and disappear to spend the night with her. Sal D'Carlo, the club's owner, still a friend of Tyson's, would have to find him and drive him back to Catskill at four or five in the morning in time to get a couple of hours sleep before his daily training session.

In December of 1988, two women did file charges against the heavyweight champion, based on alleged incidents that took place at Bentley's nightclub on Manhattan's East 40th Street. A twenty-four-year-old woman, whom the police would not identify at the time, said she and her girlfriend were at the bar when Tyson grabbed her arm and pulled her toward him. She told him, "I have a man," but Tyson would not let that discourage him. He replied, "I am the man." She walked away, but a few minutes later she said Tyson again approached her, this time grabbing her breasts and buttocks. A loud exchange followed, and Tyson's friends came and took him away. But about an hour later, according to the police account of the woman's complaint, Tyson once more approached her and threatened to punch her in the mouth, at which point she got her coat and left Bentley's, filing charges later that day.

Tyson often goes to the club, which was also frequented by Eddie Murphy, New York Mets star Darryl Strawberry and New York Giants star Lawrence Taylor. Tyson generally arrives in his Rolls, with a large entourage. Cutting the waiting line outside, as befits his celebrity status, he pays the admission charge for all his friends. He then moves around the club, hits the dance floor, and swigs Dom Perignon champagne straight from the bottle, often racking up a $600 bar bill in a single night.

Several days after the first complaint was filed against him, a second woman also filed charges against Tyson from an incident she said occurred on the same weekend, also at Bentley's. Lori Davis, twenty-nine, said she was dancing in the club's disco lounge when "someone grabbed my behind under my dress." She said she spun around and screamed, " 'Try that again and I'll slap the shit out of you.' Then it dawned on me that I was screaming at the Heavyweight Champion of the World." She said Tyson tried to make a joke of the incident, raising his hands in the air and saying, "Whoa, whoa, OK, OK, we have a live one here." She said Tyson's two male companions giggled as they viewed the scene. Davis, a professional woman who works as a recreational therapist, filed a lawsuit against Tyson. Howard Weitzman, Tyson's attorney, said his client had no "recollection" of the incident. Tyson was served with papers. On April 19, 1989, the other woman, Sandra Moore of Brooklyn, New York, filed a $4.5 million lawsuit against Tyson, accusing him of assault and battery by "violently and forcibly grabbing . . . and fondling and embracing her against her will." Both cases were still pending as of May.

Tyson's pattern with women has been one of aggression. Even Robin Givens, in a December 1988 *People* magazine interview, noted Tyson's aggressive behavior, but seemed to admire it nonetheless: "He grabbed me on our first night together, picked me up and carried me to his apartment. When I tried to break away and go, he wouldn't let me. He just put his arm between me and the door, and then he picked me up and shook me. . . . His arm was so solid, so sturdy, it felt like you could depend on an arm like that forever. . . . There's something about Michael that's dangerous. As we all know, that's part of the attraction. It's like enjoying scary movies or roller coaster rides." London's *News of the World* reported that Givens later confided in a friend, "Mike makes love brutally—like a street fighter. I just wish he'd be more gentle." Even after they were divorced, while he ran from woman to woman, he still looked upon Givens as his property. Givens reportedly told a friend, "He [Mike] won't leave me alone. . . . He told me, 'You're tormenting me, you're making me miserable. I can't stand the thought of you being with someone else. You still belong to me.' "

A radically different view of Mike Tyson was offered in a confidential interview with the author by a woman he has been seeing regularly since December 1988. Twenty-two years old, college-educated, a Los Angeles resident, this well-raised young black woman prefers to keep her relationship out of the limelight. She said she and Mike enjoy quiet evenings at her apartment, brunches at local restaurants, movies and long drives when he is in town. The two spoke by phone virtually every day when Tyson was in Las Vegas training for the Bruno fight, and she sees a tender side to Mike Tyson. "He needs a friend. He just needs someone to love him. I told him that's what I'm there for. I know I'll always love him no matter what he decides to do. I'll always be there for him, because he needs a simple human being that leads an everyday life just to be his friend, and to care."

Of their physical relationship, she says, "He just makes me very comfortable. I mean, I haven't touched another guy after him. I don't want anybody else. I don't even desire anybody else. When he's with me he's concerned about how I feel. He's very warm. The whole night he holds me." Sexually, Mike is "excellent. He's my fantasy. He's definitely, like they say, 'Iron' Mike," she blushingly confesses. "He makes me want him. He makes me feel like I just want to do anything for him." After one lovemaking session, she recalls saying to herself, "I just proved Robin wrong. She's crazy not to want to be with him." The first night they spent together was Christmas night in 1988. (Tyson had spent Christmas eve in Los Angeles with Robin.) "We went back to his place," she recalls, "and I knew it was going to happen. It was our first date, and I wanted to be with him. Everything was perfect, the way he came on to me. He was like a baby, like a little baby, but still a man. He just said he wants me. I said I want you, too, but it's just our first date. But it happened. He didn't push me. As a matter of fact, I'm the one that helped him take off his clothes! I don't sleep with every Tom, Dick and Harry. I can count on my hand the times I've been in love, the guys I've dated. I wouldn't trade him for anybody. If it doesn't work out, I'll wish him the best, but I'll always love him."

Mike is hardly settled down. Reliable reports say his bedroom energy rivals his energy in the ring, and there are countless tales of sexual high jinks. In Las Vegas for a Julio Caesar Chavez fight, Tyson was bumming around with Canada's fighting Hilton brothers, themselves a wild and wacky bunch of rowdies. They had become friendly years before, when the Hiltons were in residence at Catskill. On this particular night, they were all out drinking and when they got back to their suite, they decided to play a prank on Tyson. An associate of theirs, a young man who worked for their promoter, was asleep in the next room. The Hiltons knew this, but Tyson did not. The young man was blond, and wore his hair fairly long. The Hiltons told Mike they had a blond in the next room, in the bed waiting for him. They failed to tell him it was a guy. The libidinous champion opened the door and was ready for action. He jumped on top of the sleeping figure and began "humping" the body through the blanket. Not surprisingly, the young man was quickly roused from his slumber, and recoiled in horror when he saw that it was Tyson pounding away at him. Tyson, seeing it was a guy, was equally repulsed, and the Hiltons fell on the floor, convulsed in laughter.

Because of his active and often indiscreet sex life, Tyson's friends became concerned for his safety, and by the end of 1988 he had reportedly been tested, at their urgings, for AIDS at least three times, all the tests producing negative results. There have always been lots of young women around, making themselves readily available just for the "honor" of being with the champ. He reportedly bragged to Jose Torres that at one orgy, in Philadelphia, he had twenty-four women in one night, something which sounds, on the surface, unbelievable. "It was outrageous," Torres said. "Mike boasted about it himself, and witnesses confirmed it. I know Mike has had hundreds of girls, but I found it very scary hearing him brag about that orgy. He couldn't have known . . . whether they were clean or not. I was in constant fear of him catching AIDS. He just didn't seem to care what sort of girl he went with." Ruth Roper was said to have been extremely concerned during the time Robin was married to

Mike about her daughter contracting a disease, since the women obviously knew Mike was not exactly being faithful to his marriage vows. And yet, as he turned the ripe old age of twenty-three, and despite his professed born-again Christianity, Mike Tyson shows no signs of slowing down—in the ring . . . or in the bedroom.

In the ring, he is considered the best. Jersey Joe Walcott says, "I think he is a great fighter and a great champion. He would have done well in any given time. I'm sure he would have done well in my time when all the great fighters of the forties were around." Jake LaMotta says, "What I've seen so far, he impressed me very, very much. At the rate he's going right now, he could very easily be the greatest heavyweight champion of all time." Willie Pep acknowledges, "There's nobody around to beat him. He's a black Marciano. He can fight, he's tough, and if he gets in shape, nobody's going to lick him for a while." Former world champion Jack "Kid" Berg terms Tyson "a terrific fighter. I think he's a great fighter, and I think there will be nobody who can touch him." The great trainer, Ray Arcel, says, "He could have fit in at any time in the heavyweight ranks. He could punch hard enough to have beaten anybody if he could hit them. The guy's a natural fighter. Unfortunately, he has no opposition. The talent we have in the heavyweight ranks is the poorest that we've ever had. But you have to give credit where credit is due. He's the best we have in the heavyweight ranks right now."

"Tyson is a terrific young fighter," says Eddie Futch, "but I'd like to see him with a better caliber of competition to really determine whether he's a great fighter or not. His weaknesses have been shown in fights like a very terrible fight with 'Bonecrusher' Smith. Tony Tucker showed what a boxer could do with him. If he'd come along in the time of Ali and Foreman and Frazier and those guys, it might be a very different story. I think he has the potential to be the greatest of all, because he has two things going for him: terrific hand speed and the power, combined. He can lose 11⅔ rounds of a fight and then take you out with one shot."

* * *

Outside the ring, his press notices have not been as glowing as those he generates when he's fighting. Columnist Steve Jacobson, writing in *Newsday*, said, "Tyson never had to learn to live in society; misbehavior was swept under the ring for years by people guiding him because he had championship potential. He excused himself as 'a product of my environment.' When is an athlete to be held responsible for himself? The argument that justifies the inherent violence in boxing because it offers a way out of the gutter falls apart in Tyson's hands. A silk suit and a heavy bank account don't always hide the individual." In the same newspaper, Wally Matthews talked of "Tyson's increasingly besmirched personal image. . . . Ever since he was the prize pupil of Cus D'Amato's stable as a fourteen-year-old, Tyson has listened to no one but himself and his street instincts. The blame . . . lies not only with [Tyson], but also with D'Amato and Cayton and his late partner, Jim Jacobs. In their desire to mold the former juvenile delinquent into a heavyweight champion, D'Amato, Jacobs and Cayton traded off something far more important—Tyson's development as a responsible member of society. The reason, of course, is that the three used their wealth and influence to ensure that Tyson never had to take responsibility for any of his transgressions."

Mike Lupica, in the New York *Daily News*, called Tyson "a dangerous hood [who] needs plenty of help." Veteran boxing official and manager Marty Cohen, who helped bring Michael Dokes back from cocaine addiction to a top-ten ranking in 1988 and 1989, said of Tyson, "They built a Frankenstein to a point where they can no longer control the Frankenstein. . . . He's going to wind up killing himself or somebody else or going to an asylum." Phil Berger, in the *New York Times*, observed, "With Tyson, things happen, and the more they happen the deeper grows the feeling that whatever bad endings await Mike Tyson, the chances are they will happen outside the ring." Mike Katz, in the New York *Daily News*, said, "Tyson's character seems [to be] developing along wrong lines. He is a bully. He is disloyal. He is arrogant. . . . Obviously, Cus did not have enough time. The lessons have not been learned." Katz went on to say Tyson's real nature "has been well-camouflaged." In a wonderful, to-the-point column on Tyson's twenty-second birthday, three days after his defeat of Spinks, Katz addressed Tyson directly. The column was called "Happy Birthday, Ingrate" and in it Katz outlined many of the instances of disloyalty that Tyson was either a party to or directly responsible for. "Outside the ring you've become a disappointment," Katz told the champion. "You're no Muhammad Ali, who was a man of the people, a man of great soul. . . . You've turned your back on too many people who were kind to you, who got you out of the ghetto and tried to get the ghetto out of you. You call them 'Jews in suits.' . . . You're beginning to sound like Don King. . . . You know what a lucky puppy you've been. Heavyweight champion at twenty, a millionaire by twenty-one. Go ahead, sue [Bill Cayton] and Jimmy's widow. . . . All he ever did was join with Jimmy in making you rich and famous in what must be one of the best jobs of managing a fighter in history."

Tim Layden, who covered Tyson at newspapers in both Albany and New York, has said, "The strongest feeling I'm left with as to the kid's whole life is that he's more a victim than a criminal." Certainly in many ways, this may be true, but Mike Tyson has, despite his naivete, willingly allowed himself to be used and manipulated by a succession of people. He knew full well the implications of his complaint against Jacobs and Cayton, his signing agreements with King in violation of his contract, his seeking to break a contract he renegotiated just months earlier with Cayton. In many ways he is like the bad driver on the highway who causes a twenty-car wreck behind him but emerges unscathed and keeps merrily rolling along, oblivious to the carnage left in his wake. "I want to be mentioned in the same breath with Marciano and Louis and Ali," he has said, but he needs to learn that what these men had in common, outside their greatness in the ring, was character. Mike Tyson is still young. He still has time to change the "bad intentions," but that time continues to run down.

As recently as April 10, 1989, another incident involving Tyson was reported to police in Los Angeles. According to Michael Devine, a parking lot attendant, Tyson and several companions pulled into the lot adjacent to the Palace nightclub, where the champion and his buddies were heading shortly after midnight. When they drove into the parking spot reserved for the club's owner, Devine informed them they couldn't park in that particular spot. According to Devine's criminal complaint filed with police, Tyson then hit him three times (presumably not with full force) in the stomach. "It's bad enough working at a parking lot," said Devine. "When Mike Tyson hits you, it hurts." But Devine had no witnesses, and Tyson had two friends willing to testify the champion had not touched Devine, and so, on May 14, charges were dropped. Los Angeles Assistant District Attorney Timothy Hogan, after meeting with Tyson (accompanied by Don King and attorney Weitzman), said the champion "understood that he pretty much precipitated this incident by his conduct that night."

Tyson often chooses questionable company. His recent pal has been Lloyd Daniels, a hotshot high school basketball star from Brooklyn who was tossed out of five schools, then blew his chance to play college basketball when he was caught by police—and TV cameras—in a drug raid on a Las Vegas crack house. On May 11, 1989, Daniels was critically wounded in a drug-related street shooting in New York.

Despite all this, Tyson was nevertheless presented with an honorary doctor of humane letters degree on April 25, 1989, by Central State University in Ohio, an all-black college, which cited him, based on some convoluted reasoning, as an inspiration to young people. The very next day, back in upstate New York, Tyson was arrested by Albany police for drag racing in his new Lamborghini. He was clocked by police at 71 miles per hour in a designated 30 MPH zone. Tyson's racing buddy, twenty-two-year-old Mark Johnson, was also clocked at 71 MPH in his 1988 Chevy Blazer. Three weeks later, Johnson was arrested for cocaine dealing, to which he pleaded not guilty, and was held on $20 thousand bail. Another example of the company Tyson chooses to keep.

Sometimes, when he is alone, when the public bravado is laid aside, Mike thinks about losing. If he fights long enough, he knows it is bound to happen—someday. He has read the words of Don Jordan, another champion in another era, who said, "Every man knows when he fights he must lose." It is not likely—if Mike can manage to settle his legal disputes, get his personal life on an even keel, and stay active in the ring—that any of today's heavyweights will beat him. But out there, somewhere, he knows there is a hungry youngster who also has the spark, the spark that someday will become the roaring blaze.

As a boy, Tyson sat with D'Amato in the Catskill house and watched Larry Holmes, in his greatness, defend his title. D'Amato told Tyson how one day he would fight and beat this champion, and tutored the disbelieving youngster on the techniques he would use to do just that. And so it came to pass. And now Mike Tyson thinks of the young boy, name unknown, who stopped him one day, pulling on his arm until the heavyweight champion turned and looked into the boy's eyes. What did he want, asked the champion. "I just want to see what you look like," replied the boy, barely a teenager, "because someday I'm going to beat you." Mike Tyson remembers that look, those eyes. And he takes the memory of that encounter more seriously than most people might imagine.

ABOUT THE AUTHOR

Peter Heller was born in 1947 in New York City, where he attended the High School of Art & Design and New York University. He joined ABC News as a writer in 1968, and has subsequently worked there as a TV sportscaster, publicist for ABC Sports, and is the sports producer for news segments for "Good Morning America." He was nominated for an Emmy Award for his sports producing. His first book, *In This Corner . . . : 40 World Champions Tell Their Stories*, was critically acclaimed following its publication in 1973.

In addition, he has been a boxing judge for the New York State Athletic Commission and judged several of Mike Tyson's early fights. He is the comanager (with Judd Maze) of world-ranked heavyweight contender "Big" Art Tucker, and his boxing articles have appeared in all the major boxing magazines during the last 20 years.

SPORTS FAVORITES

☐ **BAD INTENTIONS** *The Mike Tyson Story* **by Peter Heller.** The hard-hitting biography that tells perhaps the most remarkable story in the annals of boxing—of a thirteen-year-old boy who was ripped from his roots and shaped by a master to be one thing and one thing only . . . the heavyweight champion of the world. "Rings true throughout."—*Kirkus Reviews*   (166558—$4.95)*

☐ **SEMI-TOUGH by Dan Jenkins.** This superb bestseller, the prequel to *Life Its Ownself,* is "Funny, marvelous, outrageous . . . Dan Jenkins has written a book about sports, but not about sports . . . It mocks contemporary American values, Madison Avenue, racial attitudes, writers like me . . . Women abound. I loved it." David Halberstram, *The New York Times Book Review*   (137930—$3.95)*

☐ **INSTANT REPLAY: THE GREEN BAY DIARY OF JERRY KRAMER edited by Dick Schaap.** From the locker room to the goal line, from the training field to the Super Bowl, this is the inside story of a great pro football team . . . "The best behind-the-scenes glimpse of pro football ever produced."—*The New York Times*   (146301—$3.95)*

☐ **EVERYTHING YOU ALWAYS WANTED TO KNOW ABOUT SPORTS And Didn't Know Where to Ask by Mickey Herskowitz and Steve Perkins.** Here is the book that answers every question a sports fan ever had in the back of his mind and tells the truth about the whispered rumors of the sports world.   (124715—$2.75)

☐ **EAT TO WIN: The Sports Nutrition Bible by Dr. Robert Haas, with Foreword by Martina Navratilova.** In this #1 Nationwide bestseller, a world-class nutritionist reveals the secrets of the breakthrough diet that gives top athletes that unbeatable edge. "A winning recipe for energy, strength, speed and endurance!"—*The New York Times*
                                                          (155092—$4.95)*

☐ **LEONARD MARSHALL: THE END OF THE LINE by Leonard Marshall and Dave Klein.** A riveting autobiographical chronicle of an athlete's spectacular success. Marshall, New York Giants all-pro defensive end, tackles even the most challenging subjects—from personal problems to NFL controversies. "Exceptional!"—*Publishers Weekly*   (154762—$4.50)*

*Prices higher in Canada

Buy them at your local

bookstore or use coupon

on next page for ordering.